W9-BZA-321

DENNETT AND HIS CRITICS

JB

PHILOSOPHERS AND THEIR CRITICS

General Editor: Ernest Lepore

Philosophy is an interactive enterprise. Much of it is carried out in dialogue as theories and ideas are presented and subsequently refined in the crucible of close scrutiny. The purpose of this series is to reconstruct this vital interplay among thinkers. Each book consists of a contemporary assessment of an important living philosopher's work. A collection of essays written by an interdisciplinary group of critics addressing the substantial theses of the philosopher's corpus opens each volume. In the last section, the philosopher responds to his or her critics, clarifies crucial points of the discussion, or updates his or her doctrines.

DENNETT AND HIS CRITICS

Demystifying Mind

Edited by

Bo Dahlbom

BLACKWELL
Oxford UK & Cambridge USA

Copyright © Basil Blackwell Ltd 1993

First published 1993

First published in USA 1993

Blackwell Publishers
238 Main Street, Suite 501
Cambridge, Massachusetts 02142
USA

108 Cowley Road
Oxford OX4 1JF
UK

All rights reserved. Except for the quotation of short passages for the purposes of criticism and review, no part of this publication may be reproduced, stored in a retrieval system, or transmitted, in any form or by any means, electronic, mechanical, photocopying, recording or otherwise, without the prior permission of the publisher.

Except in the United States of America, this book is sold subject to the condition that it shall not, by way of trade or otherwise, be lent, resold, hired out, or otherwise circulated without the publisher's prior consent in any form of binding or cover other than that in which it is published and without a similar condition including this condition being imposed on the subsequent purchaser.

Library of Congress Cataloging-in-Publication Data

Dennett and his critics : demystifying mind/edited by Bo Dahlbom.
   p. cm.
Includes bibliographical references and index.
ISBN 0-631-18549-6
1. Dennett, Daniel Clement. 2. Consciousness. 3. Mind and body.
4. Intentionality (Philosophy) I. Dahlbom, Bo, 1949– .
B945.D394D46 1993
126–dc20   92-43145
                                          CIP

British Library Cataloguing in Publication Data

A CIP catalogue record for this book is available from the British Library.

Typeset in 9½ on 11 pt Erhardt by TecSet Ltd, Wallington, Surrey
Printed in Great Britain by TJ Press Ltd, Padstow, Cornwall.

This book is printed on acid-free paper

Contents

Notes on Contributors

KATHLEEN AKINS is Assistant Professor of Philosophy at the Beckman Institute, University of Illinois, Champaign-Urbana and at Simon Fraser University, Canada. Her research is in the interdisciplinary area between philosophy and neuroscience.

P. S. CHURCHLAND is Professor of Philosophy at the University of California, San Diego, and Adjunct Professor at the Salk Institute. She is the author of *Neurophilosophy* and co-author with Terrence Sejnowski of *The Computational Brain*. She is a winner of a MacArthur Prize.

BO DAHLBOM is Associate Professor of Philosophy at the Department of Technology and Social Change, University of Linköping, Sweden. He is the author (with Lars Mathiassen) of *Computers in Context*. His next book will be *An Artificial World*, an introduction to the world of computer technology.

RICHARD DAWKINS is Reader in Zoology at the University of Oxford and a Fellow of New College. He is the author of *The Selfish Gene*, *The Extended Phenotype*, and *The Blind Watchmaker*. His next book will be *Growing up in the Universe*, based upon his Royal Institution Christmas Lectures for Children.

JERRY FODOR is Professor of Philosophy at Rutgers University and at the CUNY Graduate Center. His next book, called *Mentalese*, will deal with issues that connect theories about mental representation to theories about meaning and knowledge.

JOHN HAUGELAND is Professor of Philosophy at the University of Pittsburgh. He is the author of *Artificial Intelligence: The Very Idea*, and editor of *Mind Design*. He is now working on a book on Heidegger.

ERNEST LEPORE is Professor of Philosophy at Rutgers University. He is the co-author (with Jerry Fodor) of *Holism: A Shopper's Guide*, and is currently working on a book on semantics for natural languages.

COLIN MCGINN is Professor of Philosophy at Rutgers University. His most recent books are *The Problem of Consciousness* and *Moral Literacy*.

RUTH GARRETT MILLIKAN is Professor of Philosophy at the University of Connecticut at Storrs. She is the author of *Language, Thought and Other Biological Categories*. Her new book is called *White Queen Psychology and Other Essays for Alice*.

V. S. RAMACHANDRAN is Professor of Psychology at the University of California, San Diego, doing research in psychophysics. He has studied many visual phenomena, including stereo vision, shape from shading, motion capture, filling in, and segmentation.

RICHARD RORTY is Professor of Humanities at the University of Virginia. His most recent books are *Objectivity, Relativism and Truth* and *Essays on Heidegger and Others*.

Editor's Introduction

When other philosophers use definitions and arguments, Daniel Dennett will make his point by telling a story. So, if you ask him about his view on a specific question, he will scratch his beard and hem and haw, but only for a few seconds before going into narrative mode, launching into a wonderful story. His philosophy is in his stories. Only they can really introduce him.[1]

1 Some Stories

Fido, who has not yet been fed all day, is handed a large chunk of beefsteak, but instead of eating it he carefully gathers together a little pile of straw, puts the meat in the middle, and sits down on the meat. Now, suppose that we are able to determine that Fido's perceptual state on this occasion is the state he would normally be in when receiving a steak. But since Fido is behaving so strangely, we cannot say that this state has the content (roughly) "this is food" for him, so how do we determine its content? Fido's behavior would be appropriate to a belief that the beef was an egg and Fido was a hen, and perhaps therefore we should attribute the following content to his perceptual state: "this is an egg and I am a hen." But Fido's behavior is also appropriate to other beliefs, e.g. "this is beef, but if I pretend it's an egg I'll get twice as much beef tomorrow," or "sitting on beef improves its flavor." So, how do we ascribe content to a perceptual state when the behavior is inappropriate? (Dennett, 1969, p. 77–8).

It takes a really callous person to deny the existence of pain. Or does it? Consider the following exchange (from Dennett, 1969, p. 11):

"How old is Smith's sake?"
"Sakes don't exist in time."
"But they do exist, don't they?"
"Why not?"
"Then if Smith's sake is timeless, we'll be able to do things for it after he's dead."
"No; although a sake is timeless, it can no longer receive benefits after the death of its owner."

"Then I might only think I was doing something for Smith's sake, if all along
he was dead without my knowing it?"
"No, you'd be doing it *for* Smith's sake, only his sake would no longer have any
use for whatever you were doing."

In order to block this nonsense we would want to say that even if "sake" is a
perfectly fine noun, there are no sakes. But, you will say, sakes (whatever they are)
are very different from pains. Pains are experienced, so obviously they exist. All this
talk about sakes is not really relevant. Then, listen to the following story (from
Dennett, 1978, p. xix).

Suppose we find a society that lacks our knowledge of human physiology, and that
speaks a language just like English except for one curious family of idioms. When
they are tired they talk of being beset by *fatigues*: of having mental fatigues, muscular
fatigues, fatigues in the eyes and fatigues of the spirit. Their sports lore contains
such maxims as "too many fatigues spoils your aim" and "five fatigues in the legs are
worth ten in the arms." When we encounter them and tell them of our science, they
want to know *what fatigues are*. They have been puzzling over such questions as
whether numerically the same fatigue can come and go and return, whether fatigues
have a definite location in matter or space and time, whether fatigues are identical
with some particular physical states or processes or events in the bodies, or are
made of some sort of stuff. We can see that they are off to a bad start with these
questions, but what should we tell them? One thing we might tell them is that there
simply are no such things as fatigues – they have a confused ontology. We can
expect some of them to retort: "You don't think there are fatigues? Run around the
block a few times and you'll know better! There are many things your science might
teach us, but the non-existence of fatigues isn't one of them." (Now, how about
those pains?)

When you believe something, what is it you have in your head making up the belief?
A sentence of sorts? Well, what if a clever neurosurgeon were to put the following
sentence into your head: "I have an older brother living in Cleveland." Would you
then believe you had such a brother? Suppose you are sitting in a bar and a friend
asks you, "Do you have any brothers or sisters?" You say, "Yes, I have an older
brother living in Cleveland." "What's his name?" Now, what is going to happen?
You may say, "Name? Whose name? Oh, my gosh, what was I saying? I don't have
an older brother!" Or you may say, "I don't know his name," and when pressed you
will deny all knowledge of this brother, but still insist that you have an older brother
living in Cleveland. Well, what do you think, are beliefs some sort of sentences in
the head? (Dennett, 1978, p. 44).

Several years ago I was approached by Pentagon officials who asked me to volunteer
for a highly dangerous and secret mission. The mission involved the recovery of a
deadly warhead lodging about a mile deep under Tulsa, Oklahoma. Something
about the nature of the device and its complex interactions with pockets of material
deep in the earth had produced radiation that could cause severe abnormalities in
certain tissues of the brain. No way had been found to shield the brain from these
deadly rays, which were apparently harmless to other tissues and organs of the body.
So it had been decided that the person sent to recover the device should *leave his*

brain behind. Would I submit to a surgical procedure that would completely remove my brain, which would then be placed in a life-support system at the Manned Spacecraft Center in Houston? Each input and output pathway, as it was severed, would be restored by a pair of microminiaturized radio transceivers. All the connectivity would be preserved. At first I was a bit reluctant. Would it really work? The Houston brain surgeons encouraged me. "Think of it," they said, "as a mere *stretching* of the nerves."

When I came out of anesthesia, I opened my eyes, looked around, and asked the inevitable question: "Where am I?" The nurse smiled down at me. "You're in Houston," she said, and I reflected that this still had a good chance of being the truth one way or another. She handed me a mirror. Sure enough, there were the tiny antennae poling up through their titanium ports cemented into my skull.

"I gather the operation was a success," I said, "I want to see my brain." I was helped over to the life-support vat. I peered through the glass. There, floating in what looked like ginger-ale, was undeniably a human brain. I thought to myself: "Well, here I am, sitting on a folding chair, staring through a piece of plate glass at my own brain . . . But wait, shouldn't I have thought 'Here I am, suspended in a bubbling fluid, being stared at by my own eyes'?" (Dennett, 1978, p. 310ff, reprinted in that book of stories, Dennett and Hofstadter, 1981, p. 217ff).

The first day I was ever in London, I found myself looking for the nearest Underground station. I noticed a stairway in the sidewalk labeled "SUBWAY," which in Boston is our word for the Underground, so I confidently descended the stairs and marched forth looking for the trains. After wandering about in various galleries and corridors, I found another flight of stairs and somewhat dubiously climbed them to find myself on the sidewalk on the other side of the intersection from where I had started. I must have missed a turn, I thought, and walked back downstairs to try again. After what seemed to me to be an exhaustive search for hitherto overlooked turnstiles or side entrances, I emerged back on the sidewalk where I had started, feeling somewhat cheated. Then at last it dawned on me; I'd been making a sort of category mistake! Searching for the self or the soul can be somewhat like that. You enter the brain through the eye, march up the optic nerve, round and round the cortex, looking behind every neuron, and then, before you know it, you emerge into daylight on the spike of a motor nerve impulse, scratching your head and wondering where the self is (Dennett, 1984, pp. 74f).

2 A Radical Position

Those are just a few examples – there are many, many more – of Daniel Dennett at work, using stories to make philosophical points. He lives off his "intuition pumps," as he calls them, and he is well aware of their importance: "reflection on the history of philosophy shows that the great intuition pumps have been the major movers all along" (Dennett, 1984, p. 17).

If intuition pumps are the major movers in philosophy, they are not necessarily the prime movers, as Dennett himself observes: "An intuition pump is not, typically, an engine of discovery, but a persuader or pedagogical tool – a way of getting people to see things *your* way once you've seen the truth" (Dennett, 1980, p. 429). And

Dennett has seen the truth, that is, it is not difficult to see how his stories are motivated by, and aimed at advocating, a definite and stable philosophical position. Unlike most philosophers, Dennett is not content to repeat one or two such intuition pumps, again and again. No, his creative imagination breeds stories at a fantastic rate – but most of them seem to have, pretty much, the same message.

Behaviorism is the message. To use this worn-out label is dangerous, of course, but I have no better way to quickly place Dennett among the variety of often confusing attempts, in our century, to formulate a viable alternative to, what used to be, modern philosophy with its penchant for introspection. Dennett is one of the more *consistent* proponents of such an alternative today, and I think that when the dust settles, behaviorism will be the label we will use for this alternative. And, behaviorism, in this sense, will be regarded as the major, original contribution to philosophy, besides logic, of our century. Let me line up a few more of these rather worn-out labels to indicate what I mean when I call Dennett a "behaviorist."

Dennett is a radical, that is, he is skeptical of many of the traditional ways and methods of philosophy. The major tools in his questioning of the tradition are an unusual acquaintance with front-line scientific research in several disciplines, and, as we have already seen, a Wittgensteinian attention to, and talent for, the concrete examples of philosophical discourse.

His radicalism will not take for granted the world as it is handed down to us in language, culture, and philosophical tradition. And he is radical enough not to take too seriously his own, as well as other contemporary, attempts at charting the world. As a true radical he is in no hurry to arrive at the truth, being content not to know, not to be sure, not to have answers. To some this will give the impression that he does not care, that his thinking or feelings are not deep enough, but others will interpret it as courage and confidence. Nietzsche did not feel awe when looking up to the stars or down into his soul, but this was not because he was a more superficial thinker than Kant.

As a radical and skeptic, Dennett is a nominalist: he does not believe in essences or final truths. Where others see dichotomies and sharp boundaries, he sees differences, compromises, and conventional amplifications of contrasts. He mistrusts our intellectual powers, our ability to reason, define, and argue. But he is also practical, with a liking for engineering, at home with and happy to trust and put to good use the results of modern science. His field is the philosophy of mind or cognitive science, and he has so far shown no ambition to extend, but briefly, his philosophical wanderings outside that field. Thus, his nominalism will lead him, like it led Goodman, to a constructive view of what there is, but he will not apply that constructive view to physics – since physics is none of his business.

Dennett is a behaviorist, and in his behaviorism he brings together ideas from Wittgenstein, Ryle, and Quine, as well as from experimental psychology. Behaviorism is functionalism applied to organisms, the idea that an organism is a machine, producing behavior with a mind–brain as its control system. It is a version of naturalism, treating human beings as biological organisms bringing evolutionary theory to bear on our self-understanding. The theory of evolution will support a radical, nominalistic questioning of traditional attempts to define the essence of man, and in particular such attempts that want to draw a sharp line between our species and our ancestors. There are no sharp lines in biology, or elsewhere, except temporarily and by accident.

Dennett's behaviorism and functionalism are related to verificationism, the idea that where there can be no evidence to decide an issue, there is no issue. The notion of evidence here is borrowed from science: whatever natural scientists in their practice will count as evidence, Dennett will accept. On Dennett's understanding of science, this means that by evidence we mean intersubjectively accessible physical phenomena (whatever they are – I am not claiming that this is a particularly clear notion). Thus, Dennett's verificationism is a brand of scientism. When you practice this version of verificationism in psychology, as it is being practiced in the mainstream of twentieth-century experimental psychology, including cognitive science, you are a behaviorist. But behaviorism is also the more particular application of veɪ....cationism to psychological language, what used to be called "logical behaviorism" by philosophers in Oxford. Dennett is a logical behaviorist, that is, along with Wittgenstein, Ryle, and Quine, he thinks that the language of psychology "is a social art. In acquiring it we have to depend entirely on intersubjectively available cues as to what to say and when." (Quine, 1960, p. ix).

Functionalism can, of course, be construed as a version of verificationism – as in the pragmatism of Peirce. Both functionalism and verificationism imply an interest in relations rather than in properties, or, stronger, properties turn out to be relations. Functional roles are relational structures, and evidence are phenomena related to what they are evidence for. Such a relationism will reject the idea of intrinsic properties and all notions of "direct" experience of pheneomena, of acquaintance with qualia, or intuition of intrinsic properties. It will deny us the possibility of "grasping" an object, or "entertaining" an idea, at least in the sense of having it present in its totality, in favor of a structuralist, holistic position, according to which an object always refers us to other objects, and can only be approached through its relations to others. (I am not sure that this reduction of properties to relations makes sense in the end, but it seems to make as much sense as the notions property and relation themselves do.)

Behaviorism is often described, by Dennett and by others, as giving us a third-person view of things. This is misleading. The interesting difference is not between first and third person, but between a relational and an intrinsic view of experience. We can use one of Dennett's stories (1982, p. 9) to explain this difference:

> There was once a chap who wanted to know the meaning of life, so he walked a thousand miles and climbed to the high mountaintop where the wise guru lived. "Will you tell me the meaning of life?" he asked.
> "Certainly," replied the guru, "but if you want to understand my answer, you must first master recursive function theory and mathematical logic."
> "You're kidding."
> "No, really."
> "Well then . . . skip it."
> "Suit yourself."

Dennett uses this story to illustrate the encounter between twentieth-century analytical philosophy and the public, but this story also expresses Dennett's very modern, very American, belief in hard work. There is no free lunch, the story says, not even in philosophy, but if you are willing to work hard nothing is impossible. So, don't think that consciousness, those wonderful raw feels, qualia, subjective feelings, or whatever you want to call them, the smell of a cake in the oven, the feel of your beloved's skin, the sight of an apple orchard in bloom, the sound of a saxophone, will be yours for free. No, in order to experience them, you, or your brain, must work hard. Only by a complex process, the functioning of a complex mechanism, will such wonderful things be possible. It may seem as if all it takes to see something is to open one's eyes, but we know how misleading this impression is. Likewise, it seems as if consciousness just *is* there, that qualia are just *given* for us to savor or suffer. If they aren't (and how could they be?), then the way to explain consciousness is to look closer at the mechanisms doing the work. And when you know how those mechanisms work, how the work is done, you know what qualia are, or so says Dennett.

The purportedly interesting difference between a third- and a first-person view of something is this difference between hard work and having something for free, between hard-won interpretation and easy acquaintance. Since Dennett does not believe that there is anything in the latter category, he should really stop describing himself as taking a third-person view of things. My view of the world is always my view, and no one else's, and the distinction between a first- and a third-person account that works so well in everyday life should not be pressed into philosophical service. In post-war philosophy of science, the positivistic notion of theory-neutral observation has been abandoned. So Dennett's rejection of the notion of acquaintance should come as no surprise, but it does. People don't seem to want to accept the idea that "nothing is given."

There are many "isms" involved in this characterization of Dennett's position: radicalism, nominalism, constructivism, behaviorism, functionalism, verificationism, scientism, relationism, holism, interpretationism. But they all join together into a tight knot, tying Dennett to philosophers such as Wittgenstein, Ryle, and Quine, but also to Nietzsche, Rorty, and Derrida. This is one of those remarkably stable positions in philosophy, and Dennett has not moved an inch from it since he first saw it and nailed it (as he would put it himself) in his D.Phil. thesis (what was to become *Content and Consicousness*) at the age of twenty-three.

Dennett's many stories are supposed to nudge us in the direction of this radical behaviorism. But this position is too radical, too different from the majority view, for even the best of stories to do very well. Through the history of philosophy the distinction between intuition, sensation, or acquaintance, on the one hand, and knowledge, judgment, or description, on the other, plays a fundamental role. It is a distinction deeply engrained in contemporary common sense, and it plays an important role in our understanding of what an object is and what it is for an object to have properties. To deny this distinction is to claim that we are fundamentally alienated from reality, that we have no real *contact* with the world, our own experiences, or ourselves.

This is a frightening vision, causing anxiety and giving a glimpse of nothingness – and not only to existentialists like Heidegger. To many people it seems obviously, utterly wrong. Still, this vision has been favored by many of the major philosophers of this century: by pragmatists like Quine, by positivists like Carnap, by existentialists like Sartre, and by post-structuralists like Derrida. Indeed, it makes good sense to read this attack on man's sense of being at home in the world as only one in a series of similar attacks accompanying the progress, some would say decline, of

Western civilization. And like earlier such attacks, it will take a while before it sinks in and people get around to accepting it: surely the earth is the center of the universe and does not move, surely man is a rational being, certainly not descended from some ape, or comparable to a machine, surely our experience is really real and not a figment of our theoretical imaginations.

3   The Ways of his Critics

With this very radical philosophical position pervading most of what he does, Dennett cannot really expect to get many to agree with him. All the efforts of Wittgenstein, Ryle, Quine, and Derrida have not succeeded in making the way any smoother for this kind of philosophy. So, Dennett seems bound to be frustrated. But if he does not find enough support for his philosophical position, he can certainly look back with satisfaction on the role he has played in changing the *way* that philosophy of mind is being done. That discipline of philosophy is now dominated by people who are just as happy to describe what they are doing as cognitive science, and this change owes a lot to the example set by *Content and Consciousness*.

In spite of a general commitment to cognitive science, the variety of ways in which philosophy of mind is being done today is striking. Look only at the contributions to this volume.

Patricia Churchland, reporting on Ramachandran's intriguing experiments on filling in, gives us an example of how to do philosophy with facts (chapter 2). Dennett has argued against the rather naive view that we perceive by copying our environment inch by inch, in favor of a view of perception as using short-cuts and heuristics of various sorts. Exemplifying his view, Dennett has ventured opinions on some special cases of perception on which Churchland and Ramachandran now bring a number of experimental results to bear, accusing Dennett of speculating, and being wrong, in a domain where there are empirical results.

Churchland and Ramachandran end their contribution with a diagnosis, another commonly used method of philosophy. Rather than just showing that someone is mistaken, you go on to give the intellectual etiology of the mistake. Richard Rorty (chapter 9) gives us a more extensive specimen of a similar genre, making clear the nature of Dennett's radical behaviorism and how it comes into conflict with the views of "the new mysterians." There is, of course, something presumptuous about this way of doing philosophy, presupposing as it does that one's colleagues need to be told what is going on in the texts they read and write. But, then again, this is very much the role of the philosopher since Socrates.

Kathleen Akins' paper (chapter 7) illustrates, I think, a less presumptuous kind of educational effort. Addressing both the philosopher who would use bats to examplify the subjectivity of consciousness, and the philosopher who would use the intentional stance to ascribe beliefs to bats, she says that, interestingly enough, there is rather a lot of empirical research on bats that one should perhaps consult before saying too much about them, research results which can bring into sharper focus philosophical worries about subjectivity and the nature of beliefs. The point of this way of doing philosophy is not just to rebut a specific philosophical point, but also to enrich and change the discussion as a whole.

Churchland and Akins give us more facts, as Holmes would say, and more facts is certainly something we and philosophy need. But the typical method of philosophy is not to give more facts but to dispute, to engage in dialectics, as it used to be called, putting to use the very special philosophical competence of analyzing concepts, making distinctions, identifying basic principles and lines of reasoning, unveiling hidden premises, testing different interpretations, evaluating arguments, and so on. All the contributors to this volume do, of course, practice philosophy in this way, but none do it so explicitly as Jerry Fodor and Ernie Lepore (chapter 4) when they spin a web in which to catch Dennett's interpretationism and prove it wrong.

Dennett has always insisted that psychology – and, more recently, biology – is very different from physics, and that explanations from the intentional stance are normative, based on rationality assumptions, rather than on laws. When Fodor and Lepore argue that psychology is just like any other science in this respect, their argument illustrates yet another of philosophy's many ways. To show that many intentional explanations are just like explanations in the rest of science, they give an example – the Moon illusion – of what they claim is an intentional law.

Ruth Millikan (chapter 6) uses biology in yet a third way, differing from both Akins and Churchland. Millikan employs biological categories as a framework in which to couch conceptual distinctions and arguments, forging claims of reasoning, doing philosophy in the style of that great metaphysician Wilfrid Sellars. Her views on representation are close to Dennett's, but the way she relies on intuition to make decisive points is rather different from the way Dennett does philosophy.

Intuition is the philosophical method *par excellence*, and the painting of imaginary scenes or the setting up of thought experiments, and then asking what we see or would say, is the major alternative or complement to the philosophical dispute. Dennett has been anxious to remind us of the dangers of trusting our intuition on complex examples, to use it to decide the details of metaphysics or ontology, in the way, I think, Millikan is here using her intuition. In this she resembles John Haugeland (chapter 3), who is testing his powers of intuition on the question of being. Haugeland proceeds from Dennett's recent paper "Real Patterns," the aim of which is to help people quit ontology, to outline a far-reaching ontological project, in aim and ambition much like Heidegger's.

If Fodor and Lepore argue that explanation in psychology is like that in physics, Richard Dawkins (chapter 1), Colin McGinn (chapter 5) and Bo Dahlbom (chapter 8) are all trying to show that the difference between psychology and physics is even greater than Dennett wants to say. Psychology has its laws, says McGinn, but they are the laws of logic, and mind is logical in its very nature. No, says Dawkins, much of what goes on in mind is terribly illogical, due to the fact that our minds are so susceptible to viruses, ideas that unexamined invade our minds and take control. Dahlbom has a more positive view of these viruses, thinking of them as socially constructed artifacts, subject to control by society if not by every individual. Thinking involves the use of such artifacts, and is therefore social rather than natural.

The contributions by Dawkins, McGinn, and Dahlbom all illustrate yet another way of doing philosophy: trying to change the perspective. Metaphors and surprising juxtaposition of ideas are the means employed by this type of philosophy. We are survival machines for our genes and memes, and some ideas are viruses.

Psychology is really logic, psychological laws are the laws of logic. Minds are artifacts, thinking is the use of tools, a craft that is becoming industrialized. The typical ambition of this philosophy is, as McGinn puts it, to "open up some new lines of enquiry rather than arrive at any firm conclusions."

The philosophers, biologists, and psychologists speaking up about the mind in this book have different philosophical positions to advance, but more striking is, I think, the differences in the way they go about doing this. Positions and ways will normally depend on each other, of course, but still they are often distinct enough for it to make sense to ask which is most important to a philosopher: the fundamental position or the way philosophy should be done. And I am not sure what the answer is in Dennett's case.

One could, of course, argue that Dennett's preference for stories, and the indeterminacy they give to his views, is an obvious reflection of his radical behaviorism and its Quinean belief in the indeterminacy of meaning. But then one must add that Dennett himself is convinced that his stories make his views more determinate than could be done with definitions and principles. Yet, there is something intriguing in seeing a connection between his increasing insistence on the indeterminacy and holism of meaning and his method of telling narratives to make an idea clear. But then again, there is no similar connection in Quine.

4 An Optimistic Style

When we read philosophy we do it for our interest in the issues, of course, but also for the satisfaction of dealing with these issues in a certain style. When we become engrossed in Quine's philosophy, for example, it is only partly because we worry whether "gavagai" means "rabbit" or "undetached rabbit part," and it is perhaps mainly because we enjoy the company of Quine and his style, his particular outlook on the world, and the particular mode and mood in which he expresses that outlook. We may find his radical behaviorism outrageous, but it will seem less outrageous if we sympathize with his style.

As it is with Quine, it is with Dennett. When peddled second-hand, as in the April 20, 1992 *Newsweek* coverage "Is the Mind an Illusion?" Dennett comes off as something of a villain: a science-crazed, insensitive mechanist, with a bleak and inhumane world view, a rather superficial engineer compared to deep and serious thinkers like Thomas Nagel and John Searle. But people who hear Dennett speak, or read him first-hand, are almost invariably fascinated. They are being educated, intrigued, and entertained. They are so fascinated, it often seems, that they fail to fully appreciate the radicalness of his philosophy. But in appreciating his style, they accept his philosophy in a way that matters more, I think, than whether they accept his behaviorism or not.

By a philosophical style I mean the attitude philosophers have to their own philosophies, or to philosophy in general, as it is expressed in the way they present their views, the mood in which they think. Are they serious? Angry? Tragic or ironic? Cautious or bold? Complaining? Styles are not easy to describe. You take them in half-consciously, and when you try to describe them, they prove to be complex objects. When we discuss them we seem to be discussing the person rather than the philosophy – as if the two could be distinguished. But to really appreciate the role of philosophy, we have to be aware of the different styles, the different attitudes philosophers have to philosophy.

The styles express what they want to do with philosophy, what their deepest ambition and values are, as Rorty puts it, and how they feel about that ambition. Philosophers are after wisdom, truth, of course, and sometimes fame, but their particular style will reveal additional motives: a need to believe and share beliefs, to find in philosophy a cause and a firm foundation to stand on; a wish to surprise and stir, to use philosophy to shock us out of our beliefs into enlightenment; an ambition to change the world, to use philosophy in politics; an ambition to entertain, to induce a more playful spirit; or an exhortation to take life more seriously, a mission to teach, to educate, and so on.

What I find most striking about Dennett as a philosopher, speaking now of his style, is his *optimism*. I read him in order to be a part of those good spirits, to experience with him the enthusiasm and belief in making progress, in philosophy as elsewhere. I read him for his rationalism, for his impatience with mysteries and intellectual laziness, and I read him for his confidence in his own very radical position. If you are bored and frustrated by the rather childish extravagances that philosophers seem so fond of, if you are not interested in card house construction projects, then you have a friend in Dennett, and you will savor his direct, unaffected, down to earth, yet elegant and professional, philosophical style.

5   Theories

When Dennett is described as a radical behaviorist, a conspecific of Quine and Ryle, he comes out very much as a philosopher. Undeterred by what has been going on in cognitive science, it seems, he has been steadfastly advocating an extreme empiricism. When Noam Chomsky, in the early 1960s, dragged linguistics and psychology out of their behavioristic hole, Quine, Putnam, Goodman, and others among the second generation analytical philosophers were up there on the barricades defending Skinner and behaviorism against the new tide. Looking back now it seems as if Dennett would have been on their side, on the side of philosophy, against a developing science.

Today, with connectionism, brain science and Darwinism, it is empiricism that dominates cognitive science, and Dennett can be comfortably on the side of science. But that seems more like a stroke of luck than anything else. Like Quine, Dennett describes his philosophy as "naturalized," as a "chapter of psychology," and like Quine, Dennett will only accept what psychology is saying as long as it is talking the language of empiricism. Don't mistake Dennett's interest in science for a *belief* in science. In spite of being genuinely interested in science, feeling perhaps most at home with scientists, and not afraid of contributing theories and hypotheses for experimental testing, both in biology and psychology, Dennett is a philosopher and nothing else. He is using science to produce a more convincing package for his radical behaviorism.

Be that as it may, the result has become an unusually rich and exciting version of empiricism. And, to get to the punch line, at last, it is the many layers of this philosophical package, and the way they are wrapped together, not the radical behaviorism, nor, in the end, the stories, that make Dennett such a fascinating philosopher to read. When Dennett is described as a radical behaviorist, I am confident that we have correctly identified the essence of his philosophy. But it is somewhat ironic that a philosopher who is such a critic of the idea of essences should be stuck with an essence himself. Similarly, when Dennett is described as a story-teller, there is an irony there too. Stories are pedagogical devices, and as such they are incidental ornaments to the real thing. Now, for all his interest in intuition pumps, Dennett has a view of evolution denying the importance of both essences and ornaments.

"Isms" are the essences of philosophy, and taking "isms" seriously means being caught in an Aristotelian, essentialistic way of thinking. No wonder nothing much changes in philosophy, if there is no evolution of the species. For someone as intrigued as Dennett is, by Darwin's non-essentialistic theory of evolution, it must be painful to constantly hear people asking what species of philosopher he is. Likewise, for someone as strongly a believer in adaptation as the important mechanism of evolution, in the function of things, Dennett must find it painful to be getting requests for stories when it is his many *theoretical* innovations, the taxonomy of stances, the intentional systems theory, the consciousness of time, elbow room, hoping for hieroglyphics, free-floating rationales, abstracta and illata, centers of narrative gravity, virtual machines, real patterns, multiple drafts, heterophenomenology, the Baldwin effect . . . that does all the real work in his philosophy.

6 Another Story

It is now twenty years since I first read *Content and Consciousness*. Impressed by Quine's program for a "naturalized philosophy" and excited by the radical power of his behaviorism, I found in Dennett's writings the program practiced with wit and gusto and a richness of provocative ideas and details. I was particularly fascinated by the evolutionary theory of content, promising contact with and a hold on reality, thus overcoming the circularity of formal semantics.

For discussion at a meeting of the weekly faculty colloquium, in the phenomenologically oriented department where I was a beginning graduate student, I chose the section of *Content and Consciousness* that I liked the most, section 11 on pain. I am sorry to say that Dennett and I, his poor defender, were laughed out of school. Three years later, I knocked on Joe Lambert's door at the UC Irvine campus in southern California, asking for Professor Dennett. I had been admitted as a graduate student there, and in my application I had motivated my choice of university by reference to what I had read on the jacket of *Content and Consciousness*.

But, alas, Daniel Dennett was no longer assistant professor at Irvine. He had left a few years earlier and was now at Tufts University in Boston, on the other side of the continent (where he still remains). Had they not seen in my application that Dennett was the only reason I wanted to come to Irvine? No, they only remembered my quip about being from Göteborg, where Volvo, of legendary high quality, was being produced, and Bill Ulrich had more or less admitted me on that quip, so happy was he with his Volvo.

"Let's talk to Dan," was Lambert's suggestion. Stammering and stuttering, I explained to "Professor Dennett" over the phone how much I appreciated his work and that I was now in California and so on. "Well, why don't you come *here*?" was his immediate response. "We don't have a PhD program at Tufts, but you can be a visiting scholar working with me, and I have a big house, the third floor is not really used, you can stay there as long as you like."

So the editor of *Dennett and His Critics* is a friend of Dennett. And maybe that is why, when I took on the job of editing this book, I was not really interested in doing a *Dennett* book. I encouraged the contributors to concentrate on their own themes rather than write explicit criticism of Dennett's philosophy. I wanted a book with a rich and varied content, bringing out the best in the contributors, and the most exciting ideas in the philosophy of mind today. The result is, I believe, a happy compromise. There is a lot of Dennett in this book, both about him and by him, as there should be, but there are also intriguing, alternative conceptions to Dennett's conception of the mind.

ACKNOWLEDGMENTS

I am grateful to the Swedish Council for Planning and Coordination of Research for financial support, to Kathleen Akins, Linus Broström, Stephan Chambers and Ernie Lepore for encouragement and advice, to all the contributors for the excitement they brought and the grace with which they received my editorial suggestions, to Susan Dennett for checking my English, to Sue Ashton for exemplary copy-editing and to Daniel Dennett for permission to tamper with some of his stories for the purpose of this introduction.

Bo Dahlbom

NOTE

1 I have taken the liberty of retelling a few of his stories, mixing quotation with paraphrase, with the source given. If you ask Dennett for his philosophy in general, you will get something like the "Self-Portrait" (forthcoming), an essay which first provoked me to venture on this more unorthodox kind of introduction. Those who are baffled by my attempt may find his own more illuminating.

REFERENCES

Dennett, D. C. (1969) *Content and Consciousness.* London: Routledge & Kegan Paul and New York: Humanities Press.

Dennett, D. C. (1978) *Brainstorms: Philosophical Essays on Mind and Psychology.* Montgomery, VT: Bradford Books and Hassocks, Sussex: Harvester.

Dennett, D. C. (1980) The milk of human intentionality. *Behavioral and Brain Sciences*, 3, 428–30.

Dennett, D. C. (1982) Philosophy according to Nozick. *New Boston Review*, 7, 9–11.

Dennett, D. C. (1984) *Elbow Room: The Varieties of Free Will Worth Wanting.* Cambridge, Mass: Bradford Books/MIT Press and Oxford University Press.

Dennett, D. C. and Hofstadter, D. R. (1981) *The Mind's I: Fantasies and Reflections on Self and Soul.* New York: Basic Books and Hassocks, Sussex: Harvester.

Quine, W. V. (1960) *Word and Object.* Cambridge, Mass.: MIT Press.

1

Viruses of the Mind

RICHARD DAWKINS

The haven all memes depend on reaching is the human mind, but a human mind is itself an artifact created when memes restructure a human brain in order to make it a better habitat for memes. The avenues for entry and departure are modified to suit local conditions, and strengthened by various artificial devices that enhance fidelity and prolixity of replication: native Chinese minds differ dramatically from native French minds, and literate minds differ from illiterate minds. What memes provide in return to the organisms in which they reside is an incalculable store of advantages – with some Trojan horses thrown in for good measure . . .

Daniel Dennett, *Consciousness Explained*

1 Duplication Fodder

A beautiful child close to me, six and the apple of her father's eye, believes that Thomas the Tank Engine really exists. She believes in Father Christmas, and when she grows up her ambition is to be a tooth fairy. She and her schoolfriends believe the solemn word of respected adults that tooth fairies and Father Christmas really exist. This little girl is of an age to believe whatever you tell her. If you tell her about witches changing princes into frogs she will believe you. If you tell her that bad children roast forever in hell she will have nightmares. I have just discovered that without her father's consent this sweet, trusting, gullible six-year-old is being sent, for weekly instruction, to a Roman Catholic nun. What chance has she?

A human child is shaped by evolution to soak up the culture of her people. Most obviously, she learns the essentials of their language in a matter of months. A large dictionary of words to speak, an encyclopedia of information to speak about, complicated syntactic and semantic rules to order the speaking, all are transferred from older brains into hers well before she reaches half her adult size. When you are preprogrammed to absorb useful information at a high rate, it is hard to shut out pernicious or damaging information at the same time. With so many mindbytes to be downloaded, so many mental codons to be duplicated, it is no wonder that child brains are gullible, open to almost any suggestion, vulnerable to subversion, easy prey to Moonies, scientologists and nuns. Like immune-deficient patients, children are wide open to mental infections that adults might brush off without effort.

DNA, too, includes parasitic code. Cellular machinery is extremely good at copying DNA. Where DNA is concerned, it seems to have an eagerness to copy, like a child's eagerness to imitate the language of its parents. Concomitantly, DNA seems eager to be copied. The cell nucleus is a paradise for DNA, humming with sophisticated, fast, and accurate duplicating machinery.

Cellular machinery is so friendly towards DNA duplication that it is small wonder cells play host to DNA parasites – viruses, viroids, plasmids and a riff-raff of other genetic fellow travelers. Parasitic DNA even gets itself spliced seamlessly into the chromosomes themselves. 'Jumping genes' and stretches of 'selfish DNA' cut or copy themselves out of chromosomes and paste themselves in elsewhere. Deadly oncogenes are almost impossible to distinguish from the legitimate genes between which they are spliced. In evolutionary time, there is probably a continual traffic from 'straight' genes to 'outlaw', and back again (Dawkins, 1982). DNA is just DNA. The only thing that distinguishes viral DNA from host DNA is its expected method of passing into future generations. 'Legitimate' host DNA is just DNA that aspires to pass into the next generation via the orthodox route of sperm or egg. 'Outlaw' or parasitic DNA is just DNA that looks to a quicker, less cooperative route to the future, via a sneezed droplet or a smear of blood, rather than via a sperm or egg.

For data on a floppy disc, a computer is a humming paradise just as cell nuclei hum with eagerness to duplicate DNA. Computers and their associated disc and tape readers are designed with high fidelity in mind. As with DNA molecules, magnetized bytes don't literally 'want' to be faithfully copied. Nevertheless, you can write a computer program that takes steps to duplicate itself. Not just duplicate itself within one computer but spread itself to other computers. Computers are so good at copying bytes, and so good at faithfully obeying the instructions contained in those bytes, that they are sitting ducks to self-replicating programs: wide open to subversion by software parasites. Any cynic familiar with the theory of selfish genes and memes would have known that modern personal computers, with their promiscuous traffic of floppy discs and e-mail links, were just asking for trouble. The only surprising thing about the current epidemic of computer viruses is that it has been so long in coming.

2   Computer Viruses: a Model for an Informational Epidemiology

Computer viruses are pieces of code that graft themselves into existing, legitimate programs and subvert the normal actions of those programs. They may travel on exchanged floppy disks, or over networks. They are technically distinguished from 'worms' which are whole programs in their own right, usually traveling over networks. Rather different are "Trojan horses," a third category of destructive programs, which are not in themselves self-replicating but rely on humans to replicate them because of their pornographic or otherwise appealing content. Both viruses and worms are programs that actually say, in computer language, "Duplicate me." Both may do other things that make their presence felt and perhaps satisfy the hole-in-corner vanity of their authors. These side-effects may be "humorous" (like the virus that makes the Macintosh's built-in loudspeaker enunciate the words "Don't panic", with predictably opposite effect); malicious (like the numerous IBM viruses that erase the hard disk after a sniggering screen-announcement of the impending disaster); political (like the Spanish Telecom and Beijing viruses that protest about telephone costs and massacred students respectively); or simply inadvertent (the programmer is incompetent to handle the low-level system calls required to write an effective virus or worm). The famous Internet Worm, which paralysed much of the computing power of the United States on November 2, 1988, was not intended (very) maliciously but got out of control and, within 24 hours, had clogged around 6,000 computer memories with exponentially multiplying copies of itself.

"Memes now spread around the world at the speed of light, and replicate at rates that make even fruit flies and yeast cells look glacial in comparison. They leap promiscuously from vehicle to vehicle, and from medium to medium, and are proving to be virtually unquarantinable" (Dennett, 1990, p. 131). Viruses aren't limited to electronic media such as disks and data lines. On its way from one computer to another, a virus may pass through printing ink, light rays in a human lens, optic nerve impulses and finger muscle contractions. A computer fanciers' magazine that printed the text of a virus program for the interest of its readers has been widely condemned. Indeed, such is the appeal of the virus idea to a certain kind of puerile mentality (the masculine gender is used advisedly), that publication of any kind of "how to" information on designing virus programs is rightly seen as an irresponsible act.

I am not going to publish any virus code. But there are certain tricks of effective virus design that are sufficiently well known, even obvious, that it will do no harm to mention them, as I need to do in order to develop my theme. They all stem from the virus's need to evade detection while it is spreading.

A virus that clones itself too prolifically within one computer will soon be detected because the symptoms of clogging will become too obvious to ignore. For this reason many virus programs check, before infecting a system, to make sure that they are not already on that system. Incidentally, this opens the way for a defense against viruses that is analogous to immunization. In the days before a specific anti-virus program was available, I myself responded to an early infection of my own hard disk by means of a crude "vaccination." Instead of deleting the virus that I had detected, I simply disabled its coded instructions, leaving the "shell" of the virus with its characteristic external "signature" intact. In theory, subsequent members of the same virus species that arrived in my system should have recognized the signature of their own kind and refrained from trying to double-infect. I don't know whether this immunization really worked, but in those days it probably was worth while "gutting" a virus and leaving a shell like this, rather than simply removing it lock, stock, and barrel. Nowadays it is better to hand the problem over to one of the professionally written anti-virus programs.

A virus that is too virulent will be rapidly detected and scotched. A virus that instantly and catastrophically sabotages every computer in which it finds itself will not find itself in many computers. It may have a most amusing effect on one computer – erase an entire doctoral thesis or something equally side-splitting – but it won't spread as an epidemic.

Some viruses, therefore, are designed to have an effect that is small enough to be difficult to detect, but which may nevertheless be extremely damaging. There is one type, which, instead of erasing disk sectors wholesale, attacks only spreadsheets, making a few random changes in the (usually financial) quantities entered in the rows and columns. Other viruses evade detection by being triggered probabilistically, for example erasing only one in 16 of the hard disks infected. Yet other viruses employ the time-bomb principle. Most modern computers are "aware" of the date, and viruses have been triggered to manifest themselves all around the world, on a particular date such as Friday 13th or April Fool's Day. From the parasitic point of view, it doesn't matter how catastrophic the eventual attack is, provided the virus has had plenty of opportunity to spread first (a disturbing analogy to the Medawar/Williams theory of ageing; we are the victims of lethal and sub-lethal genes that mature only after we have had plenty of time to reproduce (Williams, 1957)). In defense, some large companies go so far as to set aside one "miner's canary" among their fleet of computers, and advance its internal calendar a week so that any time-bomb viruses will reveal themselves prematurely before the big day.

Again predictably, the epidemic of computer viruses has triggered an arms race. Anti-viral software is doing a roaring trade. These antidote programs – "Interferon," "Vaccine," "Gatekeeper" and others – employ a diverse armory of tricks. Some are written with specific, known, and named viruses in mind. Others intercept any attempt to meddle with sensitive system areas of memory and warn the user.

The virus principle could, in theory, be used for non-malicious, even beneficial purposes. Thimbleby (1991) coins the phrase "liveware" for his already-implemented use of the infection principle for keeping multiple copies of databases up to date. Every time a disk containing the database is plugged into a computer, it looks to see whether there is already another copy present on the local hard disk. If there is, each copy is updated in the light of the other. So, with a bit of luck, it doesn't matter which member of a circle of colleagues enters, say, a new bibliographical citation on his personal disk. His newly entered information will readily infect the disks of his colleagues (because the colleagues promiscuously insert their disks into one another's computers) and will spread like an epidemic around the circle. Thimbleby's liveware is not entirely virus-like: it could not spread to just anybody's computer and do damage. It spreads data only to already-existing copies of its own database; and you will not be infected by liveware unless you positively opt for infection.

Incidentally, Thimbleby, who is much concerned with the virus menace, points out that you can gain some protection by using computer systems that other people don't use. The usual justification for purchasing today's numerically dominant personal computer is simply and solely that it *is* numerically dominant. Almost every knowledgeable person agrees that, in terms of quality and especially user-friendliness, the rival, minority system is superior. Nevertheless, ubiquity is held to be a good in itself, sufficient to outweigh sheer quality. Buy the same (albeit inferior) computer as your colleagues, the argument goes, and you'll be able to benefit from shared software, and from a generally larger circulation of available software. The irony is that, with the advent of the virus plague, "benefit" is not all that you are likely to get. Not only should we all be very hesitant before we accept a disk from a colleague. We should also be aware that, if we join a large community of users of a particular make of computer, we are also joining a large community of viruses – even, it turns out, *disproportionately* larger.

Returning to possible uses of viruses for positive purposes, there are proposals to exploit the "poacher turned gamekeeper", principle, and "set a thief to catch a thief." A simple way would be to take any of the existing anti-viral programs and load it, as a "warhead," into a harmless self-replicating virus. From a "public health" point of view, a spreading epidemic of anti-viral software could be especially beneficial because the computers most vulnerable to malicious viruses – those whose owners are promiscuous in the exchange of pirated programs – will also be most vulnerable to infection by the healing anti-virus. A more penetrating anti-virus might – as in the immune system – "learn" or "evolve" an improved capacity to attack whatever viruses it encountered.

I can imagine other uses of the computer virus principle which, if not exactly altruistic, are at least constructive enough to escape the charge of pure vandalism. A computer company might wish to do market research on the habits of its customers, with a view to improving the design of future products. Do users like to choose files by pictorial icon, or do they opt to display them by textual name only? How deeply do people nest folders (directories) within one another? Do people settle down for a long session with only one program, say a word processor, or are they constantly switching back and forth, say between writing and drawing programs? Do people succeed in moving the mouse pointer straight to the target, or do they meander around in time-wasting hunting movements that could be rectified by a change in design?

The company could send out a questionnaire asking all these questions, but the customers that replied would be a biased sample and, in any case, their own assessment of their computer-using behavior might be inaccurate. A better solution would be a market-research computer program. Customers would be asked to load this program into their system where it would unobtrusively sit, quietly monitoring and tallying key-presses and mouse movements. At the end of a year, the customer would be asked to send in the disk file containing all the tallyings of the market-research program. But again, most people would not bother to cooperate and some might see it as an invasion of privacy and of their disk space.

The perfect solution, from the company's point of view, would be a virus. Like any other virus, it would be self-replicating and secretive. But it would not be destructive or facetious like an ordinary virus. Along with its self-replicating booster it would contain a market-research warhead. The virus would be released surreptiously into the community of computer users. Just like an ordinary virus it would spread around, as people passed floppy disks and e-mail around the community. As the virus spread from computer to computer, it would build up statistics on user behavior, monitored secretly from deep within a succession of systems. Every now and again, a copy of the viruses would happen to find its way, by normal epidemic traffic, back into one of the company's own computers. There it would be debriefed and its data collated with data from other copies of the virus that had come "home."

Looking into the future, it is not fanciful to imagine a time when viruses, both bad and good, have become so ubiquitous that we could speak of an ecological community of viruses and legitimate programs coexisting in the silicosphere. At present, software is advertised as, say, "Compatible with System 7." In the future, products may be advertised as "Compatible with all viruses registered in the 1998 World Virus Census; immune to all listed virulent viruses; takes full advantage of the facilities offered by the following benign viruses if present..." Word-processing software, say, may hand over particular functions, such as word-counting and string-searches, to friendly viruses burrowing autonomously through the text.

Looking even further into the future, whole integrated software systems might grow, not by design, but by something like the growth of an ecological community such as a tropical rainforest. Gangs of mutually compatible viruses might grow up, in the same way as genomes can be regarded as gangs of mutually compatible genes (Dawkins, 1982). Indeed, I have even suggested that our genomes should be regarded as gigantic colonies of viruses (Dawkins, 1976). Genes cooperate with one another in genomes because natural selection has favored those genes that prosper in the presence of the other genes that happen to be common in the gene pool. Different gene pools may evolve towards different combinations of mutually compatible genes. I envisage a time when, in the same kind of way, computer viruses may evolve towards compatibility with other viruses, to form communities or gangs. But then again, perhaps not! At any rate, I find the speculation more alarming than exciting.

At present, computer viruses don't strictly evolve. They are invented by human programmers and if they evolve they do so in the same weak sense as cars or aeroplanes evolve. Designers derive this year's car as a slight modification of last year's car, and they may, more or less consciously, continue a trend of the last few years – further flattening of the radiator grill or whatever it may be. Computer virus designers dream up ever more devious tricks for outwitting the programmers of anti-virus software. But computer viruses don't – so far – mutate and evolve by true natural selection. They may do so in the future. Whether they evolve by natural selection, or whether their evolution is steered by human designers, may not make much difference to their eventual performance. By either kind of evolution, we expect them to become better at concealment, and we expect them to become subtly compatible with other viruses that are at the same time prospering in the computer community.

DNA viruses and computer viruses spread for the same reason: an environment exists in which there is machinery well set up to duplicate and spread them around and to obey the instructions that the viruses embody. These two environments are, respectively, the environment of cellular physiology and the environment provided by a large community of computers and data-handling machinery. Are there any other environments like these, any other humming paradises of replication?

3 The Infected Mind

I have already alluded to the programmed-in gullibility of a child, so useful for learning language and traditional wisdom, and so easily subverted by nuns, Moonies and their ilk. More generally, we all exchange information with one another. We don't exactly plug floppy disks into slots in one another's skulls, but we exchange sentences, both through our ears and through our eyes. We notice each other's styles of moving and of dressing and are influenced. We take in advertising jingles, and are presumably persuaded by them, otherwise hard-headed businessmen would not spend so much money polluting the air with them.

Think about the two qualities that a virus, or any sort of parasitic replicator, demands of a friendly medium, the two qualities that make cellular machinery so friendly towards parasitic DNA, and that make computers so friendly towards computer viruses. These qualities are, firstly, a readiness to replicate information accurately, perhaps with some mistakes that are subsequently reproduced accurately; and, secondly, a readiness to obey instructions encoded in the information so replicated.

Cellular machinery and electronic computers excel in both these virus-friendly qualities. How do human brains match up? As faithful duplicators, they are certainly less perfect than either cells or electronic computers. Nevertheless, they are still pretty good, perhaps about as faithful as an RNA virus, though not as good as DNA with all its elaborate proofreading measures against textual degradation. Evidence of the fidelity of brains, especially child brains, as data duplicators is provided by language itself. Shaw's Professor Higgins was able by ear alone to place Londoners in the street where they grew up. Fiction is not evidence for anything, but everyone knows that Higgins's fictional skill is only an exaggeration of something we can all do. Any American can tell Deep South from Mid West, New England from Hillbilly. Any New Yorker can tell Bronx from Brooklyn. Equivalent claims could be substantiated for any country. What this phenomenon means is that human brains are capable of pretty accurate copying (otherwise the accents of, say, Newcastle would not be stable enough to be recognized) but with some mistakes (otherwise pronunciation would not evolve, and all speakers of a language would inherit identically the same accents from their remote ancestors). Language evolves, because it has both the great stability and the slight changeability that are prerequisites for any evolving system.

The second requirement of a virus-friendly environment – that it should obey a program of coded instructions – is again only quantitatively less true for brains than for cells or computers. We sometimes obey orders from one another, but also we sometimes don't. Nevertheless, it is a telling fact that, the world over, the vast majority of children follow the religion of their parents rather than any of the other available religions. Instructions to genuflect, to bow towards Mecca, to nod one's head rhythmically towards the wall, to shake like a maniac, to "speak in tongues" – the list of such arbitrary and pointless motor patterns offered by religion alone is extensive – are obeyed, if not slavishly, at least with some reasonably high statistical probability.

Less portentously, and again especially prominent in children, the "craze" is a striking example of behavior that owes more to epidemiology than to rational choice. Yo-yos, hula hoops and pogo sticks, with their associated behavioral fixed actions, sweep through schools, and more sporadically leap from school to school, in patterns that differ from a measles epidemic in no serious particular. Ten years ago, you could have traveled thousands of miles through the United States and never seen a baseball cap turned back to front. Today, the reverse baseball cap is ubiquitous. I do not know what the pattern of geographical spread of the reverse baseball cap precisely was, but epidemiology is certaintly among the professions primarily qualified to study it. We don't have to get into arguments about "determinism;" we don't have to claim that children are compelled to imitate their fellows' hat fashions. It is enough that their hat-wearing behavior, as a matter of fact, *is* statistically affected by the hat-wearing behavior of their fellows.

Trivial though they are, crazes provide us with yet more circumstantial evidence that human minds, especially perhaps juvenile ones, have the qualities that we have singled out as desirable for an informational parasite. At the very least the mind is a plausible *candidate* for infection by something like a computer virus, even if it is not quite such a parasite's dream-environment as a cell nucleus or an electronic computer.

It is intriguing to wonder what it might feel like, from the inside, if one's mind were the victim of a "virus." This might be a deliberately designed parasite, like a present-day computer virus. Or it might be an inadvertently mutated and unconsciously evolved parasite. Either way, especially if the evolved parasite was the memic descendant of a long line of successful ancestors, we are entitled to expect the typical "mind virus" to be pretty good at its job of getting itself successfully replicated.

Progressive evolution of more effective mind-parasites will have two aspects. New "mutants" (either random or designed by humans) that are better at spreading will become more numerous. And there will be a ganging up of ideas that flourish in one another's presence, ideas that mutually support one another just as genes do and as I have speculated computer viruses may one day do. We expect that replicators will go around together from brain to brain in mutually compatible gangs. These gangs will come to constitute a package, which may be sufficiently stable to deserve a collective name such as Roman Catholicism or Voodoo. It doesn't too much matter whether we analogize the whole package to a single virus, or each one of the component parts to a single virus. The analogy is not that precise anyway, just as the distinction between a computer virus and a computer worm is nothing to get worked up about. What matters is that minds are friendly environments to parasitic, self-replicating ideas or information, and that minds are typically massively infected.

Like computer viruses, successful mind viruses will tend to be hard for their victims to detect. If you are the victim of one, the chances are that you won't know it, and may even vigorously deny it. Accepting that a virus might be difficult to detect in your own mind, what tell-tale signs might you look out for? I shall answer by imagining how a medical textbook might describe the typical symptoms of a sufferer (arbitrarily assumed to be male).

(1) The patient typically finds himself impelled by some deep, inner conviction that something is true, or right, or virtuous: a conviction that doesn't seem to owe anything to evidence or reason, but which, nevertheless, he feels as totally compelling and convincing. We doctors refer to such a belief as "faith."

(2) Patients typically make a positive virtue of faith's being strong and unshakable, *in spite of* not being based upon evidence. Indeed, they may feel that the less the evidence there is, the more virtuous the belief (see below).

This paradoxical idea that lack of evidence is a positive virtue where faith is concerned has something of the quality of a program that is self-sustaining, because it is self-referential (see the chapter, "On viral sentences and self-replicating structures" in Hofstadter, 1985). Once the proposition is believed, it automatically undermines opposition to itself. The "lack of evidence is a virtue" idea would be an admirable sidekick, ganging up with faith itself in a clique of mutually supportive viral programs.

(3) A related symptom, which a faith-sufferer may also present, is the conviction that "mystery," *per se*, is a good thing. It is not a virtue to solve mysteries. Rather we should enjoy them, even revel in their insolubility.

Any impulse to solve mysteries could be seriously inimical to the spread of a mind virus. It would not, therefore, be surprising if the idea that "mysteries are better not solved" was a favored member of a mutually supporting gang of viruses. Take the "Mystery of the Transubstantiation." It is easy and non-mysterious to believe that in some symbolic or metaphorical sense the eucharistic wine turns into the blood of Christ. The Roman Catholic doctrine of transubstantiation, however, claims far more. The "whole substance" of the wine is converted into the blood of Christ; the appearance of wine that remains is "merely accidental," "inhering in no substance" (Kenny, 1986, p. 72). Transubstantiation is colloquially taught as meaning that the wine "literally" turns into the blood of Christ. Whether in its obfuscatory Aristotelian or its franker colloquial form, the claim of transubstantiation can be made only if we do serious violence to the normal meanings of words like "substance" and "literally." Redefining words is not a sin but, if we use words like "whole substance" and "literally" for this case, what word are we going to use when we really and truly *want* to say that something did actually happen? As Anthony Kenny observed of his own puzzlement as a young seminarian, "For all I could tell, my typewriter might be Benjamin Disraeli transubstantiated . . . ."

Roman Catholics, whose belief in infallible authority compels them to accept that wine becomes physically transformed into blood despite all appearances, refer to the "mystery" of the transubstantiation. Calling it a mystery makes everything OK, you see. At least, it works for a mind well prepared by background infection. Exactly the same trick is performed in the "mystery" of the Trinity. Mysteries are not meant to be solved, they are meant to strike awe. The "mystery is a virtue" idea comes to the aid of the Catholic, who would otherwise find intolerable the obligation to believe the obvious nonsense of the transubstantiation and the "three-in-one." Again, the belief that "mystery is a virtue" has a self-referential ring. As Hofstadter might put it, the very mysteriousness of the belief moves the believer to perpetuate the mystery.

An extreme symptom of "mystery is a virtue" infection is Tertullian's "*Certum est quia impossibile est*" ("It is certain because it is impossible"). That way madness lies. One is tempted to quote Lewis Carroll's White Queen who, in response to Alice's "One can't believe impossible things" retorted "I daresay you haven't had much practice . . . When I was your age, I always did it for half-an-hour a day. Why, sometimes I've believed as many as six impossible things before breakfast." Or Douglas Adams's Electric Monk, a labor-saving device programmed to do your believing for you, which was capable of "believing things they'd have difficulty believing in Salt Lake City" and which, at the moment of being introduced to the reader, believed, contrary to all the evidence, that everything in the world was a uniform shade of pink. But White Queens and Electric Monks become less funny when you realize that these virtuoso believers are indistinguishable from revered theologians in real life. "It is by all means to be believed, because it is absurd" (Tertullian again). Sir Thomas Browne (1635) quotes Tertullian with approval, and goes further: "Methinks there be not impossibilities enough in religion for an active faith." And "I desire to exercise my faith in the difficultest point; for to credit ordinary and visible objects is not faith, but perswasion."

I have the feeling that something more interesting is going on here than just plain insanity or surrealist nonsense, something akin to the admiration we feel when we watch a ten-ball juggler on a tightrope. It is as though the faithful gain prestige through managing to believe even more ridiculous things than their rivals succeed in believing. Are these people testing – exercising – their believing muscles, training themselves to believe impossible things so that they can take in their stride the merely improbable things that they are ordinarily called upon to believe?

While I was writing this, the *Guardian* (July 29, 1991) fortuitously carried a beautiful example. It came in an interview with a rabbi undertaking the bizarre task of vetting the kosher-purity of food products right back to the ultimate origins of their minutest ingredients. He was currently agonizing over whether to go all the way to China to scrutinize the menthol that goes into cough sweets. "Have you ever tried checking Chinese menthol . . . it was extremely difficult, especially since the first letter we sent received the reply in best Chinese English, 'The product contains no kosher' . . . China has only recently started opening up to kosher investigators. The menthol should be OK, but you can never be absolutely sure unless you visit." These koshner investigators run a telephone hotline on which up-to-the-minute red-alerts of suspicion are recorded against chocolate bars and cod-liver oil. The rabbi sighs that the green-inspired trend away from artificial colors and flavors "makes life miserable in the kosher field because you have to follow all these things back." When the interviewer asks him why he bothers with this obviously pointless exercise, he makes it very clear that the point is precisely that there *is* no point:

> That most of the Kashrut laws are divine ordinances without reason given is 100 per cent the point. It is very easy not to murder people. Very easy. It is a little bit harder not to steal because one is tempted occasionally. So that is no great proof that I believe in God or am fulfilling His will. But, if He tells me not to have a cup of coffee with milk in it with my mincemeat and peas at lunchtime, that is a test. The only reason I am doing that is because I have been told to so do. It is doing something difficult.

Helena Cronin has suggested to me that there may be an analogy here to Zahavi's handicap theory of sexual selection and the evolution of signals (Zahavi, 1975). Long unfashionable, even ridiculed (Dawkins, 1976), Zahavi's theory has recently been cleverly rehabilitated (Grafen, 1990a,b) and is now taken seriously by evolutionary biologists (Dawkins, 1989). Zahavi suggests that peacocks, for instance, evolve their absurdly burdensome fans with their ridiculously conspicuous (to predators) colors, precisely *because* they are burdensome and dangerous, and therefore impressive to females. The peacock is, in effect, saying: "Look how fit and strong I must be, since I can afford to carry around this preposterous tail."

To avoid misunderstanding of the subjective language in which Zahavi likes to make his points, I should add that the biologist's convention of personifying the unconscious actions of natural selection is taken for granted here. Grafen has translated the argument into an orthodox Darwinian mathematical model, and it works. No claim is here being made about the intentionality or awareness of peacocks and peahens. They can be as sphexish or as intentional as you please (Dennett, 1983, 1984). Moreover, Zahavi's theory is general enough not to depend upon a Darwinian underpinning. A flower advertising its nectar to a "skeptical" bee could benefit from the Zahavi principle. But so could a human salesman seeking to impress a client.

The premise of Zahavi's idea is that natural selection will favor skepticism among females (or among recipients of advertising messages generally). The only way for a male (or any advertiser) to authenticate his boast of strength (quality, or whatever it is) is to prove that it is true by shouldering a truly costly handicap – a handicap *that only a genuinely strong* (high-quality, etc.) male could bear. It may be called the principle of costly authentication. And now to the point. Is it possible that some religious doctrines are favored not *in spite of* being ridiculous but precisely *because* they are ridiculous? Any wimp in religion could believe that bread *symbolically* represents the body of Christ, but it takes a real, red-blooded Catholic to believe something as daft as the transubstantiation. If you can believe that you can believe anything, and (witness the story of Doubting Thomas) these people are trained to see that as a virtue.

Let us return to our list of symptoms that someone afflicted with the mental virus of faith, and its accompanying gang of secondary infections, may expect to experience.

(4) The sufferer may find himself behaving intolerantly towards vectors of rival faiths, in extreme cases even killing them or advocating their deaths. He may be similarly violent in his disposition towards apostates (people who once held the faith but have renounced it); or towards heretics (people who espouse a different – often, perhaps significantly, only very slightly different – version of the faith). He may also feel hostile towards other modes of thought that are potentially inimical to his faith, such as the method of scientific reason which may function rather like a piece of anti-viral software.

The threat to kill the distinguished novelist Salman Rushdie is only the latest in a long line of sad examples. On the very day that I wrote this, the Japanese translator of *The Satanic Verses* was found murdered, a week after a near-fatal attack on the Italian translator of the same book. By the way, the apparently opposite symptom of "sympathy" for Muslim "hurt," voiced by the Archbishop of Canterbury and other Christian leaders (verging, in the case of the Vatican, on outright criminal complicity) is, of course, a manifestation of the symptom we diagnosed earlier: the delusion that faith, however obnoxious its results, has to be respected simply because it *is* faith.

Murder is an extreme, of course. But there is an even more extreme symptom, and that is suicide in the militant service of a faith. Like a soldier ant programmed to sacrifice her life for germ-line copies of the genes that did the programming, a young Arab or Japanese is taught that to die in a holy war is the quickest way to heaven. Whether the leaders who exploit him really believe this does not diminish the brutal power that the "suicide mission virus" wields on behalf of the faith. Of course suicide, like murder, is a mixed blessing: would-be converts may be repelled, or may treat with contempt a faith that is perceived as insecure enough to need such tactics.

More obviously, if too many individuals sacrifice themselves the supply of believers could run low. This was true of a notorious example of faith-inspired suicide, though in this case it was not "kamikaze" death in battle. The Peoples' Temple sect became extinct when its leader, the Reverend Jim Jones, led the bulk of his followers from the United States to the Promised Land of "Jonestown" in the Guyanan jungle where he persuaded more than 900 of them, children first, to drink cyanide. The macabre affair was fully investigated by a team from the *San Francisco Chronicle* (Kilduff and Javers, 1978).

> Jones, "the Father," had called his flock together and told them it was time to depart for heaven.
> "We're going to meet," he promised, "in another place."
> The words kept coming over the camp's loudspeakers.
> "There is great dignity in dying. It is a great demonstration for everyone to die."

Incidentally, it does not escape the trained mind of the alert sociobiologist that Jones, within his sect in earlier days, "proclaimed himself the only person permitted to have sex" (presumably his partners were also permitted). "A secretary would arrange for Jones's liaisons. She would call up and say, 'Father hates to do this, but he has this tremendous urge and could you please . . . ?'" His victims were not only female. One 17-year-old male follower, from the days when Jones's community was still in San Francisco, told how he was taken for dirty weekends to a hotel where Jones received a "minister's discount for Rev. Jim Jones and son." The same boy said: "I was really in awe of him. He was more than a father. I would have killed my parents for him." What is remarkable about the Reverend Jim Jones is not his own self-serving behavior but the almost superhuman gullibility of his followers. Given such prodigious credulity, can anyone doubt that human minds are ripe for malignant infection?

Admittedly, the Reverend Jones conned only a few thousand people. But his case is an extreme, the tip of an iceberg. The same eagerness to be conned by religious leaders is widespread. Most of us would have been prepared to bet that nobody could get away with going on television and saying, in all but so many words, "Send me your money, so that I can use it to persuade other suckers to send me their money too." Yet today, in every major conurbation in the United States, you can find at least one television evangelist channel entirely devoted to this transparent confidence trick. And they get away with it in sackfuls. Faced with suckerdom on this awesome scale, it is hard not to feel a grudging sympathy with the shiny-suited conmen. Until you realize that not all the suckers are rich, and that it is often widows' mites on which the evangelists are growing fat. I have even heard one of them explicitly invoking the principle that I now identify with Zahavi's principle of costly authentication. God really appreciates a donation, he said with passionate sincerity, only when that donation is so large that it hurts. Elderly paupers were wheeled on to testify how much happier they felt since they had made over their little all to the Reverend whoever it was.

(5) The patient may notice that the particular convictions that he holds, while having nothing to do with evidence, do seem to owe a great deal to epidemiology. Why, he may wonder, do I hold *this* set of convictions rather than *that* set? Is it because I surveyed all the world's faiths and chose the one whose claims seemed most convincing? Almost certainly not. If you have a faith, it is statistically overwhelmingly likely that it is the same faith as your parents and grandparents had. No doubt soaring cathedrals, stirring music, moving stories and parables, help a bit. But by far the most important variable determining your religion is the accident of birth. The convictions that you so passionately believe would have been a completely different, and largely contradictory, set of convictions, if only you had happened to be born in a different place. Epidemiology, not evidence.

(6) If the patient is one of the rare exceptions who follows a different religion from his parents, the explanation may still be epidemiological. To be sure, it is *possible* that he dispassionately surveyed the world's faiths and chose the most convincing one. But it is statistically more probable that he has been exposed to a particularly potent infective agent – a John Wesley, a Jim Jones or a St Paul. Here we are talking about horizontal transmission, as in measles. Before, the epidemiology was that of vertical transmission, as in Huntington's Chorea.

(7) The internal sensations of the patient may be startlingly reminiscent of those more ordinarily associated with sexual love. This is an extremely potent force in the brain, and it is not surprising that some viruses have evolved to exploit it. St Teresa of Avila's famously orgasmic vision is too notorious to need quoting again. More seriously, and on a less crudely sensual plane, the philosopher Anthony Kenny provides moving testimony to the pure delight that awaits those that manage to believe in the mystery of the transubstantiation. After describing his ordination as a Roman Catholic priest, empowered by laying on of hands to celebrate Mass, he goes on that he vividly recalls

> the exaltation of the first months during which I had the power to say Mass. Normally a slow and sluggish riser, I would leap early out of bed, fully awake and full of excitement at the thought of the momentous act I was privileged to perform. I rarely said the public Community Mass: most days I celebrated alone at a side altar with a junior member of the College to serve as acolyte and congregation. But that made no difference to the solemnity of the sacrifice or the validity of the consecration.
> It was touching the body of Christ, the closeness of the priest to Jesus, which most enthralled me. I would gaze on the Host after the words of consecration, soft-eyed like a lover looking into the eyes of his beloved . . . Those early days as a priest remain in my memory as days of fulfilment and tremulous happiness; something precious, and yet too fragile to last, like a romantic love-affair brought up short by the reality of an ill-assorted marriage. (Kenny, 1986, pp. 101–2)

Dr Kenny is affectingly believable that it felt to him, as a young priest, as though he was in love with the consecrated host. What a brilliantly successful virus! On the same page, incidentally, Kenny also shows us that the virus is transmitted contagiously – if not literally then at least in some sense – from the palm of the infecting bishop's hand through the top of the new priest's head:

If Catholic doctrine is true, every priest validly ordained derives his orders in an unbroken line of laying on of hands, through the bishop who ordains him, back to one of the twelve Apostles . . . there must be centuries-long, recorded chains of layings on of hands. It surprises me that priests never seem to trouble to trace their spiritual ancestry in this way, finding out who ordained their bishop, and who ordained him, and so on to Julius II or Celestine V or Hildebrand, or Gregory the Great, perhaps. (Kenny, 1986, p. 101)

It surprises me, too.

4 Is Science a Virus?

No. Not unless all computer programs are viruses. Good, useful programs spread because people evaluate them, recommend them and pass them on. Computer viruses spread solely because they embody the coded instructions: "Spread me." Scientific ideas, like all memes, are subject to a kind of natural selection, and this might look superficially virus-like. But the selective forces that scrutinize scientific ideas are not arbitrary or capricious. They are exacting, well-honed rules, and they do not favor pointless self-serving behavior. They favor all the virtues laid out in textbooks of standard methodology: testability, evidential support, precision, quantifiability, consistency, intersubjectivity, repeatability, universality, progressiveness, independence of cultural milieu, and so on. Faith spreads despite a total lack of every single one of these virtues.

You may find elements of epidemiology in the spread of scientific ideas, but it will be largely descriptive epidemiology. The rapid spread of a good idea through the scientific community may even look like a description of a measles epidemic. But when you examine the underlying reasons you find that they are good ones, satisfying the demanding standards of scientific method. In the history of the spread of faith you will find little else but epidemiology, and causal epidemiology at that. The reason why person *A* believes one thing and *B* believes another is simply and solely that *A* was born on one continent and *B* on another. Testability, evidential support and the rest aren't even remotely considered. For scientific belief, epidemiology merely comes along afterwards and describes the history of its acceptance. For religious belief, epidemiology is the root cause.

5 Epilogue

Happily, viruses don't win every time. Many children emerge unscathed from the worst that nuns and mullahs can throw at them. Anthony Kenny's own story has a happy ending. He eventually renounced his orders because he could no longer tolerate the obvious contradictions within Catholic belief, and he is now a highly respected scholar. But one cannot help remarking that it must be a powerful infection indeed that took a man of his wisdom and intelligence – now President of the British Academy, no less – three decades to fight off. Am I unduly alarmist to fear for the soul of my six-year-old innocent?

ACKNOWLEDGMENT

With thanks to Helena Cronin for detailed suggestions on content and style on every page.

REFERENCES

Browne, Sir T. (1635) *Religio Medici*, I, 9, p. 11.
Dawkins, R. (1976) *The Selfish Gene*. Oxford: Oxford University Press.
Dawkins, R. (1982) *The Extended Phenotype*. Oxford: W. H. Freeman.
Dawkins, R. (1989) *The Selfish Gene*, 2nd edn. Oxford: Oxford University Press.
Dennett, D. C. (1983) Intentional systems in cognitive ethology: the "Panglossian paradigm" defended. *Behavioral and Brain Sciences*, 6, 343–90.
Dennett, D. C. (1984) *Elbow Room: The Varieties of Free Will Worth Wanting*. Oxford: Oxford University Press.
Dennett, D. C. (1990) Memes and the exploitation of imagination. *The Journal of Aesthetics and Art Criticism*, 48, 127–35.
Grafen, A. (1990a) Sexual selection unhandicapped by the Fisher process. *Journal of Theoretical Biology*, 144, 473–516.
Grafen, A. (1990b) Biological signals as handicaps. *Journal of Theoretical Biology*, 144, 517–46.
Hofstadter, D. R. (1985) *Metamagical Themas*. Harmondsworth: Penguin.
Kenny, A. (1986) *A Path from Rome*. Oxford: Oxford University Press.
Kilduff, M. and Javers, R. (1978) *The Suicide Cult*. New York: Bantam.
Thimbleby, H. (1991) Can viruses ever be useful? *Computers and Security*, 10, 111–14.
Williams, G. C. (1957) Pleiotropy, natural selection, and the evolution of senescence. *Evolution*, 11, 398–411.
Zahavi, A. (1975) Mate selection – a selection for a handicap. *Journal of Theoretical Biology*, 53, 205–14.

2

Filling in: Why Dennett is Wrong

P. S. CHURCHLAND AND V. S. RAMACHANDRAN

It comes as a surprise to discover that the foveal area in which one has high resolution and high-acuity vision is minute; it encompasses a mere 2° of visual angle – roughly, the area of the thumbnail at arm's length. The introspective guess concerning acuity in depth likewise errs on the side of extravagance; the region of crisp, fused perception is, at arm's length, only a few centimeters deep; closer in, the area of fused perception is even narrower. The eyes make a small movement – a saccade – about every 200–300 milliseconds, sampling the scene by shifting continuously the location of the fovea. Presumably, interpolation across intervals of time to yield an integrated spatiotemporal representation is a major component of what brains do. Interpolation in perception probably enables generation of an internal representation of the world that is useful in the animal's struggle for survival.

The debut demonstration of the blind spot in the visual field is comparably surprising. The standard set-up requires monocular viewing of an object offset about 13–15° from the point of fixation (figure 2.1). If the object falls in the region of the blind spot of the viewing eye, the object will not be perceived. Instead, the background texture and color will be seen as uniform across the region. This is generally characterized as "filling in" of the blind spot. The existence of the perceptual blind spot is owed to the specific architecture of the retina. As shown in figure 2.2, each retina has a region where the optic nerve leaves the retina and hence where no transducers (rods and cones) exist. This region is the blind spot. Larger than the fovea, it is about 6° in length and about 4.5° in width.

Relying on two eyes, a perceiver – even a careful and discerning perceiver – will fail to notice the blind spot, mainly because the blind regions of the two eyes do not overlap. If light from a thimble, for example, falls in the blind spot of the left eye, it will nevertheless be detected normally by the right retina, and the viewer sees a thimble. Even in the monocular condition, however, one may fail to notice the blind spot because of objects whose borders extend past the boundaries of the blind spot tend to be seen as filled in, as without gaps.

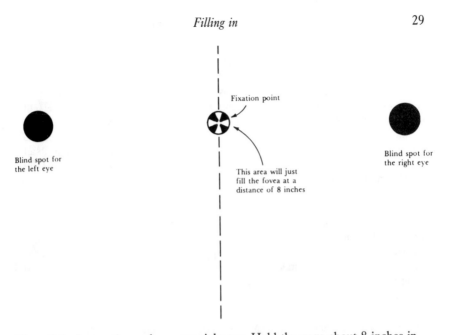

Figure 2.1 Instructions: close your right eye. Hold the page about 8 inches in front of you. Hold the page very straight, without tilting it. Stare at the fixation point. Adjust the angle and distance of the paper until the black spot on the left disappears. Repeat with the left eye closed. (Reproduced with permission from Lindsay and Norman, 1972.)

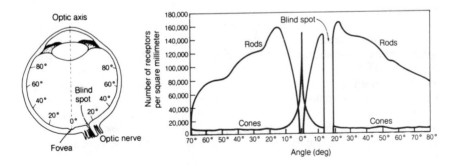

Figure 2.2 (Left) The human eye. The blind spot (optic disk) is that region on the retina where the ganglion cells leave the retina and project to the lateral geniculate nucleus of the thalamus. (Right) The packing density of light-sensitive cones is greatest at the fovea, decreasing sharply in the peripheral field. Rod density is greatest in the region that immediately surrounds the fovea, and gradually decreases in the more peripheral regions. Notice that the region of the blind spot is in the peripheral field, and is larger than the foveal area.

1 Dennett's Hypothesis

What is going on when one's blind spot is seen as filled in – as without gaps in the scene? Is it analogous to acquiring the non-visual representation (belief) that Bowser, the family dog, is under the bed, on the basis of one's visual perception of his tail sticking out? Or is it more akin to regular visual perception of the whole Bowser in one's *peripheral but non-blind field?* That is, is the representation itself a visual representation, involving visual experiences? In *Consciousness Explained* (1991, p. 356) Dennett favors the first hypothesis, which he sums up in his discussion of filling in: "The fundamental flaw in the idea of 'filling in' is that it suggests that the brain is providing something when in fact the brain is ignoring something."

We understand Dennett to mean that in the monocular condition the person may represent that there is a non-gappy object, say a vertical bar, in his visual field, but not because his brain generates a non-gappy *visual* representation of the vertical bar. In explicating his positive view on filling in, Dennett invites us to understand filling in of the blind spot by analogy to one's impression on walking into a room wallpapered with pictures of Marilyn Monroe:

> Consider how the brain must deal with wallpaper, for instance . . . Your brain just somehow represents *that* there are hundreds of identical Marilyns, and no matter how vivid your impression is that you see all that detail, the detail is in the world, not in your head. And no figment gets used up in rendering the seeming, for the seeming isn't rendered at all, not even as a bit map. (Dennett, 1991, pp. 354–5)

If, as instructed, we are to apply this to the case of filling in of the blind spot, presumably Dennett's point is that no matter how vivid one's impression that one sees a solid bar, one's brain actually just represents that there is a solid bar. Dennett's claim, as he clarifies later, is that the brain ignores the absence of data from the region of the blind spot. In what follows, we shall show that, contrary to Dennett, the data strongly imply that at least some instances of filling in do indeed involve the brain "providing" something.

One preliminary semantic point should be made first to forestall needless metaphysical tut-tutting. Hereafter, in discussing whether someone's perception of an object, say an apple, is filled in, we shall, *as a convenient short-hand*, talk about whether or not "the apple is filled in." In availing ourselves of this expedient, we do *not* suppose that there might be a little (literal) apple or (literal) picture of an apple in someone's head which is the thing that is filled in. Rather, we refer merely to some property of the brain's *visual* representation such that the perceiver sees a non-gappy apple.

Very crudely speaking, current neurobiological data suggest that when one sees an apple, the brain is in some state that can be described as representing an apple. This representation probably consists of a pattern of activity across some set of neurons, particularly those in the visual cortex, that have some specific configuration of synaptic weights and a specific profile of connectivity (P. M. Churchland, 1989). Given this general characterization of a representation, the question we want to address can now be rephrased: does filling in an apple-representation consist in the visual cortex generating a representation which more closely resembles the standard case of an apple-representation of an apple in the peripheral visual field? Or does it consist, as Dennett (1991) suggests, in a non-visual representation rather like one's non-visual representation of the dog under the bed?

Our approach to these questions assumes that *a priori* reflection will have value mainly as a spur to empirical investigation, but not as a method that can be counted upon by itself to reveal any facts. Thought experiments are no substitute for real experiments. To understand what is going on such that the blind spot is seen as filled in (non-gappy), it will be important to know more about the psychological and neurobiological parameters. In addition to exploring filling in of the blind spot, other versions of visual filling in, such as the filling in experienced by subjects with cortical lesions, can also be studied. Although a more complete study would make an even wider sweep, embracing modalities other than vision, for reasons of space we narrow the discussion to visual filling in.

2   Psychophysical Data: The Blind Spot

To investigate the conditions of filling in, Ramachandran (1992) presented a variety of stimuli to subjects who were instructed to occlude one eye and fixate on a specified marker. Stimuli were then presented in various parts of the field in the region of the subject's blind spot. If a bar extends to the boundary on either side of the blind spot, but not across it, will the subject see it as complete or as having a gap (figure 2.3)? Subjects see it as complete. If, however, only the lower bar segment or only the upper bar segment is presented alone, the subject does not see the bar as filled in across the blind spot (figure 2.4). What happens when the upper bar and the lower bar are different colors; e.g. upper red, lower green? Subjects still see the bar as complete, with extensions of both the red and green bar, but they do not see a border where the red and green meet, and hence they cannot say just where one color begins and the other leaves off. (For the explanation of non-perception of a border in terms of semi-segregated pathways for functionally specific tasks, see Ramachandran, 1992.)

Ramachandran also found that spokes extending to but not into the blind-spot boundary were filled in, demonstrating that filling in can be very complex. Suppose there is a kind of competition between completion of a black bar across the blind spot, and completion of an illusory contour lengthwise across the blind spot. Will the illusory contour or the real contour complete? Ramachandran discovered that in this test, the illusory contour typically completes (figure 2.5).

Ramachandran next explored the relation between subjective completion of a figure, and that figure's role in illusory motion (figure 2.6). The basic question is this: does the brain treat a filled-in bar like a solid bar or like a gappy bar? In the control case, the upper gappy bar is replaced with the lower gappy bar (delay about 100–200 ms). Because the gap in the upper bar is off-set with respect to the gap in the lower bar, subjects see illusory motion in a diagonal direction from left to right. In the experimental (monocular) condition, the gap in the upper bar is positioned so that it falls in the subject's blind spot, and the subject sees a completed bar. Now when the upper bar is replaced by the lower bar to generate illusory motion, subjects see the bar moving vertically, *non-diagonally*, just as one does if a genuinely solid bar is replaced by the lower bar. This experiment shows that the brain treats a

Figure 2.3 Subjects are presented with a display consisting of two vertical bar segments, separated by a gap of about 5°, and this gap is positioned to coincide with the subject's blind spot. Fixation is to the right for left eye viewing. Subjects report seeing an uninterrupted bar.

completed bar just as it treats a genuinely non-gappy bar in the perception of illusory motion.

According to Dennett's characterization of filling in (1992, p. 356), the brain follows the general principle that says, in effect, "just more of the same inside the blind spot as outside." Several of Ramachandran's results are directly relevant to this claim. If filling in is just a matter of continuing the pattern outside the blind spot, then in (figure 2.7), subjects should see an uninterrupted string of red ovals, as a red oval fills the blank space where the blind spot is. In fact, however, subjects see an interrupted sequence; that is, they see two upper red ovals, two lower red ovals, and a white gap in between. In a different experiment, subjects are presented with a

Figure 2.4 If only the lower segment of the bar is presented, subjects do not complete across the blind spot.

display of "bagels," with one bagel positioned so that its hole falls within the subject's blind spot (figure 2.8). The "more of the same" principle presumably predicts that subjects will see only bagels in the display, as one apparently sees "more Marilyns." So the blind spot should not fill in with the color of its surrounding bagel. In fact, however, this is not what happens. Subjects see bagels everywhere, *save in the region of the blind spot*, where they see a disk, uniformly colored.

3 Psychophysical Data: Cortical Scotomata

A lesion to early areas of visual cortex (V1, V2; i.e. areas 17,18) typically results in a blind area in the visual field of both eyes. The standard optometric test for determining scotomata consists in flashing a point of light in various locations of the visual field. Subjects are instructed to indicate, verbally or by button-pressing, when they see a flash. Using this method, the size and location of a field defect can be determined. Ramachandran et al. (forthcoming) explored the spatial and temporal characteristics of filling in of the scotoma in two patients (BM and JR).

BM had a right occipital pole lesion caused by a penetrating skull fracture. He had a paracentral left hemifield scotoma, 6° by 6°, with clear margins. JR had a right occipital lesion caused by hemorrhage and a left visual field scotoma 12° in width and 6° in height. The locations of the lesions were determined by magnetic resonance (MR) scanning. Both patients were intelligent and otherwise normal neurologically. Vision was 20/20. BM was tested 6 months and JR 8 months after the lesion events. Neither experienced his scotoma as a gap or hole in his visual

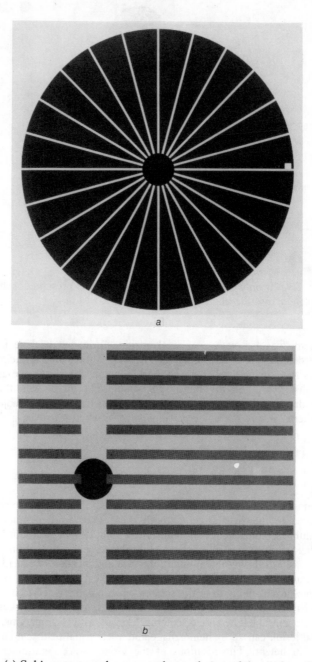

Figure 2.5 (*a*) Subjects reported perceptual completion of the spokes. (*b*) An illusory vertical strip was displayed so that a segment of the illusory contour fell on the blind spot. Subjects reported completion of the illusory strip rather than completion of the horizontal lines.

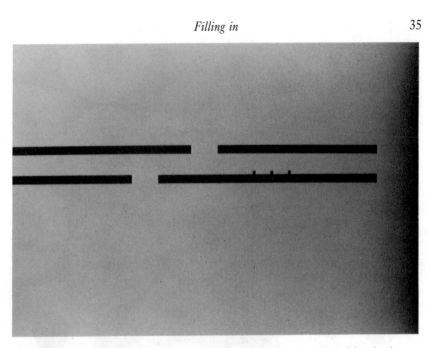

Figure 2.6 To generate illusory motion, the upper bar is replaced by the lower bar. When the gaps in both bars are located outside the blind spot, subjects see diagonal movement. When the gap in the upper bar coincides with the subject's blind spot, the movement appears to be vertical.

Figure 2.7 If the display is positioned so that a circle falls in the blind spot, subjects report a gap, not completion.

Figure 2.8 The display consists of yellow bagels and a fixation marker. The hole in one bagel (labeled *b*) coincides with the subject's blind spot. Subjects report seeing a yellow *disk* at this location, indicating that the yellow bagel is filled in.

field, but each was aware of the field defect. For example, each noticed some instances of "false" filling in of a real gap in an object. Additionally, they noticed that small, separable components of objects were sometimes unperceived, and noticed as missing. For example, one subject mistook the Women's room for the Men's room because the "Wo" of "Women's" fell into the scotoma. Seeing "Men's", the subject walked directly in and quickly discovered his mistake.

In brief, the major findings of Ramachandran et al. are as follows:

1 A 3° gap in a vertical line is completed across the scotoma, the completion taking about 6 seconds. The duration was determined by asking the patients to press a button when the line segment was completely filled in. Even with repeated trials, the latency remained the same.

2 One patient (JR) reported that his perception of the filled-in line segment persisted for an average of 5.3 seconds after the upper and lower lines were

turned off. The delay in completion as well as the persistence of "fill" is intriguing, and it is not seen in non-traumatic blind spot filling in.

3 When the top and bottom segments of the line were misaligned horizontally by 2°, both patients first reported seeing two misaligned segments separated by a gap. After observing this for a few seconds, they spontaneously reported that the upper and lower line segments began to drift towards each other, moving into alignment, then slowly (over a period of about 10 seconds) the line segments filled in to form a single line spanning the scotoma (figure 2.9). The realignment and visual completion took 6.8 seconds on average.

4 When viewing dynamic 2-D noise (e.g. "snow" on a television screen), one patient reported that the scotoma was first filled in with static (non-flickering) noise for 7 or 8 seconds before the random spots began to move and flicker. When the noise was composed of red pixels of randomly varying luminance, JR reported seeing the red color bleeding into the scotoma almost immediately, followed about 5 seconds later by the appearance of the dynamic texture.

5 When a vertical column of spots (periodicity >2°) was used instead of a solid line, both patients clearly saw a gap. When the spacing was reduced (periodicity <0.3°), patients reported seeing completion across the scotoma of a dotted line. These conditions were repeated using Xs instead of spots, and the results were comparable (figure 2.10). Presenting a wavy, vertically oriented sinusoidal line (0.5 cycle/degree) with a gap matching the height of the patient's scotoma, both patients reported clearly seeing a non-gappy sinusoidally wavy line.

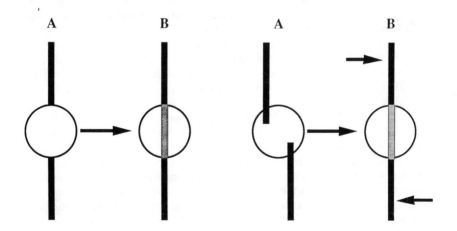

Figure 2.9 Schematic illustration of the stimuli shown to patients. The circle represents (roughly) the region of the patient's scotoma; fixation was approximately center field. (Left) Two bar segments were displayed on either side of the scotoma. The bar was vividly completed; the process of completion took about 6 seconds. (Right) The vertical bar segments were misaligned in the horizontal plane. After a few seconds of viewing, patients reported the lines moving toward each other until they became colinear. They then gradually began to complete across the scotoma.

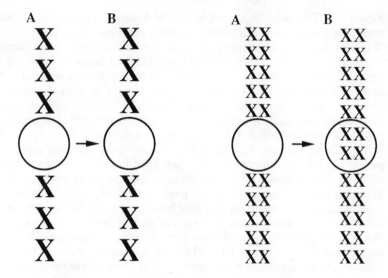

Figure 2.10 (Left) A column of large Xs was not completed across the scotoma. (Right) A column of small Xs did complete. If the column consisted of small horizontal line segments, the results were similar.

6 Each patient reported seeing illusory contours filled in across his scotoma. The experiment was similar to that performed with normal subjects (see again figure 2.5), save that the display was positioned so that the scotoma lined up with the gap in the stimuli. First, two horizontal line segments bordering the scotoma were presented, and as expected, they completed across the gap. Next, when an aligned array of horizontal lines were presented, the horizontal bars did not complete across the gap, and instead patients saw the vertical illusory strip complete across the scotoma.

7 Patients were presented with a checkerboard pattern, both fine (<0.3°) and coarse (>1.5°) grained, which were readily filled in. When the checkerboard texture was subjected to counterphase flicker (7.5 Hz flicker; 0.6 check width), BM completed the flickering checks. JR, however, reported that as soon as the pattern was made to flicker, he saw non-flickering stationary checks inside his scotoma, with the result that the margins of his scotoma became "entopically" visible. After about 8 seconds, JR saw the dynamic checks everywhere, including his scotoma.

8 To determine whether these filling in effects might be seen in patients with laser-induced paracentral *retinal* scotomata, the tests were repeated on two such patients. Ramachandran and colleagues found that (a) gaps in bars were not completed; (b) there was no motion or completion of misaligned bars; (c) coarse checkerboard patterns did not complete; (d) fine-grained 2-D random-dot textures were completed. This suggests that many of the completion effects are of cortical origin.

In the lesion studies, the time course for filling in, together with the subject's reports, indicate that the completion is a visual phenomenon rather than a non-visual judgment or representation. For example, when their spontaneous reports were tested with comments such as "you mean you *think* that the checkerboard is uniform everywhere", the patients would respond with emphatic denials like "Doctor, I don't merely *think* it is there; I *see* that it is there." Insofar as there is nothing in the visual stimulus corresponding to the filled in perception, it is reasonable to infer, in contrast to Dennett, that the brain is "providing something," not merely "ignoring something." The visual character of the phenomenon also suggests that in looking for the neurobiological mechanism, visual cortex would be a reasonable place to start.

4 Psychophysical Data: Artificial Scotomata

Ramachandran and Gregory (1991) discovered a species of filling in readily experienced by normal subjects, and conditions for which can easily be set up by anyone. The recipe is simple: adjust the television set to "snow" (twinkling pattern of dots), make a fixation point with a piece of tape, roughly in the middle of the screen, and place a square piece of gray paper, about 1 centimeter square and roughly isoluminant to the gray of the background, at a distance of about 8 centimeters from the fixation point (in peripheral vision). Both eyes may be open, and after about 10 seconds of viewing the fixation point, the square in peripheral vision vanishes completely. Thereafter, one sees a uniformly twinkling screen. Insofar as this paradigm yields filling in that is reminiscent of filling in of the blind spot and cortical scotoma, it can be described as inducing a kind of artificial blind spot. Hence Ramachandran and Gregory called it an "artificial scotoma" (figure 2.11).

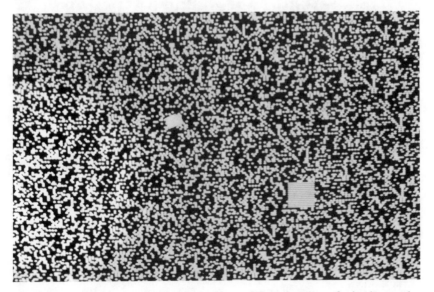

Figure 2.11 Display for artificial scotoma conditions consists of a background texture, fixation point, and small segment in the peripheral field with a different texture, roughly isoluminant to the background.

By using a computer to generate visual displays, many different arrangements of background texture and artificial scotomata can be investigated. In exploring the variety of conditions for filling in of an artificial scotoma, Ramachandran and Gregory found a number of striking results, several of which we briefly outline below:

1 Subjects tended to report filling in from outside the gray square to the inside, with a time scale of about 5–10 seconds.
2 Once subjects reported filling in to be complete, the background twinkles were then turned off. Subjects now reported that they *continued* to see twinkling in the "scotomic" square for about 3–4 seconds after the background twinkles disappeared.
3 Suppose the background screen is pink, twinkles are white. The "scotomic" square is, as before, gray, but within the square, dots are moving not randomly but coherently, left to right. Subjects report seeing a completely pink screen after about 5–10 seconds, but report that the dots in the square continue to move coherently from left to right. After a few more seconds, however, they report seeing uniformly random twinkles everywhere. Note that the artificial scotoma is in peripheral vision, where resolution is much poorer than in the foveal region (see again figure 2.2). The twinkles that are filled in look just the same as the twinkles elsewhere in the peripheral field.
4 If the screen is covered in text, the peripheral square comes to be filled in with text (figure 2.12).

Figure 2.12 The filling in of the artificial scotoma can be complex. In this condition, subjects report that the text fills in.

5 If a smaller square with black borders is inscribed within the region of the gray square, subjects report that the inner area does not fill in with background texture.

Many other experiments in artificial scotomata are now underway in Ramachandran's laboratory, and those few cited here mark only the first pass in exploring a salient and intriguing visual phenomenon. For our purposes here, it is perhaps enough to note that so far as we can determine, the results from artificial scotoma experiments do not confirm Dennett's hypothesis that, for phenomena such as filling in, "we can already be *quite* sure that the medium of representation is a version of something efficient, like color-by-numbers [which gives a single label to a whole region], not roughly continuous, like bit-mapping" (Dennett, 1991, p. 354).

5 Psychophysics and The Krauskopf Effect

Krauskopf (1963) discovered a remarkable filling in phenomenon. In his set-up, a green disk is superimposed on a larger orange disk. The inner boundary (between green and orange) is stabilized on the retina so that it remains on exactly the same retinal location no matter how the eyes jitter and saccade, but the outer boundary moves across the retina as the eyes jitter and saccade. After a few seconds of image stabilization, the subject no longer sees a green disk; instead, the entire region is seen as uniformly orange – as filled in with the background color.

Using the Krauskopf image stabilization method to explore further aspects of the filling in phenomenon, Thomas Piantanida and his colleagues have found more remarkable filling in results. It is known that adaptation to yellow light alters a subject's sensitivity to a small flickering blue light; more exactly, flicker sensitivity is reduced in the presence of a yellow adapting background. *Prima facie* this is odd, given that "blue" cones are essentially insensitive to yellow light (it is the "red" and "green" cones that are sensitive to yellow light). Piantanida (1985) asked this question: is blue flicker sensitivity the same if yellow adaptation is obtained by subjective *filling in of yellow* rather than by actual yellow light illuminating the retina?

To get a perception of yellow in an area where the retina was not actually illuminated with yellow light, Piantanida presented subjects with a yellow bagel, whose inner boundary was stabilized on the retina (using a dual Purkinje eye tracker) and whose outer boundary was not stabilized. The finding was that the yellow background achieved by image stabilization was *as effective* in reducing "blue" cone flicker sensitivity as an actual yellow stimulus. This probably means, therefore, that the reduction in flicker sensitivity as a function of perceived background is a cortical rather than a retinal effect. The most likely hypothesis is that cortical circumstances relevantly like those produced by retinal stimulation with yellow light are produced by yellow filling in, and hence the adaptation effects are comparable.

There is a further and quite stunning result reported by Crane and Piantanida (1983) that is especially relevant here. They presented subjects with a stimulus consisting of a green stripe adjacent to a red stripe, where the borders between them were stabilized, but the outside borders were not stabilized. After a few seconds, the colors began to fill in across the stabilized border. At this point, some observers described what they saw as a new and unnamable color that was somehow a mixture of red and green. Similar results were obtained with yellow and blue. Produced extra-retinally, these visual perceptions of hitherto unperceived colors resulted from experimental manipulation of filling in mechanisms – mechanisms that actively do something, as opposed to simply ignoring something.

Dennett says of the blind spot: "The area is simply neglected" (1991, p. 355). He says that "the brain doesn't have to 'fill in' for the blind spot, since the region in which the blind spot falls is already labeled (e.g. 'plaid' or 'Marilyns' or just 'more of the same')" (p. 355). Part of the trouble with Dennett's approach to the various filling in phenomena is that he confidently prejudges what the neurobiological data at the cellular level will look like. Reasoning more like a computer engineer who knows a lot about the architectural details of the device in front of him than like a neurobiologist who realizes how much is still to be learned about the brain, Dennett jumps to conclusions about what the brain does not need to do, ought to do, and so forth.

In sections 6 and 7 below, we discuss neurophysiological data that conflict with Dennett's claim that "There are no homunculi, as I have put it, who are supposed to 'care about' information arising from the part of the visual field covered by the blind spot, so when nothing arrives, there is no one to complain" (p. 357). And again: "The brain's motto for handling the blind spot could be: Ask me no questions and I'll tell you no lies" (p. 356). While Dennett's idea may seem to have some engineering plausibility, it is really a bit of *a priori* neurophysiology gone wrong. Biological solutions, alas, are not easily predicted from reasonable engineering considerations. What might, from our limited vantage point, have the earmarks of sound engineering strategy, is, often as not, out of kilter with the way Nature does it.

6   The Blind Spot and Cortical Physiology: The Gattass Effect

There are upwards of twenty cortical visual areas in each hemisphere of monkeys, and probably at least that many in humans. Many of these areas are retinotopically mapped, in the sense that neighbouring cells have neighbouring receptive fields, i.e. neighborhood points in the visual field will be represented by neighboring cells in the cortex. In particular, visual area V1, has been extensively explored (figure 2.13). The receptive field size of V1 cells is about 2–3°, and hence is much smaller than the size of the blind spot (about 6° × 4.5°).

Ricardo Gattass and his colleagues (Fiorani et al., 1990; Gattass et al., 1992; Fiorani et al., 1992) were the first to try to answer the following question: how do V1 cells corresponding to the region of the blind spot for the right eye respond when the left eye is closed and a stimulus is presented to the open right eye (and vice versa)?

For ease of reference hereafter, by "Gattass condition" we denote the set-up in which the experimenter records from single cells in V1 in the general area corresponding to the optic disk when the stimulus is presented to the contralateral (opposite side) eye. Call the V1 region corresponding to the optic disk of the contralateral eye, the optic disk cortex, "ODC." The optic disk is that region of retina where no transducers exist, corresponding to that part of the visual field where the blind spot resides. Remember that if a cortical region corresponds to the

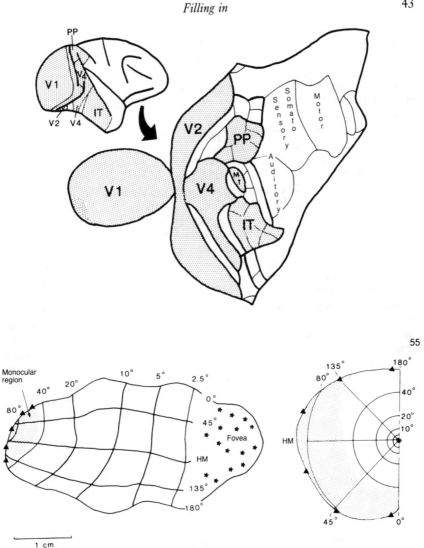

Figure 2.13 (Upper) Visual areas in the cerebral cortex of the macaque, as seen in a lateral view of the right hemisphere, and (arrow) in an unfolded 2-D map. The primary visual cortex (V1) is topographically organized. Lines of eccentricity (semicircles in the visual field drawing on lower right) map onto contours that run approximately vertically on the cortical map (lower left). Lines of constant polar angle (rays emanating from the center of gaze in the visual field) map onto contours that run approximately horizontally on the cortical map. The foveal representation (asterisks) corresponding to the central 2° radius, occupies slightly more than 10 percent of V1. The monocular region (stipple) in the visual field occupies a very small region of the cortical map. (Reproduced with permission from Van Essen and Anderson, 1990.)

optic disk for the contralateral eye, it will correspond to normal retinal area for the ipsilateral (same side) eye. See figure 2.14 for projection patterns.

The seemingly obvious answer to Gattass' question – and the answer Gattass and his colleagues expected – is that the ODC cells will not respond in the monocular condition to stimuli presented in the contralateral blind spot. That is, one would predict that the cells in that region are responsive only to stimuli from the non-blind region of the ipsilateral eye. This is not what they found. Applying standard physiological mapping techniques to monkeys, and using the conventional bars of light as stimuli, they tested the responses of ODC cells (left hemisphere) with the left eye closed. As they moved the bar of light around and recorded from single cells, they found that neurons in the ODC area responded very well. That is, cells corresponding to the blind spot gave consistent responses to a bar of light passing through the blind sector of the visual field. The response data did, however, show that the ODC was somewhat less neatly mapped by contralateral stimuli (i.e. in the blind spot) than by ipsilateral stimuli (i.e. in the non-blind field).

For some cells, an excitatory receptive field – presumably an interpolated receptive field – located *inside* the ODC could be specified. Exploring further, they found that sweeping bars on only one end of the blind spot yielded poor responses or none at all. In other cells, they discovered that the sum of responses to two bar segments entering either end of the blind spot was comparable to the response for a single non-gappy bar. This indicates that some cells in the Gattass condition exhibit discontinuous receptive fields, presumably via interpolation signals from other neurons with neighboring receptive fields. To study the relevance of neighboring relations, Gattass and his colleagues masked the area immediately surrounding the optic disk during stimulus presentations to the blind spot region of the visual field. They discovered that responses of the ODC neurons were abolished in the masked condition (figures 2.15 and 2.16). Fifteen out of 43 neurons (mostly from layer 4cα) were found to exhibit interpolation properties across a region of the visual field at least three times the size of the classic receptive field.

7 Artificial Scotomata and Cortical Physiology: The Gilbert Effect

How do cortical cells respond when their receptive field corresponds to the area of an artificial scotoma, such as the kind Ramachandran and Gregory studied? (For ease of reference, we shall hereafter call these cortical neurons "artificial scotoma" or AS cells.) Or when the area of both retinas from which they receive projections is lesioned? (Hereafter, we shall call these cortical neurons "retinal lesion" or RL cells.) These questions have been addressed by Charles Gilbert and colleagues of Rockefeller University. Recording from V1 in monkeys, they discovered that the receptive fields of cortical cells surrounding the cortical RL cells expanded in several minutes so that collectively they covered that part of the visual field normally covered by the RL cortical cells (Gilbert and Wiesel, 1992).

A similar result was found in the artificial scotoma experiments in cats (Pettet and Gilbert, 1991). The cortical cells in V1 surrounding the AS cortical cells very quickly expanded their receptive fields to include the area normally in the domain of the AS cells. The receptive field expansion was of the order of 3–5 fold. It was observed as soon as tests could be made (2 minutes), and it was reversible, in that

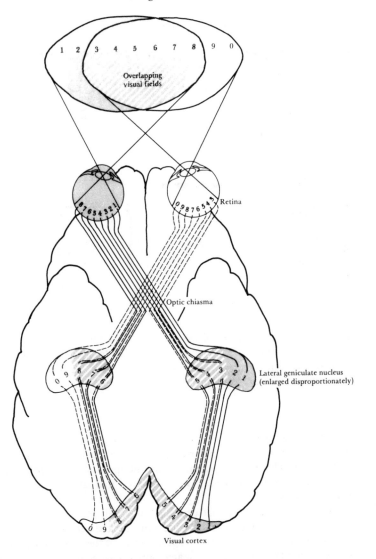

Figure 2.14 Schematic illustration of the projection pathways from the retina to the cortex, showing which parts of the visual field are represented in specific parts of the lateral geniculate nucleus (LGN) and the visual cortex. Notice that the left *hemifield* projects to the right (contralateral), which in turn projects to the right hemisphere. The blind spot of the left eye corresponds approximately to the region coded as "3," which is part of the central region where the fields of the two eyes overlap. By tracking "3" from the field, to the retina, to the LGN and the cortex, one can track the pathway for a particular stimulus in the blind region of the left eye. (Reproduced with permission from Lindsay and Norman, 1972.)

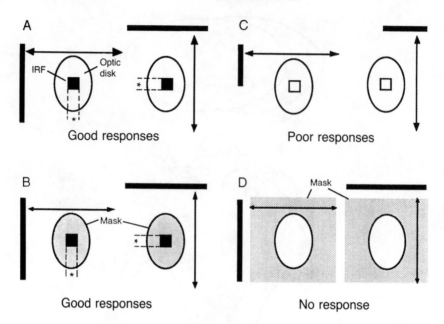

Figure 2.15 Summary of responses of cortical neurons in the optic disk cortical region to bars and masks of varying sizes. IRF: Interpolated receptive field. Asterisks indicate locations where stimulation with long bars elicited responses. (Reproduced with permission from M. Fiorani et al., 1992.)

once the experimental condition was removed and a standard, non-scotomatic stimulus was presented, normal mapping of cortical cells was restored. Although the neurobiological basis for this modification/interpolation in receptive field properties has not yet been determined, it is conjectured that lateral interactions within the cortex are probably crucial.

The Gattass effect, together with the Gilbert effect, are important evidence that the receptive fields of cortical cells are dynamic and can be modified on very short time scales. What precisely this means in terms of the neurobiological mechanisms of visual experience will require many more experiments. In any case, it is unlikely that the results are irrelevant to determining whether the brain merely ignores the blind spot or whether there is an active process related to filling in. As we try to track down the neurobiology of visual awareness, the discoveries in neuroscience are important clues to the nature of visual processing and to that component of the processing relevant to visual awareness.

Do the results from Gattass et al. and Gilbert et al. mean that, contrary to Dennett's assurances, filling in *is* rendered as a bit-map? No. The choices here are not exhausted by Dennett's alternatives "bit map or color-by-number." We suspect that neither the bit-map metaphor nor the color-by-number metaphor is even remotely adequate to the kind of representation and computation in nervous

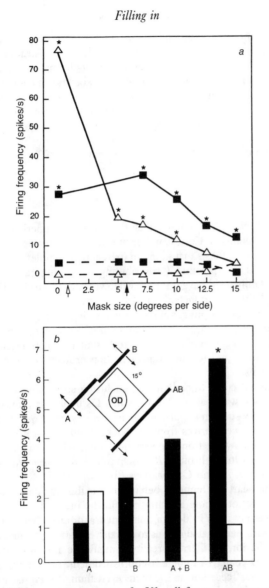

Figure 2.16 (*a*) Mean response rate of a V1 cell for ten presentations of the stimulus under different masking conditions. Triangles and filled squares linked by continuous lines show response to ipsilateral and contralateral eye, respectively, in paired trials. The lower (dotted) lines show the mean spontaneous activity where each eye is opened separately. The size of the ipsilateral classic receptive field is shown by an outlined arrow, and the diameter of the optic disk (OD) by a filled arrow. (*b*) Black bars: mean response frequency of the same neuron to stimulation over a mask 15° per side. Open bars show the mean spontaneous activity in paired trials without stimulation. (Reproduced with permission from M. Fiorani et al., 1992.)

systems. Indeed, the very lability of a neuron's response properties and receptive field properties means that the bit-map metaphor is misleading. In order to understand more clearly how to interpret the results from Gattass and colleagues, and from Gilbert and Wiesel, much more needs to be known about interpolation in neural networks and about the interaction of neurons within a mapped region and between regions. The fact is, very little is known at this point about the detailed nature of neural computation and representation, though we are at a stage where computer models highly constrained by neurobiological and psychophysical data can yield important clues (Churchland and Sejnowski, 1992).

8 Conclusion

In *Consciousness Explained*, Dennett brilliantly and quite properly debunks the idea that the brain contains a Cartesian Theater wherein images and the like are displayed. But the hypothesis that filling in (perceptual completion) may sometimes involve the brain's interpolating ("contributing something rather than ignoring something") certainly need have no truck whatever with Cartesian Theaters, either implicitly or explicitly, either metaphorically or literally, either *sotto voce* or *viva voce*. Given the data from psychophysics and neurophysiology, we hypothesize that (a) the brain has mechanisms for interpolation, some of which may operate early in visual processing; (b) brains sometimes visually represent completions, including quite complex completions; and (c) such representation probably involves those interpolation mechanisms.

How did Dennett come to embrace a conclusion so manifestly contrary to the data, some of which was readily available when his book was published? And why does "filling in" play such an important role in *Consciousness Explained*? According to our analysis, the answer derives from the background behaviorist ideology that is endemic in Dennett's work from the very beginning – from his first book, *Content and Consciousness* (1969), through *Brainstorms* (1978), *Elbow Room* (1984), *The Intentional Stance* (1987), and *Consciousness Explained* (1991).

Simplified, the heart of Dennett's behaviorism is this: the conceptual framework of the mental does not denote anything real in the brain. The importance of the framework derives not from its description of neural or any other reality; rather, it is an organizing instrument that allows us to do fairly well in explaining and predicting one another's behavior, the literal unreality of qualia etc. notwithstanding. How is it that the framework manages to be a useful instrument, despite the unreality of its categories? Because, according to Dennett, even though there is nothing *really* in the brain that corresponds to visual awareness of red, there is *something or other* in the brain which, luckily enough, allows us to get on pretty well in making sense of people's behavior on the pretense, as it were, that the brain really does have states corresponding to awareness of red. As for filling in, Dennett's rhetorical strategy hoists it as *paradigmatic* of a mental thing that we mistakenly assume to be real.

Dennett's discussions regarding the dubiousness of selected old time intuitions often fall upon receptive ears because some categories such as "the will and "the soul" probably do not in fact correspond to anything real, and because neuroscience is bound to teach us many surprising things about the mental, including that some of our fundamental categories can be improved upon. The sweeping behaviorism–instrumentalism, however, does not follow from these observations about revisability of psychological concepts – nor even from the eliminability by cognitive neuroscience of *some* concepts that turn out to be the psychological counterpart of "phlogiston", "impetus", and "natural place". Thus one may readily concur that qualia cannot be little pictures displayed in the brain's Cartesian Theater and that the self is not a little person tucked away in the folds of frontal cortex. These debunking treats are, however, just the teaspoon of sugar that helps the medicine go down. And the medicine, make no mistake, is behaviorism. The elixir is *Gilbert Ryle's Ghost-Be-Gone* (Ryle, 1949). Taken regularly, it is supposed to prevent the outbreak of mental realism. Drawing on AI's conceptual repertoire of the "virtual machine," Dennett has systematically argued *against* the neural reality, and *for* the merely instrumental utility, of mental categories generally. Dennett's engaging exposition and brilliantly inventive metaphors tend to mask the fact that this less palatable message is indeed the main message (see also McCauley, forthcoming).

This brief excursion through Dennett's behaviorism and instrumentalism may help explain why he is found defending assorted theses that are highly implausible from a scientific perspective: the brain does not fill in; there is nothing whatever ("no fact of the matter") to distinguish between a misperception and a misrecollection; there is no time before which one is not aware of, say, a sound, and after which one is aware; human consciousness is a virtual machine that comes into being as humans learn to talk to themselves, and so forth (Dennett, 1991).

Scientific realism, in contrast to Dennett's instrumentalism (P. M. Churchland, 1979, 1989) proposes that we determine by empirical means – by converging research from experimental psychology, neuropsychology, and neuroscience – what hypotheses are probably true, and hence what categories truly apply to the mind–brain. Some categories may be largely correct, for example "visual perception;" some, for example "memory," "attention," and "consciousness" appear to be subdividing, budding, and regrouping; and some may be replaced by high-level categories that are more empirically adequate. At this stage, it is reasonable to consider sensory experiences to be real states of the brain, states whose neurobiological properties will be discovered as cognitive neuroscience proceeds (P. S. Churchland, 1986, 1988; P. M. Churchland, 1989).

Perhaps Dennett's main achievement consists in showing the Cartesian dangers waiting to ensnare those who refer to perceptual filling in by means of the expression "filling in." If so, then the achievement is primarily semantic, not empirical. Furthermore, his aim could be satisfied merely by instructing us on the dangers, without requiring also that the very description "filling in" be expunged as untrue of what goes on in the brain. In any case, one might well wonder whether Dennett overestimates the *naïveté* amongst scientists. To judge from the literature (see references below), those who scientifically study perceptual completion phenomena understand perfectly well that filling in involves no Cartesian Theaters, ghosts, paint, little pictures, putty knives or homunculi. At the very least, they are no more addled by metaphor than is Dennett when he refers to the brain as "editing multiple drafts." Taken as a linguistic prohibition rather than an empirical hypothesis about the mind–brain, Dennett's thesis that "the brain does not fill in" sounds uncomfortably like a quirky edict of the "word-police."

ACKNOWLEDGMENTS

For helpful discussion at many stages, we thank Paul Churchland, Francis Crick, Peter Dayan, Bo Dahlbom, Ricardo Gattass, Read Montague, Diane Rogers-Ramachandran, Adina Roskies, and Oron Shagrir.

Postscript: Filling In – Facts and Fallacies

The basic facts are these: on the cortical surface at V1 there exists a 2-D, retinotopically organized representation of the visual field: it is as close to being a literal picture as one could possibly wish, save that no one is literally looking at it. Certain small areas of that 2-D surface fail to receive information from one or other retina, information that is received by the rest of the surface. The failure is chronic in the case of the blind spot, and temporary in the case of "artificial scotoma." But in both cases, the deprived areas regularly show vigorous representational activity, activity of the very same kind displayed elsewhere on that surface, activity driven by the activity of the cells immediately adjacent to the stimulus-deprived area. Such interpolated activity has a measurable time course, and it can even survive for some seconds the cessation of the surrounding activation. The results from Gattass and from Gilbert show that the brain is not merely ignoring something, as Dennett insists, but providing something, as he denies. Although the precise computational role of the cells' responses is not yet clear, the general point that the brain has mechanisms for filling in seems far better supported by the evidence than Dennett's opposite hypothesis. Assuming data are relevant at all to this question – and it is hard to see how they can fail to be – then Dennett's refusal to budge an inch on the "no filling in" hypothesis in the teeth of countervailing data has a hint of "Flat Earthiness."

Although Dennett does not try to defend his hypothesis against the Gattass and Gilbert data showing the existence of active filling-in mechanisms, he does raise a lot of dust about other cases, such as the wallpaper case and viewing a cat behind a picket fence. The structure of his argument is that if these cases do not involve literal filling in, then neither can the blind spot or artificial scotoma case. The assumption that assorted cases must be psychophysically and neurobiologically uniform is fallacious. The basic neurobiological point is that there may be many different kinds of perceptual completion, at many different stages of processing, employing different mechanisms. Some probably operate early in the system, such as blind spot filling in, others may kick in later. Some cases may be very like perceiving a whole object, and others may not. There may be a wide range of kinds of completion – kinds that are distinct psychophysically, computationally, and neurobiologically. Other cases are interesting, to be sure, and the results of physiological experiments would be especially interesting. But the existence of other cases does not gainsay the basic experimental results of Gattass and Gilbert.

If no homunculus exists to look at a filled-in representation, why would the brain bother filling in? This seems to be Dennett's motivating question. Having failed to imagine a reason, his answer is: "it wouldn't." Our answer is: first, *go with the facts*. If, as it seems, the brain does sometimes fill in, the reason may be because the filled-in representation is used in some subsequent stage of processing. Intermediate levels of processing probably have some use for the kind of cellular response seen by Gattass and by Gilbert, and what we need to discover now is exactly what each processing stage involves. This does not seem like a metaphysically dangerous answer. On the contrary, the answer seems rather benign and neurobiologically plausible. Obviously, it is fallacious to conclude from the absence of a homunculus that no such intermediate level representation *could* be needed.

REFERENCES

Churchland, P. M. (1979) *Scientific Realism and the Plasticity of Mind.* Cambridge: Cambridge University Press.
Churchland, P. M. (1989) *A Neurocomputational Perspective.* Cambridge, Mass.: MIT Press/Bradford Books.
Churchland, P. S. (1986) *Neurophilosophy.* Cambridge, Mass: MIT Press/Bradford Books.
Churchland, P. S. (1988) Reduction and the neurobiological basis of consciousness. In A. J. Marcel and E. Bisiach (eds), *Consciousness in Contemporary Science,* Oxford: Oxford University Press.
Churchland, P. S. and Sejnowski, T. J. (1992) *The Computational Brain.* Cambridge, Mass.: MIT Press/Bradford Books.
Crane, H. D. and Piantanida, T. P. (1983) On seeing reddish-green and yellowish-blue. *Science,* 221, 1078–9.
Dennett, D. C. (1969) *Content and Consciousness.* London: Routledge & Kegan Paul.
Dennett, D. C. (1978) *Brainstorms.* Cambridge, Mass.: MIT Press/Bradford Books.
Dennett, D. C. (1984) *Elbow Room.* Cambridge, Mass.: MIT Press/Bradford Books.
Dennett, D. C. (1987) *The Intentional Stance.* Cambridge, Mass.: MIT Press/Bradford Books.
Dennett, D. C. (1991) *Consciousness Explained.* Boston: Little, Brown.
Fiorani, M., Gattass, R., Rosa, M. G. P. and Rocha-Miranda, C. E. (1990) Changes in receptive field (RF) size of single cells of primate V1 as a correlate of perceptual completion. *Society for Neuroscience Abstracts,* 16, 1219.
Fiorani, M., Rosa, M. G. P., Gattass R. and Rocha-Miranda, C. E. (1992) Visual responses outside the "classical" receptive field in primate striate cortex: A possible correlate of perceptual completion. *Proceedings of the National Academy of Sciences,* 89, 8547–51.
Gattass, R., Fiorani, M. Rosa, M. G. P., Pinon, M. C. F., Sousa, A. P. B. and Soares, J. G. M. (1992) Changes in receptive field size in V1 and its relation to perceptual completion. In R. Lent (ed.), *The Visual System from Genesis to Maturity.* Boston: Birkhauser.
Gilbert, C. D. and Wiesel, T. N. (1992) Receptive field dynamics in adult primary visual cortex. *Nature,* 356, 150–2.
Krauskopf, J. (1963) Effect of the retinal image stabilization on the appearance of hetrochromatic targets. *Journal of the Optical Society of America,* 53, 741.
Lindsay, P. H. and Norman, D. A. (1972) *Human Information Processing.* New York: Academic Press.
McCauley, R. N. (forthcoming) Why the blind can't lead the blind: Dennett on the blind spot, blind sight, and sensory qualia.
Pettet, M. W. and Gilbert, C. D. (1991) Contextual stimuli influence receptive field size of single neurons in cat primary visual cortex. *Neuroscience Abstracts,* 431, 12.
Piantanida, T. P. (1985) Temporal modulation sensitivity of the blue mechanism: measurements made with extraretinal chromatic adaptation. *Vision Research,* 25, 1439–44.
Piantanida, T. P. and Larimer, J. (1989) The impact of boundaries on color: stabilized image studies. *Journal of Imaging Technology,* 15, 58–63.

Ramachandran, V. S. (1992) Blind spots. *Scientific American*, 266, 86–91.

Ramachandran, V. S. (in press) Filling in gaps in perception. *Current Directions in Psychological Science.*

Ramachandran, V. S. and Gregory, R. L. (1991) Perceptual filling in of artificially induced scotomas in human vision. *Nature*, 350, 699–702.

Ramachandran, V. S., Rogers-Ramachandran, D. and Damasio, H. (forthcoming) Perceptual "filling in" of scotomas of cortical origin.

Ryle, G. (1949) *The Concept of Mind.* New York: Barnes and Noble.

Van Essen, D. C. and Anderson, C. H. (1990) Information processing in primate vision. In S. F. Zornetzer, J. L. Davis and C. Lau (eds), *An Introduction to Neural and Electronic Networks.* San Diego: Academic Press.

3
Pattern and Being

JOHN HAUGELAND

Dennett's landmark "Real Patterns" is an essay in *ontology*: its topic is the being of entities.[1] Ostensibly, it is prompted by questions about the reality of intentional states, and about the implications of Dennett's own seminal account in "Intentional Systems."[2] But these are pretexts: the issue is not intentionality at all, except in passing, but rather *being*. Intentional states – beliefs, desires, and the like – frame the discussion, motivating it in the introduction, and secured by it in the conclusion. But all the main points are made in a more general way, in terms of *patterns*. Intentional states are just a special case, and there can be other special cases as well, the status of all of which we will be able to understand once we understand the ontology of patterns more generally. In the same spirit, I too will mention the intentional only incidentally, and will focus instead on the general case. (Also, I will take it for granted that the reader is familiar with Dennett's work, especially the two articles just cited.)

1 Two Levels: Patterns and their Elements

From the beginning, Dennett's ontological investigation of patterns exhibits a perplexing vacillation between two levels. It can be brought to the fore with the following question: what are the *entities* the status of which is to be illuminated? Are they the patterns themselves, or are they rather the elements (components) of the patterns? This distinction should not be confused with another: namely, that between patterns considered abstractly or concretely. For instance, a melody is a pattern of notes, varying relative to one another in pitch and timing. Abstractly, the melody need be in no particular key, register, or tempo, not to mention at any date or location. But in any concrete instance (of which there can be arbitrarily many), these and all other characteristics must be determinate. The vacillation is between the pattern and its elements, the melody and the notes, not between the abstract form and its concrete instances.

On the one hand, the title, "Real Patterns," suggests that it is the patterns themselves, rather than their component elements, whose ontological status ("reality") is to be explained and defended. This interpretation is reinforced by the initial example of a visible pattern of dots within a frame: the status of the dots is never questioned, but only that of the pattern of black and white stripes that they make up. Dennett says: "I take it that this pattern, which I shall dub *bar code*, is a real pattern if anything is" (p. 31) and then asks the essential question: "what does it mean to say that a pattern in one of these frames is real, or that it is really there?" (p. 32). Again, the invocation of mathematical randomness, or the incompressibility of a bit-map (pp. 32f), presupposes the bits or the "data". Only the status of the pattern itself is in doubt: "A pattern exists in some data – is real – if there is a description of the data that is more efficient than the bit map, whether or not anyone can concoct it." (p. 34).

On the other hand, Dennett introduces his catalog of "different grades or kinds of realism" about beliefs by asking: "When are the elements of a pattern real and not merely apparent?" (p. 30). Indeed, in assimilating the intentional stance to radical interpretation and radical translation (pp. 30 and 46), Dennett is inevitably (and willingly) committed to the brand of holism that understands intentional items in terms of the ordered wholes they participate in, not any wholes they may comprise. That is, the intentional items, such as beliefs and desires, are not themselves the relevant patterns, but are rather the elements of the relevant patterns. Hence, to inquire after the ontological status of intentional states is to inquire after the status of pattern elements, not patterns. These are the two levels between which Dennett vacillates.

It is tempting to suppose that the opposition must somehow be false, that the ontological status of the pattern and its elements must go hand in hand, because (as one wants to say) "each is defined in terms of the other." In so far as this is right, however, it is a posing of the problem rather than a solution. The problem is: how can such a "going hand in hand" make non-trivial (non-question-begging) sense? In resolving this problem, it should become clear for the first time what patterns have to do with *ontology*.

2   To Be is not Just to "Count As"

It is important to avoid at the outset a tempting false start. What, after all, are the bits in a bit-map, or the pixels in a picture? As was pointed out above, these elements are taken for granted – their "reality" is not in question – when we ask about the status of mathematical or visual patterns of them. But, of course, their status *as bits or pixels* is not at all independent of those patterns. A particular flipped flip-flop or black dot on white paper would not *count as* as a bit or pixel except in so far as it is a component in some relevant mathematical or visual pattern. Likewise, nothing could *count as* this sort of mathematical or visual pattern except in so far as it is a pattern of such bits or pixels. Accordingly, it seems, the patterns and their elements are defined in terms of one another, and their respective statuses go hand in hand.

But this misses the point: the *being* of the bits or pixels is not at issue at all, but only whether the terms "bit" or "pixel" apply to them – that's what "counting as" a bit or pixel means. Thus, whether it's a pixel or not, the dot is still there; its status as an entity (viz., a dot) is quite independent of whether it counts as a pixel in some visual pattern. The corresponding approach to intentional states would be to say that they are (for instance) structures in the brain, identifiable neurophysiologically or syntactically, but so related to one another in an overall pattern that they also *count as* beliefs and desires. The being, the "reality," of such states would be nothing other than that of those brain structures – for they would be identical. Such an account (a version of token-identity theory) would be ontologically straightforward and familiar, and it might well be Fodor's view, or even Davidson's; but it surely isn't Dennett's.

It bears mentioning, therefore, that the analogy that Dennett still proposes between beliefs and centers of gravity (pp. 27–29) is completely misleading, and should be discarded. A center of gravity is nothing other than a spatial point at a time, or a point trajectory through time. Hence, its ontological status is exactly on a par with that of any other spatial point or trajectory, including the center of the smallest sphere containing all the socks Dennett has ever lost. Whether a given point or trajectory *counts as* a center of gravity, or a lost sock center, depends on its position relative to certain masses or socks; but its *being* is spatial, and independent of what else it counts as.[3] Accordingly, the greater usefulness, in scientific calculation, of centers of gravity does not confer on them any further *ontological* status; they are no more "real" than lost sock centers – just more worth keeping track of. This is not at all analogous to the claim about beliefs: as just noted, Dennett never suggests that beliefs are simply a subset of the set of all brain structures (or computational states, or anything else independently specifiable) which, because of their participation in some pattern, also *count as* intentional.

3   Patterns in the Life World: Two Ways to be Special

Centers of gravity and bit patterns, however, are merely preparatory for Dennett's richest and most developed example: patterns in the Life world.[4] Although the lessons will ultimately be quite different, Life looks at first to be little more than a kinetic variant of a pattern of pixels. Thus, much as a black dot is a black dot, whether or not it counts as a pixel in some image, so also a Life cell is a Life cell, whether or not it counts as a component in a glider, eater, or other pattern in the Life plane.[5] Moreover, the same point can be made at successive higher "levels." For instance, if a Turing machine is implemented (as can be done) as a higher-order pattern of gliders, eaters, and so on, then each glider is the glider it is, whether or not it also counts as (say) a token on the tape of that Turing machine. Though its status as a tape token depends on its participating in the higher-order pattern, its status as an *entity* – a glider, as it happens – does not.

A glider, as its name suggests, moves across the plane from moment to moment; so it cannot be identified with any fixed set of cells or cell states; but, somewhat like a trajectory, it might plausibly be identified with a temporal sequence of sets of cell states. The trouble with such an identification is that it ignores the *motivation* for picking out this particular kind of sequence. Thus, there are any number of definable sequences of sets of cell states – which, when they occur, are all equally "actual" or "real."[6] But some few of these kinds of sequence, including gliders, are very special. Roughly, they *persist* as reidentifiable non-empty configurations against an empty background.

One way to think about this special persistence is *from below*, as a consequence of the kinetic law governing cell state changes in the Life world. This law entails that if, at a given time, all the cells in the Life world are off except those that would be on for a single glider at that time, then the sequence of sets of cell states for that glider will occur in the future of that world – that is, the glider will persist. Further: the effect of the kinetic law is entirely local, which means that the glider will persist for as long as those cells sufficiently nearby are all off (what's happening far away doesn't matter at the moment). To put it another way, the law guarantees that once a glider sequence is started, and so long as it is not interfered with, it will continue. Very few of the definable sequences of sets of cell states have this feature of guaranteed persistence; hence those that do are special.[7]

A different way to think about persistence is to consider, not what makes it possible (and rare), but what makes it noteworthy or important – to ask, in effect, what's so *special* about persisting configurations. Dennett speaks of their "*salience as real things*," and says this means that one can "proceed to predict – sketchily and riskily – the behavior of larger configurations or systems of configurations" (p. 40). In other words, persistent patterns and structures are special because they can be relied upon as *components* of higher-order patterns or structures, such as tokens on Turing machine tapes. This is to think about the persistence or, more broadly, the *specialness* of certain patterns *from above*, in terms of what they participate in or contribute to.

In a Life-world implementation of a Turing machine tape, the gliders are, at the same time, patterns and components of patterns. They fall, therefore, on both sides of Dennett's initial vacillation. As we shall see, it is precisely in this double or bivalent position, with "specialness from above," that patterning can have ontological import – that is, confer status as an entity. But this will require more careful attention to the notion of "pattern."

4   Patterns as Recognizabilia, and the Concept of Recognition

Relatively early in his article, Dennett inserts a remarkable passage, one with little evident connection to the remainder of the text.

> I propose that the self-contradictory air of "indiscernible pattern" should be taken seriously. We may be able to make some extended, or metaphorical, sense of the idea of indiscernible patterns (or invisible pictures or silent symphonies), but in the root case a pattern is "by definition" a candidate for pattern *recognition*. (p. 32).

Nowhere in the ensuing discussion, however, does he tell us anything about what pattern recognition *is*, or why it should have this definitive significance. On the contrary, no sooner has he acknowledged the implication of an "unbreakable link to observers or perspectives" than he turns instead to "discernibility-in-principle" and the mathematical definition of randomness – two ideas that seem as observer independent and non-perspectival as one could hope to find. Tracing this ambivalence will show, by steps, that Dennett understands "pattern" in two different ways, that he needs *both* of them to make his ontological point, and that this is what "stances" are all about. But, to get there from here, we first have to ask what it means to *recognize* something.

Recognizing, as the quoted passage indicates, is *at least* discerning or discriminating. To recognize something is to respond to it in a way that distinguishes it from other things; to recognize is to tell apart. But differential response cannot be the whole story, for two deeply related reasons. First, what is recognized is always some determinate item, feature, or characteristic of the confronted situation, whereas a given response can equally well be taken as a response to any of several distinct things. Secondly, recognition, unlike response, is a normative notion: it is possible to *mis*recognize something, to get it *wrong*, whereas a response is just whatever response it is to whatever is there. These are related because: only insofar as something determinate is supposed to be recognized, can there be an issue of recognizing *it* rightly or wrongly; and it is only as that which determines rightness or wrongness that the object of recognition is determinate.

Thus, in order to understand recognition, as distinct from mere differential response, we must understand these interrelated phenomena of object determinacy and normativity. Consider an automatic door; it responds to an approaching pedestrian by opening, and to the pedestrian's passing through by closing again. Of course, it might respond identically to a wayward shopping cart, or a large enough piece of plaster falling from the ceiling; and we can even imagine it being triggered by the magnetic fields of a floor polisher passing near its control box, across the hall. Are such incidents *misrecognitions?* Has the door *mistaken* plaster or a floor polisher for a pedestrian, say? Obviously not, for pedestrians, plaster, and polishers are nothing to a door. Therefore, even in the usual case, we cannot say that it has recognized a pedestrian.

Should we conclude instead that it recognizes pressure on its floor pad, the current in some wire, or – in the limit – a force adequate to open it? Again, no; for if the possibility of error is systematically eliminated, then it's vacuous to speak of correctness or recognition at all. Rather, whenever the door opens, there is an extended set of relevant causal factors (some proximal, some distal) any of several of which might equally well be identified as "the" factor to which it responded – depending on what we're interested in at the time. But since the door doesn't get any of them right or wrong – it just responds as it does – none of the responses amounts to recognition. The same can be said about a trout striking at a fly (whether natural or hand-tied) and, in my view, about a hound chasing a rabbit (whether across a field or around a racetrack).

If, on the other hand, opening for anything other than a pedestrian would amount to an *error* (regardless of what pressures or currents did or didn't intervene), then, in the ordinary case, the pedestrian (and not any pressure or current) would be the *object* of the response; that is, the system would *recognize* pedestrians. (This is just what the situation would be if the "system" were a human employee). To put it more generally, if some specific causal factor can be singled out as making the difference, from case to case, between correct response and error, then, in any given non-erroneous case, this same factor also can be singled out as *the object* recognized. And likewise vice versa: if a response has a determinate proper object – if it is a recognitive response – then, absent that object, the response is an error. In sum, recognition, object determinacy, and the possibility of mistake belong together.

Thus, to comprehend the full content of the suggestion that patterns be regarded as candidates for recognition, we will need to understand the normative standards according to which they can stand individually as criteria for *correct* recognitions.

5 Two Senses of "Pattern": Recognizabilia versus Orderly Arrangements

There are really two notions of "pattern" at work in Dennett's article. On the one hand, there is the idea that patterns are "by definition" candidates for discernment or recognition; on the other, there is the idea that a pattern is some sort of orderly or non-random arrangement – the opposite of chaos. The first idea invites an operational or practical definition, via an account of recognizing and correctness; the second invites an explicit or theoretical definition, in terms of what's arranged, what arrangements are possible, and which of those arrangements are orderly. The mathematical definition, as well as all the pixel examples, are of this latter sort. The obvious question is: why have both? In particular, why bother with the looser operational definition when the explicit theoretical definition is available?

One advantage of the "operational definition" in terms of recognition is that it does not presuppose or depend on any determination of what the pattern is a pattern *of*. The mathematical definition, by contrast, only makes sense if the "bits" – or, more generally, the possible types and relations of its elements – are specified in advance. But recognition needs no such prespecification: you just have to "know one when you see one." For instance, when I recognize the faces of my friends, or the expressions on their faces, or the genre of a book, there are no particular bits or other elements that these are patterns of. A delighted smile is not a pattern of epidermal cells, still less of pixels or light waves; if anything, it's a concurrence of cheek lift and brow movement, of lip shape and eye sparkle. But these are not more antecedently determinate than smiles themselves, perhaps less so. Smiles, as the definition suggests, are what they are because we recognize them to be, and not the other way around. Likewise, the recognizable mystery or romance in a novel is not a pattern of words, still less of letters, but of something more like characters, situations, and mood – again, because readers reliably take them so.

The recognition-based definition is liberating in a second respect as well: it is not oriented exclusively to the "internals" of the recognized pattern. Thus, when I recognize something as a reassuring or a cautionary gesture, my response is influenced not only by the specific character of the gestural motions, but also, and perhaps largely, by the circumstances in which they are made. "Context dependence" of interpretations is, of course, familiar; but it is frequently understood on a broadly inferential model:

1 any instance of *I*, in context *C*, would be (or count as) an *R*.
2 Here is an instance of *I*; and
3 It is in context *C*.
4 So, here is an *R*.

This presumes, however, that *C* and *I* are identifiable as such independently, and that the recognition of *R* is then just drawing a conclusion – not really a *recognition* at all. But very often, I think, context-informed phenomena (gestures are but one example) are recognized for what they are, quite apart from any *independent* recognition of the context or of anything which is "in" the context. Indeed, the inferences, if any, can just as easily go in the other direction. Joint recognizability of instance-cum-context yields a notion of pattern notably divergent from that of an orderly arrangement of parts.

In the meantime, determinate prespecification of the bits or elements, as required by the mathematical definition, can be a philosophical embarrassment, in more than one way. First, many relevant patterns – conspicuously including the behavioral patterns that support intentional interpretation – do not seem to be made up of well-defined bits or elements. Just which causal commerce with the environment amounts to perception and action is by no means specifiable in advance, nor can it be precisely delineated in any case. Secondly, the account of patterns as orderly arrangements of predeterminate elements is an invitation to metaphysical reductionism: the thesis that these patterns are "nothing but" their elements as arranged. Clearly, however, (whatever else one thinks about it) this runs counter to Dennett's motivating insight that "real patterns" might be of distinctive ontological status and interest. Thirdly, if (in spite of all the foregoing) an attempt were made to merge the two notions of pattern, such that recognizable patterns must at the same time *be* arrangements of prior elements, then, arguably, their recognizability would have to be *via* prior recognition of those elements; and that would be a version of epistemological foundationalism.

No sooner are these observations made, however, than the outline of a *rapprochement* becomes roughly visible. For if the independent identifiability of the elements of an orderly arrangement pattern is problematic, and if, at the same time, the identity of a recognition pattern can be context dependent, then the one hand may wash the other. Rather than merging (so as to coincide), the two notions of pattern join forces, to mutual advantage. In this larger conception, the "elements" of an orderly arrangement need no longer be thought of as *simple* ("elementary"), like bits or pixels, or even independently identifiable. On the contrary, they might be quite elaborate, elusive, and/or subtle, so long as some relevant creatures are (or can learn to be) able to recognize them. This recognizability, in turn, can perfectly well depend, in part, on their participation in the arrangement (= the context) of which they are the elements.

In effect, we have "patterns" at two different levels, one level for each of Dennett's two definitions, but in such a way that (artificially simplified cases aside) each requires the other. That is, both definitions are integral to a single unified account. What's more, this one integral account reveals how Dennett's ambivalence between the two notions of "pattern" is deeply connected with his initial vacillation between considering patterns and considering their elements; for both involve the same distinction of "level." But we still must see how their integration enables his ontological insight.

6 The Two Levels and the Normativity of Recognition

Recognition, we noted, is subject to normative appraisal, and has a determinate (purported) object. These related characteristics are what distinguish it from mere differential response. But what they are and how they are possible has yet to be explained. If, however, recognizable patterns are understood as elements of orderly arrangement patterns, then the resources may be available to supply that explanation. For the elements of an orderly arrangement are by no means arbitrary: the order itself, in conjunction with the other elements, imposes strict constraints on what any given element can be. In particular, it sharply – as a rule, uniquely – limits which among the causal antecedents of a response could possibly be such an element. This limitation, in other words, picks out a single factor in the causal background of the response as having a special status and importance, *vis-à-vis* the larger orderly arrangement; and then, if that single factor could be identified as its *object*, the response would amount to a recognition.

To pick out which factor, if any, would have the status of object, however, is not yet to show that any factor *does* have that status. For that, something else about the larger, two-level picture must be brought out, something in terms of which responses can be deemed right or wrong according as they track that object. Or, to put it differently, it is yet to be shown how this singled-out factor, the candidate object, can serve as a *criterion* for the *correctness* of the response.

Return to the Life world. Since a universal Turing machine can be implemented in it, so can any other computer architecture, and any program on any such computer – indeed, in many different ways. Dennett imagines a chess-playing system implemented (several levels down) in a vast "galaxy" of gliders, eaters, and so on; and then imagines setting it up to play against itself (p. 41). The point of the exercise is that an outsider might adopt any of a variety of perspectives on this assemblage, including, at the highest level, the intentional stance.

> one can shift to an ontology of chess-board positions, possible chess moves, and the grounds for evaluating them; then, adopting the intentional stance toward the configuration, one can predict its future *as* a chess player performing intentional actions – making chess moves and trying to achieve checkmate. Once one has fixed on an interpretation scheme, permitting one to say which configurations of pixels count as which symbols . . . one can use the interpretation scheme to predict, for instance, that the next configuration to emerge from the galaxy will be such-and-such a glider stream (the symbols for "*RxQ*", say). (p. 41)

There are, in fact, three distinct perspectives or levels mingled in this dense passage: (a) the chess ontology (board positions, possible moves, etc.); (b) the ontology of symbols for chess moves ('*RxQ*'); and (c) the intentional ontology (actions, tryings, and the like).

Focus, for the moment, on the chess ontology; certain subpatterns in this galaxy *are* chess pieces and positions, and appropriate changes in them are chess moves. What makes them so? Clearly the basic requirement is that, understood as chess phenomena, they be found reliably to accord with the rules of chess – the pieces must be those defined for chess, they must start in the standard starting positions, the moves must be legal (and not too bad), and so forth. Implicit in these are also certain "enabling" prerequisites, such as that the pieces and positions be reidentifiable, that they be changeable in the ways permitted by the rules, that they be otherwise reliably stable, and so on. Consistent with those, anything whatever can serve as a chess set, including, but by no means limited to, subpatterns in a galaxy of flashing cells in the Life plane.

Chess phenomena, constituted as they are in accord with these preconditions, are a perfect example of what was earlier described as *specialness from above* – something's being noteworthy *as a pattern* not by virtue of how it's built out of elements, but by virtue of how it participates in or contributes to something else. Hence, in our larger unified account, chess pieces, locations, and moves, would fill the bill as *recognition* patterns, functioning as elements in the orderly arrangement pattern defined by the rules of the game.[8] The rules of chess, moreover, are paradigmatically normative. Consequently, at least for domains with this particular structure, a credible source is at hand for the corresponding derivative norms of recognition. Two main things, therefore, remain to be shown. First, how this derivation works; that is, how the standards that govern chess phenomena as such induce norms for the recognition of those phenomena. And, secondly, how the account, introduced in terms of rule-governed games, can be seen to generalize to other domains as well.

7   Chess players and their Commitments

A fundamental limitation of Life-world chess is that one can at best observe it as an outsider; there is no provision for interactive input to the system, hence no way to play against it. So consider instead a more congenial system, such as a computer that accepts opponents' moves via keyboard input, and continuously displays the current position on a screen. Again, what makes these display patterns *chess* pieces is not that they look like old-fashioned chess pieces to us (indeed, they may not), but that they are positioned and moved according to the rules. Only this time we're not just observing, we're *playing* – so some of those moves are our own. What difference does that make?

If you want to play chess, you have to play by the rules, and insist that your opponent also plays by the rules – you have to *commit yourself* to the game proceeding in accord with the rules. In any given instance, that means you have to be able to tell what the current position is, what move is being made (considered), and whether that move is (would be) legal in that position. And you must be resolved to resist if it isn't. In other words, in taking on a commitment to the legality of the game, you inevitably also take on a commitment to *recognizing* the pieces, positions, and moves – recognizing them *correctly* – for only in that way can legality be maintained. This is how norms that govern chess phenomena as such can induce norms for the recognition of those phenomena.

More specifically, a concord of two potentially discordant factors is required. If we ask *which* recognitions are correct, and why, we might answer that those recognitions are correct that find the positions to be stable and the moves legal – because these are the conditions on there being chess phenomena to recognize at all. But this risks vacuity; for if there were no *other* constraint on correct recognition, then arbitrary patterns could be gratuitously "recognized" as the moves of any legal game you like. The first leaf falling today could be white's opening, P–K4; the second leaf could be black's reply, also P–K4; and so on, at tournament level. Obviously, the recognitions must be *beholden* somehow to what is ostensibly being recognized, yet in such a way that the criteria of correctness are induced from above.

Here lies the true import of the phrase "you know one when you see one": recognition is essentially a *skill*. It can be easy or arduous to acquire; but, once mastered, it can be performed reliably and consistently. What's more, competent practitioners can almost always tell when they're having difficulty; and, in such cases, they can much improve their performance by taking extra care, making multiple attempts, asking for help, and so on. This conscientious, sometimes painstaking, practical exercise is the concrete way in which recognition holds itself to its object. The constitutive standards for a given domain – e.g. the rules of chess – set conditions jointly on a range of responsive dispositions and a range of phenomena: if they are both such that the former consistently find the latter to accord with the standards, then the former are recognition skills and the latter are objects in the domain. But such eventual concord is anything but vacuous: it is rare and, in general, a considerable *achievement*.

It amounts to an achievement precisely because skillful practitioners – *observers* are a special case – can tell if it isn't working, and sometimes rectify it. Thus, whatever form the chess pieces, positions, and moves take, players who play with them would have to be able to tell if pieces were disappearing, positions randomly changing, or the moves illegal. And not only could they tell, but they wouldn't stand for it. At first, an apparent breach would elicit a more thorough examination, double checking, perhaps excuses or explanations, all geared to correcting the recognitions, in case there were some mistake. But these attempted corrections are themselves just further exercises of the same recognitive skills constituted along with the recognizable phenomena according to the standards for the domain. This means that the efforts may well not succeed: it may turn out that the alleged chess phenomena are not reliably stable or legal after all, which is to say, they may not be chess. Thus, insistence on the constitutive standards is on pain of giving up the game. The fact that this could happen is what makes it an achievement when it doesn't.

More generally, if a larger arrangement pattern is constitutive for the domain of its elements, and is as such insisted upon by skillful practitioners, it can induce the norms by which those elements can themselves be recognition patterns. That is, the elements can be *criterial* for the correctness of their own recognition, and in that sense *objects*.

8   Ontology without Equivocation (to wit, on "Real")

The term "object" brings connotations of "objectivity" and "autonomy": an object is an entity "in its own right," quite apart from us – which is *why* it can stand over against us as a criterion, hence *why* we can be wrong about it. Though Dennett does not use the word "object" in this privileged way, he unmistakably endorses these connotations in his pervasive talk of ontology, realism, and "salience as real things." His purpose, of course, is to explicate and defend his own longstanding position on the ontological status of intentional entities, a position he now wants to call mild, intermediate, or semi-realism. I am not happy with any of these expressions. I do agree with Dennett's final assessment that the view itself is clearer than the labels (p. 51); but that, it seems to me, is not merely a credit to the view, but also a discredit to the labels.

Let us begin by considering the reality of chess pieces. The first temptation, always, is to think of chess pieces as the familiar manipulable figurines – conventionally shaped lumps of wood, plastic, or whatever – and these, of course, are paradigmatically real. Being *real*, after all, is being *thingly*, being in the manner of the *res*; and the cohesive, enduring corporeal lump is the paradigm thing. We should, however, be very hesitant to identify chess pieces with things.

Traditional metaphysics interprets the thing as substance; the individual perduring bearer of multiple variable properties.[9] The substantial thing is *independent* in a strong sense, as that which needs nothing else in order to be.[10] This gives the metaphysical meaning of *"property"*: that which is "proper to" or "owned by" a substance all by itself, that which a substance "has" regardless of anything else.[11] In the case of corporeal substances, their spatiotemporal continuity and integrity is the basis of their identity and individuality; and their properties include mass, shape, hardness, temperature, and the like. By contrast, market price, functional role, ecological niche, and so on, are *not* properties of things: they can never "belong to" an individual independently and all by itself.[12] The fact that this ontological understanding remains vague in important respects, and has evolved in a variety of distinct traditional directions, should not blind us to its very considerable specificity and definiteness. It is anything but tautologically empty and noncommittal.

What then about chess pieces – rooks, pawns, knights – are they substantial things? Manifestly not. A chess piece is "defined," *what it is* is determined, by how it moves around the chess board in relation to other pieces, how it threatens, protects, captures, and is captured by them. Apart from its participation in chess, a *rook* makes no sense, and could not be: to be a rook is to play the part of a rook in a chess game. That is why patterns in the Life plane or on a computer display can *be* rooks. The point is not that such patterns are "insubstantial," so at least some rooks are. Rather: *no rook is a substance.* No matter how the metaphysical notions of independence and property are worked out, they will not apply to rooks. Nothing about a rook is determinate, not even its "rookness," apart from its participation in a chess game.

It is equally important to resist the thought that rooks, in contrast to corporeal things, are "abstract." In so far as abstraction concerns the consideration of properties apart from any particular instantiations in things, then it has nothing to do with chess pieces. But if we broaden the abstract/concrete distinction to mark the difference between general characteristics or possibilities and their determinacy in particular individuals, then rooks can be considered either way. Considered in the abstract, rooks – any rook, "the" rook, rooks as a type – always start in a corner of the board, move only along ranks and files, tend to be more valuable than knights, and so on. But at a particular point in a particular game, this particular rook is a fully concrete individual: everything that can be determinate for a rook is determinate for this one – the particular square that it's on, the particular other pieces that are threatening or blocking it, its particular history of prior moves, its particular strategic value in the current position, etc., etc.[13]

Must we not acknowledge, however, still speaking of this particular rook, that it is *identical to* – the very same entity as – this particular lump of black plastic? Further, having granted that the lump of plastic is a thing, must we not concede after all that the rook, this particular rook token, is a thing too – the very same thing? Whatever the fate of token identity theory in other domains, I believe it is demonstrably false for chess pieces. Chess imposes quite definite identity conditions on its pieces, and they simply do not coincide with those for lumps of plastic. For instance, a game begun with the plastic set in the garden, can, after lunch, be carried on with the ivory set in the library. Now, the rule for castling stipulates that one cannot castle with a rook that has previously moved, even if it has since returned to its original square. And, clearly, for one continuing game, black's queen-rook would be the *same* piece in the garden and in the library; that is, black couldn't move it in the garden, and then castle with it later in the library, claiming that it was a *different* rook. But the plastic and ivory lumps are quite distinct (all day long); hence neither can be identical with that (or any) rook.[14]

Dennett's double notion of pattern gives us also another way to see past the token identity theory. As the account has been emerging, individual chess pieces are recognition patterns serving as the elements of rule-constituted games, themselves understood as orderly arrangements. But recognition patterns need have no separate identifiability at all (e.g. as patterns *of* anything else), apart from their recognizability in context. There must, of course, be ways of double-checking these recognitions, perhaps from multiple angles or by multiple observers (with insistence on the rules inducing the normative force). Even so, ultimately, it is (or can be) *just* a matter of recognition – knowing one when you see one. If, with all due care and attention, that can't be made to work, then the game breaks down, and objectivity vanishes. But until then, everything's fine. In other words, there need in principle be no determinate candidate in any *other* domain (such as corporeal substances or arrangements of pixels) for token identification.

So, are chess pieces *real*? It depends on how the term is meant. If it's used in its strict (metaphysical) sense, then, no, chess pieces are not at all real, not even a little bit. But if it's used in one of its more colloquial senses, to pick out all and only what there is – what there "really" is, as opposed to the posits of hallucinations, superstitions, and false pretenses – then, of course, there really are chess pieces, lots of them, all over the world. On neither reading, however, is the reality of chess pieces "intermediate" or "halfway": they are not *substances* at all, but they are genuine, full-fledged *entities*, one hundred percent. As far as I can see, the idea of "mild realism" depends on running together these two distinct senses of "real" and, consequently, is much more likely to confuse than to illuminate.[15]

9　Stance and Being

It would be a misunderstanding, therefore, to take the analogy between intentional states, on the one hand, and patterns and game phenomena, on the other, as a way of mitigating or watering down the ontology of the mental – as if to say they're "no more real" than these. The distinctions among the ways of being, and, in particular, between the being of the intentional and the being of the physical, are, of course, central to the account; and it is to illuminate these that patterns and games are discussed. But the inner coherence and genius of Dennett's position lies not in the analogies among these distinctions, but the underlying unity that binds them all together, that makes them all distinctions among *ways of being*.

Famously, Dennett introduces and explicates intentionality in terms of what he calls "the intentional stance." A *stance*, on the face of it, is a kind of posture or attitude that somebody can take toward something, a specific way of regarding and dealing with it. That intentional systems should be defined in terms of a possible attitude toward them has misled many into thinking the point is to downgrade their status, to imply that the intentional is somehow secondary, observer relative, or artificial – in contrast, say, to the physical. But, in this respect, Dennett puts the intentional and the physical exactly on a par: each is understood in terms of a possible stance. To be sure, the physical stance is importantly different from the intentional; but it is a stance, none the less. And there are others: Dennett discusses also the design stance, and later considers the possibility of a moral or personal stance.[16] Presumably, he would be equally receptive to stances for evolutionary biology, cultural anthropology, macro-economics, and so on.

Officially, a stance is a strategy that one might adopt in order to predict and explain the behavior of something. Which stance one adopts in a given case is, of course, constrained by which strategies can be expected to work; but it is otherwise optional – a pragmatic decision, based on interests and purposes. Thus, a person might be treated as a physical object when calculating elevator loads, as a designed system when performing surgery, as an intentional system when offering coffee, and so on. The phenomena predicted and explained from the respective stances are not the same. Purposive action, for instance, is not the same as physiological movement; and both are distinct from physical motion. Indeed, each stance has its own peculiar vocabulary, and, in general, even its own observational and explanatory methodology. So, from the design stance, one speaks of what the various structures and processes are *for*, and explains how their organized complexes *work*; and, in this context, one can say also that something is malfunctioning, the wrong size, out of kilter, or broken – terms that make no sense from either the intentional or the physical stance.

But a stance is more than just an attitude toward or a perspective on things, more even than a method and terminology for dealing with them. Adopting a stance is *taking a stand*. Why? Because it is this alone – *commitment* to constitutive standards – that allows that toward which the stand is taken to stand out as phenomena, to stand over against us as objects. Such standards determine the *being* of the objects: what it is for them to be, *and* what is possible and impossible for them. Practitioners' insistence that the objects accord with the standards presupposes an ability to tell whether they do, and a resolve not to stand for it if they don't, either by finding out what went wrong and fixing it, or (failing that) by "giving up the game." Only in the light of this commitment can it be said non-vacuously, when things go right, that *phenomena* have been discovered, that *objects* have been constituted.[17] Only against a genuine and determinate possibility of failure can there be any meaningful success.

Dennett discusses only the intentional stance in any detail. For the intentional domain, *rationality* is the constitutive standard ("rationality is the mother of intention," IS, p. 19). Although Dennett speaks of a *presumption* of rationality, rather than a commitment to it, the force is the same.

The presumption of rationality is so strongly entrenched in our inference habits [about people] that when our predictions prove false, we at first cast about for adjustments in the information-possession conditions (he must not have heard, he must not know English, he must not have seen *x*, been aware that *y*, etc.) or goal weightings, before questioning the rationality of the system as a whole. In extreme cases personalities may prove to be so unpredictable from the intentional stance that we abandon it. (IS, p. 32)

In other words, for intentional attribution, we *insist upon* rationality: in confronting apparent breaches of the standard, we first attempt to rectify them (e.g. explain them away in terms sanctioned by the standard itself); and, failing that, we give it up. This, I claim – and I intend it fully in the spirit of Dennett's stances – is the essence of all science, and, indeed, of all objective knowledge.

10   Outer and Inner Recognition: Knowledge and Understanding

To bring out the essential shape of "Real Patterns," I have so far suppressed the noise in it. Yet noise is an integral component of Dennett's insight. Intentional systems, as he is constantly reminding us, do not have to be *perfectly* rational, just mostly (i.e. a lot better than chance). Ultimately, in fact, the notion of "perfect rationality" (or, for that matter, perfect accord with constitutive standards more generally) need not be well defined. This is one of several respects in which the "chess stance" can be misleading, if taken as more than an introductory example; for digital games are quite exceptional in the explicit precision with which their constitutive standards can be articulated, and the corresponding absoluteness of the demand for compliance. Even physics, notable as it is for ontical precision, is less well spelled out in its ontological foundations than is chess, and more tolerant of anomalies in its concrete practice.

To see the possibility of unarticulated (perhaps inarticulable) constitutive standards, we turn again to Dennett's definition of "pattern" in terms of recognition, only this time from the inside out. What we have hitherto called "recognition patterns" are patterns that can be recognized, so to speak, from the outside, when the pattern as a whole is present. These have served, in the two-level account, as the elements of a larger "arrangement pattern," which is the global structure of the domain as prescribed by its constitutive standards. In principle, however, there need be no articulate specification of these standards; all that is really essential is an ability to tell, in any given case, whether the standards are being met. Thus, for chess, it would suffice in principle if the players could tell which moves were legal, regardless of whether they could spell out the rules that define legality – or, indeed, whether there were any such rules.

So we can distinguish two fundamentally different sorts of pattern recognition. On the one hand, there is recognizing an integral, present pattern from the outside – *outer recognition* we could call it. On the other hand, there is recognizing a global pattern from the inside, by recognizing whether what is present, the current element, fits the pattern – which would, by contrast, be *inner recognition*. The first is telling whether something (a pattern) is *there*; the second is telling whether what's there *belongs* (to a pattern). When chess players recognize pieces, positions, and moves, it is outer recognition of the constituted phenomena; when they recognize these phenomena as legal or illegal, it is inner recognition of the constitutive standards. What these have in common, as species of *recognition*, is that "you can tell by looking" – that is, in both cases, it's the exercise of a practical, learnable *skill* (not an inference or a rule-application).

What is crucial for objectivity is that the two recognitive skills be distinct. (They cannot, of course, be independent, inasmuch as what is recognized in the one way is constitutive for what is recognized in the other.) In particular, skillful practitioners must be able to find them in conflict – that is, simultaneously to outer recognize some phenomenon as present (actual) and inner recognize it as not allowed (impossible). For only in the face of such potential discord does it make sense to *insist* that the patterns accessible to outer recognition accord with the pattern accessible to inner recognition; and only on the strength of such insistence can the latter pattern be a *standard* according to which the former are constituted as *objects*.

The essential but perhaps elusive distinction between these two recognitive skills is reflected in the equally essential but sometimes elusive distinction between knowledge and understanding. Roughly, knowledge is outer recognition, understanding inner. That is, phenomena are *known* in so far as they are recognized as present with their respective characteristics and relations; they are *understood* in so far as they are recognized as being in accord with the standards constitutive for their domain. If understanding is lord of the domain, explanation is concierge: to *explain* a phenomenon is to show it in, to exhibit its allowability according to the standards, to let it be. This is what lies behind Dennett's saying that a stance is a strategy for explanation. A stance, as a commitment to the relevant standards, as made concrete in the respective recognitive skills and insistence on their concord, is nothing other than a strategy for showing that the observable phenomena fit the overall constitutive pattern. The centrality of explanation in the philosophy of science has exactly the same provenance.

Herein lies also, I think, the ultimate limitation of the *intentional* stance. For, if the foregoing is correct, then neither knowledge nor understanding is possible for a system that is itself incapable of adopting a stance – that is, insisting that objects accord with constitutive standards. By this test, neither extant animals nor current computers can know or understand *anything*. This jibes with – I suspect, accounts for – widespread intuitions to the effect that "genuine" or "full-fledged" intentional states cannot properly be ascribed to animals and/or computers. "They may exhibit," one wants to say, "behavioral regularities that are best characterized as informed goal directedness; but they don't *understand* what they're doing at all." Dennett has hoped to demystify such notions as belief and desire by assimilating them to the posits of the intentional stance, being careful all the while to acknowledge the differences of degree between more and less sophisticated intentional systems. But "beliefs" and "desires," in the complete absence of any understanding, indeed the absence of any possibility of understanding what they are about, could hardly be of the same order as what we ordinarily understand by these words. So the differences are not of degree; and the demystification fails.

Yet, in a larger sense, it succeeds. For the true achievement lies not in the account of the intentional stance in particular, but in the account of stances and objectivity in general. If the so-called "intentional states" ascribed in the so-called "intentional stance" are not genuinely *intentional*, that indicates no worse than a misnomer – and certainly not a misidentification or mischaracterization of an important domain of objective inquiry. But, further, if intentionality proper is ever to be understood as an objective phenomenon, then it too must be constituted in accord with a standard-setting stance. Whether this stance, as itself a stance toward standard-setting as such, must be in some unique way a stance toward itself and its own finitude, can here be left open. In that direction lies the existential analytic of dasein, an undertaking which Dennett has only just begun.

NOTES

1   Dennett, Daniel C. (1991) Real patterns. *Journal of Philosophy*, 88, 27–51; parenthetical page references in the text are all to this article, unless otherwise indicated.

2   Dennett, Daniel C. (1971) Intentional systems. *Journal of Philosophy*, 68, 87–106; reprinted as chapter 1 of Dennett's *Brainstorms*. Cambridge, Mass.: MIT Press (1978). Page references will be to this latter edition, and be indicated with the initials "IS."

3   This is not, of course, to pretend that spatial being is unproblematic, nor that it is unconnected with physics and/or everyday life. The point is merely that counting as a center of gravity or a lost sock center is not, on the face of it, an ontological determination.

4   Note that "the Life world" here refers to the realm of possible structures and processes in the two-dimensional formal system called "The Game of Life"; it has nothing to do, not even as a pun, with Husserl's *Lebenswelt*.

5   Though Dennett makes nothing of it (nor will I), it is interestingly difficult to say just which cells (at a time) are components of a pattern such as a glider or an eater. Clearly, they must include not just the cells that are "on" there and then, but also at least some of the adjacent "off" cells; for were those not off, it would be a different pattern. But exactly which cells need to be in which states is not always clear, and may even depend on spatial and temporal context – as when an eater is in the process of consuming something else.

6   The phrase "when they occur" is what differentiates this example from trajectories. A given trajectory through space–time may or may not be the center of gravity for some extended mass; but there's no sense in which the trajectory itself "occurs" or not, depending on this – it's just "there," as a one-dimensional manifold, either way. A sequence of sets of cell states, by contrast, actually *occurs* only if the relevant cells are in fact in the relevant states in the relevant temporal order; otherwise, it isn't "there," it isn't "realized" at all.

7   Actually, since Life is deterministic, every configuration has a guaranteed future, as long as it's not interfered with; and one might say that this total future amounts to one "pattern" which persists. But gliders and a few other patterns persist in the much stronger sense that they are periodic: that is, the *same* momentary configurations (perhaps translated) recur in the same order indefinitely.

8   Whether anyone could, in fact, recognize them as implemented in the Life plane is a separate question; but the essential point could be made as well with a less formidable implementation.

9   Compare this with Quine's definition: "To be is to be the value of a bound variable," meaning that identifiable unity of which an arbitrarily complex open sentence is true.

10 In part I, principle 51, of his *Principles of Philosophy*, Descartes writes: "By *substance* we can understand nothing other than a thing which exists in such a way as to depend on no other thing for its existence" (Cottingham, Stoothoff, and Murdoch translation).

11 Relational properties, if not rejected as incoherent, can be conceived as proper to a plurality of substances – but, again, *proper to them*, regardless of anything else. Extrinsic properties, properties that individuals have by virtue of their relations to others, are then not, stricly speaking, *properties* at all, but rather abbreviated ways of speaking about pluralities.

12 This, no doubt, is why philosophers from time to time try to explain them away – they're not "really real."

13 In just this spirit, I believe also that Dennett should avoid speaking (as he does, e.g., on p. 29) of beliefs as *abstract objects*. Beliefs, of course, do not belong to the *thing* category any more than chess pieces do; but, in the broadened sense of the abstract/concrete distinction, surely beliefs can be disucssed either in abstraction or in the concrete. Thus,

one might (as in logic) consider beliefs only with regard to their content, "abstracting away" from the degree of conviction with which they are held, the source of the evidence on which they are based, their reception as good news or bad news, and so on. Concretion for beliefs, by contrast, is to be fully determinate in all such possible regards.

14 The rules for *en passant* and stalemate also depend on the identity of pieces from move to move. I think the same argument implies that there is no piece identity from one game to another, and hence that there are no chess pieces at all except in the midst of games – in the box, there's just plastic. This is to say, in another terminology, that the that-it-is of a chess piece (its being "in play") is just as dependent on chess as is its what-it-is (its "chess role"). Note that token identity theory for chess pieces breaks down just as thoroughly when the pieces "are" Life-plane or screen-pixel patterns as when they "are" lumps of plastic; in other words, this "are" cannot be the "is" of identity, but must be something else. Perhaps we should say that the pixels or plastic "serve as" or "implement" the pieces, or some such.

15 A further confusion possibly lurking in the progression from "milder than mild" to "industrial strength" realism is the suggestion that ontologies come in "degrees," arrayed along a single dimension. But I see no reason whatever to suppose that the respective ways of being ("reality") of intentional states, functional components, physical particles, chess pieces, everyday paraphernalia, works of art, institutions, people, and whatever else there is, form a one-dimensional series in any interesting sense.

16 See "Mechanism and Responsibility," in *Brainstorms*, ch. 12, pp. 240–3.

17 This suggestion that objectivity is contingent on a commitment (eventually) to "give up the game," if it cannot be made to work in practice, is similar in structure and intent to Popper's proposal of falsifiability as the mark of the scientific; but it is, so to speak, a level up (ontological rather than ontical). Thus, Popper addressed his criterion to *hypotheses* (particular candidate bits of doctrine), thereby presupposing an already constituted vocabulary for expressing the hypotheses, and an already constituted methodology for testing them. A *stance*, by contrast, effectively *is* a vocabulary and a methodology, coupled with a demand for what will in fact be found – or, more to the point, what will *not* be found. Hence, what is up for rejection in case of failure is not any particular hypothesis but rather the entire constituted domain (at least in the current situation).

4

Is Intentional Ascription Intrinsically Normative?

JERRY FODOR AND ERNEST LEPORE

In a short article called "Mid-Term Examination: Compare and Contrast" that epitomizes and concludes his book *The Intentional Stance*, D. C. Dennett (1987) provides a sketch of what he views as an emerging Interpretivist consensus in the philosophy of mind. The gist is that Brentano's thesis is true (the intentional is irreducible to the physical) and that it follows from the truth of Brentano's thesis that:

> strictly speaking, ontologically speaking, there are no such things as beliefs, desires, or other intentional phenomena. But the intentional idioms are "practically indispensable," and we should see what we can do to make sense of their employment in what Quine called an "essentially dramatic" idiom . . . . Not just brute facts, then, but an element of interpretation . . . must be recognized in any use of the intentional vocabulary. (Dennett, 1987, p. 342)[1]

In this context, "making sense of" the prevalence of the intentional idiom is *not* explaining why it should be indispensable if there are no beliefs or desires for it to refer to. Nor is it specifying the truth conditions of intentional ascriptions; Dennett thinks that, strictly speaking, no intentional ascriptions can be true. Rather, the project in "Mid-Term Examination" and his earlier paper "Intentional Systems" is to make clear the sense in which intentional attribution inevitably involves "an element of interpretation." The discussion that follows treats these two papers together.

According to Dennett, there are two schools of Interpretivism, two ways in which one might reveal the element of interpretation in content ascription. These are Projectivvism and Normativism:

> Here two chief rivals have seemed to emerge: one or anther Normative Principle, according to which one should attribute to a creature the propositional attitudes it "ought to have" given its circumstances, and one or another Projective Principle, according to which one should attribute to a creature the propositional attitudes one supposed one would have oneself in those circumstances. (Dennett, 1987, pp. 342f)

The Normative Principles will be our main concern; they include such "principles of charity" as that *most of* the beliefs ascribed to a creature are true (*a fortiori*, that most of them are coherent) and thus imply the holist thesis that there can be content attribution only where there is a *multiplicity* of beliefs. Before we turn to Normativism, however, we will briefly discuss the Projectivist alternative.

1 Projectivism

Projectivism can be construed as proposing a first approximation to a theory of the logical form of belief sentences (for discussion, see Stich, 1983). Roughly, "John believes that it's raining" is equivalent, in Smith's mouth, to "John is in the state that would normally cause me (Smith) to say that it's raining."[2] It is notoriously difficult for this sort of account of belief ascription to get the details right (for example, there are problems about paraphrasing sentences that contain indexicals in complements to verbs of propositional attitude); but, for present purposes, we can put these relatively technical issues to one side. We want to suggest just two main criticisms of the Projectivist story.

First, Projectivism seems hopelessly unable to construe sentences that existentially quantify over the contents of propositional attitudes (as opposed to sentences that actually cite their contents). Consider the following kind of case: Smith's three-year-old hears him prattling on about the analytic/synthetic distinction, and it occurs to the child that Smith must have some beliefs about this distinction that he, the child, does not understand and could not express. On the present analysis, this thought – which intuition might plausibly take to be true – is self-contradictory, since it entails both that Smith is in some state that would normally lead the three-year-old to say that... blah, blah, blah, analytic/synthetic, blah, blah, blah...; and that there is no such state.

Or consider you and your Twin-earth twin *after* you have noticed that what he calls "water" isn't H_2O, and hence that the belief he expresses by uttering the form of words "water is wet" isn't the belief that water is wet. (For the original Twin examples, see Putnam, 1975). Perhaps you would like to say that there is nevertheless *some or other* belief that your twin uses that formula to express. But how *can* you say this, knowing, as you do, that the belief he expresses isn't one that it's possible for *you* to entertain? (According to the standard story, you can entertain the belief that your twin uses the form of words "water is wet" to express only if you are causally connected to XYZ – which, by assumption, you aren't.)

So you can't coherently believe that there is something that your twin means by what he says when he utters "water is wet." It would make *no sense* for you to believe this, given the Projectivist analysis of belief ascriptions. Turnabout is fair play, of course; your twin can use the same considerations to exempt himself from thinking that there is anything *you* mean by *your* utterances of "water is wet." It would be understandable if you were to find this consequence of Projectivism offensive.

These aren't merely technical difficulties. The problem is that, if the Projectivist account of the (putative) interpretive element in belief attribution is right, then what *you* can believe depends on what *your interpreter* can say. But if anything is metaphysically independent of anything, surely your repertoire of potential beliefs is independent of anybody else's repertoire of potential speech acts. There is, no doubt, an "element of interpretation" in talk about mountains; where does the mountain end and the valley begin, after all? But only a megalomaniac could suppose that whether there are mountains depends on whether he can say that there are.

The second objection is that Projectivism can't *explain* the putative "element of interpretation" in intentional ascription; on the contrary, Projectivism must *presuppose* it in order to count as a species of Interpretivism.

Consider the following line of inquiry. Why isn't the Projectivist actually a *Realist* about the intentional, albeit a Realist who disagrees with the usual assumptions about the polyadicity of propositional attitude predicates? That is, why isn't a Projectivist just a Realist who thinks that believing (and the like) is a *four*-place relation (between a creature, its mental state, the propositional object of its mental state, and an interpreter), as opposed to the more conventional view that it's a *three*-place relation (between a creature, its mental state, and the propositional object of its mental state)? Notice that, *so far*, there is no incompatibility between Realism and this view of the polyadicity of intentional ascriptions.[3]

Relativizing intentional ascriptions to an interpreter doesn't, *in and of itself*, impugn their objectivity. For, *prima facie*, there is a fact of the matter about whether John *is* in the sort of state that would normally cause Smith to say that it is raining; and if he is, then, according to the Projectivist analysis, Smith's claim that John believes that it's raining is just straightforwardly *true*.[4]

The obvious reply would be that there is no fact of the matter – that it is a question for interpretation – as to whether the state that John is in *is* the same state (is a token of the same state type) as the one that normally causes Smith to say that it's raining. (Or, equivalently for these purposes, there is no fact of the matter – it's a question for interpretation – whether what John does when he's in that state is to count as saying what Smith does when Smith utters the form of words "it's raining.") This does make Projectivism a species of Interpretivism; but it also gives up on the idea that intentional ascriptions are interpretive *because* they are projective. On the contrary, what we've just seen is that the order of analysis must go the other way around: only when it is given an Interpretivist reading does Projectivism fail to represent attitude ascriptions as fully factual. But then, *a fortiori*, it can't be that the Projectivist analysis *per se* accounts for the "element of interpretation" in intentional ascription.

So much for the discussion of Projectivism. We turn now to the consideration of Normativism, the other form Interpretivism can take according to "Mid-Term Examination."

2   Normativism

Normativism is the claim that the attitudes that an interpreter attributes to a creature are constrained by the requirement that, in general, the creature should be represented as having the beliefs it ought to have and the desires whose satisfaction would be in its interest. There are, presumably, two sorts of reasons for supposing that Normativism is a species of Interpretivism. For one thing, by definition, Normativists believe that some of the constitutive principles of content attribution are *normative*; and, at least on some views of what normativity amounts to, this would all by itself suffice to make such attributions not fully factual. Secondly, as we understand Dennett, it is central to his argument for Interpretivism that (at least some of) the normative principles constitutive of content assignment are idealized and heuristic; that they are *not* really satisfied by flesh and blood intentional systems. It is because the conditions for intentional ascription require that we treat fallible creatures *as if* they were fully rational that "an element of interpretation" enters in when intentional states are ascribed.

We propose to question both the argument from Normativism to Interpretivism and the argument that Normative principles are inextricably involved in content attribution. First, however, *which* normative principles? Consider the following:

1 *The truth principle*: Necessarily, intentional ascriptions represent a creature's beliefs as mostly true (by the interpreter's lights).
2 *The coherence principle*: Necessarily, intentional ascriptions represent a creature's beliefs as mostly coherent (by the Interpreter's lights).
3 *The closure principle*: Necessarily, if a creature is represented as believing p, and p entails q, then the creature must be represented as believing q.
4 *The probity principle*: Necessarily, intentional systems mostly desire what it would be good for them to have.

Our reading is that Dennett endorses (1) and (2). Dennett also endorses (3) as an appropriate idealization governing intentional ascription (see Dennett, 1978, p. 11; 1987, p. 21 and pp. 94–5). However, Dennett's argument for (3) serves equally well as an argument for (2); and the latter is clearly the weaker and more plausible option. Similarly, Dennett's argument for (1) also serves as an argument for (4), a principle that he explicitly endorses. Having said all this, it simplifies the exposition to ignore these distinctions except where they matter. We propose henceforth to do so.

Dennett's Evolutionary Argument for the Truth Principle

What shows that content ascription is required to represent intentional systems as believers (/tellers) of truths? Dennett proposes an evolutionary argument; or, at least, he seems to:

> Suppose we travel to a distant planet and find it inhabited by things moving about its surface, multiplying, decaying, apparently reacting to events in the environment, but otherwise as unlike human beings as you please. Can we make intentional predictions and explanations of their behavior? If we have reason to suppose that a process of natural selection has been in effect, then we can be assured that the populations we observe have been selected in virtue of their design: they will respond to at least some of the more common event-types in this environment in ways that are normally appropriate. (Dennett, 1978, p. 8)

Dennett later adds that:

> there is no point in ascribing beliefs to a system unless the beliefs ascribed are in general appropriate to the environment, and the system responds appropriately to the beliefs. An

eccentric expression of this would be: the capacity to believe would have no survival value unless it were a capacity to believe truths. (Dennett, 1978, p. 17)

Let's, for the moment, ignore the caveat "eccentric;" we'll presently come back to it. Suppose that the doctrine is simply that, on the one hand, since our cognitive capacities are evolved, they must have been selected and, on the other hand, only a cognitive system that generally endorses truths would *be* selected since no other kind of cognitive system would have survival value. So, all of this being the case, the truth principle must hold of our beliefs.

The evolutionary assumptions required to run this sort of argument are, in our view, very dubious; that a system is selected does not require that all of its subsystems have survival value; some of them may be vestigial.[5] That a disposition to believe mostly truths is *ipso facto* at a competitive advantage with respect to any and every capacity to believe mostly falsehoods is, in fact, not obvious (for discussion, see Stich, 1990); and so forth. However, let's put these issues to one side. For, even if the empirical assumptions of the evolutionary argument were impeccable, it doesn't appear to yield either of the conclusions that Dennett wants. What Dennett wants is that Normativism should entail Interpretivism, and that principles like (1) and (4) should be *necessary* (they should hold of intentional systems as such). It is, to put it mildly, not obvious that either consequence follows from the evolutionary story.

Problems with Dennett's Evolutionary Argument for the Truth Principle

It would look to be a matter of fact whether a creature has an evolutionary history; and it would also look to be a matter of fact whether part of the evolutionary story about the creature is that it is at competitive advantage in virtue of the character of its cognitive capacities. But if these are matters of fact, and if being selected for one's cognitive capacities is, as Dennett apparently maintains, at least a *sufficient* condition for being mostly a believer of truths,[6] then it would seem to be a matter of fact – and not a matter of interpretation – whether *we* are believers of mostly truths. Epistemologists should be able to settle the issue of skepticism once and for all by consulting the fossil record.

It is, in short, puzzling how Dennett thinks an appeal to the Darwinian theory – which is, after all, a causal story about the *mechanisms of speciation* – could reveal an "element of interpretation" in content ascription. Interpretivism is, *inter alia*, the view that, strictly speaking, we don't really have beliefs and desires. But, one supposes, what a creature *doesn't really have* can't help it much in its struggle for survival. It is for exactly this reason that, unlike Dennett, most people who take an evolutionary line on intentionality are correspondingly Realist (not to say reduction-ist) about content (Millikan and Dretske are two examples). *Qua* Darwinists, they suppose that there's a matter of fact about what selection history a creature has and about what mechanisms served to mediate its history of selection. So they are required to suppose also that organisms can't be selected for believing truths unless they *do* believe truths.

Dennett himself is, apparently, sensitive to this sort of point; it's the burden of the caveat "eccentric" in the passage quoted above, which proceeds as follows.

An eccentric expression of [the evolutionary argument for principle (1)] would be: the capacity to believe would have no survival value unless it were a capacity to believe truths. What is eccentric and potentially misleading about this is that it hints at the picture of a species "trying on" a faculty giving rise to beliefs most of which were false, having its inutility demonstrated, and abandoning it. A species might "experiment" by mutation in any number of inefficacious systems, but none of these systems would deserve to be called belief systems precisely because of their defects, their nonrationality, and hence a false belief system is a conceptual impossibility. (Dennett, 1978, p. 17)

It's not clear to us what Dennett takes to be the bottom line; but it looks as though it may not be evolution after all that he sees as underwriting the truth principle. Maybe Dennett's position is that it's just *analytic* that a creature's beliefs are mostly true (a system of mostly false propositional attitudes wouldn't "deserve to be called a belief system").

On this reading, Dennett's defense of the claim that principle (1) is constitutive of belief attribution is just that it follows from our concept of belief that beliefs are mostly true. The up side of this sort of strategy is that it gives the opponent so little room to maneuver. The down side is the danger that the best you get is a Pyrrhic victory. Suppose it is analytic of *belief* that no creature has any beliefs unless it has mostly true beliefs (or mostly rational beliefs, or whatever). Very well, then; if the propositional attitudes we've got are mostly *not* true, it follows that they aren't beliefs. But so what? It doesn't follow that they aren't propositional attitudes or that we aren't intentional systems. Perhaps what we've got are *shmeliefs* – propositional attitudes exactly like beliefs in their functional roles, their qualitative contents (if any), and their satisfaction conditions, except that they are *not* analytically constrained by the principles of charity. To make the case worse, it might be supposed that it is *nomologically* necessary that shmeliefs are mostly true (mostly rational, or whatever); you might tell the very Darwinian story Dennett does, according to which natural selection would prefer creatures with mostly true shmeliefs to creatures with mostly false ones. Then, *ceteris paribus*, the *only* difference between a creature's having beliefs and its having shmeliefs would be that, in the latter case, there are logically possible worlds in which what the creature has are mostly false, and in the former case there aren't. It might thus be really *quite* difficult to tell beliefs and shmeliefs apart.[7]

What Dennett needs to avoid this reply is an argument that shmeliefs are conceptually (or metaphysically) impossible; in particular, that a state can't be *intentional* (can't have conditions of semantic evaluation) unless it satisfies the charity principles. This argument is surely *not* provided by the claim that "beliefs are mostly true" is analytic.

In some of his recent papers (see especially "Intentional Systems in Cognitive Ethology: the 'Panglossian Paradigm' Defended" and "Evolution, Error, and Intentionality" both reprinted in Dennett, 1987), Dennett offers a rather different line of thought that may be intended to meet this sort of criticism of his Darwinian argument for principle (1). Apparently the idea is that while, on the one hand, it is indeed the biological function of cognitive mechanisms to fix true beliefs (so a system of false beliefs is an evolutionary impossibility, so the truth principle must be true), yet, on the other hand, ascriptions of biological function themselves involve adopting the intentional stance *towards the evolutionary process* (towards "Mother

Nature," as Dennett likes to say) and must therefore exhibit "an element of interpretation" which our ascriptions of intentional states to creatures other than Mother Nature then inherit. Although "attributions of intentional states to us cannot be sustained . . . without appeal to assumptions about 'what Mother Nature had in mind'" (Dennett, 1987, p. 314), it is also true that "Mother Nature doesn't commit herself explicitly and objectively to *any* [sic] functional attributions; all such attributions depend on the mind-set of the intentional stance, in which we assume optimality in order to interpret what we find" (Dennett, 1987, p. 320). So, apparently, the hermeneutic status of intentional ascriptions (to us) derives from the correspondingly hermeneutic status of ascriptions of biological functions (to mental states), which in turn derives from the hermeneutic status of intentional ascriptions (to Mother Nature). We wouldn't want to insist that this story is circular; but nor would we want to insist that it's not.

In any event, we find it very puzzling. For one thing, there's the point we made above, which does seem to us pretty decisive. If there *are* no beliefs and desires, then, *a fortiori*, there can't be anything that beliefs and desires were selected for, and there can't be any biological (or other) functions that beliefs and desires perform. No doubt interpretation can do a lot – hermeneutics is everywhere these days. Maybe interpretation can somehow determine teleology or selectional history (though with such friends Darwin doesn't need enemies). But surely interpretation can't bestow a teleology or a selectional history *on things that don't exist.* That there is nothing that the unicorn's horn was selected for *follows from* there not having been any unicorns; there is no place for interpretation to insert a wedge, because there are no unicorns (*a fortiori*, no unicorn horns) for an interpreter to take a stance towards. It's one thing to claim that what is is text; it's a bit much to claim that what isn't is too.

Secondly, we're not really clear what the doctrine of interpretivism in biology is supposed to amount to. One would have thought that either evolutionary biology does have entailments of the form "(trait) *t* was selected for performing (function) *f*," or it doesn't. In either case, it's hard to see how our adopting the intentional stance towards evolution (or towards Mother Nature) is supposed to help. It's mysterious, in biology as elsewhere, either how you could make facts out of stances, or how stances could make facts disappear.

Perhaps an analogy will clarify the situation. Suppose it's suggested that the *ecological* function of forest cover is to prevent the erosion of topsoil; *that*, according to the suggestion, is what forest cover is *for.* (You can imagine the claim being spelled out by reference to counterfactuals, among which "no forest cover → no topsoil" would presumably be prominent.) Well, either ecology does underwrite a notion of function or it doesn't. If it does, then it's just a matter of fact what forest cover is for; but if it doesn't, we can't improve the situation by adopting the "intentional stance" towards erosion.

No doubt we could tell a fairy-tale according to which Father Erosion wants to wash away the topsoil and the Tree Fairy wants to stop him. This might be useful for mnemonic purposes, or to amuse small children. But, surely, our telling this story (or not telling it) can't be what determines whether there are ecological functions. If ecology doesn't have consequences of the form "the function of *x* is *f*" *independently* of the story about Father Erosion and the Tree Fairy, then there straightforwardly *isn't* anything that forest cover is for; if it does, then there straightforwardly *is* something that forest cover is for. Either way, our decision to adopt the intentional stance towards erosion affects the ontological status of ecological functions *not one whit*. How could it? It is *stance independent*, after all, that there is no Father Erosion. So adding the story of our ecology can't increase the number of claims that our ecology warrants (a true proposition cojoined with a false one warrants only the inferences that the true proposition does). But if the story about Father Erosion doesn't legitimize interpretivism about functions in ecology, why, exactly, does the story about Mother Nature legitimize interpretivism about functions in biology?[8]

See how the gods punish Instrumentalism: refuse to distinguish theories from fables, and soon you can't distinguish fables from theories. The moral still seems to be that if intentional ascription is to be understood in terms of evolutionary explanation, then it's an empirical rather than a conceptual question whether the truth principle holds. (We, of course, reserve the right to assert this hypothetical and deny its antecedent.)

Dennett's argument for the Closure Principle

Preliminary note: if you have an argument that a creature's beliefs are mostly true, of course, you have an argument that they are mostly coherent; so the satisfaction of principle (1) entails the satisfaction of principle (2). The satisfaction of principle (1) does *not*, however, entail the satisfaction of principle (3) (the closure principle). But, as we remarked above, the argument that Dennett gives for (3) will do equally well as an argument for (2), and we will assume that he intends that it cover both.

Dennett's argument for the closure principle goes like this:

> The assumption that something is an intentional system is the assumption that it is rational; that is, one gets nowhere with the assumption that entity x has beliefs p,q,r, . . . unless one also supposes that x believes what follows from p,q,r, . . . ; otherwise there is no way of ruling out the prediction that x will, in the face of its beliefs p,q,r, . . . do something utterly stupid, and, if we cannot rule out *that* prediction, we will have acquired no predictive power at all. (Dennett, 1978, pp. 10–11)

(Notice that the argument goes through equally well to show that an intentional system that believes *p* must not also believe not-*p*; in effect, for the coherence principle.) We take this passage to intend a transcendental argument according to which the closure principle is presupposed by the very possibility of making intentional predictions. Accordingly, *the argument fails if there is any way to warrant intentional predictions without presupposing closure.*

Much of what needs to be said about Dennett's argument for closure has already been remarked upon in the literature (see Fodor, 1981; Stich, 1981; and "Making Sense of Ourselves" in Dennett, 1987). For example, it seems unclear that anything like *perfect* closure (/coherence) is needed to meet the requirement that *some* predictive power be generated by belief/desire ascriptions.[9] We'd get *some* predictive value out of belief ascription even if it only worked, say, 87 percent of the time that a creature that believes ($p \rightarrow q$ and p) believes q. But if getting predictive power from belief/desire psychology doesn't really depend on assuming *flawless* rationality, then perhaps there is, as a matter of fact, enough closure (/coherence) around to make intentional ascription predictive. In which case, intentional ascription would rest upon rationality assumptions that are (not merely heuristic but) *true*. In which case, how would Normativism argue for Interpretivism?

Also, it seems just not to be true that successful prediction "from the intentional stance" always requires that we assume rationality. There are, for example, lots of cases in which we successfully predict someone's behavior on the assumption that he will *not* notice some consequence of his beliefs and desires. (The chess player who is reliably a sucker for a knight fork, and the like). It may be argued that such predictive successes can operate only "against a background" of presumed rationality; but this does need to be *argued* and we have, as yet, no hint as to how the argument would go. Clearly, we must have (what Dennett's account doesn't give us) *some* story about how the prediction of counter-rational behavior is even *possible*. Maybe it will turn out that the strategies that underlie predictive successes in these apparently exceptional cases will prove to be perfectly general when they are properly analyzed – hence that appeals to charity are never *essential* to intentional prediction. Let's, therefore, actually consider such cases.

Everybody knows that the Moon reliably looks larger when it's seen as being on the horizon. It *may* be that this phenomenon has a "cognitive" explanation in terms of (unconscious) judgements, inferences and the like; but also it may be that it hasn't. The psychologists themselves aren't sure. Clearly, in any event, nobody has detailed knowledge of the presumed underlying inferences, so nobody knows how much closure and coherence they do (or don't) actually exhibit. Yet we confidently predict that we and our friends and relations (and, for that matter, absolute strangers) will be subject to the illusion. And surely this is a prediction "from the intentional stance;" it's ineliminably committed to intentional contexts like "looks to be . . . when seen as . . ." How, then, are such predictions possible?

The question answers itself; the phenomenon is that the Moon *reliably* looks larger when it's on the horizon. The generalization is lawlike in that it is confirmed by its instances, supports counterfactuals, and so forth. And, given access to a *law* that relates the apparent size of the Moon to its apparent position, we don't need to appeal to principles of rationality to predict that if Smith sees the Moon as on the horizon, then he will see it as oversized.

Similarly for the guy who is suckered by knight forks. Heaven knows why he keeps falling for them; there's clearly *something* wrong with the way he plans his moves. But we don't have to know *what* is wrong, or *how much* is wrong – in particular, we don't have to know whether, or to what extent, his planning is rational – in order to predict that he'll fall for our traps; all we have to know is that his disposition to get suckered is reliable.

The long and short would seem to be that you can predict behavior from the intentional stance without committing yourself on closure and coherence *so long as there are lawful connections between the subject's behaviors and his intentional states.* We've been illustrating this point by examples of illusions and incapabilities, but in fact it is entirely general. If there is a law that makes being in intentional state A nomologically suffcient for being in intentional (and/or behavioral) state B, then, given the knowledge that a creature *is* in state A, you can predict that it will (come to) be in state B, *whether or not the transition from A to B is rational.* The upshot is that the argument that infers charity from the presuppositions for intentional prediction *fails because it begs the question against there being intentional laws.*[10]

Of course, many philosophers who think that charity constrains intentional ascription *a priori* doubt that there *are* intentional laws. We have nothing to say against their doubting this except that they are in need of an argument, and that, whatever this argument is, it mustn't itself depend on assuming that charity is constitutive of intentional ascription (as does, for example, the famous argument that Davidson, 1980, gives). In the present context, that assumption would be merely question-begging.

Here's another way to put the point. At first thought, it seems perfectly natural to suppose that if rational processes do enter into the intentional etiology of a creature's behavior – if, for example, decision-theoretic calculations bridge the gap between believing *p* and wanting *q*, on the one hand, and performing such and such an action, on the other – then a prediction that runs from premises about the creature's intentional states to conclusions about its behavioral outcomes must postulate that these rational processes transpire. But, on second thought, this surely isn't so. *The Times* shows up on the doorstep every morning; and presumably there is a decision-theoretic story about the newsboy, according to which his bringing it maximizes his expected utility. But I don't need to postulate the newboy's decision-theoretic rationality in order to predict the arrival of tomorrow's copy from the intentional stance. All I need is that his intention to deliver the paper is reliable and that, *ceteris paribus*, people reliably do what they intend to do.[11]

As a matter of fact, in this sort of case the argument typically goes the other way around. It's only *because* I have independent evidence that the newsboy reliably brings the paper that I'm prepared to infer that, probably, there is some decision-theoretic calculation according to which it is rational for him to do so; in fact, I've never actually inquired into his motives. *Pace* Dennett, rationality assumptions typically don't enter as presuppositions of intentional predictions, but rather as part of the story we tell when we start to wonder what mental processes could underlie the reliable intentional generalizations by which everyone's experience tells him that behavior is subsumed.

We want to emphasize that we aren't denying that the mental processes that mediate the production of behavior are typically rational; or that, if you want to *reconstruct the etiology* of behavior, you must explicate these rational processes. Our point is just that you don't, in general, have to reconstruct the etiology of phenomena in order to predict them.[12] The question "what do you need to assume to get a true theory of the etiology of Xs?" and the question "what do you need to assume to get true predictions about Xs?" needn't have the same sorts of answers. But if this is so, then the possibility of intentional prediction wouldn't have to depend on assuming rationality even if intentional etiological processes actually were fully rational. *A fortiori*, the possibility of intentional prediction doesn't have to depend on *counterfactual* assumptions of rationality. As long as there are intentional laws, and as long as the guy who is doing the predicting has access to the intentional laws that control the behaviors he is trying to predict, people are free to be as crazy as they like, compatible with their behavior being predictable from the intentional stance.

3 Summary and Conclusion

Here's where we take it that things stand. Dennett's argument against Intentional Realism depends on his argument for Interpretivism. His argument for Interpretivism depends on showing that either Normativism or Projectivism (or both) are true; but since Projectivism is hopeless, the argument depends, *de facto*, on showing that Normativism is true. Dennett's argument for Normativism depends, in turn, on the argument for charity, in effect, for principle (1). His argument for charity is either evolutionary or it's a transcendental argument about the conditions that have to be satisfied for behavioral prediction from the intentional stance to be possible. But the evolutionary argument yields the wrong conclusion (it makes the relation between interpretation and charity *contingent*) and the transcendental argument begs the question against intentional laws.

For all that has been shown so far, one might as well be an atomistic Intentional Realist, the putative emerging Interpretivist consensus in the philosophy of mind to the contrary not withstanding.

ACKNOWLEDGMENTS

The material in this chapter is a slightly adapted version of chapter 5 of J. Fodor and E. Lepore (1992) *Holism: A Shopper's Guide.* Oxford: Blackwell. We wish to thank Bo Dahlbom and Mark Rollins for helpful comments on an earlier draft.

NOTES

1 Among those Dennett lists as *not* party to the putative emerging consensus are Anscombe, Burge, Chisholm, Fodor, Geach, Kripke, and Searle. He might have added Barwise and Perry, Dretske, McGinn, Millikan, Stalnaker, Papineau, and many others. We are reminded of Peter de Vries' joke about the woman who was stark naked except for her clothes.

2 *Qua* species of Interpretivism, Projectivism is not a reductionist program; remember that Interpretivists accept Brentano's thesis. So there is no principled objection to a construal of "believes that" that makes essential use of semantical notions like "says that." One can imagine a reductionist (hence, of course, not Dennett) embracing an analysis in which *uttering* replaces *saying that.* So, "John believes that it's raining" in Smith's mouth comes out equivalent to something like "John is in the state that would normally cause me (Smith) to utter 'it's raining'." The points we're about to make generally hold for both kinds of Projectivist analysis, as far as we can tell.

3 For a kind of Intentional Realism that takes a similarly eccentric view of the polyadicity of attitude sentences, see Fodor (1990a).

4 One might argue that this sort of relativization of intentional ascriptions would nevertheless make them unfit for purposes of scientific explanation. But, *prima facie*, that would be a different claim from Interpretivism; the latter would follow only on the tendentious assumption that the facts that can figure in scientific explanation are the only facts there are. It is instructive, in this respect, to compare Dennett's treatment of Projectivism with Stich's (1983). The conclusions Stich derives from the Projectivist account of attitude attribution are scrupulously methodological, *not* ontological.

5 Beware the fallacy *post hoc; ergo, propter hoc. Pace* Dennett, it just isn't true that if we find a creature that has a selectional history and an intentional structure, we can assume straight off that its intentional structure was designed by its selectional history. Consider: "Sheep are stupid; sheep are selected; so sheep are selected for their stupidity." (For discussion of this sort of case, see Gould and Lewontin, 1979). To make his argument for charity even begin to run, Dennett would have to restrict it to intentional systems whose selection depended on the truth of their beliefs. (We know of no argument that people are such creatures.)

6 We're not sure whether Dennett considers it also to be a *necessary* condition. If he does, then we are presumably all at risk that a Kuhnian revolution in macrobiology will show that none of us has a mind.

7 There was a time when even a respectable philosopher might have sought to establish that we have beliefs (and not shmeliefs) by appeal to a paradigm case argument. But not, we trust, any more.

8 One way to answer this question is to bite the bullet and go Instrumentalist about Darwin. In "Intentional Systems in Cognitive Ethology: the 'Panglossian Paradigm' Defended," Dennett says that: "adaptationism and mentalism (intentional system theory) are not *theories* in one traditional sense. They are stances or strategies that serve to organize data, explain interrelations and generate questions to ask Nature. Were they theories in the 'classical' mold, the objection that they are question begging or irrefutable would be fatal" (Dennett, 1987, p. 265). So far as we can make out, Dennett's argument for these surprising claims is just that vacuous, *ad hoc*, or question begging adaptationist (/mentalist) explanations can always be devised if the data prove recalcitrant. By that standard, however, *no* theories count as being "in the 'classical' mold," physical theories included. That a theory permits of *ad hoc* defense can't be enough to make it just a stance, since if it did, all theories would be just stances.

9 The most predictivity could conceivably require is that if an agent believes p, and $p \rightarrow q$, and believes that q is relevant to the success of his plans, then the agent believes q. This is clearly still far too strong to be realistic; but at least it's weaker than the closure principle.

10 Notice, in passing, that Brentano's thesis does not imply that there are no intentional laws; Brentano tells us only that if there are intentional laws, then they must be irreducible.

11 If there are intentional laws they are surely *ceteris paribus* laws; special science laws generally are. For a recent discussion, see Schiffer (1987) and Fodor (1990b).

12 We take this to be *patently* true. Sailors reliably predict that the wind will blow south west in fair weather in the summer on the Atlantic Coast of the US. Few of them have any idea of why it works that way. (We used to know, but we've forgotten.)

REFERENCES

Davidson, D. (1980) Mental events. In *Essays on Actions and Events*. Oxford: Clarendon Press.
Dennett, D. C. (1978) *Brainstorms*. Montgomery, VT: Bradford Books and Hassocks, Sussex: Harvester.
Dennett, D. C. (1987) *The Intentional Stance*. Cambridge, Mass.: Bradford Books/MIT Press.
Fodor, J. (1981) Three cheers for propositional attitudes. In *Representations*. Cambridge, Mass.: MIT Press/Bradford Books.
Fodor, J. (1990a) Substitution arguments and the individuation of beliefs. In G. Boolos (ed.), *Meaning and Method: Essays in Honor of Hilary Putnam*. Cambridge: Cambridge University Press.

Fodor, J. (1990b) Stephen Schiffer's dark night of the soul: a review of "Remnants of Meaning." In *A Theory of Content and Other Essays.* Cambridge, Mass.: MIT Press/ Bradford Books.

Gould, S. J. and Lewontin, R. C. (1979) The spandrels of San Marco and the Panglossian Paradigm: a critique of the adaptationist programme. *Proceedings of the Royal Society*, B205, 581–98.

Putnam, H. (1975) The meaning of "meaning." In *Mind, Language and Reality.* Philosophical Papers, II. Cambridge: Cambridge University Press.

Schiffer, S. (1987) *The Remnants of Meaning.* Cambridge, Mass.: MIT Press/Bradford Books.

Stich, S. (1981) Dennett on intentional systems. *Philosophical Topics*, 12, 38–62.

Stich, S. (1983) *From Folk Psychology to Cognitive Science: The Case against Belief.* Cambridge, Mass.: MIT Press/Bradford Books.

Stich, S. (1990) *The Fragmentation of Reason.* Cambridge, Mass.: MIT Press/Bradford Books.

5

Logic, Mind, and Mathematics

COLIN McGINN

Let us think of *logic* as a systematic theory of a certain class of abstract structures – the propositional structures created by the logical constants, whatever these may be.[1] Logic is an account of the nature and laws of these structures, their constituents and interrelations – an attempt to map the geography of "logical reality." Logical theory is the study of one category of particles, the logical particles: it investigates the essence of these particles, their combinatorial powers, the laws in which they feature, the theorems that govern them. In particular, logic is concerned to articulate the way the logical particles determine the property of *validity* – what propositions follow from what other ones, and why. Since validity is a normative notion, logic is concerned with the workings of a certain kind of norm – that which governs the activity of (deductive) reasoning. Hence the centrality of the normative notion of deductive consequence in logical studies. The subject-matter of logic consists essentially in the apparatus needed to capture the relation of deductive consequence.[2]

Now suppose we have devised a fully adequate logical theory *L*, wherein the principles of logical consequence are comprehensively laid out. Then we might find ourselves wondering whether *L* could be used in accounting for other subject-matters seemingly distinct from that of logic proper. Consider some theory *T*, a set of sentences with a distinctive interpretation: we might ask whether our perfect logical theory *L* could provide an illuminating account of the subject-matter carried by *T*. Such illumination might consist in an outright definitional reduction of *T* to *L*, employing bridge principles and identity assertions; or it might, less ambitiously, supply some partial account of the entities and laws invoked in *T*. I propose, unoriginally, to call a thesis of this kind *logicism* with respect to *T*. Logicism, then, is the claim that some area of discourse can be explained or characterized in terms of logical notions – that logical structures underlie the subject-matter of the target discourse. (Of course, logic *applies* to all discourse; logicism is rather the stronger thesis that a certain body of talk is *about* logical structures.)

Logicist theses can be advanced in two kinds of spirit: instrumentally or realistically. It might be claimed merely that it is useful for certain purposes to regard the subject-matter of *T* as logical in character (instrumental logicism); or it might be asserted, more fervently, not only that it is useful so to view *T*, but also that it is literally *true* that *T* has a logical subject-matter, possibly in disguise (realist logicism). Thus logicist theses can be intended in either of the two ways in which explanatory theories are standardly intended, philosophically speaking – as predictive devices or as candid ontology.

As a further preliminary, let us also distinguish between thoroughgoing and limited varieties of logicism, total and partial logicist theses. A total logicist thesis (instrumental or realist) asserts that the entire nature of the target subject-matter can be reduced down to logic; a partial logicist thesis asserts, more weakly, merely that certain branches or aspects of that subject-matter can be so explained. Partial logicism thus allows that some supplementation, of an extra-logical nature, is going to be needed to yield the full richness of the subject-matter at issue, while insisting that the core of this subject-matter is susceptible of logicist interpretation. Total logicism, on the other hand, recognizes only the need for trivial notational transformations to take us from *L* to *T*, with nothing substantive added. In either case, the interest of the logicist thesis would lie in revealing *T* to be more logical in subject-matter than it might initially seem, with the advantages attendant upon this revelation.

Clearly, this depiction of logicism is intended to include a particular logicist thesis with which we are familiar under the name "logicism" – the thesis that mathematical discourse, specifically arithmetic, can be analyzed in terms of logic, where logic must here be taken to include set theory or property theory.[3] This is precisely the thesis that mathematical entities and truths can be reduced to logical entities and truths. But I mean to encompass more than this under the label "logicism" – I mean to include also certain claims about semantics and psychology.

With respect to semantics, we have the thesis that the sentences of natural language harbor underlying logical forms that determine (many of) their key semantic properties. The semantical logicist holds that natural-language meanings enjoy a logical structure which is revealed by the formulas of some preferred logical system – as it might be, first-order quantification theory. Thus the subject-matter of linguistics (grammar) essentially includes the subject-matter of logic. Specifically, the logical constants, with their distinctive properties, e.g. their truth-functionality, enter into the grammar and sense of natural-language sentences: semantic structure comprises logical structure. A clear example of semantical logicism would be Davidson's quantified conjunction theory of adverbial modification (see Davidson, 1980). The meanings expressed by adverbial sentences get reduced to the kinds of structures already present in logic proper.

Less obviously, I also want to include certain theses about the nature of mind – about the psychology of propositional attitudes. I am calling "logicist" such claims as that psychological explanation by beliefs and desires is ineliminably bound up with logical norms; as well as theories that construe mental states as consisting in realizations of abstract logical structures. Mental logicism, then, is any thesis that makes psychology essentially logic-involving; any thesis, that is, that regards logical structure as an indispensable part of the domain of psychology. Though this is fairly vague, I hope it is clear and familiar enough to be going on with. Since one of my later aims will be to explain and defend the idea, I won't attempt a more exact characterization at this stage. What I hope is clear by now is that my threefold grouping of logicist theses is not arbitrary or unmotivated.[4] In particular, it should suggest the possibility of interesting inter-connections, to be pursued below.

These three logicisms are most plausibly taken as theses of partial logicism only. It isn't plausible that *all* grammatical facts are logically constituted; the most that could be claimed is that all entailment-relevant compositional structure is logically explicable. Nor would it be at all plausible to suggest that the psychology of sensation is logically based, since pains and the like are not even links in chains of reasoning. And there must be more to a propositional attitude than simply its propositional content, or else we could not distinguish attitudes with the same content. Likewise, logicism in mathematics is difficult to extend naturally to geometry, and anyway notoriously requires non-logical supplementation even for ordinary arithmetic (e.g. the axiom of infinity). In each case the most that could reasonably be claimed is that a substantial core of the given subject-matter has a logical nature, so that it is at least necessary to bring logical theory to bear in order to articulate that core.

One way of formulating the modesty we need to admit is to adopt a "modular" conception of the domain under consideration: we need to see the domain as organized, non-arbitrarily, into a number of segments or systems, only some of which are logically constituted. Logicism with respect to a particular module or sub-domain might then be defended as an adequate theory of the nature of that isolable component of the wider subject-matter: say, the reasoning faculty, entailment structure, finite arithmetic. Other components or modules might then be exempted from logicist treatment, and this exemption given a motivated rationale. Lapses from the logicist ideal might then be dismissible, not as gaps in the theory, but as interference from outside the module for which we are giving a theory, or as extraneous conceptual elements. At any rate, although a claim of pure total logicism for any of linguistics, psychology or mathematics strains credulity, we need not push the view that far for it to be of interest. For partial logicism offers us a logical foundation for at least an important part of the discipline in question: so it significantly extends the reach of logical theory.

Now for each of our three chosen areas the would-be logicist will need a distinguishing factor in order to proceed from the common logical foundation to the specific super-structure of the discipline at hand. Since the three disciplines are plainly not identical, despite their shared logical core, something must differentiate them. The distinguishing factor may be conceived as what converts or transforms the common fund of logical structures into meaning or mind or mathematics, as the case may be – what you need to add to logic to get these three distinct things out of it. It is natural to understand the factors as different *relations* that pure logical forms may have to the specific theories they enter into. Thus it is the relation of linguistic *expression* that gives logical structures semantic significance – what maps those structures onto our acts of speech (of course, we can try to say more about what this relation consists in). In the case of psychology, the relevant relation is something like *realization*, or *grasping* in another idiom: this relation is what makes it the case that an abstract logical structure gets mapped onto a causal network of mental states and processes. The mind or brain has the power to incarnate logical forms in empirical events. In the case of mathematics, on the other hand, we need, not causal-empirical incarnation, but some such relation as *definional abbreviation*: the lengthy logical propositions in which the truth conditions of mathematical statements are held to consist are to be seen as expansions or analyses of those latter statements. So mathematical sentences and thoughts bear, for the logicist, the relation of *condensation* to the logical structures that define them: this relation is what takes you from logic to mathematics as it is commonly encountered. Thus, on this picture, the three disciplines have an overlapping subject-matter or shared essence, but this common ground gets specialized by virtue of three distinct relations, which serve to map the logical foundation onto three different sorts of entities: sentences, mental states, mathematical truths.

Setting our three logicist theses side by side, we can discern a unitary movement or thread in twentieth-century philosophy and associated disciplines: the idea that the study of logic can provide the key to understanding more than just the rules of valid inference. Other disciplines trace back to logic, radiate out from it, thus partaking of its clarity and power and beauty. There is a sense, then, in which Tarskian formal semantics, computational psychology and logic-based mathematics share a common presupposition or inspiration: all depend upon a logicist conception of their specific subject-matters. And no doubt the great advances made in logic during this century have added fire to this kind of logical foundationalism.[5]

But my interests here are not in the history of ideas; I am concerned to explore the relationships between our three kinds of logicism, especially between the psychological and mathematical kinds. I want to probe the consequences of explicitly conjoining mental and mathematical logicism. First, then, I shall consider propositional attitude psychology in a frankly logicist light, in order to arrive at a better understanding of various claims that have been made about it. Secondly, I shall consider what bearing logicism in psychology might have on logicism in mathematics. This second theme will be treated in a highly speculative (and tentative) manner, the aim being to open up some new lines of enquiry rather than arrive at any firm conclusions.

1 Mental Logicism

Mental logicism should be regarded as primarily an ontological thesis about the nature or essence of cognitive states: a mental state-type, such as believing that everyone loves someone, is an abstract logical property of an organism, though one whose instantiation requires the satisfaction of appropriate non-abstract conditions. Materialistics say that mental states are wholly constituted by physical states of organisms; dualists hold that mental states are non-physical traits of an immaterial substance; functionalists maintain that mental states consist in higher-order causal-role properties of input–output systems; and logicists assert that mental states are logically defined properties of rational agents – be these agents physical, immaterial, divine, or whatever. The state of believing that p is a relation to a logical object, viz. the proposition that p, and this object's constitutive properties (partly) determine the character of the corresponding belief. The proposition is *internal* to the belief, so that without it the belief would not even be a belief. Logicism takes a belief to be nothing other than a realized logical structure, so that the abstract world enters into the very constitution of the mental world; the lineaments of the latter are fixed by those of the former. Of course, the abstract structures need to be embodied or tokened in some fashion if beliefs are to possess causal powers and belong to persons, but logicism asserts that the ground of such embodiment is marginal or incidental to the essential nature of the property realized – a fact shown by the neutrality of mental states with respect to the kinds of embodying materials that could in principle do the job (physical, ectoplasmic, divine, etc). What incarnates a belief property should not be confused with what constitutes such a property.

The logicist view is a theory about the nature or structure of the rational capacity. It is a theory of one kind of *competence*, in Chomsky's sense: a cognitive system that underlies and controls performance, this latter being the upshot of more than simply the bare reasoning capacity. It describes the inner character of a particular module, considered in abstraction from outside factors – memory limitations, emotional upsets, bumps on the head, viral infections. Just as grammar can be construed as a theory of linguistic competence, so logic can be construed as a theory of rational competence. Logic thus has psychological reality, descriptive significance: it is what has to be invoked if we are to characterize the empirical nature of actual reasoning.[6]

Although they might not care to put it as baldly as I have just done, there are a number of philosophers who in effect subscribe to mental logicism as I have described it. Daniel Dennett, for example, is a kind of instrumental logicist: the "intentional stance" is logic applied, its norms employed to generate predictions of thought and action on the basis of an assumption of rationality. The mind is construed as a logical engine; or at least, according to Dennett, that is the most useful way to construe it.[7] Donald Davidson's emphasis on the "constitutive role" of rationality, taken as irreducibly normative, also involves regarding logic as definitive of mentality: there can be no (interpretable) mind without general conformity to logical norms.[8] John McDowell, following Davidson, is quite explicit about how logical norms shape the very conception we have of the mental.[9] And computationalists are swimming in the same waters, though the conflation with causal-role functionalism sometimes obscures this fact. What is common to these positions is the idea that there is no notion of thought prior to, and independent of, the imposition of logical concepts and rules onto a thinking creature. To have propositional attitudes *is* to be mappable onto a normative structure in such a way as to respect consistency and consequence, a structure essentially characterized by such notions as quantification and truth-functional composition. To believe that *p* is to be disposed to track the logical consequences of the proposition that *p*. So if it isn't logical, it isn't mental either.

It might be useful to subdivide mental logicism into four distinct theses, each intended to capture one aspect of the doctrine. These theses concern the following: (a) individuation; (b) laws; (c) interpretation; (d) origin. In turn, then, and somewhat summarily.

Individuation

What makes a belief the particular belief it is is the proposition believed, and propositions are precisely the proper subject-matter of logic. Differences of logical form as between propositions are thus sufficient to demonstrate the distinctness of the corresponding beliefs, thus tying psychological taxonomy to logical taxonomy. The propositional object of the attitude fixes its identity, so that it cannot be abstracted away and the belief left intact. Individuation goes by content. You can, indeed, abstract away the proposition and leave the *ground* of the belief, its physical realization in the brain (say): but considered in isolation from a proposition this grounding property is not a belief *that* anything, so not really a *belief* at all. The division between propositional object and realizing ground is a cut *within* the belief itself, so the proposition is not extraneous to the belief.

Laws

Nakedly stated, logicism says that psychological laws are logical laws. Correlatively, psychological explanation essentially invokes logical norms and principles, and psychological causation hinges upon the joints supplied by logical structure. A bit less nakedly, the mental logicist takes psychological laws of reasoning to be just *ceteris paribus* (henceforth "*c.p.*") laws of deductive consequence.[10] For example, it is a law of psychology that, *c.p.*, if x believes that p and also believes that if p then q, then x believes that q. You just seize hold of the pure logical law and apply it to the empirical mental world with no more nomological insurance than a little *c.p.* clause. And such laws actually work, according to the mental logicist, predicting thought and action with remarkable success, thus demonstrating the inherent logicality of the intended domain of the law. The causal transitions in mentation hinge upon the properties of the logical constants occurring in the corresponding logical laws, causal consequence recapitulating logical consequence. The causal powers of the two premise beliefs accordingly mirror the logical powers of the premises themselves.[11] And explaining why the subject formed the belief that q essentially involves observing that he rationally came to believe that q on the basis of two other things he believed: he believes that q *because* this belief was normatively required by his other beliefs. Forming a belief is thus represented as conformity to an ideal, not merely as fitting a regularity (however nomologically invariant) concerning which cognitive states in fact succeed which others (cf. McDowell, 1985). In short, people necessarily believe what they logically ought to, other things being equal.

When a domain of objects is governed by a certain sort of law, we can say that the domain constitutes a natural kind delimited by that sort of law. The taxonomic follows the nomic. Applying this familiar idea to the present case, we can say that cognitive subjects constitute a logical natural kind – the class of rational beings – in virtue of their subsumption under *c.p.* logical laws. It is because we belong to a natural kind in virtue of our subsumption under *c.p.* logical laws that the principle of rationality can be usefully employed to predict our causal transitions. It is not merely a happy accident that we are predictable from the "logical stance;" rather, it is written into our very nature as reasoning beings to fall under logical laws. The logical stance yields good predictions because of the truth of mental logicism as an ontological thesis concerning our nature as thinking beings.

Contrast our necessary logical subsumption with our much more tenuous relation to (say) ethical laws. Here, the norms do not form part of our very nature as psychological beings; they are extrinsic, not intrinsic. For, sad to say, human beings do not constitute an ethical natural kind, in the sense that their conduct is predictable from the "ethical stance." People don't always do what is right, even *ceteris paribus*. No principle of ethical charity in interpretation recommends itself as obligatory. Try to derive an empirical predictive law of human feeling, thought and action from a moral principle: seize hold of that principle, insert a *c.p.* clause into it, and see whether you obtain any nomically predictive joy. For example, suppose it is right to give money to people more needy than yourself: can we then say, "People give money to those needier than they are, *c.p.*"? Clearly not; lamentably so. Still less is failure to conform to such a law a good reason to doubt that the agent in question is subject to moral evaluation at all. Indeed, one might say that the whole point of ethical prescription and criminal law is to get people to do what they would not do as a matter of human psychological nomic necessity. By contrast, says the mental logicist, there is no need to inflict penalties on people for failure to obey logical laws, since this is something that (*c.p.*) they cannot help.

A divine being is presumably someone for whom the ethical stance is appropriate, since for him ethical norms are intrinsic to his nature, not nomological options. God is ethical in the way we are logical. But actual human beings don't fall under the kind of ethical law that successfully predicts the behavior of angels. So the relationship between the ethical ideal and the actual facts is nowhere near as intimate as that between the logical ideal and the actual facts. It is not part of the natural essence of human beliefs and desires to be ethical, while it is part of their essence to be rational. Nomologically and metaphysically, goodness is accidental to human beings. Logicism, yes; ethicism, no. Hence we must strive to be ethical, but (for the mental logicist) to strive at all presupposes that we are already rational. We are logic-driven by nature, but goodness-driven only by will.

Interpretation

This is the epistemological side of the metaphysical thesis I am sketching: in order to know what someone else thinks you have to adopt the methodological assumption that she thinks more or less rationally.[12] You have to take her cognitive transitions to be logically licensed if you are going to be able to identify what these are transitions between. Interpretation requires logical charity. Put my way, this principle says that radical interpretation must proceed by taking the subject to fall under *c.p.* logical laws. For instance, you will not be able to interpret some linguistic device as a conditional unless you take it that (*c.p.*) the subject's reasoning observes *modus ponens*. Finding too much illogicality is tantamount to giving up the interpretative project.

In my view, this familiar epistemological point should be taken as a reflection of the metaphysical nature of belief, rather than as some kind of brute methodological imperative about the conditions of knowing another's thoughts. We must be charitable about other people's reasoning *because* their thoughts are inherently logically defined states. Without mental logicism as an ontological doctrine, logical charity looks like a kind of wishful thinking – or merely a reflection of what the *interpreter* needs to assume about the world. The norms have to be written into the internal structure of the belief system if they are to condition its interpretation.

Origin

So far I have been paraphrasing some fairly familiar claims about the cognitive mind, stressing the logicist presuppositions of those claims. The point I want to make now is not so familiar and may sound a bit queer at first. It is this: the correct *explanation* of how minds originally came to have the causal structure they have is that abstract propositions are themselves logically structured in the way they are. It is *because* logical space has the abstract structure it has that minds came into existence with the causal structure they have. I mean this as a teleological explanation: it isn't that the abstract propositions *cause* minds to have the inferential architecture they have; rather, possible mental structures were selected in or out according to their conformity with logical structure. The reason our minds follow the causal tracks they do is that these tracks are designed to mirror logical relations; would-be minds that followed other tracks failed to pass evolutionary muster. Picturesquely: the genes were aiming for a casual structure in the mind that approximated to the logical structure of propositions. Soberly: rationality has selective advantage. Divinely: God first created logic and then ensured, in the light of this creation, that our minds fitted its patterns. It is because *modus ponens* is a valid rule of inference that organisms exist whose beliefs obey its prescriptions. The factual is explained, teleologically, by the normative (*inter alia*). So logic itself is part of the historical story of how minds like ours came into being. Brains are, among other things, devices for mining the survival advantages of logical relations.

In sum, then, mental logicism amounts to a kind of foundationalist thesis about the cognitive mind: mentation is erected on a bedrock of logical structure. Logical entities and relations are the *sine qua non* of mental activity. Psychology embeds logic. The mind is logical form incarnate.

2 Mind and Mathematics

I shall now consider mental and mathematical logicism together, exposing the consequences of each for the other. These are quite large, and I intend the following simply as sketchy notes towards a program. Suppose, then, that both logicist theses are true, at least as partial accounts of their target theories. Then it follows that cognition and mathematics share a common underlying essence or foundation. In both cases, it is true, some distinctive supplementation is needed to reach the two subject-matters in their full glory, but still they are both jointly rooted in logic. Mathematical truths can be derived from logical axioms and definitions, and psychological predictions can be "derived" from logical principles. Logical formalism may also be used in the expression of both psychological and mathematical laws. Thus, in the psychological case, we readily employ quantificational notation to formulate the empirical laws of thinking, substituting logical formulas into belief contexts in place of vernacular content sentences. Then we apply our theory of logical consequence to the regimented content-clauses to derive empirical predictions (*c.p.*). Psychological knowledge thus rests upon logical knowledge, rather as mathematical knowledge is held to spring from logical knowledge. Numbers and thoughts have this property in common: they are both logically based, co-derivable from prior logical elements.

This co-derivability from logic has clear consequences for the *inter*-derivability of psychology and mathematics. Each contains the materials to generate the other, roughly speaking. On the one hand, the conceptual resources of psychology suffice, when appropriately juggled, to derive the logicist portion of mathematics. These concepts include whatever belongs to the general theory of propositions, and this theory is extensively exploited in psychological explanation and prediction.[13] On the other hand, and conversely, psychology has theoretical commitments which are, at least potentially, mathematical in character. As we can work out from logic to mathematics, so we can work back through the logicist definitions from mathematics to logic – and thence to the core of rational psychology. The seeds of arithmetic are already planted in our mental make-up; there is something essentially mathematical about thought itself. The logical constants, the notions of property, of extension, of instantiation: all these and more are tacitly employed in folk psychology, and they are what number theory comes down to according to mathematical logicism. Hence the kind of mutual derivability I have noted. Now, what kind of philosophical significance might this have?

One question to consider concerns psychologism in logic and mathematics – the doctrine that logical and mathematical laws are derivative from psychological laws (a *locus classicus* is John Stuart Mill's *A System of Logic*). What I just said sounds a lot like this generally repudiated doctrine, but mental logicism gives psychologism a new twist and possibly new life (suitably reformed). For, given mental logicism, there is indeed a harmless sense in which we can grant the truth of psychologism about logic, since psychological laws really rest upon logical laws and are not prior to, or independent of, such laws. This allows logic to derive, ultimately, from itself, by way of its mental vehicle. Essentially, you just need to drop the *c.p.* clause from a psychological law in order to derive a logical law. Nor is this a bit startling, since the logical law was the initial input to the psychological law. Mental logicism is what makes psychologism of this kind possible.

It is easy to see that psychologism, so construed, has no subjectivist implications, nor does it commit any naturalistic fallacy concerning logical norms.[14] The instincts of the psychologistic philosophers of logic were not wholly misguided – or they can be reconstructed thus – though they perverted the germ of truth in their position. They got their ontological priorities the wrong way round, despite the basic correctness of the idea that logical laws mirror psychological laws. What has to be recognized is that psychological laws are not like natural laws of other kinds. The laws of physics or chemistry, say, are not amenable to logicist interpretation, since transitions between purely physical states (devoid of propositional content) are not rationally constrained. Psychological laws are inherently norm-involving, which is why logical norms are trivially extractable from them.

Much the same may be said of psychologism with respect to mathematics. If mathematics derives from logic and logic can be extracted from mind, then mathematics too can be viewed as derivable from mind (I speak loosely). But, of course, this is so only in the innocuous sense just mentioned: psychology itself has logical foundations, so deriving mathematics from psychology is really just helping oneself to those foundations – and they are not themselves inherently psychological. So we have a sort of Pyrrhic victory for psychologism – one which concedes its appeal yet draws its sting. Seeing matters from the present perspective, however, may help to explain the intuitions that have beset some psychologistically inclined philosophers of mathematics: there really is an affinity of nature between mind and mathematics, and we actually can represent mathematics as extractable from mental principles, so long as we correctly understand the status of those principles and the ground of the derivation. Right intuitions, wrong underlying metaphysics. Mental logicism offers a way of catering to the intuitions without sacrificing the objectivity of mathematics.

In the light of these reflections, perhaps we can now find room for an attractive middle position in the philosophy of mathematics. One tradition regards mathematical truth as frankly mind-dependent: thus the intuitionists who construe numbers as mental constructions. Another tradition insists that mathematical truth is objective, depending upon the mind-independent disposition of a world of abstract entities: thus the Platonists who take numbers to be denizens of a third ontological realm. Combining mental and mathematical logicism yields a position that preserves objectivity while acknowledging that mind and mathematics are intimately related. The principles of mathematics overlap with the principles of psychology, but the foundational role of logic in the latter area thwarts any subjectivist inference. There is a kinship between the two, but no collapse of the mathematical into outright mind-dependence.

A final consequence of this double logicism concerns the troubled epistemology of mathematics. How can minds such as ours come to know mathematical truths? In virtue of what knowledge-conferring link do our mathematical faculties hook up with the abstract facts we take ourselves to know? How, in particular, can a broadly causal epistemology be brought to bear on mathematical knowledge?[15] Well, begin by assuming mental and mathematical logicism, and let the resulting consanguinity sink in for a while. Then the first point to note is that just by reflecting on the structure of mind it should be possible in principle to derive those regions of mathematics susceptible to logicist treatment. For psychological knowledge itself presupposes knowledge of logical principles, by mental logicism. The materials for arriving at mathematical knowledge are thus present in the subject-matter of self-knowledge. If God could look into your mind, He would see logic lurking there, waiting to be expanded into mathematics. The basis of mathematical knowledge thus lies within; so it could in principle be generated from self-awareness, plus the ingenuity that went into writing *Principia Mathematica*.

But this observation, correct so far as it goes, does not yet offer any *explanation* of how we know logic and mathematics; it simply locates the objects of such knowledge within the mind, while presupposing epistemic access to the underlying logical principles. How are *they* known? What kind of causal link mediates between logical structures and our epistemic faculties, granted that those structures configure the mental landscape? How exactly does mental logicism make logical (and hence mathematical) knowledge possible?

The beginnings of an answer are not far to seek, once we note the necessary congruence between the logical and the causal which is definitive of mental logicism. That thesis says that mental transitions necessarily respect, and hinge upon, logical relations (*c.p.*): the causal network of mental states perforce mirrors the logical network of abstract propositions. Now suppose our faculty of self-knowledge to be sensitive to causal facts about our inner states, particularly their dispositions to cause other inner states. This will then imply, in conjunction with mental logicism, that we have a faculty that is causally sensitive to facts that are reliably, indeed necessarily, *correlated* (*c.p.*) with logical facts. So we have a faculty whose states are mediately covariant with logical relations. For example, we know our dispositions to operate with the conditional by being introspectively tuned to those dispositions; but these dispositions must track the logical relations into which propositions containing the conditional enter; *so* we are tuned to something itself internally connected to the logical facts we are endeavouring to know. We thus come to know *modus ponens* because we ourselves exemplify causal transitions that map onto the logical relations in question.[16] And now, granted mathematical logicism, we also know (or could know) mathematical truths by the same general route: we first come to know logic by exploiting the causal isomorphism entailed by mental logicism, then we apply our logical ingenuity to excogitating number theory from logic. The causal basis of both kinds of knowledge consists in the mapping between the logical and the psychological which is the heart of the thesis of mental logicism.

If this sketch for a theory of logical epistemology is on the right track, then an interesting result emerges: namely, that the truth of mental logicism is a precondition for any kind of logical or mathematical knowledge. If (*per impossibile*) human reasoning processes systematically and radically failed to mirror logical geography, so that the dispositions of mental states to cause other mental states bore no coherent relation to logical consequence, then there would simply be no causal handle for logical knowledge to get a grip on. Knowledge requires reliable correlation, causal sensitivity, but if reasoning entirely failed to correlate with logic, there would be nothing to mediate an epistemic relation between logical belief and logical fact. We would be epistemically cut off from the abstract world of logic and mathematics, since nothing in the causal facts of our psychology would bear the required relation to that world. We can know logical truth only because we embody it, so if we didn't we wouldn't. We know the logical powers of the truth-functions, say, *only* by virtue of the (non-contingent) fact that the corresponding symbols in our heads exhibit causal features that map reliably onto those logical powers. There is a strong sense in which we have to *be* logical if we are to know logic and mathematics; whereas we don't have to be (say) geological if we are to know geology. We have to be causal counterparts of logical principles, but we don't have to be causal counterparts of geological principles – for they already have their causal relation to knowers built into them. Contraposing, and taking this whole story as given, since we *do* know logic and mathematics, it *must* be the case that mental logicism is true – since its truth is a necessary condition for such knowledge. Mental logicism can actually be deduced from the fact of logical knowledge plus certain considerations in general epistemology. So mental logicism is not just good psychology; it also makes for a feasible epistemology of logic.

Clearly, there is much more to be said on these difficult matters, but I hope the above remarks serve at least to indicate a potentially promising line of thought. Certainly, this is an area in which we need all the ideas we can get. The lack of a plausible epistemology of logic and mathematics is surely one of the most conspicuous gaps in our philosophical understanding.

ACKNOWLEDGMENT

I am grateful to Bo Dahlbom for a number of helpful editorial suggestions.

NOTES

1   I will not try to unvex the issue of what makes an expression a logical constant. Actually I am not convinced that we should be more worried about this than (say) physicists are about what defines the general notion of a physical particle: there doesn't seem to be any

non-circular definition of that notion either, and its open-endedness is not widely deplored. What interesting notion does admit of non-circular definition!

2   You don't have to agree with this characterization of logic in order to get something out of the rest of the paper; I intend it chiefly to fix ideas. I shall restrict discussion to deductive logic, since this is most relevant to my present concerns; but if you believe in "inductive logic" you can include that too. As will emerge, set theory will here be included under the term "logic," though more by stipulation than principle. In fact, I think this inclusion is well motivated, but I do not need to argue the case here. I note merely that (a) model-theoretic notions of validity are set-involving; (b) the extensions of predicates are sets; and (c) second-order logic is both logic and closely akin to set theory.

3   See Whitehead and Russell (1910) for the long version of logicism. Henceforth when I say "logic" I mean to include set theory or some equivalent.

4   Perhaps it is not surprising that Quine inaugurated the logicist tradition in the philosophy of mind, in view of his early steeping in logicism about mathematics. For his seminal remarks on logic and radical translation, see Quine (1960), pp. 58–9.

5   It is orthodox to characterize post-Fregean twentieth-century philosophy in terms of a foundational interest in language – as having taken the "linguistic turn." However, the pivotal role of logic in shaping the philosophical landscape during this period suggests a somewhat different picture: drilling for logical form rather than turning to language. Perhaps the reluctance to see things this way comes from the deep departure from empiricism consequent upon assigning logic a foundational role, since logical forms are not at all closely related to the data of sense, as linguistic forms at least appear to be. The problematic epistemic status of pure logic is indeed hard to reconcile with the dominant tradition of empiricist epistemology.

6   Obviously we need logic in order to evaluate reasoning; but it is a quite different, and far more substantive, claim that logic is necessary for describing and predicting the natural facts of reasoning – for saying what actually happens. Some events occur because they logically should! Psychology is thus a very special science.

7   See Dennett (1987). Perhaps Dennett adopts an instrumentalist interpretation of mental logicism because he can't see how a physical system could really, in itself and objectively, be subject to logical norms. I think myself that instrumentalism deprives mental logicism of much of its interest and punch, and probably issues from an underlying physicalist reductionism with respect to all objective facts.

8   See various papers in Davidson, *Essays on Actions and Events* (1980); especially "Mental Events." Davidson's principle of logical charity involves (a) imposing the structure of our logic on others and (b) finding others competent in that logic. There can be no deviant logic and no deviation in the use of standard logic.

9   See McDowell (1985). McDowell conceives the structure of mental states themselves as not abstractable away from the (normative) structure formed by their propositional objects. It is illuminating to see this as a kind of logical externalism about the mind. We have become accustomed to the idea that beliefs cannot be prised off the worldly entities they are about; but now we must recognize that they cannot be detached from the logical objects that fix the form of their content. There are really two dimensions through which beliefs escape the confines of the head: the environment, and logical space. Internalist inclinations may operate against both types of externalism. Mental logicism will come more easily to those who have already absorbed the more familiar semantic externalism. I also stressed the hold of logic over psychology in McGinn (1982), pp. 19–21.

10 For some discussion of *ceteris paribus* laws in psychology, see Schiffer (1991) and Fodor (1991). Note that the c.p. qualification to people's logical omniscience is no abrogation of the thesis of mental logicism, on pain of finding virtually no laws anywhere. The detection of nomic patterns in nature constantly requires such idealization – the

permanent possibility of nomic impurity and extraneous interference. Laws purport to trace the natural properties of selected underlying structures and forces, rather than state exceptionless generalities about what is going to happen next.

11   Cf. Brian Loar's L-constraints, in Loar (1981), pp. 71ff.

12   See Davidson (1984), pp. 125–79. I would firmly distinguish logical from factual charity, agreeing with the former but disagreeing with the latter: see McGinn (1986).

13   This raises the question of how *much* of the logical apparatus needed to derive mathematics is tacitly employed in ordinary folk psychology; in particular, how much of the apparatus of set theory (if any). It should be clear, I hope, that I am *not* saying that the Frege–Russell definition of number is itself indispensably and explicitly employed in routine folk psychology – that is certainly false. No, my claim is rather (of course) that the basic conceptual ingredients of such a definition crop up ineluctably in folk psychology – the primitive notions which the definition sophisticates and combines. It may be objected that, while this is true of the strictly logical concepts employed, it is questionable whether set-theoretic concepts play such an integral role in folk psychology. I disagree. The essential notion needed in the Frege–Russell definition is that of the "extension of a concept," so that numbers come out as classes of equinumerous classes. Now it seems to me that some such notion as this is deeply embedded in any psychology worthy of the name. For it is surely essential to cognition that the mind have the capacity for *grouping* objects together. The *Gestalt* psychologists stressed this capacity in the case of perception, but it is even clearer that the possession of concepts requires an ability to group objects in thought: that, after all, is what a concept *is*. What could it mean to discern thought in a creature and yet deny that the creature could class things together? Thus the idea of a collection is fundamental in psychology, and this is the primitive root of the notion of set elaborated by logicians. Moreover, it is difficult to see how a subject with a notion of collection could fail to appreciate the basic principles governing collections. These notions seem as conceptually primitive as the basic laws of truth-functional logic. I therefore think we need to attribute basic set theory to thinkers as well as basic quantification theory; indeed, I would argue that we really can't do the latter without tacitly doing the former. Any content-based psychology must ascribe the rudiments of set theory to its subjects. Thus the raw materials of the logicist definition of number are presupposed by the very structure of folk psychology. You cannot conceive of a mind apart from these notions.

14   One of Husserl's (1970) arguments against psychologism is that if it were true logic would be subject to the same inductive empirical uncertainty as the laws of psychology. This is a good objection if, but only if, psychological laws themselves are arrived at inductively or empirically. But, according to mental logicism, psychological laws are in effect arrived at *a priori*, on the basis of logic itself and a philosophical thesis about the nature of mind. Husserl's objection lapses once the laws of psychology are awarded their rightful *a priori* status.

15   I allude here to the kind of problem formulated by Paul Benacerraf (1973). I am offering joint logicism as a way of answering Benacerraf's problem that avoids invoking mysterious faculties of mind.

16   Logic is ontologically more basic than psychology, but epistemologically psychology comes first, since our epistemic access to logic depends upon its mental incarnation. We know logic "indirectly," through its correspondence with our causal make-up. Perhaps *a priori* knowledge is generally the kind that can only be possessed by virtue of the knower's exemplification of the truths known – by his mapping appropriately onto what he knows. This gives a rather strong sense to the idea, perennially attractive, that *a priori* knowledge is, or essentially involves, a kind of self-knowledge. Interesting questions are raised by this line of thought, but I won't pursue them further here.

REFERENCES

Benacerraf, P. (1973) Mathematical truths. *Journal of Philosophy*, 70, 661–79.
Davidson, D. (1980) The logical form of action sentences. In *Essays on Actions and Events*. Oxford: Oxford University Press.
Davidson, D. (1984) *Inquiries into Truth and Interpretation*. Oxford: Oxford University Press.
Dennett, D. C. (1987) *The Intentional Stance*. Cambridge, Mass.: MIT Press.
Fodor, J. A. (1991) You can fool some of the people all of the time, everything else being equal, hedged laws and psychological explanations. *Mind*, 100, 19–34.
Husserl, E. (1970) *Logical Investigations*. London: Routledge and Kegan Paul.
Loar, B. (1981) *Mind and Meaning*. Cambridge: Cambridge University Press.
McDowell, J. (1985) Functionalism and anomalous monism. In E. Lepore and B. McLaughlin (eds), *Actions and Events*. Oxford: Basil Blackwell.
McGinn, C. (1982) *The Character of Mind*. Oxford: Oxford University Press.
McGinn, C. (1986) Radical interpretation and epistemology. In E. Lepore (ed.), *Truth and Interpretation*. Oxford: Blackwell.
Quine, W. V. O. (1960) *Word and Object*. Cambridge, Mass.: MIT Press.
Schiffer, S. (1991) Ceteris paribus laws. *Mind*, 100, 1–17.
Whitehead, A. N. and Russell, B. (1910) *Principia Mathematica*. Cambridge: Cambridge University Press.

6
On Mentalese Orthography

RUTH GARRETT MILLIKAN

How then do I see the Golden Age? . . . First there will be our old, reliable friend, folk psychology, and second, its self-consciously abstract idealization; intentional system theory. Finally there will be a well-confirmed theory at a level between folk psychology and bare biology, sub-personal cognitive psychology. We can now say a bit more about what it might be like: it will be "cognitive" in that it will describe processes of information-transformation among content-laden items – mental representations – but their styles will not be "computational"; the items will not look or behave like sentences manipulated in a language of thought.

Dennett, The Intentional Stance

"Processes of information-transformation" among "content-laden" "mental representations" but whose styles are not "computational," that do not "behave like sentences manipulated in a language of thought" – that is what I suspect too. But whether Dennett and I *really* agree depends upon a number more things – such as what "processes of information-transformation" would be, what "content-laden" means, what "representations" are, what "computation" or "manipulation" is, and what "sentences . . . in a language of thought" would be like, for a few!

The name "representation" does not come from scripture. Nor is there reason to suppose that the various things we daily call by that name have an essence in common, or if they do that anything people have in their heads could conceivably share it. What is needed is not to discover what mental representations *really are* but to lay down some terms that cut between interestingly different possible phenomena so we can discuss their relations. In part one, I will distinguish and label four different kinds of possible phenomena in the representation neighbourhood. First are "tacit suppositions." Then, each a subset of the last, are "intentional icons," "inner representations," and "mental sentences." "Intentional icons" are "contentful." "Representations" participate in "processes of information-transformation" – I shall call it "inference." But – and this will be the burden of part two – neither "mental sentences" nor any other "representations" are "computed" or, as I shall say, "calculated over."

PART ONE

1 Tacit Suppositions

There are times when the design of an organism or one of its parts is so neatly specialized to mesh with some feature of its natural environment that one might almost "read" the environmental feature off the design. In such cases the design of the organism might also be said to "presuppose" the environmental feature; in the absence of that feature the organism or part could not possibly function as designed. There are two kinds of instance in which it is particularly natural to think of such design features as "representing" environmental features.

The first is illustrated by biological clocks. In the case of diurnal clocks (diurnal circadian rhythms), for example, had the earth spun faster or more slowly the biological clock inside the animal would have needed to be adjusted accordingly, so the clock rhythm is naturally thought of as "representing" the length of a day. Likewise, the color pattern of the Viceroy butterfly, which "mimics" that of the bad tasting Monarch, might naturally be said to "represent" the Monarch's design. Mechanisms in various of the species that are adjusted to respond to subtle distinguishing features of conspecifics, predators, or prey are often thought of as containing "representations" of these in the form of "templates" for recognition: had the features been different along certain dimensions, the templates would have had to differ accordingly. Similarly, the cerebral motor cortex is said to contain a "representation" of the hand, different but connected areas of the brain receiving input from corresponding different but connected parts of the hand. Had the hand had more digits, the brain would have needed more of these areas to correspond. All these cases have in common that a certain design feature of the organism seems to "map" onto a feature of its environment (or another feature of the organism) in this sense: had the environmental feature differed along certain dimensions, the design feature would have had to differ along isomorphic dimensions to effect the same coordination or adaptation in the same way.

The second representation-like phenomenon is illustrated by a well-known feature of Marr's theory of vision. According to Marr (1982), the construction of a perceptual representation of an object in three dimensions starting from retinal stimulation patterns, works on certain suppositions about the edges of objects, about the ambient light, and about interactions between these. Some would say these assumptions were "tacitly represented" by the visual systems or in the operation of these systems. Generalizing, any environmental feature that is not explicitly represented but that must be presupposed for correct operation of an "inferencer" – a mechanism that, working properly, derives new true representations from old true representations – is naturally thought of as "tacitly represented" by or through the operation of the inferencer (compare Dennett, 1987, pp. 216–18).

In both these kinds of cases, what is said to be "represented" may in some environments be false. The tacit assumptions of Marr's reconstructions, for example, can easily be falsified in the laboratory. Indeed, it is because of the obvious possibility of something like falseness that the word "representation" surfaces. In none of these cases, however, will I use the term "representation." What we have in each of these instances, I will say, is merely a system or part that requires certain conditions, under which it was designed to operate, in order to function properly in its normal way. Its structure fits these conditions, or is a function of them, because it has been adapted to them; it does not "represent" these conditions. Rather than "representing" these conditions, I will say that the system "presupposes them for its proper operation," and that they correspond to "tacit suppositions" of the system – suppositions that may sometimes be false.

2 "Content-ladenness": Intentional Icons

A second group of items I call "intentional icons" – "intentional" as in "intentionality."[1] Intentional icons are akin to those structures mentioned above that map onto or are isomorphic to environmental features to which they are adapted. A difference, however, is that intentional icons are not built into the organism but acquired by the individual in response to the environment. Often, though not always, they are temporary adaptations to a temporary environment. They exhibit a dimension or dimensions of possible variance running parallel to possible variances in the environment. A rule of projection, in the mathematician's sense, maps the one onto the other. We can call this rule the icon's "mapping rule." That the environment corresponds to the icon in conformity with this mapping rule is presupposed for proper operation of the system containing the icon.

But intentional icons are distinguished in two other ways as well. First, there must be a mechanism in the organism whose function is to produce the icon. And there must be a way that this mechanism, when successful, actually *effects* or brings it about that the icon maps onto the environmental feature.[2] For example, although various surface patterns occurring in the outer sense organs (say, vibrating ear drums) may systematically map certain patterns in the distal environment, these surface patterns are not intentional icons. This is because no biological mechanisms have as their functions to produce these mappings. The patterns are merely natural signs. On the other hand, images on the retina of the eye are formed due to the structure of the eye lens. And the eye lens was designed by evolution for the purpose of bringing about systematic mappings between certain environmental structures and these images. The patterns are thus intentional icons; the lens is their "producer."

Secondly, there must be a mechanism (or mechanisms) in the organism that may use or be guided by the intentional icon in the performance of certain of its normal functions. When so guided, this user will not function properly in the usual way unless the icon and the environment match by the relevant mapping rule. Thus, although there are mechanisms in the skin of a chameleon whose job is to make the color of its skin match the color of its surroundings, there are no other mechanisms in the chameleon that use these colors for guidance. The colors, then, are not intentional icons. On the other hand, we need not require that the guided mechanism reside in the same individual as the icon-producing mechanism. The production and the "consumption" of the icon may be accomplished by any mechanisms *designed*, biologically or in some other way, to cooperate on the iconing project. For example, the dances that honey bees execute to guide fellow workers to nectar are paradigm cases of intentional icons.

Intentional icons do not, as such or in general, carry "natural information."[3] Nor do they "covary" with or "track" what they icon. Their definition makes no reference to how likely or unlikely they are actually to correspond to their designated environmental features, nor to how likely these features are to get mapped by them. I have no idea how reliable bees are at dancing the right dances, dances bearing the mapping relations to nectar that, historically, have led watching bees to the spot. Maybe bees are good at this and maybe they're not. But if bee dances mapped nectar locations correctly only once in ten, surely the effect would still be better than if the workers hunted for nectar independently. And the dances would still be intentional icons. Rather than being natural information, the "content" of an intentional icon is described by telling what sort of structure or feature would have to be in the organism's environment, for the icon to map onto by its mapping rule, in order for its consumer to use it successfully in the normal way, that is, the way that historically accounted for the interlocking design of producer, icon, and consumer.

Looking ahead to the possibility that thoughts are intentional icons, notice that, according to my story, the content of an intentional icon is neither a direct nor an indirect function of the stimulations, or the empirical evidence, or the prior thoughts that induce it. Its semantic value is determined by whatever mapping relation is in fact doing the work of successfully guiding the organism through its activities in its world when controlled by the representation. Or, being more accurate, we should refer not to how the organism is in fact guided, but to the general principles in accordance with which it is *designed* to be guided – designed to make icons, perhaps also to *learn* to make icons (concept formation),[4] designed to combine icons in inference, and designed to be guided by icons in action. For an organism's design, its "competence," may be very far from its actual performance. Quite special conditions are required for the correct performance of most biological devices.[5]

Intentional icons can be extremely simple devices harbored by extremely simple organisms. For example, consider simple signals, such as an animal's warning cry to its conspecifics. Count its time and place as being *part* of the signal. The time or place of the signal is now seen to map onto the time or place of the signaled event. Signal at time t_1 place p_1 corresponds to danger at t_1 and p_1. If the signal is shifted over two miles and ahead three days then the danger needs to be shifted over two miles and ahead three days for the signal to do its work. So it is possible to consider even these simple devices to be varieties of intentional icon.[6]

That one can look upon even simple signals this way should also make it clear how extremely simple an organism might be that harbors intentional icons. And it should make it clear how very local or minimal the mirroring of the environment may be that is accomplished by an intentional icon. Why, then, do I dignify these icons with the title "intentional?" How could anything exhibit intentionality that did not think? And how could anything think that did not make inferences, hence that was not, at least to an approximation, rational? Is not rationality, as Dennett claims, "the mother of intention" (1978, p. 19)? The contemporary mood is so adverse to the idea of intentionality without reason that even perception, a faculty traditionally taken as continuous from us to the lowliest animals, may be thought to be intentional only as producing a disposition to judgment and inference (Armstrong, 1968; Shoemaker, 1975; Smart, 1975).

Now the word "intentionality" was (re)introduced in modern times by Brentano for a quite definite purpose. Of course, the fact that Brentano intended "intentionality" to be the distinguishing mark of the mental doesn't help very much if we suspect that mentality comes in styles and degrees. But Brentano was rather more specific than that. He thought that what was funny about the mental was that it could be directed toward something that didn't exist. You can think about your vacation in Spain or about St Christopher, even though perhaps neither of them was or will be. And that, or the closest thing to it, is just what can happen with intentional icons. The intentional icon can be such that even though there is no environmental feature onto which it maps appropriately, still there "should" be. That is, exactly because there's not any such environmental feature, the icon will misguide its users. In this respect, false intentional icons are just like false sentences. So I call them "intentional" and speak of them as having "intentional content."

It is not uncommon for an intentional icon normally to map in accordance with a definite rule of projection onto more than one environmental feature. Despite this, it is possible to define the content of an intentional icon with considerable determinacy if you do it in the following way. Consider the content to be that mapped feature to which the icon specifically adapts the *user(s)* of the icon. It is that feature which, if removed from the environment or incorrectly mapped, will guarantee failure for its *users*. It will guarantee failure, that is, granted there occur no coincidental interventions, no helpful contingencies of a sort not historically normal for performance of the users' functions. Suppose then that in the normal case the bee dance maps not only onto the location of nectar, but also onto the direction from which the dancing bee last approached the hive. Its content concerns the location of nectar, not the direction of the dancer's approach. This is because it is only if the location of nectar is mapped wrongly that the watching bees' normal reactions to the dance will fail, barring miraculous intervention, to serve their proper functions. If the location of nectar is correctly mapped, but in fact the dancing bee's last approach to the hive was from an unusual direction, this won't affect the success of the watching bees.

Consider another example, made famous by Fred Dretske (1986). The little magnetosome, the magnetic-field-sensitive organ, in certain northern hemisphere bacteria pulls toward magnetic north, hence toward geomagnetic north, hence down, hence away from surface water, hence away from oxygen, which is toxic to these bacteria. Thus it guides them to safety. Considered as an intentional icon, the pulling of the magnetosome in a certain direction has just one intentional content. It intentionally icons the more-oxygen/less-oxygen polarity, for being wrong about *that* is what would guarantee its failure to perform its normal function. (Note that it is not one of its *functions*, for example, to move the bacterium either down or toward geomagnetic north – any more than it is one of its functions to move it toward true north, toward molten rock or toward snow (the arctic). None of these figures in a causal chain that helps to *effect* its survival. Each is merely a usual correlate of performing its true biological function.)

I have been emphasizing very simple intentional icons. But there are good reasons to suppose that animals exhibiting flexible behaviors achieve this flexibility by harboring correspondingly complex intentional icons. Dennett himself has given the argument, most clearly, perhaps, in connection with the representation of rules rather than of states of affairs, but the idea is much the same.[7] Begin, he suggests, by considering an automatic elevator that is designed to "follow" one set of "tacit rules" (tacit suppositions – section 1 above) from nine to five on weekdays and a different set during off-peak and weekend hours. To accomplish this, a clock switches it between two different hardwired control systems at the appropriate times.

> We can imagine similar systems in animals . . . for instance, an animal that is both aquatic and terrestrial, and when it is on the land it obeys one set of rules, and when it is in the water it obeys another. Simply *getting wet* could be the trigger for changing internal state from one set of rules to the other.
>
> . . . but we could have more elaborate switching machinery, so that which system of rules was transiently tacitly represented depended on complex distal features of the environment . . . then there is no apparent limit to the specificity or complexity of the state of the world . . . that could be tacitly represented by the current state of such a system. [Note that Dennett's "tacitly represented" here is, at best, my "tacitly presupposed."]
>
> . . . But as the number of possible different states . . . grows . . . this profligacy demands . . . economies achieved via multiple use of resources. For instance, where the different states are variations on a theme . . . it becomes useful – virtually mandatory – to . . . change states by *editing* and *revising*, one might say, instead of *discarding* and *replacing*. Economies of this sort require systematicity. . . . (Dennett, 1987, p. 223–4)

Now what is "systematic" accords with rules, in the sense that it is projectable to cover new cases. And what these rules govern must not be just changes in the inner states of the organism so that they proceed in an orderly fashion. The rules must govern relations *between* these inner states of the organism and the relevant "complex distal features of the environment." Only if certain transformations performed upon the one correspond to parallel transformations performed upon the other will there be a point to the systematicity. But that is the same as to say that the states are intentional icons. "Systematicity" here just corresponds to the semantic productivity which is built into the notion "intentional icon."

In the above passage, Dennett goes on to warn that "the 'syntactical' elements of such systems are to be viewed first as having an entirely internal semantics . . . 'referring' . . . not to things and events in the outer world" (p. 224). I do not understand this restriction. If the rules that the animal must follow exhibit themes with multiple variations, presumably this is because the states of the world to which the animal needs to adapt exhibit themes with multiple variations. The transformations of the animal's interior surely must correspond systematically not just to other adjustments in the animal's interior but to transformations of its world. Perhaps this is why Dennett's phrase is qualified: "viewed *first*."

Consider, for example, quite mundane perceptual capacities. To be able to negotiate physical movement among the objects in its world, an animal must be prepared to deal with any of innumerable arrangements of objects surrounding it. In the case of many sighted animals, these arrangements are mapped onto patterns of ambient light impinging on the moving animal and brought to a focus through a lens in the eye. A description of the rules by which variations (transformations) in the pattern of the light impinging on the animal correspond to variations in the arrangements of surrounding objects is exceedingly complex. But the mapping is there, and the animal uses it. It uses the pattern, presumably, by projecting it internally to become a pattern in the nervous system which again maps onto the arrangement of external objects. Only in this way could movement be guided *according* to this arrangement, guided as, in part, a function of this arrangement.

The rules in accordance with which this latter inner movement-controlling pattern maps onto the environment may be even harder to describe than the rules for the ambient light. Taking a topical example, the rules by which the order or pattern within a large complex connectionist network in the brain mapped onto the chunk of the world it represents might be nearly impossible for us to describe. "Brain writing" may indeed prove to be "illegible"[8] to the outside observer. But the inner patterning is surely there and, as such, constitutes an intentional icon having a productive semantics. Thus, whether or not it also produces a disposition to conception and inference, perception itself exhibits intentionality.

Moreover, surely this lesson carries over from perception to cognition generally. We are prepared to pack into our heads any one of an innumerable number of alternative "settings" for adapting us to whichever one of an innumerable number of ways the world might turn out to be. This could not possibly be done without system, without a productive inner semantics – without the use of intentional icons.[9]

3 "Processes of Information-transformation": "Representations"

Yet surely we must agree with Dennett that having real *thoughts*, truly being believers, is somehow connected with being rational. In any event there is surely an important distinction of kind that needs marking between simple intentional icons and human thoughts. Hormones running in the blood stream can be intentional icons; surely they are not continuous with thoughts. Indeed, perceptions that guide an animal in motion, though these may be complex and multidimensional, seem not necessarily, just as such, to be thoughts. In fact there are, without doubt, a number of quite wide distinctions of kind between the simplest intentional icons and thoughts, just which distinctions and how many being, at the moment, a matter of rather free speculation. But one distinction that seems hardly speculative is, exactly, between simple intentional icons and items that participate in processes of inference. It is to honor this distinction that I have withheld the term "representation" until now.

I call "representations" only those intentional icons that have as one of their functions to participate in *mediate* inference. *Immediate* inference, by contrast, is probably best assimilated to translation, which, of course, can be partial. Translating information from one iconic medium into another, say, from retinal patterns to connectionist neural patterns, I am not considering to be inference. Nor am I interested in moves that distill more restricted information or more general information from that already given in some single icon. Paradigmatically, moves from "A&B" to "A" are not of interest here, nor are moves from "Fido barks" to "Something barks." What makes an intentional icon into a representation is that one of its various jobs is to combine with *other* icons to produce icons carrying *new* information.[10] It is this kind of "process of information-transformation among content-laden items" that defines "mental representations" (see epigraph).

Imagine a creature that carries about in its head intentional icons that are three-dimensional maps of various places it has been – not maps in three spatial dimensions, of course, but dimensions in some neurally realizable medium. It has a map of the locale in which it last found water, and another of the locale in which it last saw lions. On each of these maps its den is marked. Now imagine that it overlaps these maps, using its den as a pivot, and arrives at a third map showing the proximity of lions to the source of water. Reacting to this new map, it seeks a new source of water rather than going back to the lion-infested source on its map. Granted that in combining the maps this way the animal's brain was functioning in a way it was biologically designed to function – that is, the combining accorded with a "competence" of the animal – this would be a paradigm case of mediate inference. As is characteristic of all mediate inference, two vehicles of information have been combined, *using a middle term*, so as to produce a third vehicle containing new information. Accordingly, the maps are "representations."[11]

Soon I will argue that mental sentences, should these occur, would be intentional icons. But it seems quite reasonable that much of our active thinking, much of our inferring, may occur in media more like maps or like models (in the lay sense) than like sentences. Such models would have to be very abstract indeed, the mathematical isomorphisms between representations and world structures being far from tangible. I have already suggested that certain very abstract patterns found in neural nets could be intentional icons. Nor is there any reason why the results of superpositional storage of information in neural nets should not be considered to yield conclusions of inference. That superimposed information gets stored correctly in the same net with certain old information clearly depends upon there being an overlap in semantics on some level – on the presence of what I am calling "middle terms."

There is also another way in which "inference," as I intend that term, might look quite unlike inference as we typically express it by presenting "arguments" in the form of a series of sentences. Intentional icons occurring in different representational media might be premises and/or premise and conclusion of a single inference. Suppose, for example, that, by combining information contained in perception of an object *seen* to be in a certain place, with information about that object as *felt* to be in that same place, one comes to believe, say, that a green apple is hard. Here the premises are percepts and the conclusion is a thought, but the motion turns on a middle term and it is inference. It is "information-transformation among content-laden items." The percepts involved in such a transaction would, accordingly, be representations.

It does not follow from this definition of "representation," however, that every creature harboring representations is rational. This is for at least two reasons. First, it is likely that many inferencers produce true conclusions from true premises by relying heavily on tacitly presupposed information about the organism's normal environment (section 1 above). This information would have to be made explicit in the premises of a correct logical reconstruction of the inference. Now "rational" is another term that is pretty much up for grabs, its long philosophical history having rather more hindered than helped. But if we reserve it for a creature *capable*, at least, of explicit *valid* mediate inference, inference in which all information bearing premises are explicit, then it may well apply, as Aristotle suggested, to just us.

The other reason that harboring representations does not imply rationality is that there is no cause to suppose that every creature capable of inference, in the sense described, is capable of recognizing the intrusion of *inconsistency* among its representations, and prepared to respond to such intrusions in a productive way. From the definition of mental representation I have given, nothing follows about consistency. Nothing prohibits an organism from harboring as large a number of contrary or contradictory representations as it pleases, due either to malfunction inside the organism or unfavorable conditions outside. The ability to recognize and elminiate contradiction in inner representations is a distinct capacity not even hinted at in laying down the definition of representation. But having a lot, at least, of this capacity should surely be required as a condition on being fully "rational." (The conclusion of this essay entails that this capacity is not as unproblematic for humans as is generally supposed. Like the ability to make inferences, the ability to recognize contradiction depends upon recognizing middle terms or, as I shall later put it, on being able to "coidentify" correctly. But in no case, I will argue, is that ability transparent. A creature that never had *any idea* when it had contradicted itself in thought, however, could hardly be accorded rationality.)

4 "Sentences . . . in a Language of Thought"

Many are prone to confuse the claim that representations "map" onto the world with advocacy of a "picture theory" of representation and hence to reject it out of hand.[12] "Compositionality," on the other hand, is all the rage. Now what is interesting about compositionality is that it allows new semantic entities to be made by rearrangement of the parts or aspects of old ones. For instance, it allows "Jane loves John" to be made out of "John loves Jane." You can, of course, think of this change as produced by rearranging the parts, ". . . loves . . .," "John," and "Jane," but a more generalized way to think of it is as an operation, in the broad mathematician's sense, performed upon "John loves Jane" – the same operation which, when performed upon "The cat ate the mouse," produces "The mouse ate the cat," and so forth. Another kind of operation recognized by mathematicians are "substitute in" transformations, for example, "John loves Jane" may be transformed into "John loves the mouse" by the same "substitute in" move that transforms "Bill hits the nail" into "Bill hits the mouse." By other substitution operations we get from "John loves the mouse" to "The cat loves the mouse" and then to "The cat eats the mouse." Various introductions of the negative are also operations, taking us, for example, from "John loves Jane" to "John does not love Jane" or from "All John's money is invested in land" to "Not all John's money is invested in land."

Each of these various kinds of operations corresponds, of course, to a parallel operation on or transformation of the arrangements that are necessary in the world for the corresponding sentences to be true. ("Transformation" must be read here in the mathematical sense, of course – transformations of arrangements in the world are not *changes*.) But where operations performed on representations correspond one-to-one to transformations performed on representeds, then (by the rule of proportion: $A : B \ as \ C : D = A : C \ as \ B : D$) there must also be a "mapping" in accordance with a rule of projection between the domains of representations and of representeds. That is, semantic compositionality just *is* one kind of "mapping." Thus as I read it, Dennett's (1987, p. 149) assurance that "[c]ertainly some very efficient and elegant sort of compositionality accounts for the essentially limitless powers we have to perceive, think about, believe, intend . . . different things" is just one more voucher for intentional icons.[13] Similarly, turning to some other fashionable words, suppose that semantic "generativity" or "productivity" or "learnability" require that semantic rules project from a relatively small number of cases to all cases. Then these require a "mapping" from representations to representeds.

It seems to follow that mental sentences would be allowed to be "representations" under the definition I have given. But what else besides representationhood should we require of "mental sentences?" Sentences are usually thought of as composed of parts that can be strung together to contribute to the meaning of the whole, and that can be recombined to yield different meanings. But how literally should we interpret "parts" and "strung together?" For example, consider the "sentences" in Sellars' "Jumblese," where a tall "T" stands for "Tom is tall" and a shaky "T" for "Tom is scared," or where writing "T" on top of "B" stands for "Tom admires Bill." Do these count as sentences? I suggest that it would prove philosophically very dull not to count them. But I do suggest that we insist on subject/predicate structure. There must be possible transformations of the icon to correspond to other subjects having the same predicate, and there must be transformations to correspond to the same subject having other predicates. Then bee dances are not sentences, for they have no subject terms, and a rabbit's danger thumps are not sentences for they never predicate of a time and place anything other than danger. Let us require also that the icon be subject to a negation transformation. Then the alarm calls of the vervet monkeys are not sentences because, although the times and places of the calls vary with the times and places of predators (subject terms), and although there are different calls for different predators (predicate terms), the vervets' calls are never negated.[14]

5 Interlude: Inner Representations and Ascriptions of Belief

I now offer a radical translation of the following words from Dennett:

> I am as staunch a realist as anyone about those core information-storing elements in the brain, whatever they turn out to be, to which our intentional interpretations are anchored. I just doubt . . . that those elements, once individuated, will be recognizable as the beliefs we purport to distinguish in folk psychology. (Dennett, 1987, pp. 70f)

Consider the relation between a bee dance showing nectar 15 degrees west of the line between sun and hive and the English sentence "There is nectar 15 degrees west of the line between sun and hive." If the bee dance is true, the sentence has got to be true too; the sentence is implied by the bee dance. The two maps, bee dance and sentence, cover, in part, the same content. But this content is mapped, in the two cases, by entirely different projection rules. The bee dance is an analogue icon, while the sentence is articulated by substitution transformations. The bee dance has one basic analogue rule for direction, transformations of the orientation of the dance corresponding to transformations of the angle relative to the sun of the nectar. The sentence transforms into sentences indicating other directions in various ways, by "6" substituting in for "5," for example, or "east" substituting in for "west." The sentence is subject to a negation transformation whereas the bee dance is not. Indeed, no two bee dances are even contraries of one another. Any set of bee dances might be true all at once, nectar being in all those places at once, lucky bees. Further, the bee dance has, as it were, no subject term or terms. There are no transforms of it that indicate relations of things other than nectar to things other than sun and hive, or that indicate alternative kinds of relations between sun and hive.

In a similar way, the correctness of an ordinary map or diagram, chart or graph, may entail the truth of various sentences, yet the common content will be projected via rules that articulate it against quite different contrasting possibilities. The space of significant transformations surrounding such icons is different; each resides in what early Wittgenstein would have called a different "logical space." Implication relations between non-propositional icons and sentences can also go the other way. What a frog's eye tells a frog's brain may not imply any definite English sentence or sentences, but English sentences can be constructed that will imply the truth of what any particular frog's eye is currently telling its brain. And so with animal danger signals, the various cries of the vervet monkeys, and so forth. In each of these cases it seems reasonable to say that one icon implies what the other says, or implies part of what it says, but that it does not make this content explicit. One represents "implicitly" what the other represents "explicitly." This accords, I believe, with Dennett's own terminology (1987, p. 216).

Granted all this, it might be that although there were no such things as mental sentences, still the contents expressed by public language sentences correctly ascribing beliefs to a person were all implicit in, in the sense of immediately entailed by, that person's mental representations. Nor does this model require that a person be capable of articulating all his or her own beliefs in propositional form, either mentally or verbally. It does not require that he or she has command of any propositional, i.e. sentence-like, representational system at all. Nor would this entail that all of a person's mental representations could be correctly described as beliefs, or that all were of a kind that belief–desire talk makes an attempt to capture. Some might be like the icons in the frog's eye, that is, implied by representations with propositional structure, but not having nearly that degree of structure themselves. But it might still be that "*core* information-storing elements in the brain" (emphasizing "core"), though not "recognizable," "once individuated," as "the beliefs we purport to distinguish in folk psychology," would strictly entail the belief-ascribing sentences through which we customarily filter their contents.[15]

This suggestion about beliefs has a consequence, however, that may be in conflict with Dennett's vision of the "intentional stance," whereby belief–desire ascription floats entirely free of reference to representations inside. If correctly ascribed belief contents are entailed by the contents of real mental representations, then belief ascription will not be involved in a reconstruction of the *entire* behavioral pattern of an agent, but in the reconstruction only of parts. Inner representations have (by my definition) a potential effect upon action. But not all of a creature's actions need be representation-controlled, nor need all failures of the representation-forming and representation-using systems be failures to represent the right content. Starting with obvious examples, surely knee jerks and reflex eyeblinks are not to be accounted for by reference to beliefs and desires. Nor are errors such as tripping or spilling one's coffee. Similarly, I suggest, errors in comprehending a sentence or reading a map, errors in perception or, generalizing this broadly, errors in recognizing one's true situation, quirks in one's expectations of and attitudes towards self or others, none are invariably accountable to mistaken beliefs or desires. In particular, taking examples not exactly at random, not all errors in making change need be so accountable,[16] nor need all quirks such as "having a thing about redheads."[17] In each of these cases it may be that the peculiarity is attributable to some glitch in the system not describable in intentional terms, not resulting from inner representation. Nor am I saying that the description in intentional terms may be indeterminate. Rather, these quirks may have no legitimate intentional descriptions, no intentional character, at all.

To try to rationalize such happenings would be not just unhelpful but plain wrong. Similarly, if inner representations are as I have described them, rationalizing away apparent inconsistency will sometimes be just plain wrong. There may often be considerable ambiguity in the behavioral evidence for inconsistency, but the real *inner* facts of the matter, as common sense also requires, may remain entirely determinate.[18]

PART TWO

6 "Computational": "Manipulated in a Language of Thought"

The notion "mental sentence" is obviously intended to rest on an analogy with public language sentences, an analogy I have tried to make more precise. I have required subject-predicate structure for mental sentences, and required that they be subject to negation transformations. But I have not required them to be composed of rearrangeable elements all of the same type (recall Sellars' Jumblese, section 4 above). The notion that sentences in a language of thought are "manipulated" or "computed" or "calculated over" is clearly supposed to rest on an analogy with the manipulations performed upon sentences or strings in a formal logical system. Again, we must ask just exactly what is supposed to be preserved in the analogy.

One thing that is clearly intended to be preserved is that the manipulation occurs in conformity with rules, and that these rules operate upon physical form rather than meaning. The image is of a Mentalese harnessed to its tasks by lawfully patterned transformations operating upon its "shapes" or "syntax." Thus, beginning with certain initial mental sentences, one arrives at different mental sentences, written down separately. And, of course, the "manipulations" that correspond to *inferences* are supposed to be truth preserving. They produce *valid* inferences.

Let me bring out two more aspects of this image, difficult to isolate because they are so deeply impressed. One is that "computation" produces a multiplicity of sentence tokens exhibiting recombinations of *recurrent* elements. That is, pairs of mental sentences in the same head often contain elements that are of the same type or that exhibit the same formal structures. Were this not so, there could be no rules, in the sense envisioned, for calculating over them. Thus mental sentences understood as "calculated over," are not just icons and representations. To be an icon token, all that is required is that had that token been different along a certain dimension or dimensions, it would have meant something different. And to be a representation token, we need add only a capacity to interact with other representations in a way that produces new icons with new contents. It is not required in either case that there be other tokens in the same brain with identical elements or aspects, to which the same mapping rules apply. Especially important, the requirement of a middle term on which inference pivots is a semantic requirement, not a syntactic one. Recall the inference that combines visual with tactual percepts to produce thoughts (section 3).

The second buried point is that where mental sentences are taken to be "calculated over," meanings are taken to be assigned to these sentences "by the typeful." That is, it is by recognizing the types exemplified in a mental sentence token that one determines the meaning. Types are equivalence classes which serve, on the one hand, as units to which meanings are assigned and, on the other hand, as units over which formal inference rules univocally apply. If meanings were not assigned by the typeful, no rules for calculating over tokens in accordance with their types could be guaranteed to preserve truth, or any other sort of semantic order.

Spelled out this way, the traditional modern analogy between thinking and the unfolding of a formal logical system is seriously flawed, I believe, in at least two ways. The first and less serious concerns the representation of rules of inference in "brain writing" v. in formal systems (section 8 below). The second and far more damaging is that there is every reason to suppose that elements of mental representations are not grouped into types in the sense required (sections 9–11). But if thought contains no such types, then there can be no formal rules that determine validity for forms of inference in Mentalese. Bluntly speaking, valid inference cannot be distinguished *a priori*. Though I will not press the matter here, I suspect that this disanalogy between mental representations and strings in formal systems undermines much of the motivation for language of thought hypotheses.

7   What Achilles Replied to the Tortoise

Dennett has often reminded us of Lewis Carroll's argument for the indispensability of tacit rules of inference for logical systems (Carroll, 1895). Although it is possible to build a logical system that has no axioms but only rules, it is not possible to build a system with no rules but only axioms. That is, the rules cannot all be represented explicitly. Dennett concludes that if it exists at all, "brain writing is a dependent form of storage" of information (1978, p. 46). It is dependent upon "tacit" information storage – tacit storage, presumably, of first major premises or rules. Thus he says of Fodor, "it seems as if he is committed to the impossible view that only explicit representation is representation, and (roughly) nothing can be believed, thought about or learned without being explicitly represented" (Dennett, 1978, p. 104).

Now in a traditional formal system, each axiom or hypothesis is written down on a separate line of paper, the system unfolding as new sentences or formulas, derived from these by rule, are written down below. In such a system, adding axioms to the system, writing down more sentences at the top of the paper, obviously will not determine *how* the axioms are to be used in order to guide further construction of the system. Rules to guide the manipulation of the strings must be given in a metalanguage. The person who uses the system reads these rules and, inspired by them, performs the appropriate transformations. If the system is unfolding in the head, however, the "user" is just another part of the head. Since representations in the head are just head-structures that vary according to how the world is, this part may itself *constitute* a representation. Taking a childish example, imagine an inference machine designed to perform inferences using universal categorical sentences as major premises and constructed in the following manner. Premises of the form *All As are Bs* are entered by constructing a sliding board between two ports, the top port being an A-shaped hole, the bottom a B-shaped hole. Sentences ascribing predicates to individuals consist of pieces of putty the colors of which name individuals and the shapes of which ("A," "B," "C") ascribe properties. These pieces of putty are gently pushed across the tops of the constructed slides, where they enter the ports through which they fit, proceeding to the bottom where they are pushed through the lower ports and change their shapes accordingly. They thus become conclusions.

Surely this image could be improved on, but the principle should be clear. There is no reason why one premise has to lie passively beside the next in a representational system. Ways the inferencing system is put together can themselves be representations, so long as it is put together that way through influence of the individual's environment, and so long as variations in how it is put together correspond, systematically, to variations in that environment.

So Lewis Carroll's point need not apply to all inferencing systems. There just might be systems in which all the rules were explicitly represented. Indeed, it seems likely that where rules are learned rather than "hardwired in" (i.e. "tacitly presupposed," see section 1 above) then they are explicitly iconed. To suppose otherwise seems to imply that the learning is not accomplished in a principled way. Principled learning would surely result in internal structures representing major premises which structures varied systematically upon themes, hence constituted intentional icons.

Could there be a system in which all of the rules were explicitly represented and all the representations were sentences? For example, could transformations functioning as negations be added to the representations in our system using colored putty and slides, thus turning these structures into sentences? I haven't an answer to that question, but thinking it through surely would require that we abandon the traditional image of the computing of mental sentences as like a formal system unfolding on paper. Would the inferencing mechanism that uses putty and slides count as "computational?" Would its major premises, assuming these might somehow be sentences, count as being "manipulated in a language of thought?"

8   Typing Rules in Formal Systems

A much deeper disanalogy to be explored between thought and formal systems concerns the grouping of tokens into types. Formal symbol tokens are grouped into types in a perfectly definite manner, each token falling under one and only one type. The rules of the system then apply to the types, and to the tokens only *as* falling under types. If the system is interpreted, the interpretations are also assigned to the types, and to the tokens only as falling under the types. This property of formal systems is so essential, so much taken for granted, that it is not even mentioned when these systems are set up or described. The hypothesis that there is a language of thought, manipulated in the mind as thinking proceeds, has this image at its very core. Little if any meaning can attach to the notion of a language of thought lacking this feature.

Consider how formal systems are traditionally set up. First you say what elementary symbols will be used: *p*s and *q*s, say, or *A*s and *B*s and *x*s and *y*s, wedges, horseshoes, parentheses, and so forth. Next you explain how to construct well-formed formulas from these ingredients, typically with the aid of recursive definitions. Then you may (but need not) lay down axioms. And last, you lay down rules (all this in the metalanguage, of course) that will move you from well-formed formulas already laid down or derived to new formulas. This laying down of symbols, of well-formedness rules, of axioms, and of inference rules, is traditionally done by displaying *tokens* of symbols, using these as examples of the types of symbols to be put down and manipulated in accordance with the system's rules. But how are other tokens of these types to be recognized? By what criterion will they be known to be tokens of the same types? Typically nothing is said about this.

One pretends, traditionally, that some suitable but unmentioned kind of sameness of shape is what binds the tokens into types. In practice, of course, this is false. In practice we take for granted certain conventional methods which do not go just by shape. They may rely *partly* on shape similarities, often defining disjoint sets of tokens – various type fonts, for example. But conventional methods also pay close attention to the intention of the symbol maker. What counts as an "*a*" is what was intended to be an "*a*", having been purposefully copied, carefully or carelessly, competently or incompetently, with or without consciously added style, on the model of earlier "*a*"s.[19] The fact that convention follows this path is assumed to be a matter of mere convenience, a concession to messy human users. In principle it is or could be shape alone that does the typing or some other point of physical similarity. Symbol types, it is supposed, are basically *physical* types.

This assumption can be challenged, and I will do so later. After all, certain physical similarities, and not others, group tokens into types only because someone, say, the general public, *reads* the tokens that way. Physical *similarities*, if salient, are so only because made so by symbol users. Similarly, if there are symbol types in mental language, these must correspond to ways the inner system "reads" mental tokens. But if the general public is human and substitutes messy conventions that turn on etiology for physical similarities when grouping symbols into types, might not the brain be human too? Indeed, I will argue that it is most unlikely that typing for mental tokens rests on physical similarity. But we can make considerable progress in understanding the problems surrounding mental typing before raising this, so let us put it aside for a while.

Although typing rules for formal systems are virtually never discussed, in fact they have considerable clout. How one does the symbol typing can actively interact with how one does the axioms and/or rules for a system. I will content myself with very simple illustrations of this, taken from the propositional calculus.

The first example concerns laws of commutativity. Standard renditions of the propositional calculus require that the equivalence of "*A&B*" to "*B&A*" and of "*A*∨*B*" to "*B*∨*A*" be either introduced as axioms, derived as theorems, or (aberrant but possible) given as special rules of inference. Suppose, however, that one were to construct a system in which the difference between left and right on the paper is ignored when grouping symbol tokens into types. No distinction is drawn between "*p*" and "*q*", nor between "*b*" and "*d*" and so forth. Similarly, "*A*⊃*H*" is the same string as "*H*⊂*A*". More interesting, "*A*∨*H*" is the same string as "*H*∨*A*" and, if we use the traditional dot instead of "&", "*A·H*" is the same string as "*H·A*". Here a symbol typing rule does duty for a couple of axioms, theorems, or rules.

For our next example, we read right–left distinctions as usual and play instead with up and down. We read "*p*" as a symbol of the same type as "*b*" except that it has been *turned upside down*. Then we use turning upside down for the negation transformation. We negate propositional constants and variables by turning them upside down; we negate strings by turning the whole string upside down. Double negation elimination now no longer appears as an axiom, theorem, or metalanguage rule. Indeed, it can't be stated. Of course, we have to be terribly careful. We must not use any symbols that are symmetrical top to bottom, or we won't be able to tell whether they have undergone the negation transformation or not. On the other hand, suppose we use the traditional symbol "∧" for conjunction. The effect is that De Morgan's laws need not be stated, are indeed unstatable, being mere fallout from the symbol-typing rules. For example, suppose that you turn "*p*" and "*q*" each upside down, put a wedge between them, and then turn the whole string over, thus saying that it is neither the case that not-*p* nor not-*q*. The result, "*p*∧*q*," is a string that is more naturally read straight off as saying, simply, that *p* and *q*.

Symbol typing, then, is an interesting game, though we are not yet prepared to play it for brain writing, since no one has any idea what kind of logical space brain-writing symbols might be written in. There is, however, one kind of effect of symbol-typing rules that does not depend on details of the properties of mental symbol space and that is important for us to consider. This is the relation between typing rules and strings that assert identities.

First we should note something the Tortoise would surely have pointed out to Achilles. In formal systems, the closest correlates in the object language to typing rules in the metalanguage are strings asserting identities. But when we consider how such an identity sentence works, it becomes clear that not all the typing rules for a system could be rendered explicit in this way. The string looks, for example, like this: "*a* = *b*." It contains a symbol token of a different type on each side of an equals sign. The effect of the string on the user is to produce a change in future reactions not of course to these exhibited *tokens*, but to other tokens of the same *type*. So behind every such identity string there must lie a prior typing rule to determine which other tokens are to count as tokens of the same types as the tokens displayed. To attempt to make explicit in the object language all the typing rules, then, would obviously lead to regress.

With regard to the converse, however, it always *is* possible to substitute a typing rule for any axiom string asserting identity, or for any rule that might be asserted in the metalanguage allowing intersubstitution of pairs of symbols. Rather than an axiom saying "*a* = *b*," or a rule saying that you may exchange tokens of "a" for tokens of "b", one could always introduce a typing rule that simply refused to recognize a difference between "a" and "b." For example, just as one can ignore the difference between a handwritten small "a" and a printed small "a" when developing and using a formal system, or between roman "a" and italic "*a*," so one might have a system in which the difference between "colour" and "color" was ignored, or between "flammable" and "inflammable," or between "spigot" and "faucet." It is generally thought (are we entirely sure?) that the rules for typing English words do not in fact count these particular words as of the same type, but there seems to be no principled reason why they could not. Such a typing rule would, of course, be less regular than one that goes slavishly according to the letters included in each word token, but all languages abound with irregularities. For example, surely the English word "schedule" corresponds to but one spoken word type despite the fact that tokens of this type contain different phonemes when pronounced in the English and American ways.

That typing rules might take the place of identity strings or substitution rules in a formal system is not disturbing. But how would we feel if it turned out that there was no principled distinction to be drawn between the man who believes Cicero is Tully and the man whose Cicero and Tully thoughts are tokens of the same type in different fonts? Or between the man who believes Cicero is Caesar and the one whose Cicero and Caesar thoughts are tokens of the same type in different fonts!? This possibility I propose now to explore in more detail.

9 Mental Typing Rules, or Identity Beliefs?

First we note that for brain language, no distinction can be drawn among (a) typing rules, (b) metalanguage rules allowing interchangings or, as I shall say, "coidentifyings," of certain terms and (c) *axioms* asserting identities. (Strings asserting contingent identities will be discussed soon.) For formal systems, the distinction between (a) and (b) turns on whether the coidentifying rules are unstated because governed by prior implicitly understood conventions, or whether they must be stated because they modify conventions. But for brain language there are no conventions; there is only, as it were, the private user. So there is no analogue to the distinction between (a) and (b). Moreover, surprisingly, there is no analogue to the distinction between (a) (implicit typing rules) and (c) (identity axioms written at the top of the paper). This is because there is no distinction in the brain parallel to that between what is written on the paper and what is written in the structure of the reader. One structure responsible for brain coidentifying patterns is on a par with any other; all are equally "written" in the brain. Write an identity sentence in neuron patterns instead of in graphite, and the distinction between sentence and interpreting mechanism collapses. If some neuronal mechanism effects that the mental "a"s get coidentified with the mental "*a*"s – or the "Tully"s with the "Cicero"s – this mechanism *is* an identity sentence. What is the alternative? That to be an identity sentence it would have, literally, to be physically shaped like this: *Tully* = *Cicero*?

But for exactly the same reasons that (a), (b) and (c) cannot be distinguished, a question arises how to distinguish between introducing *new* identity strings into a brain – new identity beliefs – and merely altering its typing rules. And that is a worrying result. For customarily we think of introduced identity beliefs as being "synthetic," as valid or true depending on how the world is, whereas we think of typing rules as more trivial even than "analytic." Decisions about typing rules are like choosing which type font to use, choices that are totally arbitrary unless, perhaps, from an engineering standpoint. The worrying problem is this: if (a) there is nothing to determine whether brain tokens are of the same type except whether the brain identifies or distinguishes them, and (b) introducing an identity string into the brain is indistinguishable from changing the brain's typing dispositions, then (c) no distinction exists for the brain between a shift in identity beliefs and a shift in brain-writing notation. Walk to the brink now and peer over. Is there any footing below?

Suppose that you have confused Tweedledum and Tweedledee in your mind; you think there is only one Tweedle. Surely it is possible to say here as well that you have a false identity belief, that you believe that Tweedledum is Tweedledee. After all, every time you meet Tweedledum you take him to be Tweedledee – or is it vice versa? Yet you have just one symbol type in your head for both men, so your identity belief that Tweedledum is Tweedledee has the logical form "a = a" not "a = b." So a false identity belief is just a place where the brain's notational system happens to contain a single thought type that has been assigned double or equivocal meaning. Turning this over, if one falls into the false identity belief that Tweedledum is Tweedledee, hence coidentifies tokens of the thought *Tweedledum* with tokens of the thought *Tweedledee*, since tokens of these thought types are behaving exactly as though they were all tokens of the *same* type, nothing prevents the meaning assigned to each of these types from sliding across the join, so to speak, producing just one type with one equivocal meaning. Expressed as an identity belief, one's belief has then become analytic: Tweedledum is Tweedledum.

Something, one hopes, has gone wrong. Where there is *genuine* identity belief, and not just confusion of mind, the set of tokens one is disposed to coidentify divides along some line or lines, and the meanings assigned to the separate divisions stay with them, unaffected by any coidentifying dispositions that may be superimposed. Something *beneath* mere coidentifying dispositions should determine the types to which meanings attach. What we seem to need is something at least *like* a distinction between necessary and contingent dispositions to coidentify. One possibility, of course, would be to look where Quine looked for this kind of distinction (Quine, 1960, ch. 2). We might look for coidentifying dispositions that cannot be disrupted no matter what kind of barrage hits the sensory surfaces.[20] Or we might suppose that certain coidentifying competencies are wired into the brain at birth. It is natural, for example, to suppose that the brain might be wired such that it is optional whether it coidentifies, say, mental "a" with mental "a," but not optional whether it identifies "a" with "a," these latter tokens being physically identical.

But, on the other hand, why suppose that the brain *has* any built in or unalterable coidentifying competencies? After all, earlier we suggested that physical sameness may not be a basis on which the brain coidentifies tokens. Worse, we can wonder what the *relevance* of built in or unalterable dispositions would be to brain language typing as it determines meaning assignments. Why should how the brain was born or how it can or can't be altered affect what its brain language tokens currently mean? What is to prevent the brain from altering its representational system as it goes along?

10   Acts of Coidentifying

In trying to untangle this snarl, it will help first to have thought more about what coidentifying options the brain might in fact have, about how it might go about grouping tokens into types. Supposing the grouping of tokens into types rests on what the brain takes to be the same, we begin by asking what kind of response to a pair of symbols *constitutes* such a taking. Later we can ask whether some of these takings might be something like "analytic" or "mandatory" while others are not.

Naïvely, it might seem that the question about brain-writing types could be put more directly. Why not just ask, for any symbol token in the language of thought, what physical variations of it are possible without affecting the way that the symbol is read? Won't the limits of these variations delimit which physical forms *must* fall within the same brain-language type? There are two reasons why not, a little initial one, and a big and very final one. The initial reason is that there is not the slightest reason to suppose that the brain has a single "reader" before which all its representations march, hence to suppose that no matter where in the brain a representation token occurs, its way of being read imposes on it the same limits of physical form. Surely the writing in one part of the brain might be slightly bigger or have a higher voltage than that in another? Would this imply that different parts of the brain used merely cognate languages? Indeed, are any two brain sentence tokens ever *literally* passed before the same brain reader? If not might there be then as many languages as the brain contains token sentences? One begins to sense that there is something badly wrong with this line of questioning. Notice too how it ignores our earlier worry that typing might not rest on sameness of physical form.

The second reason shows *why* this line of questioning is wrong. In assuming that sameness of type is manifested primarily in token interchangeability, it bypasses the root of the question about typing: what is it for sameness of type to be recognized? To suppose that token interchangeability manifests sameness of type makes sense only if one supposes that the reader parts of the system recognize sameness of type by reacting the same. But, in fact, reacting the same way is not the primary way that a reader recognizes sameness of type. Consider a person manipulating symbols to derive theorems in a logical system. Does such a person do the same thing again whenever the same symbol, say, the same variable or constant, is encountered again? The reaction depends, rather, on the context in which the variable or constant is found, and for strings, on what other strings are already available for combining with this string. In the primary case, reader reactions are to *pairs* of strings, not to single strings or single terms.

Recognition of type identity is paradigmatically manifested when the reader combines two strings to yield a third. Such combinings or "mediate inferences" invariably require an *overlap* in the two strings, a "middle term." The middle term has to be "the same" for a rule of mediate inference to apply. That is, the two strings must contain tokens falling under the same type. Consider, for example, the rule that moves one from the string $p{\supset}q$ and the string p to the string q. Applying this rule manifests grasp that the tokens of p in the two premise strings are tokens of the same type. Correctly applying this rule also requires that a new token of q be produced, that is, a new token of the same type as the third token in the first premise. But what determines that this part of the rule has been followed correctly is not whether the shapes of the old and new tokens are the same or whether the tokens are interchangeable, but whether these tokens would be recognized, say, each as interacting by rule with a token of $r \supset \sim q$ to produce, respectively, $\sim(p \cdot r)$ and $\sim r$. Interchangeability is not just irrelevant but undoubtedly quite wrong as an indicator of sameness of type. Suppose, for example, that the symbols in the desire box prove to be larger than those in the belief box, so that they just wouldn't fit right if one interchanged them. Still, surely if the desire *I am warm* interacts with the belief *If I put on my coat I am warm* to produce the desire *I put on my coat* then the two tokens of *I am warm* must be counted as of the same type.

Consonant with this, the basic act of recognizing that an object encountered in perception or thought on one occasion is the same as that encountered on another is never mere sameness of reaction (Millikan, 1984, ch. 15; 1991c; in press a, sections 10–11). For example, this act is not accomplished by "applying the same concept again," not at least as this phrase is usually understood. To suppose that it is, is implicitly to assume that mere presence of a sameness between acts of thought constitutes recognition of sameness in *content*: the sameness of two acts of thought constitutes a thought of the sameness of their objects. Compare this with Hume's mistake in supposing that a succession of impressions is the same as an impression of succession (Millikan, 1991c). On the contrary, recognition that elements within two intentional icon tokens represent the same occurs only when these icons are used jointly, pivoting on the "overlap" or "middle term," to produce a new icon or an adapted action. For example, our creature that overlapped a map of the relation of water to its den with a map of the relation of lions to its den to determine the relation of water to lions, recognized, in performing that act, that these maps showed a place in common, its den. Similarly, every act of mediate inference postulates the sameness of whatever its middle term tokens stand for in the two premises.

But there is a secondary kind of act we should count as grasping that an object presented twice is the same. This act prepares for a primary act of coidentifying by reacting to the two presentations to produce icons containing elements of the same type. For what it is for two tokens to be of the same type is for there to be a *competence* to coidentify them. This implies that there is, after all, a *sense* in which reacting the same way by "applying the same concept" again is a recognition of sameness, but only granted that "applying the same concept" *means* constructing icons containing elements one knows to coidentify. But then "applying the same concept again" need not imply any *physical* sameness of reaction.

What relations other than similarity might then be brought to the task of grouping thought tokens into types? Compare here natural languages. When anaphora is used, that two tokens are to have their referents coidentified is indicated not by token similarity but by a relation: "I told *John* that *he* was to go." Nor is token similarity in natural languages always an indication that referents *are* to be identified. Homonyms abound, numerous people have the same given names, and so forth. How is it indicated, say, which tokens of "Alice" go with which other tokens of "Alice" for purposes of coidentifying? However it is done, if we have ways of telling which identical "Alice" tokens outside us do and don't go with which others, mightn't the mind have ways of telling which identical "Alice" tokens inside it do and don't go with which others? Consider also indexicals. How do we know which public language indexicals go with which other indexicals for purposes of coidentifying? Were similarity the relevant factor, "this is this" could never be informative, which surely it sometimes is. Must not the brain too have systems by which it coidentifies indexicals?

Indeed, why suppose that the brain pays attention to token similarity at all? Maybe it goes *entirely* by other relations. Imagine, for example, that the brain groups tokens into types by wiring them together so that whenever one token of the type lights up, they all do. Or perhaps different tokens are merely different lightings up of the same individual symbol, its place in a variety of iconic structures being held by external connections that can be activated either simultaneously or alternatively (connection-ism). As an antidote to the weight of tradition which pulls same language-of-thought-type toward same "shape," let us speak instead merely of "coidentity nets" where the brain is disposed (better, "has a competence") to coidentify a set of thought tokens.

11 Why Mental Meaning is not Dished out by the Typeful and Valid Inference is not Known *a priori*

The question tabled earlier whether a necessary/contingent distinction might be drawn along Quinean lines for the brain's typing dispositions now appears in this form. Are some of the links in the brain's coidentity nets wired in at birth, or not biologically designed to be broken? If so, do these littlest or base nets function as true types in the image of types in a logical system? Do they function, that is, as base units to which meanings are permanently affixed, unaffected by superimposed coidentifying dispositions that incorporate them into wider nets? Then acts of coidentifying among tokens in the same base net would be identifyings that couldn't in principle go wrong. Not that the tokens involved might not themselves be equivocal, but if so, their being coidentified would not be the *cause* of the equivocation. These would be nets within which identity of reference was "transparent" (Campbell, 1987/88). Whether because they are netted by innate wiring or for some other reason, that tokens should *somehow* group themselves into types within which coidentifyings are immune to error, and immune also to the hazard of introducing equivocation, is at the core of the notion of language-like types. And that notion is in turn at the core of the vision of inner representations as items that "look or behave like sentences manipulated in a language of thought." Are there then any such base identity nets?

An interesting case to examine first, because it appears to involve compulsory acts of coidentifying, is perceptual tracking. For example, in accordance with principles that are now well understood, objects moving in the visual field are seen *as* moving, and seen *as* disappearing and appearing again from behind obscuring objects. To see an object *as* moving is of course to see it *as the same object again*, tracked by the eyes over time. This seeing-as results when certain relations obtain among one's retinal images, images which can be surprisingly discontinuous both in time and in space without obscuring the effect. Nor is the effect overridden by knowledge that the movement is illusory, that its appearance is caused, for example, by blinking dots on a TV screen. Evans (1981) and Campbell (1987/88) have speculated about the relation among the thought tokens of a person who, while perceptually tracking an object, thinks to herself "this . . . this . . . this." Do these thought tokens have the same Fregean senses or not? Similarly, we can ask, are they of the same Mentalese type or not?

Surely there are not any identity nets involving indexicals more basic than those wired together by this sort of perceptual tracking? Yet it is possible for a person unknowingly to *lose* track and to wire such tokens together wrongly. Imagine a person losing track and apparently, but wrongly, perceiving the same squirrel eating first six and then seven more brazil nuts. The result is an indelible memory of the squirrel who ate 13 whole brazil nuts at a sitting. If the identified thought tokens, "this" and then "this" again, were each univocal in reference at the start, then the coidentifying act was in error. And if these tokens were equivocal, their being coidentified causing their meanings to blend, that equivocation was still the *result* of the coidentifying and not something prior. So identity nets constructed through perceptual tracking, though apparently mandatory, are not then base nets in a sense that can mirror linguistic types.

But it is often thought that indexicals are odd. Perhaps in the sense of "type" we need here, each indexical thought token is a type all of its own. That is why two such tokens can never be coidentified without some risk of error. Indexical thought tokens are assigned their meanings not, as it were, inside the mind, but through their contextual relations to the world outside. Correctly reidentifying the objects of thought indexicals, then, calls for abilities that loop through the world. Tracking, for example, only works correctly in those contingent external conditions under which the perceptual organs and tracking mechanisms were designed to operate. But thoughts other than indexicals might still come in well-behaved types.

Let us turn directly then to the case that transfixes. Suppose that thought contains mental names, tokens of these being hardwired into base identity nets strictly according to physical kinds. Surely these nets would determine types in the sense that we need; coidentifying within these nets could not in principle go wrong?

Now there are two ways God might have created Babel in the Tower. He might, straightfacedly, have made the languages spoken all sound different. Then each man would have known immediately that he couldn't understand any of the others. Or God might have created languages that all sounded alike but shifted the meanings around. Then each man would have mistakenly believed that he did understand the others, causing far more confusion and fun. Similarly, the brain might be hardwired to understand certain physically same thought tokens as meaning the same, but what charm is there against Babel at the level of the mental-language *producers*? Might they not *produce* tokens that were alike but that meant different things?

We have explicitly focused, so far, entirely upon the *users* of mental language tokens, as though they were exclusive determiners of the language's typing structure. Yet our look at indexicals a moment ago implicitly introduced another dimension, for what the mental indexical means obviously depends, at least in large part, on its origin. That is why it is obvious that even obligatory coidentifying of indexicals during tracking cannot be infallible coidentifying. Focusing on uses of mental representations is a good antidote to the current trend that focuses exclusively on origins, seeking the determiners of mental content in "natural information" or in "covariation" between cause and representation. But it is time now to correct the imbalance.

Mental representation, as I have described it (sections 2 and 3 above), rests on cooperation between representation producers and representation consumers or interpreters. If there are mental names, they are not like symbols in a logical system, determined to be referential constants by virtue of falling under types antecedently *labeled* as constants and endowed with reference by fiat. A mental name could acquire representational status only through the emergence of a systematic method of producing it – producing it in icons that mapped onto the world in accordance with determinate rules of projection. That was our first special requirement on intentional icons (section 2 above). A mental name exists only when its thinker has a competence to reiterate it in a variety of different correct and grounded *whole* representations, "grounded" meaning that there are systematic ways of producing such representations so as to accord with their mapping rules.[21] But to have that sort of capacity implies that one has certain ways of correctly reidentifying the referent of the name when that referent, or signs of it, show up again. For there to be representation at all, it is necessary that producer and interpreter should get together. Which tokens are to mean the same as which must be agreed on at the two ends. However the coidentity net wiring is done, what the representation readers will read as the same, the producers must have a competence to produce as the same, or there is no representation at all.

It doesn't follow, however, that errors in coidentifying are impossible or even uncommon. That a brain, or any other biological system, has ways of doing something, has a competence, has the ability to do something, tells us nothing about how reliable that ability is. We have ways of walking, a competence to walk, but this does not keep us from tripping. We have ways of tracking, but it doesn't follow that we never lose track. Besides tracking we have numerous other ways of reidentifying things, such as memorizing people's faces, remembering their names, recognizing their voices and signatures, gleaning identifying information about them, and so forth. Similarly for various other sorts of objects, natural kinds, and properties. But every one of these ways can fail if the environment is not cooperative, and some ways are very risky indeed.[22]

What follows then is actually the reverse. There is no immunity anywhere to the introduction of confusion in thought through acts of coidentification, not even if the coidentified thoughts are mental names that are compulsorily coidentified, and coidentified because physically identical. Suppose, for example, that seeing her on the street, I mistake Jane, who walks with a cane, for Alice. I do so because my reidentifying abilities fail me in a certain uncooperative part of the world: Jane looks just too much like Alice. Now my thought "that woman" when looking at Jane is surely a thought of Jane. I am tracking or prepared to track Jane. I have an ability to coidentify my percept of Jane with other percepts of Jane, and thus my thought is of *her*. I know how, by tracking, to coidentify the token *that woman* with various other tokens *that woman* in the making of grounded representations. Yet I think I am seeing that *Alice* now walks with a cane: *that woman, Alice, walks with a cane.* Tradition says here that I make only a false judgement, and since "that woman" and "Alice," following the corresponding English expressions, are naturally taken to be thought tokens of different types, it seems clear enough how judging them the same or coidentifying them, either one, could be an error. But now let us thicken the plot. Suppose that I lean on the false belief that Alice walks with a cane to identify her on numerous other occasions. The real Alice, meanwhile, has permanently moved to

Sun Valley. Remembering that Alice was playing tennis only a year ago, I think it sad that she aged so fast. In making this last inference I coidentify two identical mental name tokens "Alice" in a way, let us suppose, that is biologically mandatory. Yet the direct result is a confusion in thought, an equivocation. Is the trouble that one of the premises was false? If so, which one? And which of the two women is the conclusion about?

Mental names are, after all, basically amalgams of indexicals. If coidentifying can go wrong in the case of mental indexicals, it can also go wrong in the case of mental names. I conclude that sameness of reference or meaning is never transparent for thought. From which it follows that validity in mediate inference is never given to thought entirely *a priori*. Putting this in Campbell's terms (1987–8), there is no such thing as completely "manifest sameness of reference."

In thought there are no base identity nets within which coidentifications are immune to error. It follows that there is no analogue in thought to the symbol types of logical systems. This, coupled with the strong suspicion that thoughts are not grouped into identity nets by physical similarity, and the fact that the premises of inference in thought need not lie beside one another but might actively push one another about, leads me to declare, with Dennett, that although there must be such things as mental representations, "their styles will not be 'computational'; the items will not look or behave like sentences manipulated in a language of thought" (Dennett, 1987, p. 235)

ACKNOWLEDGMENTS

I am much indebted to Bo Dahlbom and to Bill Lycan for helpful comments on earlier drafts. This paper was prepared while the author was a Fellow at the Center for Advanced Study in the Behavioral Sciences where financial support was provided by the National Endowment for the Humanities #RA-20037-88 and the Andrew W. Mellon Foundation.

NOTES

1 In this essay I discuss only one of two kinds of "intentional icons" defined in Millikan (1984) (see also Millikan, in press b), namely, indicative intentional icons. Equally important are imperative intentional icons, but I shall try to get by here without them.

2 This may or may not involve the feature's being a cause of the icon that maps it. For example, the orientation of the magnetosome in Dretske's favorite bacterium (Dretske, 1986) is an intentional icon of the direction *away-from-oxygen*, but oxygen has nothing to do with the causes of its orientation (see Millikan, 1991a). Similarly, intentional icons may map onto future features of the environment.

3 In the sense of "natural information" defined in Dretske's *Knowledge and the Flow of Information* (1981).

4 See Millikan (1984), chs 9, 18 and 19.

5 This is why massive redundancy of function is the norm everywhere in the life world, as is early death rather than reproduction. For discussion, see Millikan (1992).

6 In Millikan (1984) I called these simple icons "intentional signals." Intentional signals usually indicate time or place with the *same* time or place, but one could imagine, say, an

animal signal, the "t_1" part (the now part) of which indicated danger five mintues from t_1, or winter within a month of t_1, or the p_1 part of which meant *somewhere-between-p_1-and-the-food-supply*.

7   "Styles of Mental Representation," in Dennett (1987); see especially pp. 220–25. In my official terminology, representations of rules are "imperative intentional icons" (Millikan, 1984, ch. 6).

8   Compare "Brain Writing and Mind Reading," in Dennett (1978), p. 43.

9   On the necessity of a productive semantics or "articulateness" for inner representations, see also Millikan (1991a).

10 In the last section, in order not to complicate matters too much, I defined "intentional icon" in a manner including only what I prefer to call "indicative intentional icons" (Millikan, 1984, ch. 6). Here I am making another simplification. "Representations," as I really prefer to use that term (Millikan, 1984), are intentional icons that, in order to perform some of their functions, must be "identified." The act of identifying occurs whenever two icons, either indicative or imperative, that overlap in content, are joined so as to produce either another intentional icon *or* action based on the two icons taken together. For example, the use, together, of the sight and the feel of the same object to produce a coordinated manipulation of it, granted that sight and touch yield intentional icons, involves an act of identifying, hence involves visual and tactual "representations." (I discuss the act of identifying below, but only as it pertains to indicative icons and inference.)

11 Could a bee, having watched dances of fellow bees showing nectar at two different locations relative to the hive, put these two dances together and fly directly from one of these locations to the other? In this unlikely event, bee dances would be representations.

12 For example, here is Fodor quoting Millikan (1991a): "'A second suggestion follows from the suggestion that representations are like maps' . . . Yeah, well. The last time I looked, the consensus was pretty general that picture theories of meaning had hopeless semantic indeterminacy problems of their own. (The relevant considerations have been common currency at least since Wittgenstein's *Investigations*; for discussion see *Language of Thought* . . ." (Fodor, 1991, p. 295). A discussion of the relevant considerations also introduced the theory of intentional icons in Millikan (1984, ch. 5). According to picture theories, that the represented is mapped by the representation in accordance with a rule is what *constitutes* the representation–represented relation; that is all this relation consists in. I assume that the reader too is acquainted with "the relevant considerations" that doom this view.

13 Sometimes people require recursivity for "compositionality." I suspect that recursivity is neither a pervasive nor a particularly important aspect of thought. It is not infinite productivity but productivity at all that matters.

14 The importance of the cooperating structures subject, predicate, negation, is examined in detail in Millikan (1984, chs 16–19).

15 I am assuming without argument a point on which Dennett and I agree. Belief-having creatures must make inferences. But in truth this is only a decision on the usefulness of a certain terminology. I have a botanist friend who claims to be trying to condition her venus flytraps. She whistles and stamps and then touches their traps whenever she enters the greenhouse, and she says that they close at her touch because they believe she's a fly. That then is a use of "believes" that is not just possible but actual, and who is to say it's not literal?

16 Compare Stich (1981) and Dennett, "Making Sense of Ourselves," and "Reflections: When Frogs (and Others) Make Mistakes" in Dennett, 1987.

17 See Dennett, "Beyond Belief," in Dennett, 1987, p. 148.

18 This is not intended as an argument for full determinacy of belief content. For example, malfunctions producing representations that are illegible to their own inner interpreters

certainly cause indeterminacy. And so does sufficient disruption of the systems responsible for "coidentifying," discussed below.

19 For discussion of this etiological principle in grouping words and other symbols into types, see Millikan (1984, ch. 3) and Kaplan (1990).

20 We could even tidy this up a bit by stipulating that the disruptions intended accord with normal functioning of the sensory and cognitive systems *as* such systems, that is, with competencies, thus relieving Quine's anxieties about the disruptive effect of various kinds of shock.

21 This point accords with Gareth Evans' "generality constraint" (Evans, 1982, p. 100; Millikan, 1993, and in press a). Ways of iterating grounded judgments containing a mental name may rest on understanding a public language. In Millikan (1984) I show how understanding a language is continuous with ordinary perception.

22 For more details, see (Millikan, in press a).

REFERENCES

Armstrong, D. M. (1968) *A Materialist Theory of the Mind.* London: Routledge.

Campbell, J. (1987–8) Is sense transparent? *Proceedings of the Aristotelian Society*, N. S. 88, 273–92.

Carroll, L. (1895) What the tortoise said to Achilles. *Mind.* Reprinted in I. M. Copi and J. A. Gould (eds), *Readings on Logic*, New York: MacMillan, 1964.

Dennett, D. C. (1978) *Brainstorms.* Montgomery, VT: Bradford Books.

Dennett, D. C. (1987) *The Intentional Stance.* Cambridge, Mass.: Bradford Books/MIT Press.

Dretske, F. (1981) *Knowledge and the Flow of Information.* Cambridge, Mass.: Bradford Books/MIT Press.

Dretske, F. (1986) Misrepresentation. In R. Bogdan (ed.), *Belief: Form, Content, and Function*, New York: Oxford, 17–36.

Evans, G. (1981) Understanding demonstratives. In H. Parrett and J. Bouveresse (eds), *Meaning and Understanding*, Berlin: deGruyter. Reprinted in Evans (1985).

Evans, G. (1982) *The Varieties of Reference.* Oxford: Clarendon Press.

Evans, G. (1985) *Collected Papers.* Oxford: Clarendon Press.

Fodor, J. A. (1991) Replies. In B. Loewer and G. Rey (eds), *Meaning in Mind: Fodor and his Critics.* Oxford: Blackwell.

Kaplan, D. (1990) Names. *Proceedings of the Aristotelian Society*, Suppl. Vol. 93–119.

Marr, D. (1982) *Vision.* San Francisco: W. H. Freeman and Co.

Millikan, R. G. (1984) *Language, Thought and other Biological Categories.* Cambridge, Mass.: Bradford Books/MIT Press.

Millikan R. G. (1991a) Compare and contrast Dretske, Fodor and Millikan on teleosemantics. *Philosophical Topics*, 18 (2), 151–61.

Millikan, R. G. (1991b) Speaking up for Darwin. In B. Loewer and G. Rey (eds), *Meaning in Mind: Fodor and his Critics.* Oxford: Blackwell, 151–64.

Millikan, R. G. (1991c) Perceptual content and Fregean myth. *Mind*, 100, 439–95.

Millikan, R. G. (1992) Explanation in biopsychology. In J. Heil and A. Mele (eds), *Mental Causation*, Oxford: Oxford University Press.

Millikan, R. G. (1993) Knowing what I'm thinking of. *Proceedings of the Aristotelian Society*, Suppl. Vol.

Millikan, R. G. (in press a) On unclear and indistinct ideas. In James Tomberlin (ed.), *Philosophical Perspectives*, vol. VII, Reseda, Calif.: Ridgeview Publishing.

Millikan, R. G. (in press b) The green grass growing all around. In R. G. Millikan, *White Queen Psychology and Other Essays for Alice*, Cambridge, Mass.: Bradford Books/MIT Press.

Quine, W. V. (1960) *Word and Object.* Cambridge, Mass.: MIT Press.

Shoemaker, S. (1975) Functionalism and qualia. *Philosophical Studies*, 27, 291–315.

Smart, J. J. C. (1975) On some criticisms of a physicalist theory of color. In Chung-yin-Chen (ed.), *Philosophical Aspects of the Mind-Body Problem*, Honolulu: University of Hawaii.

Stich, S. P. (1981) Dennett on intentional systems. *Philosophical Topics*, 12, 38–62.

7
What is it Like to be Boring and Myopic?

KATHLEEN AKINS

I see before me sitting on the laboratory bench a human brain – or rather a preserved human brain, readied for dissection, sporting a halo of straight pins and cheery red flags. I await the bell. When it rings, I will have one minute to identify whatever neuroanatomical structure is marked by the red flag bearing the numeral "8" – and around me stand thirty odd other students in front of "their" brains, similarly at the ready. Surveying the room, I cannot help but wonder: did any of these dear souls, whose brains now sit before us, ever foresee that one day *they* would be central players in this Kafka-esque scene?

Yet even as I ponder this question, I cannot quite grasp it. Looking at this very brain – cold, gray, and granular, stuck with pins and flags – it seems odd to think that *this* was once a *someone*, a thinking and feeling person. Stranger still to realize that there but for the grace of God go I, our roles reversed, this brain's and mine. I know, of course, that this is true. This brain was once very much a person and, in some sense, I as an experiencing subject, am just such a brain as well. Still, I cannot quite comprehend this fact. How exactly is it possible?

1 Resolving a Tension

The problem of consciousness, simply put, is that we cannot understand how a brain, *qua* gray, granular lump of biological matter, could be the seat of human consciousness, the source or ground of our rich and varied phenomenal lives. How could that "lump" be conscious – or, conversely, how could I, as conscious being, be that lump? Moreover, because we cannot comprehend how a brain can be conscious at all – *the very fact of physically embodied consciousness* – it makes little intuitive sense to think that any *particular* facts about the brain would prove helpful in this regard. We now know, for example, that the brain is not an amorphous mass but an entity of enormous physiological and anatomical complexity, that the human brain has (by a low estimate) 10^{12} neurons with an estimated 10^{15} connections running between them. This piece of knowledge, however, does not meet with our intuitive problem.

In virtue of learning that the brain is quite complex, we do not thereby understand how the brain could be conscious. Similarly, if it were discovered that the human brain has certain unique functional properties (say, a capacity for self-referential reflection) or that a certain kind of neural event occurs only during episodes of awareness (perhaps the synchronous firing of neurons in the visual areas of the brain in response to visual stimulation) these would be intriguing discoveries. *But they would not dispel our sense of mystery.* How could these neural events, no matter how unusual or unique, bring about phenomenal experience? Physiological facts and the puzzle of consciousness seem to pass each other by. This is one side of the story, the problem of consciousness as portrayed by common intuition.

On the other side of the story, we, in our various materialist guises, believe that science must surely tell us *something* about consciousness. Granting the tenet that the mind *is* the brain, it surely follows that many facts about the brain are also facts about conscious experience. Moreover, there are certain cases in which purely physiological facts *do* seem to give us insight into the experience of other subjects. For example, because we know that the retinal cells of the macaque monkey are insensitive to light in the infra-red range, we think it unlikely that these mammals experience any visual phenomena resulting from perceived infra-red light. Just as we *Homo sapiens* cannot see the infra-red light, we can be relatively certain that the macaque's visual experience does not contain episodes of this type. Similarly, when we realize that certain species of animals do not have the kind of retinal receptors necessary for trichromatic color vision, we no longer attribute to them visual perceptions of a "colored" world – perceptions, say, of the red, pink and orange hues of the setting sun.[1] Scientific facts, it seems, *can* tell us something about conscious experience, although exactly what science can say is not clear.

It is this tension, between our inability to comprehend how a material brain can be conscious at all (and hence to understand how physical facts could give us insight into phenomenal experience) and the realization that facts about consciousness both ought to be, and to some extent *seem* to be, accessible from the natural sciences, that is reflected in Nagel's work on consciousness (1979a, 1986). In his famous article "What Is It Like to Be a Bat?," that is, Nagel's primary concern was with the first side of this tension: he sought to justify our intuitive sense of mystery by drawing a distinction between objective and subjective facts. Roughly speaking, objective facts are those with which science is concerned: the way things are in themselves, a way that is independent of our (or any other subject's) perceptions of them. Thus to give an objective or scientific characterization of an event is to transcend its mere appearance, to abstract away from how the event is perceived given the particularities of the individual observer (e.g. where the individual stands relative to the event observed) and of the type of perceptual process used (e.g. human vision). The essential property of an objective characterization, says Nagel, is thus not intersubjectivity *per se* but externality or detachment: "the attempt is made to view the world not from a place within it, or from the vantage point of a special type of life and awareness, but from nowhere in particular and no form of life in particular" (Nagel, 1979b, p. 208).

In contrast, subjective facts – facts about phenomenology, conscious experience, "what it is like" for a certain creature – are essentially tied to a point of view. Unlike, say, the phenomenon of lightning, which has both an objective nature that can be apprehended from many different points of view (i.e. as a sudden discharge of electrical energy) as well as a subjective one (its appearance *to us* as a blinding flash), conscious experience admits of no distinction between its appearance and the experience in and of itself. Conscious experience exists *as* appearance and hence as an appearance *to* some subject. (Says Nagel, 1979a, p. 173: "It is difficult to understand what could be meant by the *objective* character of an experience, apart from the particular point of view from which its subject apprehends it. After all, what would be left of what it was like to be a bat if one removed the viewpoint of the bat?") Of course, if, as Nagel claims, there is no objective nature to phenomenal experience – nothing that can be observed from several different points of view – then it is clear why the third person perspective of science is of little help in understanding phenomenal experience. Says Nagel, "any shift to greater objectivity – that is, less attachment to a specific viewpoint – does not take us nearer to the real nature of the phenomenon: it takes us farther away from it" (Nagel, 1979a, p. 174)[2]

The other side of the tension – the conviction that science *can* explain certain aspects of consciousness – surfaces in Nagel's suggestion about an "objective phenomenology." Perhaps, ventures Nagel, there might be properties of phenomenal experience that admit of scientific or objective scrutiny. On the face of it, of course, this is a very odd position for Nagel to advance: how could there be a third-person understanding of that which admits of only first-person experience? It was, after all, this very property of the subjective, its existence as appearance, that was to explain why we cannot comprehend embodied consciousness.

In explaining an "objective phenomenology," Nagel puts forward two different ways to incorporate the results of science. First, in "What Is It Like to Be a Bat?," he speaks of the "structural features" of our perceptions, presumably in contrast with their qualitative or intrinsic properties. If we could provide a description of these structural properties, Nagel says, then some kind of neurophysiological or reductive account might then be given.[3] (For example, one might give a description of the *logical* space of colors and then map that logical space onto a scheme for its physical realization, say as in Paul Churchland's (1989) color state space.) In *The View from Nowhere*, however, the project is a bit different: by abstracting away from the particular features of the human experience, we are to derive a conception of a point of view that, while still essentially perspectival, admits of many different instantiations. What we want to construct, in other words, is a general description – a picture of what it *is* to have a point of view, whether one's own or that of the bat.

Note that, on either conception, an objective phenomenology is intended only to give science its rightful due, *not* to entirely bridge the gap between the objective and subjective. No matter how far advanced, says Nagel, an objective phenomenology will always leave something out, namely the "particularity" or "specific qualities" of an individual's experience. *That* we could never comprehend. So it is this promise of a permanent explanatory gap that is intended to reconcile an objective phenomenology with the special nature of conscious experience. Some aspects of conscious experience must forever lie beyond our grasp.

The problem Nagel's view encounters in making room for scientific explanation – its apparent inconsistency – arises, I think, from the very nature of his task. Confronted with the tension between two prima facie competing intuitions, Nagel *begins* with a justification of our sense of puzzlement, with a general argument about the limits of scientific knowledge. Consider, however, exactly what this would require, the demands of the project. On the one hand, in order to justify the essential mysteriousness of consciousness, the theory must show that the mystery is, *in principle*, one that science could never diffuse. It must give us good reasons to believe that there are some facts about conscious experience that will remain inaccessible to scientific investigation. On the other hand, in protecting such facts from scientific scrutiny, the theory must be careful not to deny the explanatory contributions science *can* make, the very insights scientific investigation will provide. What the theory must justify, in other words, is a certain principled divide – between those facts about consciousness that will be accessible to science (and hence human understanding), and those that will not.

Part of the problem with establishing such a divide is just that science itself has little to offer, at least not by way of present evidence for the broad negative claim. That is, in order to establish that certain properties of phenomenal experience would still be unexplained even with all the possible scientific evidence in hand, one would need, at the very least, a small but representative subset of data on which to draw. But the sciences that seem likely to shed light on the nature of consciousness (neurophysiology, neuroethology, neuroanatomy, and the like) are still in their infant states: they have yet to produce anything like a "complete" body of data on any species whose members are vaguely plausible candidates for conscious experience. (Surely neither the sea slug nor the leech!) So to date, we have not been in a position to judge – not even in a single case – what kinds of facts about conscious experience withstand empirical investigation and what kind do not. Such a divide must be discerned, then, on *a priori* grounds.

What, then, are the problems of an *a priori* argument? A theory that attempts to delineate what we can and cannot know about phenomenal experiences must inevitably take sides on any number of fundamental philosophical issues. It will necessarily prove to be (what one might call) "metaphysically expensive." Looking back at Nagel's theory, for example, the reader is asked to grant the following: the distinction between objective and subjective facts (as opposed to objective and subjective *descriptions* of the world), a characterization of science as trying to obtain a non-perspectival, sense-independent account of the physical world (a characterization that seems dubious for the sciences at issue, namely for biology, neurophysiology, neuroethology), the assimilation of phenomenal experience or "what it is like" with having "a point of view" (a pivotal notion that is left largely undischarged). The point here is not that only a conservative philosophy will do – on the contrary. Rather, the point is that, if progress can be made without the requirement of characterizing the nature of scientific practice, our knowledge of the world, the nature of the phenomenal realm, and so on, then *that* would be the more plausible strategy to adopt. Perhaps, for the present, we should simply set aside our puzzlement about how physically embodied consciousness is possible and approach the problem from the other side.

The strategy of this paper is to take the other route available: to follow our suspicion that science has something to say, and to simply ask what that might be. If one examined an admittedly incomplete body of scientific data – in this case, all the available literature on the neurophysiology and behavior of the bat – what would we learn about this particular case? What would we come to know about a bat's phenomenal experience – what it is like to be a bat – and what would we understand about phenomenal experience in general? The alternative route, in other words, is to accept Nagel's challenge – to pursue an "objective phenomenology" whatever that turns out to be – to see how much we can learn about the phenomenal world of the bat.[4]

The advantage thereby gained is that we can avoid, at least temporarily, the metaphysical entanglements to which the more *a priori* approach is prone. For example, there is no need to discern the nature of scientific practice as a whole, in order to draw any conclusions about the particular case at hand, the phenomenology of the bat. We can simply *use* the results of science as given. Similarly, we can remain agnostic about the existence and character of any explanatory "gap" and concentrate upon what *can* be known, given the evidence currently available. And, finally, this empirical route allows us to investigate the kind of undischarged notions that often arise in discussions of human consciousness: for our purposes, Nagel's notions of a "point of view," the "structural" and "qualitative" features of conscious experience, "subjective" and "objective" facts and so on. In other words, the strategy allows us to see how these abstract notions meet with the concrete case, and to ask whether they hold up to the explanatory task. These are the theoretical advantages of the strategy. Now let us turn to the bats.

2   The Informational Problem: The Auditory World

When we think about the sonar system of bats – not about "what it is like," phenomenologically, to have echo location but rather about the information-processing task that is performed by the sonar system – the temptation is to think of sonar perception as being somehow similar to human vision.[5] Since the early 1930s, when Donald Griffin first thought to plug the ears of a bat, we have known that the bat's self-produced cries and its auditory system are essential to its perception of the external world: without its ears for guidance, the bat flies about, colliding at random with various objects.[6] For the airborne bat, echo location is a primary means of spatial perception. Hence it is natural to think that the information that the bat gains through auditory processing is probably very similar to what we obtain by visual means. What the bats' ears do for them, our eyes do for us. Richard Dawkins in *The Blind Watchmaker* provides a good illustration of this intuitive view. In describing the bat's sonar system, he writes:

> [the bat] uses sound to perceive, and continuously update its perception of, the position of objects in three-dimensional space, just as we use light. The type of internal model that it needs, therefore, is one suitable for the internal representation of the changing positions of objects in three-dimensional space . . . Bats and we *need* the same kind of internal model . . . The fact that bats construct their internal model with the aid of echoes, while we construct ours with the aid of light, is irrelevant. (Dawkins, 1986, p. 34)

In other words, the intuitive view starts with an assumption about human vision, namely that its central task (although probably not its only one) is the perception of objects in three-dimensional space. Roughly speaking, light from a source (the sun or an artificial source) falls upon objects in the world and is reflected and absorbed by those opaque surfaces; then, via that reflection, some of this light arrives at our eyes, producing an image on the back of the retina. From there, the task of the visual system is a kind of "reconstruction." It tries to figure out, from the properties of the retinal image (plus, presumably, some tacit assumptions about the nature of the world), what the world is like – the nature of the environmental surfaces from which the light was originally reflected – and from there, the shape, location, and identity of any objects within the visual field.[7] (This is a view of vision that is more or less in accord with our understanding of ourselves: with what we think we see, when we stand with our eyes open, surveying the world.) The second premise of the intuitive view is simply that, because the bat also requires spatial perception to maneuver about the world, it too must have a sensory system concerned with the location and identification of the world's furniture. Here, it is the bat's own sonar signal that is reflected from the distal objects, and hence, the auditory system that must discern the various properties of any objects within the sonar field.

No one, I take it, would want to claim that bat audition is *exactly* like human vision – that it performs precisely the same information tasks. Based upon only the crudest of considerations, namely the size of the bat's brain (the size of an aspirin tablet!), it seems clear that there must be *some* disparity between the computational powers of the two neural systems. And given this disparity, there are probably many aspects of human visual processing that are not tractable given the bat's limited computational space. Something must be given up. So, what the bat must have, most people would probably say, is some kind of "downgraded" version of the human visual process. Perhaps it is a system that yields an "image" that has less spatial acuity than our own (like the difference between, say, a sharp photograph and one that is out of focus), or less detail (the difference between a photograph and a sketch of the same scene), or perhaps with a narrower field of "view" (like a picture taken through a keyhole instead of through the "wide-angle lens" of human vision), or . . . . Still, it seems plausible that the purpose of the bat's audition is object perception, the construction of representations of the shape, location, and category of objects in three-dimensional space.

When one stops to think about it, however, there is something very puzzling about this claim, something about the bat that requires explanation. Look around you. Among all the fuzzy (and not so fuzzy) creatures both vertebrate and invertebrate that inhabit the earth, the bat is a rarity.[8] Even for nocturnal species, evolution has "chosen" vision as the primary system of spatial perception. Most nocturnal animals (think here of the cat family, of owls, and rodents) have specialized visual systems to guide their activity in the dark – to detect prey, to maneuver about, to obtain information about the distal environment. Bats, on the other hand, rely upon sonar navigation in their nocturnal flights: while they also have eyes – they are not blind even if somewhat myopic[9] – they use audition as a central means of spatial perception. So why, one ought to ask, are bats so unusual? All things being equal – if sound and light were equally suited to the task of spatial perception – one would expect to find as many species adapted for echolocation as for vision. There must be some *reason*, then, why the bats are such an anomaly of adaptation. Thus, before we simply assimilate the function of the bat's auditory system to the human visual system, we need to solve this puzzle – to ask about *spatial perception* through *auditory* processing in the *bat*. We need to find out about the specific problems that arise in using sound (as opposed to light) to gain spatial information and about the kinds of spatial information the bat's behavioral repertoire requires.

Begin, then, by adopting the physicist's view of the world, a world that is not inhabited by the human ontology of middle-sized objects, of tables and chairs, but by more basic "furniture" and its interactions – the properties of sound and light, the variety of mediums they might pass through, the kinds of surface properties sound and light make contact with, and so on. Given this starting point, consider what the world of sound is like, how it differs from the visual world, and the informational problems inherent in auditory spatial perception in virtue of those properties.[10]

Most obviously, sound and light are quite different commodities. Light is electromagnetic energy, the narrow section of the electromagnetic spectrum between about 380 and 780 nanometers in wavelength, to which human visual receptors are responsive. It can be interpreted as either a transverse waveform or as a stream of photons, depending upon the phenomenon to be explained. In virtue of these properties, it is easy to see why light (on earth) makes a good source of spatial information.

For one, the sun provides a single light source that is reflected and absorbed by surfaces in the environment. The sun produces, as it were, a "bath" of light particles that surrounds the objects of the world, one that is directed and predictable in its spectral properties. Moreover, within the spectral range of electromagnetic radiation to which mammalian eyes are receptive, there are very few natural phenomena or objects that self-produce light that can interfere with the sun's illumination (fire and luminescent organisms being notable exceptions). The pattern and spectral characteristics of the light that reaches the receptors, then, can be used for, among other things, discerning object shape and texture (from shading information given the directedness of sunlight) and material composition (using the spectral composition of the reflected light).

Secondly, because light has such short wavelengths, in the nanometer range, it will be reflected by even very small objects, thus rendering them visible to the observer. Short wavelengths also guarantee a minimum of diffusion – the scattering of light – except under those conditions when the air itself is filled with small particles, say, in a fog or in a dust storm.

Thirdly, given the organic building blocks widely provided by nature, the development of a receptor for light is a fairly small investment, neurologically/ evolutionarily speaking. There are many organic molecules that are sensitive to (change their shape in response to) electromagnetic radiation, thereby providing the first link in an electrochemical neural system.

Finally, the wave property of light allows light to be easily focused through a lens or small hole. This latter property is extremely important for spatial perception because it allows the position of the light receptor to receive information about the spatial position of the light source. In the normal course of events, that is, a receptor embedded into a flat surface receives light travelling towards it from all directions (except from behind it); so the receptor response does not indicate the angular direction of the light source. The addition of a lens (or a pinhole opening), however, eliminates this problem: light travelling through a lens in a straight line must fall in a specific spot given the lens properties. Thus the spatial position of the receptor indicates the spatial position of the light source in the visual field. What is important here is that this simple informational relation can easily be taken advantage of by even the most neurologically simple organism. For example, the proverbial "fly detector" of the frog is a retinal ganglion cell activated by any small circular area of neural activation that moves across the retinal receptors; a looming shadow or predator detector can be made by monitoring the retina for any areas of "darkness" (lack of activity) that grow rapidly larger (a pattern that occurs when a large creature looms closer) and so on. Importantly, this simple correlation – between the position of the retinal receptor and the position of light source in the world – is an easy source of spatial information (position and depth plus shape) as well as of (rough) object categorization. When the fly goes by, that is, the frog "knows" where to swipe with his tongue as well as that he ought to.

Sound, on the other hand, makes for a fairly messy world. Unlike light, sound is vibration that originates with the deformation of an elastic solid (e.g. a tuning fork) and then propagates through a medium (such as air) in longitudinal waves. (The vibrations to which the human ear is sensitive are long compression waves with frequencies between 20 and 20,000 hertz.) The first problem, then, is that sound does not originate, like most natural light, from one reliable, principal source – there is no analogous homogeneous "bath" of sound that surrounds minute objects on the earth's surface.[11] For example, stop right now and concentrate on the many sounds occurring in the room around you. Even in a deserted and seemingly quiet office, I can now hear the hum of the air conditioning, a telephone ringing one floor above, a chirping bird outside my window, the computer's fan, rustling noises as I shift in my seat, etc. There is, when one stops to listen, an entire world of sound – sounds emanating from multiple directions, of numerous frequencies and intensities, that come into being each time an appropriate deformation occurs.[12] One consequence of this is that an organism that uses sound to retrieve spatial information must actively produce its own sound instead of relying on a passive receptive system, in order to ensure the kind of constant and predictable sound signal from which spatial information can be discerned. (Think here of an underground miner, finding his way around with only a head lamp for illumination.) Moreover, the organism must send a sound signal *out* to the environment and then wait to receive it *back*. Finally, the organism also faces numerous problems of interference from all the sounds that fall within the sensitivity range of its receptors – from random background noises and the signals of conspecifics in close roosting quarters, plus interference from its very own signals (one hears, as it were, the sound on the way out, as well as on the way back). These are all problems that need solution.

Secondly, because the propagation of sound waves involves the vibration of a medium, an actual movement of mass, sound waves have a high absorption rate – one that depends upon the nature of the medium, and the intensity and wavelength of the signal. Short wavelength (high-frequency) signals and low-intensity signals are most easily absorbed by a medium of propagation; longer wavelengths and high-intensity signals fare better. What this means then is that the frequency characteristics of the signal, plus an organism's ability to alter the intensity of the sound, will have a significant effect on the range over which a sonar signal can travel and on the nature of the echoes that return. (If one projected, say, a signal containing a number of different frequencies at a uniform intensity, one could loose, through absorption, all the high-frequency information in the returning signal.) So, what goes around, comes around. The characteristics of the signal that the organism sends out will determine, in part, the kind of signal that the organism gets back.

Thirdly, sound vibrations, given their comparatively long wavelengths, are subject to high diffraction and diffusion. They bend around barriers instead of bouncing off them, they disperse in random directions (in fact, given a smooth enough surface, the scattering will be so complete as to make the barrier "invisible" to an echo-locating system – the auditory equivalent of glass). This is a fact that has a number of consequences for spatial processing, most of which are not particularly good. On the positive side, sound, unlike light, can travel around corners. One can hear what one cannot see, certainly an advantage for avoiding predators or tracking prey. On the down side, there seems to be no simple or informationally *immediate* way to precisely discern the spatial location of a sound source given the signal. For one, it is no simple task to focus a sound signal, the way a lens or pinhole can focus light.[13] Given a small aperture, for example, sound waves simply bend as they pass through the opening. Thus, when sound waves enter the ear, squeezing through the narrow canal opening, they diffract in all directions. Where a sound wave lands, once in the ear, gives no immediate information about where in the external world it originated from. Hence, unlike the retina, on which the position of an active receptor correlates with a position of the light source in visual space, auditory receptors do not yield immediate spatial information. Such data must be extracted by neural computation, based upon other features of the auditory signal.

High diffraction is also problematic because it tends to hinder echo formation. In order for a wave to be reflected from a target, its wavelength must be smaller than the size of that object (or, given that most objects are not spherical, smaller than the leading edge of the object). This makes life difficult for an organism that preys on small flying insects. One might think the trick would be to use sonar signals with a very short wavelength, so that they will be reflected by even the smallest objects. But the problem is that short wavelength signals do not make good travellers – even at high intensity, short wavelength sound waves are easily absorbed by the atomsphere. So, the selection of any particular broadcasting frequency will always involve a trade-off between range (how far the signal can travel) and "grain" (the spatial resolution that will be possible given the size of the objects that reflect the sound wave). There is no one signal frequency, even at high intensity, that will provide fine spatial information for small distant objects.

Fourthly, the type of medium that carries a sound wave vibration makes a difference to the signal, to its velocity of propagation. (This is the principle behind ultrasound.) For example, the velocity of sound through dry air at STP is 331.4 meters per second, in sea water it is 1,540 meters per second, and in fresh water, the velocity of sound is 1,401 meters per second. In this respect, sound does not differ from light. Indeed, this is the very fact about light that allows it to be focused by a lens: the "inner" edge of the light wave strikes the lens surface and slows, while the "outer" edge continues at its airborne velocity until it makes contact with the lens, thus causing the light to bend towards the slower moving side. (Think here of a treaded army tank, moving along in a straight line, when suddenly it hits a patch of mud with one tread.) For sound, however, this same property has none of the beneficial consequences, at least for the average small creature (see note 13 above). Moreover, if a sound signal is to be used for fine-grained information about range –

i.e. a calculation of the distance to an object based upon the time that it takes for the echo to return – any change in the medium of propagation must be considered. In this particular case, the case of bats, changes in air pressure, temperature and in humidity (say, if there is rain or fog) will affect the signals of bats that prey on airborne insects (such as moths), while bats that hunt for fish (by flying over the surface of the water and using sonar to detect fish just under the surface) must contend with signals that use dual mediums, water and air.[14] One can see, now, why evolution failed to fasten upon sound as its central strategy for spatial perception: compared to the relative compliancy of light, sound presents many problems.[15] The question about the bat's auditory function, then, is this: how does the bat overcome the inherent difficulties of this information-processing problem? What is the strategy that makes tractable, in only a bat-size brain, the extraction of spatial information from sound?

3 The Behavioral Strategy and the Signal Characteristics

The central strategy used to extract spatial information from sonar signals by echo-locating bats is the parallel sequencing of signals and behavior: the signal characteristics of the bat's outgoing cry are matched to the informational require-ments of each stage of the bat's behavioral sequence. The bat's present behavior and its perceived state of the world, in other words, determine the kind of cry it makes, and this affects the type of information received in response. As a consequence of actively producing the sonar signal, what the bat *says* will determine, in no small part, what it *hears*.

The Behavioral Strategy

Across all species of echo-locating bats (and there are quite a number of different species, exemplifying a variety of sonar systems), sonar is used primarily during the pursuit of prey: in order to locate and track insects, moths, and other airborne prey, or to catch a fish swimming just beneath the surface (Simmons, 1989). Moreover, the behavior of each of these species during "the hunt" follows a similar pattern: initially the bat flies around *searching* for something of interest, say by flying around in the open air and "looking for" insects (the Search phase); then, once some prey is located, the bat must approach the insect and track it until the bat gets close enough to grab it (the Approach and Tracking phase); finally, once the prey is within reach, the bat must somehow make the final approach and get the insect into its mouth (the Terminal phase) (Griffin et al., 1960). Each of these stages of behavior (for any species) follows a fairly set routine (altered, of course, to fit the specific movements of the prey in each case). For example, the Little Brown bat (*Myotis lucifugus*), as it enters the Terminal phase of pursuit, often uses a somersault maneuver to grab the prey, a moth or, as in figure 7.1 a mealworm tossed into the air by the experimenters. The bat makes the final approach in such a way that its wing makes contact with the moth/mealworm. It then hits the mealworm with its wing, while somersaulting backwards, catching the prey in its tail pouch. And finally – dinner! – it bends over and eats the mealworm. The Little Brown bat also uses a number of alternative Terminal techniques: "the mouth catch" and "the tail membrane catch"

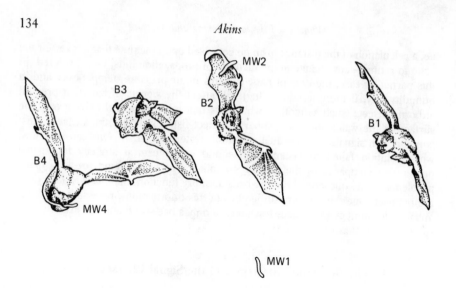

Figure 7.1 The filmed sequence of the Little Brown bat using a somersault technique to capture a mealworm. The sequence progresses from right to left, with the bat marked B1 and the mealworm MW1. (Reproduced with permission from Camhi, 1984; taken from Webster and Griffin, 1962.)

are two examples (Webster and Griffin, 1962; Webster and Durlach, 1963; Webster and Brazier, 1968). This is the standard behavioral pattern of the hunting bat – a stereotypic sequence of activities performed over and over again. Hence, the "boring" bat.

The Signal Sequence

During each of these three hunting phases, the bat's sonar signal is altered to meet the informational needs of the moment. What, then, are the sonar characteristics and how do they change with the behavioral sequence? First, the general properties of the sonar signal.

There are two signal types, CF and FM signals The two kinds of sonar signals used by bats are *constant frequency* (CF) signals, in which the cry is broadcast at one unchanging frequency or unchanging frequency combination, and *frequency modulated* (FM) signals that involve a "sweep" through a range of frequencies, starting with the highest "note" and progressing down through a series of signals to the lowest frequency sound. The constant frequency signal is ideally suited to measuring the *relative velocity* of the bat and its prey using the phenomenon of Doppler shift. This is the phenomenon whereby the frequency of the sound increases when the source and the observer are moving towards each other (a positive relative velocity), and decreases when the source and observer move apart (a negative relative velocity). (Thus the familiar sound of a train as it approaches the railway crossing and then crosses and travels away – a high pitch growing louder followed by a low one becoming softer.) Relative velocity is calculated by comparing the frequency of the outgoing signal (the *broadcast frequency*) with the frequency of the echo – a calculation that is made easy by the unchanging frequency of the CF sonar cry. The FM signal, on the other hand, is better suited to determining fine-grained *range* information, the *distance* to the target calculated by measuring the time between the outgoing cry and the echo's return (how long the echo takes reflects how far the sound has traveled). In an FM signal, each specific frequency marks a distinct place within the sweep, such that it can be used as a timing marker for the outgoing and incoming cries. The first occurrence of a certain frequency in the cry can serve to "start the timer," as it were, while the next occurrence of that frequency in the echo "stops the clock."[16] In this way, fine-grained timing information is possible.

FM and CF signals contain harmonics   When a bat emits a CF or FM signal it contains a fundamental frequency plus two or three harmonics.[17] This means that the frequency range of the signal – and hence its informational value – is greatly broadened. It gives the bat the best of both worlds: high-frequency sounds for more fine-grained spatial information about near objects and lower-frequency signals for coarse-grained information about more distant ones. Moreover, by selectively altering the intensity of the various harmonics (the "loudness" of the parts of the cry), the bat can "focus" the signal towards specific aspects of the environment (e.g. by putting energy into the higher harmonics, the return signal will contain more information about the texture of a close object). Actually, this makes the situation sound better than it is, for despite this widening of the frequency range by the use of harmonics and even though the sound is emitted at the deafening intensity of about 100 decibels, the bat's sonar signal still cannot travel very far. Even on a good day – when there is low humidity and an uncluttered field of "view" – even when the lowest harmonics are intensified, the bat is rather myopic: the furthest that most bats can "see" is about 3 meters.

The type of signal used is species-specific   Both the CF and FM signals are used alone and in combination, the species of bat determining the basic type of signal used. There are numerous species of bats, living in diverse environments, pursuing a variety of prey. Some species hunt for insects in dense forests, while others forage in the open air; the diet of bats ranges from nectar and fruit, to insects, small vertebrates (such as reptiles and rats), and surface-feeding fish (Schnitzler and Henson, 1980). Compare the informational requirements of these diverse "life-styles," e.g. the sort of motion analysis required to intercept a fluttering moth with the requisite pattern analysis of waves on a lake's surface needed to locate a surfacing fish; or the demands of high-speed navigation through a tangle of branches in pursuit of an insect as compared to the far less hairy demands of searching above an open field for a moth. Thus one finds species of bats that have FM signals, others with CF signals, and other species that use a combination signal, a long CF signal followed by a short FM "tail." For example, the Little Brown bat, *Myotis lucifugus*, which catches insects in the open air, has an FM cry; the Mustached bat, *Pteronotus parnelli*, which pursues insects in dense vegetation, emits a CF-FM cry (the CF component is thought useful in identifying a fluttering moth against the high background clutter of the vegetation); and the fish-catching bat,

Noctilio leporinus, uses a CF and CF-FM signal while searching for prey (presumably for detecting surface ripples) and an FM signal for pursuit (Suga, 1990).

These are the general characteristics of the bat's sonar signals. When a particular bat approaches a target, as I said above, it changes its sonar signal in response to the phase of the pursuit, but exactly what changes are made and what are their consequences? In what follows we will look at the Mustached bat, *Pteronotus parnelli*, that emits a combination CF-FM signal, and examine the changes to its signal throughout its hunt. (Much of the material that follows is drawn from Schnitzler and Henson, 1980.)

The search phase As the Mustached bat flies around searching for an edible insect, it emits a rapid sequence of short signals known as "chirps." In the search phase, these chirps are emitted at a relatively slow rate 8–12 chirps per second. During this time, the CF-FM signal has a long CF component and a short FM tail. The fundamental frequency is just under 30 kHz, but the second harmonic, at about 59.5 kHz, receives the most energy. Thus, as a low-frequency signal, the cry is biased towards information about distant objects – what one would expect during the search phase.[18]

The approach phase Once an insect comes into "view," the Mustached bat points its head at the target, directing its cry, and follows its prey. As it does so, its cry alters along a number of dimensions. For one, the bat increases the number of chirps (short cries) per second in inverse proportion to the distance to the target – the closer the bat gets, the more frequently it chirps. Thus, as the bat closes in on its target, the signals become more physically dense – and presumably informationally rich as well. For another, the composition of the CF-FM signal changes: the CF component is shortened in length and the FM "sweep" is broadened, passing through a wider range of frequencies. In effect this shifts the informational focus of the signal. The signal becomes better suited to the extraction of fine-grained information about distance and texture (Simmons et al., 1975) but less well suited to information about velocity. Thirdly, the bulk of the signal's energy, which in the search phase resided in the second harmonic, is now shifted to the third and fourth harmonics. This means that it is the high-frequency sounds – those signals that have high spatial resolution but that travel only short distances – that are emphasized. In this way the content of the echo quickly shifts to fine-grained spatial information about nearby objects.

The approach phase also sees a change in the broadest frequency. As the bat makes progress towards its prey and as its relative velocity increases, the sonar echo comes back at a *higher* frequency (the Doppler effect). In response, the bat *lowers* its outgoing call (this is known as Doppler compensation), and by lowering the cry, the echo always returns with a frequency (for the second harmonic) at or slightly above 61.0 kHz. So no matter how quickly the bat overtakes its prey, the frequency of the signal remains almost constant. On the other hand, if the frequency of the cry comes back substantially *lower* than broadcast frequency, the Mustached bat does *not* respond with an increase in frequency. (The bat lowers its voice, as it were, but never raises it.) Evolution, it seems, has determined that anything that flies faster than the bat – that gets away from it – is probably not catchable. (Or for that matter, edible!) So it does not pay to track those objects with a negative relative velocity.

The terminal phase In the last stages of the pursuit, as the bat slows down to approach the insect and grab it, it emits a rapid burst of shortened chirps, up to 100 per second in the Mustached bat. These are cries that consist almost entirely of a brief FM tail. As soon as the prey is captured, the signals entirely cease.

While this gives the general sequence for the progression of the signal throughout the hunt, it should be noted that, within this basic framework, the bat adjusts its signal to the situation at hand. For example, if the moth makes a number of evasive movements and manages to lose the bat briefly, the approach phase continues until once again the bat has its prey almost within reach. Or if, at the last moment, the moth side-steps the bat, either the rapid chirps of the terminal phase continue or else its signals might revert back to those of the approach phase. Moreover, the Mustached bat also tailors its signal to the *kind* of objects/targets approached. Bats then, while they have stereotypic behaviors and signal sequences, are not genuinely "boring," for they adapt their signals and behavior to the situation at hand.

Sender/Receiver Properties

Like any well-engineered system, there is a symbiotic relationship between the properties of the bat's sonar signals and the properties of the mechanisms that receive them. The bat's auditory system, in other words, is such that the transduction/sensory mechanisms "match" the sonar signals: they act as signal filters to either reduce the noise in the known incoming signal or to "shape" those sounds in some other beneficial way. In this way many of the problems inherent in the sound world begin to find solution, right at the transduction level or in the initial sensory steps. The following are some examples of these sender/receiver compatibilities.

1 When the bat tracks its prey, say a moth fluttering in front of it, the bat follows the prey with its nose. It directs its sonar signal in a high-frequency, intense and directed beam towards the moth, keeping the signal aimed on its prey throughout the moth's evasive movements, with the beam firmly focused just *below* the midline of the target. Given the way the bat's vocal system is constructed, this small sound field, focused upon the moth, has a center circular region of high sound intensity plus midlobes on either side of softer sounds (Figure 7.2A). When this signal is received back by the bat, the sound field is filtered first by the bat's outer ears or pinnae. The low-intensity "lobes" around the circular area of the sound fields are absorbed by the ears, leaving only the circular region of sound, rather like the visual field (only smaller) of a single eye (Grinnel and Schnitzler, 1977; Schnitzler and Grinnel, 1977). At the mid-brain level of sensory reception this signal is further refined. Here the receiver is maximally sensitive to signals returning just *above* the midline (Henze and O'Neill, 1990). This serves to balance the skewed sender properties so that the sound field becomes, in effect, a circular region with the highest intensity sounds directly in the middle, with decreasing concentric regions (Figure 7.2B). Filtering at the mid-brain also changes the composition of this sound field. The neurons of the mid-brain area are tuned such that sharp borders between the rings of decreasing intensity are produced. In effect, the sound field is now a circular region, the central area of highest intensity being focused upon the moth, with sharp concentric regions of decreasing intensity. The bat thus achieves its own

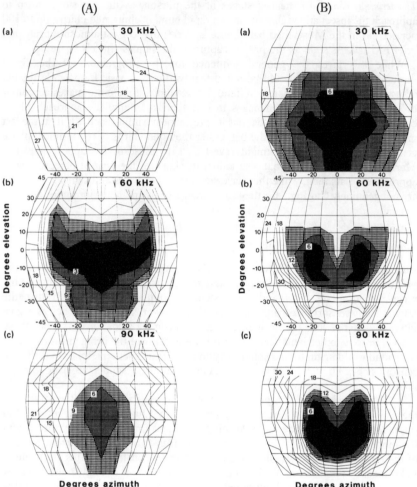

Figure 7.2 (A) The sound patterns of the emission signal measured at the fundamental frequency, (a) 30 kHz, (b) 60 kHz, and (c) 90 kHz. (B) A projection of sound contours for the combined emission and reception of the sonar system. (Adapted with permission from Henze and O'Neill, 1991.)

private version of our public "sun" – a directed "flashlight" beam of sound with uniform "spectral" and intensity properties.

2 The basilar membrane in the inner ear of the bat (the transduction mechanism) is selectively tuned to – most sensitive to – the second harmonic of the echo, to returning sounds somewhere between 61.0 and 61.5 kHz. It is least sensitive to frequencies around (and below) 59.5 kHz or the second harmonic of the vocalization, the resting broadcast frequency. Exactly which frequencies are filtered

or enhanced is a function of the individual bat: the basilar membrane is "personalized" to accommodate the slightly different broadcasting frequency of each individual. Like us, a bat has its own distinct voice (and, yes, on the whole, male bats have the lower voices) (Suga et al., 1987). As a result of these factors, the basilar membrane serves to filter out the sound of the bat's cry (below 60 kHz) and selectively enhances the echo of its own voice as it bounces back from distal objects. Thus the bat reduces interference from its own voice and from the cries of others.

3   Although the basilar membrane acts as a selective filter, this alone could not solve the interference problem. The Mustached bat, as I said earlier, issues a deafening cry – at its most intense – at about 100 decibels. (By way of contrast, this is louder than a symphony orchestra, about the same as a rock concert or the pounding of a jack hammer, and somewhat quieter than a jet engine.) Needless to say, this is a difficult interference problem: one cannot solve the problem by having an insensitive receiver, transducer neurons that respond only to sounds above 100 decibels, for this would create a bat that was "blind" to everything but its own voice (the echo always returns at a diminished amplitude)! Nor given the frequency similarity of the outgoing and incoming signals, would a "notch" filter be physically feasible. Rather, some sort of "intermittent" mechanism is needed, one that works during the production of the cry. This is, in fact, the sort of mechanism in play. The middle-ear muscles contract in tandem with the call, effectively blocking the tympanic membrane during that time. In effect, the bat is intermittently deaf but it enables the bat to process the signals returning from the world. It should be noted, however (the reasons for this will soon be made clear), that the middle-ear muscles take time to relax. After the chirp is complete, there is a period of 5–8 ms during which the muscles relax back to their uncontracted state (Henson, 1970; Suga and Jen, 1975).

4   The Beginnings of Subjectivity

Out of the physicist's view of the auditory world, the bat's signal characteristics and its sender/receiver properties, the "subjective world" of the Mustached bat, begins to emerge. We can see how the informational character of the signal changes over the course of the hunt and start to understand what that probably means for the bat's auditory experience. More specifically, at this stage, without access to most of the details of how the bat processes the neural signals, several strong negative constraints can be discerned: we can infer, with fair reliability, what information the bat lacks given the properties of the physical world and the signals produced. For example, if we know that a sound signal with a certain frequency F can travel only about 6 feet, then we know that an echo of frequency F does not provide any information about objects at a distance of greater than 3 feet (i.e. 6 feet there and back). We can also make some reasonable assumptions about the positive characteristics of the bat's auditory perceptions given only these kinds of "external" facts. For example, one can assume that if the bandwidth of the signal suddenly broadens, then the bat probably makes use of this increased informational capacity, for otherwise it is unlikely that such a change would have taken place. Because we have a general picture of the kind of information the bat will need (e.g. the velocity, range, and type of target) and we have some idea about how such information is tied to the characteristics of the signal, we can make a reasonable judgment about what information is going to be used by the bat and when this is likely to occur.

We know, for one, some general characteristics of the bat's auditory field. For example, we can infer that when the bat is using sonar navigation, its "auditory field" is a small circular area directly in front of the bat's nose. Like our own visual field which shifts position whenever the head, eyes, or body move, the bat's auditory field also moves along with its nose and head. Moreover, the mid-brain processing produces in the bat's auditory field an analogue of the human retinal fovea, that central area of our retina densely packed with sensory receptors that produces a high-resolution image of the world. In the bat, the mid-brain processing produces a central area of high intensity in the auditory signal and this in turn yields a central area with increased "depth of field" – the bat will be able to "see" further in this central region. However, unlike our visual system in which the decreased acuity (and increased rod density) of the peripheral retina causes our visual image to "fade towards gray" in the peripheral regions, the mid-brain filtering of the bat produces sharp boundaries between the intensity regions of the auditory field. For the bat, the auditory field will have a number of distinct concentric intensity regions. We also know that although the chirp of the bat is *very* loud, it is not deafened by its own outgoing cry. In fact, its own voice, in the outgoing phase, is heard only indistinctly given the middle-ear muscle contractions. On the other hand, because the bat's basilar membrane is "personalized," it hears its own returning cry far more distinctly than the chirps of anyone else. The sound of its own signal is, in one sense, more interesting than any other.

The data also give us a picture of how, specifically, the bat's auditory access to the world changes across time as it pursues its prey – as it searches for prey, then tracks the "edible," and finally comes close enough to grab its dinner. We know, for example, the following facts about the bat's sensory state as it closes in on the prey:

Myopia   The closer the bat gets to its target, the smaller becomes its depth of field. In the search phase of the hunt, recall, it is the second harmonic (low-frequency, further travelling FM sound waves) that receives the greatest energy. But as the bat gets closer, particularly in the final phase, the energy shifts to the high-frequency harmonics, sound waves that are more easily absorbed. So as the bat nears the target, the echoes contain information about only progressively closer objects. The bat can "see" furthest in the search phase, then, shorter and shorter distances thereafter.

Detail   In the last moments of the approach, there is an increase in range and texture information about the target. Because the bandwidth of the FM tail broadens in the terminal phase, the bat receives very fine-grained range information. In addition, because the higher harmonics (short wavelengths) are emphasized, there is high spatial resolution as well – two things which when taken together give the bat detailed information about the *texture* of the target.[19] Again, this is something like human vision. The closer the bat gets, the more detail it can discern.

Constant frequency   Because the bat compensates for the Doppler shift by lowering its voice, the frequency of the echo remains constant. So, contrary to what one might guess (this is certainly what *I* guessed), the bat does not keep track of how fast it is going by listening to the rising or lowering frequency of the echo: increasing frequency does *not* indicate higher speed. Rather, it is the comparison between the outgoing cry and the returning constant frequency signal that determines velocity.

Intensity and object size   As the bat closes in on its target, the echo becomes louder and louder. Not only do the sound waves have less distance to travel (hence suffer less absorption), but the subtended angle of the target increases (the target surface area looms larger). (Think of playing a trumpet against a wall.) One might imagine then that the bat has an auditory analogue of visual looming. In vision, the closer you get the *larger* the object appears; perhaps in echo location, the closer the bat gets, the *louder* the echo sounds. This is not, however, how it is for the bat: target size and target range are disambiguated. Remember that after the bat emits its cry, there is a period of 5–8 ms during which the contracted middle-ear muscles relax. During this time – before the muscles have fully relaxed – echoes from nearby objects will return. The cries bouncing back from objects at a distance of about 2 meters will take about 8 ms to return, so they will arrive when the muscles are almost entirely relaxed. Echoes from nearby objects, on the other hand, return sooner – they will make it home around the 5 ms mark or when the muscles are still almost fully contracted. The net effect, then, is that the muscles are *more* contracted – admit less sound – for the echoes of near objects and are *less* contracted – admit more sound – for the echoes of far objects. Hence, closeness of the object alone will not effect the loudness of the echo. Increased volume is accounted for only by object *size*, or subtended angle.

A disappearing world   Because Doppler compensation in the bat occurs only in one direction (the bat lowers its voice but never raises it) objects moving away from the bat will produce echoes that are well below 61 kHz (in the second harmonic). This means that the echo will fall in a frequency range to which the basilar membrane (the "receiver") is least sensitive, so objects that move away from the bat will simply *disappear*. Indeed, the faster the object moves away from the bat, the more quickly it will "evaporate." (Consider how odd our experience would be if human vision had an analogous mechanism. Imagine standing by the side of the road watching cars go by. The car comes towards you, getting bigger and bigger, but when it passes, the car almost instantly vanishes! Cyclists, however, take a little longer to disappear while pedestrians simply fade slowly away.) Unlike for us, however, this mechanism makes sense in the bat because the sonar system is used primarily during flight. It is always flying *forward*, directing the sonar signal in a small beam ahead of itself, *towards* the objects in its path. Hence, most objects will have a positive relative velocity and be potentially "visible."

All these facts about the bat's auditory access to the world have been deduced almost in the absence of the neurological facts, of the details of signal processing. How then do things look once we know something about the bat's auditory cortex?

5   Cortical Processing

The auditory cortex of the Mustached bat, as you can see from Figure 7.3a, takes up a large portion of its brain. Figure 7.3b shows an enlargement of this area, a

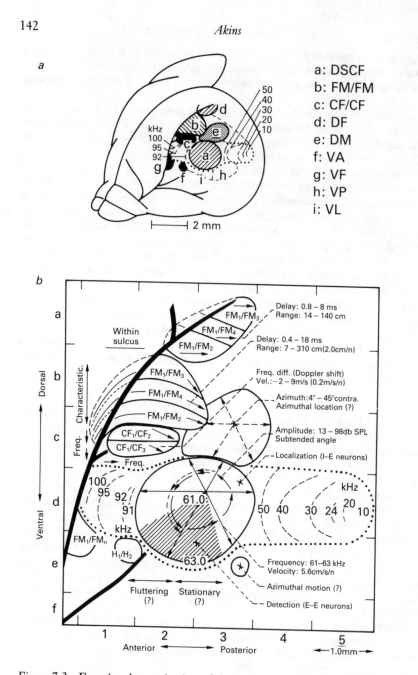

Figure 7.3 Functional organization of the auditory cortex of the Mustached bat. (*a*) The dorsolateral view of the left cerebral hemisphere. Note the large amount of cortex devoted to sonar processing. (*b*) An enlargement of the auditory cortex, showing, among other areas, the FM/FM areas, the DSCF area, and the CF/CF areas. (Reproduced with permission from Suga, 1988.)

more detailed picture of the various neurophysiological maps that have been found. This is not, of course, what the brain looks like to the naked eye (if only nature were so accommodating). Rather, these cortical areas are determined by electrophysiology: an electrical probe is inserted into the brain, the bat is presented with various auditory stimuli, and then, by recording the rate at which a given neuron fires, the "preferred" stimulus for each neuron is determined. For example, when a neuron is responsive over a range of sound frequencies, there will be one particular frequency that provokes the most vigorous neural activity.

In many sensory areas, such as the ones shown here, the neurons form an orderly "map" based upon their preferred stimuli. One might find, say, an area of cortex, all of the cells in which respond to sound amplitude, where the neurons are arranged along an axis in order of increasing preferred amplitude. Other maps are "two dimensional": they contain neurons that respond along two different dimensions of the stimulus, again with a preferred value for each property. Such maps, spread along the surface of the cortex, come in a variety of kinds: some use roughly polar coordinates, some have vaguely Cartesian coordinates, while others use non-orthogonal coordinate systems. For the most part, such maps are irregularly shaped, with "skewed" or "stretched" spatial dimensions. (While the irregularity of such maps may initially seem confusing, such skewed arrangements usually make functional sense: they allow proportionally larger areas of cortex to be devoted to signals of greater importance to the organism. In this way the irregularity of the map facilitates fine-grained processing of more salient properties – a feature we will see in the various cortical areas of the Mustached bat.)

In the primary auditory cortex of the Mustached bat, a number of such maps have been discovered.[20] Here we will look at three major kinds of area: the Doppler shift constant frequency (DSCF) area, the constant frequency (CF/CF) areas, and two areas that contain FM/FM neurons (the FM/FM area and the DF area) (Figure 7.3b).

The DSCF Area

The DSCF area covers about 30 per cent of the primary auditory cortex. Using roughly polar coordinates, the map plots signal frequency against signal amplitude. Using an analogy of Suga's (1990), think of a bicycle wheel. Radiating out along the spokes, the preferred frequencies of the neurons start at about 61 kHz and extend out to about 63 kHz at the periphery; going around the wheel – going around in both directions out from one particular spoke – the preferred amplitudes increase. (The cortical areas to either side of the DSCF area serve to extend the frequency range, out to over 100 kHz in one direction and down to about 10 kHz in the other direction.) The DSCF, then, is devoted to frequencies at and just above the reference frequency of the bat's cry.

Despite the name of this area, the DSCF is probably *not* used for calculating prey velocity (from the Doppler shift of the constant frequency signals). Instead, the central circular region seems to play some role in the bat's ability to make fine-grained frequency and amplitude discriminations, discriminations needed for a variety of functions. One theory here, is that because the CF signals carry information about the wingbeat of insects, the DSCF might be used to locate fluttering prey against background clutter or to determine the orientation and species of the prey (these are all capacities of the Mustached bat that have been confirmed by experimental observation). When the constant frequency sonar signal is reflected by the beat of an insect's wings, both the amplitude and the frequency of the echo changes. As the insect flies towards or away from (i.e. perpendicular to) the bat, the beating of the wings acts like an "acoustic mirror" resulting in sharp amplitude peaks or "glints" in the echo. Also, as the wings beat back and forth, there is a small repetitive change (AC component) in the frequency of the echo caused by Doppler shift (in effect the wing movement serves to very slightly increase or decrease the relative velocity). Both these modulations carry information about the species of insect being pursued because each species has a characteristic wingbeat rate. Here, the repetition rate of the amplitude glints encodes the frequency of the insect's wingbeats, while the small repetitive frequency shifts carry information about insect wingbeat plus the size of the insect's wings. Further, the pattern of echo glints carries information about the target orientation (Schnitzler et al., 1983). It is thought that this DSCF area, with its fine-grained processing of frequency and amplitude of the echo around the reference frequency, might contribute to these processing tasks. (This hypothesis has been confirmed in part by the presence of neurons in the DCSF that respond in a phase-locked fashion to the beating of the insect's wings – a synchronous discharge of neurons to the upper and lower frequencies of the Doppler shift.)[21]

Apart from this hypothesized function, however, the DSCF has some better-established features. For one, these neurons, by responding to the amplitude of the signal, indicate the *subtended angle* of the target – the size of the target. (Recall the dissociation of range and size brought about by middle-ear contraction.) For another, the neurons of the DSCF are "wired" in two distinct ways so as to create specialized areas. All neurons in the DSCF, that is, receive an excitatory input from the opposite or contralateral ear. (There is a DSCF area in each of the brain's two hemispheres. So all neurons in the right hemisphere DSCF area receive excitatory input from the left ear and all neurons in the left hemisphere DSCF are excited by input from the right). Input from the same ear, however, can either excite or inhibit. Neurons with excitatory input from both ears (E-E neurons) (shadowed section of DSCF in Figure 7.3b) multiply the signals and thus prove optimal for detecting weak echoes; neurons that receive one excitatory input from the contralateral ear but inhibitory signals from the ipsilateral ear (E-I neurons) will respond preferentially to sounds from one side, the localization of echoes. Thus, there are two distinct areas of DSCF, one for the *localization* of the sounds and the other for the *detection* of weak echoes.

CF/CF Area

It is here, in the two parts of the CF area (CF_1/CF_2 and CF_1/CF_3), that the neurons record information about the velocity of the prey, through maps that plot frequency against frequency: the frequency of the outgoing stimuli and the frequency of the incoming echo. Each neuron in this area responds to a *pair* of stimuli, a combination of two CF signals: first a fundamental (or CF_1) tone of the bat's cry, then either second or third harmonic signal (the CF_2 or CF_3 component) from the echo. Neurons in CF/CF areas do not respond to the single components alone, but only to a specific paired combination. (This explains, in part, why the fundamental tones are so important. As I said above, the fundamental component of the cry is emitted at very low intensity – so low, in fact, that only the bat itself can hear its own fundamental tones. Because neurons in the CF/CF area require a paired signal (the fundamental and the harmonic), there is less chance of interference from the signals of other bats in the cave – of responding to your neighbor's sonar signal instead of your own.) For most of these neurons, the relation between the CF_1 and CF_2 component is not a perfect harmonic difference. The neurons are tuned to specific frequency *differences*, differences that translate into relative velocity measures (e.g. a CF_1/CF_2 neuron tuned to signals of 30 kHz and 61 kHz respectively is therefore tuned to a relative velocity of 2.84 ms^{-1}). The range of velocities represented in the CF/CF area as a whole is between 8.7 and -2 ms^{-1}, with the largest number of neurons devoted to the important range of 0–4 ms^{-1}.

The FM/FM and DF Areas

Neurons in these two FM areas are also sensitive to pairs of stimuli. Here they respond to *time differences* – the delay between the first signal of the outgoing cry and the second signal of the returning echo. Hence, FM neurons are tuned to *range*, the distance to the target (e.g. a 1 ms delay correlates with a range of 17.3 c). (Actually FM/FM neurons have a very complex response profile: they are also tuned to the specific frequencies of the two components and most are tuned to specific amplitudes as well – hence target size.) As with the CF/CF neurons, the first signal is an FM_1 signal or a fundamental frequency; the second time-delayed signal can be an FM_2, FM_3 or FM_4 signal (these pairs are arranged in separate clusters in each FM area). Again, the first and second components are not usually perfect harmonic variants, for even though the Mustached bat uses Doppler shift compensations during flight, the FM echo will commonly arrive back at a slightly higher frequency (a positive Doppler shift.) The frequency of the second component, then, is usually slightly higher than a perfect harmonic of the fundamental tone.

In both these FM/FM areas, the neurons are arranged along an axis of preferred delay; that is, along an axis of *distance* to the target. (So, as the bat gets closer to its target, the activity of the neurons actually shifts across the surface of the cortex.) In the FM/FM area, that range is 7–310 c (practically the full range over which the bat can "see" with sonar signals); in the DF area, distances between 14 and 140 c are represented. These, then, are some of the processing characteristics of the primary auditory cortex of the Mustached bat.

6 The Bat's Point of View?

The strategy adopted at the beginning of this essay was to explore the prospects of explaining at least *some* aspects of the bat's subjective experience. Now, having assembled in the last four sections an explanation of the bat's informational problem, facts about the bat's behavior (including the emission of its sonar signal), and a description of the signal processing in primary auditory cortex, the time has finally come to return to Nagel's question, "what is it like to be a (Mustached) bat"? What can we infer about the bat's phenomenal experience?

Recall that when Nagel asked his question about the phenomenology of the bat, he equated the bat's experience – the "something it is like" to be a bat – with having a point of view. If the bat is conscious at all and if it perceives the world by audition (as opposed to by vision), then there is some way that the world seems to the bat – presumably, an auditory kind of "seeming." This way of putting the matter, however, fails to separate two distinct questions about the bat's experience.

We can all agree, I think, that the bat is located in – flies about – a world of spatiotemporal material particulars, a world of trees and caves and small flying insects; we can also agree that some of the bat's neural states are caused by the properties of those objects or, more specifically, by the spatial properties of those particulars. But this is only to describe the bat *as we see it*, as located in and causally interacting with *our* world of objective particulars. In other words, this description of the bat alone is not sufficient to attribute *to the bat* a certain perspective on an independent world – to ascribe to it a representation of the spatial world, its properties and objects, *as* objective, *as* distinct from the bat itself. To say of the bat that *it* perceives a world, one that contains objects and properties is to make a further claim about the bat's conceptual scheme.

The two very different questions that we need to distinguish then are these. First, one can inquire about "the very feel" of the bat's auditory phenomenology, whatever it is like to be a bat in virtue of having a sonar system. This is a question which is neutral with respect to the issue of the bat's perceptions of the world: whether or not, for the bat, there *is* a world of objects and properties or, indeed, any world at all conceived of as distinct from the bat itself. Let this be the question "what is it like to be a bat?" The second question is a direct query about the bat's *conscious perceptions of the world*: on the assumption that the bat's conceptual scheme includes an independently existing world of objects and properties, *how does the world, perceived by auditory means, seem to the bat?* In other words, one can also ask about the bat's *species-specific perspective on a world*, one that the bat obtains through its sonar system. It is this latter question – a question that presupposes a certain conceptual ontology – that seems to best sit with Nagel's view that we can equate the bat's *subjective experience* with the bat's *point of view*. That is, if Nagel takes the problem of grasping a bat's acoustic phenomenology as the very same problem as that of understanding a bat's point of view, this seems to presuppose that there is *something on which the* phenomenology *is* a point of view. (Nagel, I realize, would not agree. But we can turn the tables by re-phrasing Nagel's own complaint. Just as Nagel asked "what would be left of what it is like to be a bat if one removed the viewpoint of the bat?", we can reply by saying: "it is difficult to understand what could be meant by *a point of view* apart from a point of view *on something or other*: after all what would be left of a point of view, if it were on nothing at all?" In other words, if one grants that a subject is necessary for a point of view, then surely an *object* is required as well.) Let this be the question, then, "what is the bat's point of view?"[22]

Both of these questions will be addressed in turn, but in this section I will take up the latter one: what has science told us about a bat's point of view? First, what the empirical data makes plausible – in particular, what the processing properties of the bat's primary auditory cortex strongly suggest – is that what the Mustached bat *hears* is probably not what we *see* – not even what we see, minus little bits and pieces or with less spatial detail or with a narrower field of view. When the bat flies across the night sky, in all likelihood it does not use its sonar system to construct representations of the objects around it: an image of the large oak tree to the left, another bat over to the right, the ground and bushes below and so on. Even during the chase, when the bat focuses its sonar beam upon the moth, it is unlikely that the bat ever gains a real-time image of its prey: it probably does not "see" an insect of a certain type, a moth about 2 inches across, with a fuzzy body and long antennae, zig-zagging through space, its wings aflutter. Unlike our own visual perceptions, in other words, the bat's sonar experience is probably neither imagistic nor – more importantly – an experience *of* a world of objects and properties. *Hence it seems plausible that the bat may not have a point of view at all.*

To illustrate why science points in this direction, return to the data on cortical processing and a story that draws it together. Imagine that *you* are the bat – or rather, that you are the bat's wingflapper located in the frontal cortex. It is your job to man the motor controls, to steer the bat given the instruments on the control panel in front of you, namely by watching a couple of lights, some digital meters, and a compass-like dial. These are instruments that receive input from the primary auditory cortex alone, that show the summed neural activity of its various regions. You are to maneuver the bat, in other words, on the basis of what the auditory cortex "sees." But what exactly do the instruments show? How are they wired to the neural activity of the auditory cortex?

The first four instruments are hooked up in various ways to neurons in the DSCF. First, there is a yellow light which is wired to the excitatory-excitatory (E-E) neurons. When the bat is randomly searching for prey, the light remains off. But as soon as the summed activity of the E-E neurons reaches some fixed point (i.e. when the echo rises above a "whisper"), the yellow light starts to flash. The yellow light indicates, in other words, that something or other has come into "view."

Secondly, there is a compass-like dial on the panel that monitors the activity of the inhibitory-excitatory neurons. By analyzing the pattern of activity across the neural population as a whole, the dial provides a rough read on the direction of the prey. The arrow indicates, in egocentric coordinates (i.e. relative to the bat's nose), the position of the weak echo.

Thirdly, there is a metronome-like instrument, one that is hooked up to the neurons in the central region of the DSCF. Recall that these are the neurons that are phase-locked to the beating of the insect wings. The tick-tock of the metronome, then, beats time with the wings: a sort of "yum-yum" meter from which you can discern the "edibility" of the prey.

And, fourthly, there is a gauge that monitors the amplitude signals of the central DSCF and thereby shows the subtended angle of the insect.

Then there are the digital meters, three in all. The first two meters on the panel are connected to the two large FM/FM areas and – sure enough – they indicate distance to the target. One meter is the "distance meter" because it monitors the FM area, that area which represents distances between 7 and 310 c. So it encompasses all the distances to the prey throughout the chase. The second meter is the "accuracy meter." As the bat draws nearer to its prey, the accuracy meter (connected to the DF area) gives a more subtle indication of target range.

The third digital meter is a simple speedometer. It is hooked up to CF/CF areas of auditory cortex and thus indicates velocities between -2 and $+9$ ms^{-1}, giving particularly accurate information about speeds at around $+4$ ms^{-1}, the speed at which you normally fly.

This is what the instruments on the control panel show – or, more correctly, this is how things look from the neurophysiologist's point of view. This is what an outside observer could know about the instrument panel. What *you* see, however, in your role of the wingflapper, is much more simple. You see only the lights and dials, not the wiring behind the scenes, and this is what will guide your behavior.

Most of the time you can spend your time just flapping the wings at random, making the bat circle around, waiting for something to happen on the control panel. More specifically, you are waiting for the yellow "alert" light to come on. When it does, you need to turn your attention to the direction dial. Watch the needle for movement, then flap and orient so that the needle points dead ahead. Of course, this is a little tricky – you have to keep the needle centred on the direction dial while keeping one eye on the "distance meter" (to check your progress), while at the same time adjusting your speed appropriately so as to close in on your potential prey. Now comes the interesting part. Once "that something" is a little closer, you can find out whether it's even worth catching. Is it edible or not? Here, the oscillations of the metronome will tell you whether dinner is in sight.

Of course, it's not the case that things always go as planned. What if the metronome fails to oscillate, if it says *nothing at all*? This means that whatever is out there, it is *not* fluttering, so you'd better put on the brakes. Have a look at the amplitude gauge for subtended angle, check the accuracy meter for distance, and make a guess about the size. How big is that thing anyway? Hmmm . . . If its *very* big and it's getting closer all the time, you could be in trouble. What's more, the identification of large things is not your kind of job. (Is it a cave wall or *what*?!) So pull the bat sharply up and left and put in a call to another sensory area for help . . . This, then, is the wingflapper's tale.

There are, of course, no lights and dials in the frontal cortex of the bat. Nor is there a bat homunculus, the wingflapper, who reads the instruments and sends out the appropriate motor commands. Still, the story makes for a useful fiction because it makes vivid one essential point, namely just how small the gap between the bat's sonar input and its motor output might be: how little intermediary processing is required to translate (in the mathematical sense) the auditory information of the primary cortex into motor commands.

Looking back at the neural activity of the auditory cortex as represented by the lights and dials on the instrument panel, that is, one sees how closely the sonar sensory system is tied to the bat's motor needs: on the basis of this cortical information alone, we can almost imagine how to "drive" the Mustached bat, or at least, how to drive the bat during the hunt for airborne prey. To put this another way, although you, as the wingflapper, were asked to perform the appropriate tasks – you were asked to imagine *reading* the instrument panel and *deciding upon* the *appropriate* motor responses – all of your decisions and actions might have been performed by a reasonably simple control system. For example, the compass-like dial of the direction instrument could have directly controlled the line of flight using a translation of the compass directions into the suitable coordinates of the motor system. Similarly, one could specify a series of default settings for motor control to be used whenever certain sensory conditions arise; such that, say, in the presence of large looming objects (i.e. for certain values of the amplitude gauge, the accuracy meter, and the speedometer), the bat would turn sharply, up and away. The story did not require, in other words, an intelligent hand on the controls, an intentional agent who attempts to determine *what is out there* (the state of the external world) and then, on that basis, decides *what ought to be done*. Hence, there is no need to attribute to the bat any intermediary processing steps nor any of the representational capacities that would thereby be required. The input–output "loop" of the bat, it seems, might be very short indeed.

More generally, what we see in the primary auditory cortex of the bat is an extension of the same informational "strategy" employed in the emission of the sonar signal. There, the bat's solution to a complex processing problem was to match, sequentially, the informational characteristics of the signal to the informational requirements of the bat's hunting behavior. In the auditory cortex, we can again see how the bat's behavioral demands tightly constrain the informational properties of the sensory system: for the most part, the cortex encodes only highly filtered information about specific properties of the prey: its relative velocity, size, range, location, and "edibility." What the auditory cortex seems "interested in," one might say, is only that information necessary to locate, track, and catch the bat's dinner. Putting all this together then – the bat's hunting behavior, its signal, and the properties of the auditory cortex – the function of the bat's sonar system, as portrayed by the wingflapper's story, is this: *to secure, sequentially, highly filtered information that can be used, on line, to guide the bat's flight.* By and large, what the sonar system does is to direct the very rapid and stereotyped movements of the bat's prey-catching behavior by providing, "on demand," just that spatial information currently required.

More specifically, if one looks back over the science, there were two aspects of the data that strongly suggest this function for the sonar system. First, there is the "specificity" of the neurons in the primary auditory cortex. To say that a (sensory) neuron is informationally "specific" is to say that when it processes an incoming signal there is information *loss*; because the neuron responds to only particular aspects of a complex stimulus, its signal contains information about only those specific properties. For example, think of the response properties of neurons in the FM/FM areas of bat auditory cortex. These are neurons that will fire whenever there is a pair of stimuli with a certain distinct profile – two stimuli separated by a certain time delay with a particular frequency "mismatch" between a fundamental tone and its harmonic, each stimulus falling within a certain amplitude range. Given a response from an FM neuron, one can infer that a pair of stimuli with roughly those properties has occurred. Then again, the response of an FM neuron does not tell us, say, how many harmonics each signal contained, or their pattern of frequency modulation, or the amplitude of the signals except at a certain point in the signal sweep and so on. Much information about the acoustic properties of the original stimuli (and much of the information about those properties encoded by the basilar membrane in the bat's ear) has simply been lost, discarded in the interest of discerning the distance between the bat and its prey. Hence the specificity of the FM neurons. In the same way, looking again at the neurons in the other areas of the primary auditory cortex, one sees neurons with a similar informational character – informationally specific neurons that "trade" rich information about the acoustic stimulus for specific information about the properties of the prey. As I said above, what makes this property of the cortical neurons "suspicious" is just that the neurons seem to encode only the information needed by the bat in order to catch the prey, that is, to drive motor control. And this suggests that the bat may require (at least for this aspect of its behavior) little else except this kind of rudimentary information encoding.

In addition, the specificity of the bat's cortical neurons raises the possibility that the bat may not even possess, from its sonar information, the necessary "building blocks" for complex spatial representations. We know, that is, that the information-rich representations of human vision – or, more generally, the complex spatial representations of any neurobiological system – require at least the following three conditions: first, there must be a complex stimulus, one that contains the "raw goods" from which informationally rich representations can be constructed; secondly, the neural system must have a way of encoding the complex properties of stimulus at the transduction level; and thirdly, higher-level "modules" or information processors must have access to this encoding. One needs, that is, a complex stimulus, a way of encoding its complexity, and access to the information thus encoded. What such a system requires at low levels, then, are informationally *general* neurons, ones that respond across a wide variety of properties of the original stimulus and thus jointly encode very detailed information about the original stimulus. (For example, in human vision, the complex stimulus is the visual image on the retina, and the transduction mechanisms – the rods and cones – encode much of the pattern's complexity. At the level of the primary visual cortex, the "simple cells" of layer IV, taken together, still encode most of the properties of the original stimulus.) The suspicion, then, about the bat's primary auditory cortex, is that, even at this very low level of cortical processing, the raw materials of complex spatial representations are no longer present. Hence they are not accessible to higher-level processes. For the various FM/FM areas and the CF/CF regions (although perhaps not for the DSCF), much of the requisite acoustic detail has already been filtered out. Perhaps, then, the bat neither has nor needs the capacity to produce complex sonar representations.

The second telling aspect of the data is that it yields little reason to suppose that the bat's sonar system is designed for the large-scale *integration* of information over time. We know that any system that produces a representation of a stable objective world on the basis of continuously changing input must use massive integration. Again, take our visual system as an example. As you look out at the world, the patterns of light on your retinas are in constant flux. Usually this is the result of your own motion – you constantly shift your gaze, focusing first on this and then on that – but at other times, objects in the world move of their own accord. Somehow or other, amidst all this changing retinal information, the visual system produces a perception of an apparently stable, unified, continuous, and independent world. And this is only possible, I take it, through the system's massive integration of its present informational states with its previously constructed spatial representations.

In contrast, as the wingflapper story illustrates, the bat's auditory system seems designed for sequenced *non-integrated* information processing. First – an old point – as the bat progresses through his prey-catching routine, the informational *content* of the signal changes across time in tandem with its informational *needs*. Information that is not needed at the end of the behavioral sequence is simply "dropped" in virtue of the kinds of signals produced at this stage. (Recall how in the Search phase of the hunt, the bat has broad information about target range, for its "depth of field" extends past 2 meters, plus information about wingbeat, orientation, and prey size; by the Terminal phase, when the sonar signal consists almost entirely of the FM tail, the bat has very precise information about the target range, but probably little else.) Secondly, simply looking at the bat's behavioral repertoire, it seems that very little of the sonar information extracted during prey-catching will be of any use to the bat at a later time: given its behavioral repertoire, that is, there is very little need for the bat to store and integrate sonar data. For example, there is no reason for the bat to remember exactly where in the sonar field the insect (now in front of him) first appeared; nor will the bat need to recall exactly which evasive maneuvers a certain moth (recently consumed) performed; nor, once the bat has determined that an insect *is* edible, need it ever recall that *this* moth was of a particular "edible" kind. In fact, it need never remember this moth, *qua* re-identifiable particular, at all. So, for both these reasons – the signal sequencing and the bat's circumscribed use of the acoustic information – it seems unlikely that sonar information is saved and integrated into perceptions of a stable objective world.[23]

To sum up, then, what science suggests is that the sonar system of the bat is probably *not* concerned with the representation of three-dimensional objective particulars.[24] But if this is true, it makes little sense to attribute *to the bat* a phenomenal point of view, conscious mental states which are about objects and their properties. There being, that is, no particulars *for it*, we should not ascribe to the bat perceptions *of* those particulars: a perception of this moth, or of this moth *as* a certain type, or of the bat's favorite landing place, or of the layout of its cave.[25] Because there are no objects that the bat perceives, there are no objects for the bat to perceive *in a certain bat-like way*. So to attribute a point of view to the bat – a species-specific perspective from which to view the world – only imposes an ontology where there is little evidence that one exists.

7 But What is it Like?

There are no doubt many readers who, at this point, will feel that the central issue has yet to be raised. After all, even if the bat does not have a point of view in this strong sense, an experience *of the world*, could not the bat have *some kind* of phenomenological experience none the less? Surely it is still like something to be bat, even if the bat's sonar perceptions are somewhat "limited" – or so one might wonder.

Elsewhere I have argued (Akins, 1993) that the above question, for all its appearance, may not be as coherent as it seems. If it is a question about the possibility of a "purely qualitative" phenomenology – about conscious but non-intentional experience – I am not sure that we have even a vague conception of what this might mean. Still, putting this problem aside for now, it does seem that, after having a good look at the available facts, we have come closer to understanding the bat's subjective state, and this regardless of whether such "subjectivity" is consciously experienced by the bat or not.

More specifically, the view of the bat's "inner life" that emerged from the scientific data was not "the view from nowhere" that Nagel feared. Recall that Nagel worried that an objective description of the world moves us, step-wise, away from the individual's subjective experience – that beginning with the point of view of an individual,

> [the] movement toward greater objectivity involves, first, abstraction from the individual's specific spatial, temporal, and personal position in the world, then . . . gradually from the forms of perception and action characteristic of humans, and away from the narrow range of a human *scale* in space, time, and quantity, toward a conception of the world which as far as possible is not the view from anywhere within it. (Nagel, 1979b, p. 206)

On the contrary, what science provided was exactly such an entry into a bat's "subjective world," roughly, an understanding of the kind of sensory access to the "outside" or the external world that is available from the "inside" of the bat (the bat's "subjective world" being a notion that I am using as neutral with regard to the bat's conception of self or of objective, re-identifiable particulars).[26] Moreover, this was a scientific investigation that advanced in exactly the opposite direction, that began with "the physicist's view" and then by steps marched the reader back towards the specific perceptual experience of an individual bat.

The project began, that is, with some basic questions about the nature of the auditory world, the informational properties of sound and the problems those would engender for spatial processing. Then, based upon some knowledge of the Mustached bat's behavioral patterns and the properties of its sonar signal over time, some rough inferences were made about what information the Mustached bat was likely to have and at what times. We could estimate, for example, how far the bat could possibly "see" at different points in the hunt, the spatial resolution of the acoustic field, and how "things" would "disappear" from view under certain conditions. The next move involved a characterization of the first few stages of neural processing, starting at the transduction level. Through this, we gained a further refinement of the bat's "perspective," for it marked the transition between the information we could see as *theoretically* available to the bat given the signal, and the information *actually* retained for use at various levels of neural processing. For example, at the transduction level, we saw how the basilar membrane acted as a signal filter, to enhance the bat's own sonar echoes and to minimize those of its conspecific's and how the contraction of the ear muscles filtered out intensity information. Several cortical connections further down the line, at the level of the primary auditory cortex, our understanding of the bat's "subjective world" was again transformed. We could see that the bat had access to specific properties of the external world (although not *as* properties of objects), properties that included the velocity of the target (between -2 and $+9$ ms^{-1}), its subtended angle, and its distance (up to 3 meters) from the bat. Finally, although the story of the wingflapper was used for a negative purpose – to show that the bat lacks certain representational capacities – and moreover was composed of three parts fiction to every one part of substantiated fact, it none the less illustrated how, theoretically, such cortical information can be used: how the sensory processes of the *species* can be applied to the inner life of a specific *individual*, a single bat located in time and space.

On a less positive note, it was disappointing to see how very little insight into the bat's subjective state was gained by the addition of this neurophysiological data. Prima facie, the neurophysiology ought to have been the most important part of the story; yet it failed to advance our understanding of the bat's inner life very much past what had already been discerned in section 4, "The Beginnings of Subjectivity." Still, the reason so little progress was made stems from what we did not know: the information we gained about cortical processing was unenlightening only because it served to raise complex questions about the global nature of the bat's cortical function – questions about how that information was later used, the relation of the primary cortex to motor control, secondary sonar areas, and other sensory modalities. And without answers to those questions no further story could be told.

Even to construct the cartoon-like fiction of the wingflapper's story, numerous representational questions had to be decided simply *by fiat* in order to gain some semblance of a unified and coherent "perspective" for the bat. For example, in constructing that story, the frontal cortex was arbitrarily selected as the residence of the homunculus, a choice that gave the wingflapper a specific "take" on the world. The same kind of story could have been told from the vantage point of some other cortical area, say from one of the primary auditory areas, one of the other sensory "modules" or from any of the other cortical functional sites. In each case, a different story would have unfolded – another "subjective world" – a story in accordance with the external information available at that particular site.

Certain decisions were also made about how to "string the wires" from the auditory areas to the frontal cortex, about what information would be preserved in transmission and about how the informational properties of the neural population (i.e. as opposed to the properties of the individual neurons) would be processed and represented at the frontal site. Take as an example the activity of the E-E neurons in the DSCF and how that was portrayed, namely by a single yellow light on the control panel. Presumably when a bat is flying around looking for insects, the E-E neurons respond to whatever – and all – objects that reflect the bat's sonar signals. So if there were a number of insects directly ahead of the bat (or some branches of a tree in the background behind a fluttering moth, etc.) the E-E neurons would register this fact: the population would respond to all the echoes present, resulting in a pattern of activity across this area of cortex. In the wingflapper story, however, the yellow light on the instrument panel was assigned a "trigger" level, the threshold of activity for the population which turns on the yellow light. So, on this wiring scheme, the frontal cortex lost a great deal of information available in the DSCF, information about all the "background" activity below the level of the threshold (i.e. the activity caused by various other objects) as well as about the actual rate of firing that triggered the yellow light. In effect, the wiring to frontal cortex reduced the bat's perceptual world to a single sound source, one that was either present or not. Needless to say, some other "wiring diagram" might have been used.

Finally, in selecting the frontal cortex as "the" seat of consciousness, many difficult questions about the bat's world – about a unified perspective or a single subject or a "self" – were avoided. By turning a blind eye towards the difficult representational questions that would inevitably arise, the wingflapper just became "the" bat. No questions were asked about the consequences of interaction between the frontal cortex and other functionally distinct areas, about how motor control might be shared, how different representational schemes might be reconciled, how conflicting and "absent" information might be resolved and so on. No hint was given of how a unified perspective might emerge or, indeed, what this would mean.

And, finally, no problems were raised about how the bat distinguishes itself *as* a self, *as* distinct from the rest of the world. All these very difficult representational questions were simply ignored.

In order, then, to tell a more complete story about the inner life of the bat, numerous representational questions about the nature of cortical function would first need to be answered. Understanding the function of primary auditory cortex did give us some hint of the "subjective world" to come, but being only the very first part of a complex story, it largely served to raise as many questions as it answered. Thus, in the end, it was the objective facts about auditory signals and signal processing that provided our initial insight into the bat's "subjective world," and when the project came up short, it was unanswered questions about representational matters that were responsible. Despite what Nagel feared, science did not take us "further away" from the bat's conscious experiences, nor were the problems that brought the investigation to a (temporary) close, problems about inaccessible subjective facts or the intrinsic properties of the bat's experiences or the phenomenological "feel" of the bat's perceptions.

8 Conclusion

This essay began by outlining a tension between two competing intuitions about consciousness. On the one hand, there is our native sense of puzzlement about how it is possible that a subject of phenomenal experience can be physically embodied at all and hence about how physical facts can yield insight into that conscious experience. On the other, given our materialist view that the mind is the brain, it seems plausible that science ought to be able to tell us *something* about the nature of conscious events. In dealing with this tension, the strategy was to set aside the common puzzlement and to begin by taking up the positive project – to see what science would say.

Given the strategy, it was entirely foreseeable that the mystery of physically embodied consciousness would be left unaddressed – and unfortunately this was so. Some physical processes, such as those that occur in the human visual cortex, give rise to conscious events; other physical events such as pouring water into a pitcher or starting the lawnmower do not. And looking at the neurophysiology, behavior, and environment of the Mustached bat did not explain this puzzle. Similarly, the above science shed no light on the question of what *kinds* of neural processes give rise to conscious experience: why it is that some neural events, such as visual perceptions, are present to consciousness while others, such as the neural mechanisms of stereopsis or depth perception, are not. Neither of these problems seem likely to be resolved by this method alone, by looking at the scientific literature about one particular species. Moreover, it was because these questions were not addressed that, in the end, no stand could be taken on whether it is like anything at all to be a bat – whether the "subjective world" of a Mustached bat, acquired in virtue of its species-specific sonar processing and the "particularity" of the situated individual, is sufficient for phenomenal experience. All these are further problems that need to be addressed, but not, I suspect, by examining the data on a single species or even through "pure" scientific inquiry alone. My guess is that these are as much conceptual problems as scientific and perhaps the very questions themselves must change before satisfactory answers can be given.

What the strategy made readily apparent, however, is that many of the notions commonly used in speaking of phenomenal experience – the notions of "point of view," "structural properties," "self," "subjectivity," "objectivity," and the like – are firmly tied to representational questions. By taking a concrete case and attempting to piece together a coherent picture of a subject's experience, the representational nature of these notions was brought into sharp relief. The bat, we found, may fail to have a point of view, but this is to say that the bat lacks certain representational capacities, a conception of a world of objective particulars. Moreover, given what the bat is missing, it would seem that to understand a creature with a genuine point of view would require asking further representational questions: what would it be to represent objects *qua* objects, to distinguish oneself from the rest of the world, to re-identify a particular? And exactly how would these capacities be instantiated: what kind of functional or computational capacities would count as, say, seeing a particular *as* a particular? In other words, both the concept of a "subjective world" and that of a "point of view" are (at least in part) representational notions. And if we have made progress on the former – if we now know a little something about what it is like to be a bat – there is good reason to think that progress on the latter could be made as well.

ACKNOWLEDGMENTS

This essay began as dissertation section and has appeared in draft form in a number of guises. For their very helpful comments along the way, I would like to thank Dale Jamieson, Mark Bekoff, Donald Griffin, Daniel Dennett, Kim Sterelny, David Braddon-Mitchell, Bo Dahlbom, and the Spatial Representation Group at King's College, Cambridge. I would especially like to thank Brian C. Smith and Joseph Malpeli – and Martin Davies for all his help with this final version.

NOTES

As a graduate student, I worked for several years with Daniel Dennett at The Center for Cognitive Studies at Tufts University. Part of my job during that time was to unearth "telling" neurophysiological work; although, once found, Dan and I would often disagree about exactly what philosophical consequences could be drawn. In a volume devoted to Dennett's work, then, it seemed fitting to present one body of research that he and I often discussed – the neuroethology of bats – and to trace out what I take to be (some of) its theoretical consequences. Although this contribution is not directed towards Dennett's work (pedagogically, it takes issue with Nagel's views), many of its conclusions are at odds with Dennett's views about consciousness, the intentionality of mental states and the relation between these two phenomena.

1 See Dennett (1991), p. 443. In these examples, Dennett's tactic for the attribution of perceptual states to other creatures is to start with our own experiences and then "adjust downwards" as required by the physiological and behavioral data.
2 What then of the experience of subjects other than oneself? Given a subject who is sufficiently similar to you, behaviorally and physiologically, you can imagine how things

would be *for you*, if you were in that subject's particular situation. You can *adopt* that subject's point of view, in other words, through a kind of empathetic projection. Of course, given an "alien" subject, one with whom you have little in common, there will be scant basis for an ascription of your own familiar phenomenology. Hence the problematic nature of our relation to the bat and to all other alien creatures as well: if we cannot adopt their alien point of view, we will never comprehend their phenomenal worlds. We will probably never know what it is like to be a bat.

3   In essence, this would give away the game, for if there is a mystery about how a brain could be conscious *at all*, then it ought to be equally mysterious how one could have this or that kind of conscious event.

4   Two warnings about the data presented here are in order at the outset. First, the research presented is not assumed to be immutable or entirely accurate. Many of the findings cited are from recent sources that may or may not stand the test of time; no doubt other parts of the data have already been shown to be inaccurate or incorrect. This does not matter, however, as the project is not to see if we can ascertain what it is *really* like to be a (moustached) bat but rather to see what can be deduced about a bat's point of view given a body of something like objective scientific "facts." The second proviso concerns the selection of research findings. While what we now know about the neurophysiology and behavior of the bat is but a small part of what could be known, there is already an enormous body of experimental literature. Inevitably, the story that follows incorporates only a small subset of that data, one that has seemed revealing of the bat's world.

5   It is not unusual, for example, for Nagel's query, "what is it like to be a bat?" to be seen as equivalent to the question "what would it be like to *hear* the world as opposed to "*seeing* it?" The emphasis, in this latter question, is on the *modality* of the experience, audition – whether a shift in modality *alone* would make for a difference in phenomenology. If you could hear what you can see, what would that be like? The informational equivalence of the two systems is presupposed.

6   Actually, when Donald Griffin first suggested that bats navigate by echo location, his discovery was greeted with complete disbelief by the US Navy. After all, who could believe that a mere bat could be using a sonar system that was clearly more sophisticated than any the Navy had yet to produce?

7   What I am describing here is the view of vision as "inverse optics," the theory first proposed by David Marr (1982).

8   Although not a strict anomaly. Oil birds (a nocturnal species) and Cave Swiftlets (a diurnal species) are both cave roosting birds that have rough echo location systems that use a series of relatively low-frequency "clicks." In addition, certain species of dolphins (e.g. the harbour and the Bottlenose dolphins), porpoises, and whales (e.g. sperm and killer whales) are water-dwelling mammals that use sonar navigation.

9   Not very much is known about the visual system of bats, although see Pettigrew (1988) for a short but surprising summary article on this subject. Comparing the spatial resolution of both the visual and sonar systems of several species of bats, Pettigrew finds that the visual system is not always inferior to the sonar system over the spatial range within which hunting takes place. Moreover, he suggests that vision and sonar navigation might have a symbiotic relation in bats – vision stepping in for those spatial representation tasks for which sonar is ill suited and vice versa.

10 This way of thinking about the problem was suggested to me by Camhi (1984). Much of what follows draws upon that work, although I have chosen to emphasize somewhat different properties of the auditory world.

11 Actually, there is "ambient" sound – but underwater. Recently, a passive underwater sonar system has been developed at The Scripps Institute that uses ambient noise or what the Scripps researchers call "daylight sound" – the constant hiss caused by the

oscillations of myriads of bubbles near the ocean's surface. The system uses a parabolic acoustic mirror 4 feet in diameter to focus the sounds, with a shielded microphone at the center to measure the sound intensity at that spot.

12   This is why sound is such a good source of information about the presence (or lack thereof) of objects of certain types: the rhythmic crunch of the underbrush signals the presence of a heavy animal and so on.

13   While the passive underwater system developed by Scripps (see note 11 above) solves the problem of focus by using an acoustic mirror, the mirror is 4 feet in diameter – not a very practical solution for your average organism (imagine carrying around your very own satellite dish!).

14   Given the refractive index of water, more of the sound signal will be reflected at the water's surface than will travel through the water and reflect off the fish. So, it is likely that the information about the prey is discerned primarily through the surface properties of the water – through ripples and waves as the fish break the surface, a view confirmed by Suthers (1965).

15   For an entirely contrary view about the evolutionary pressures involved in the development of echo-location systems, see Norris and Evans (1988). These authors argue that sound has many advantages over light as a medium for spatial navigation/representation.

16   Actually, because the returning FM signal will be Doppler shifted and because it is the harmonics of the fundamental frequency that are used in timing the echo delay, one does not want to wait for the return of the *very same* frequency. More will be said about these complications below.

17   Harmonics are multiples of the fundamental frequency. As used in the bat literature, the first harmonic is the fundamental frequency, the second harmonic is twice the frequency of the fundamental, the third harmonic is three times the frequency and so on.

18   But if distance is the crucial factor, why is it that the fundamental frequency is not emphasized, a sound which would travel further? As I said above, there is a trade-off between range and grain, how far the signal travels versus how small an object will reflect the sound. Why, then, have the fundamental tone around 31 kHz? As we will see later, the fundamental frequency is used as a "cue" by the neural system to mark the time of the outgoing call; because the fundamental tone is produced at so low an intensity, only the bat that produces the tone can hear it, thus eliminating much interference caused by the cries of other bats.

19   In recent work, Simmons et al. claim that the Big Brown bat can perceive an echo-delay change of as little as 10–12 *nanoseconds*, which is equivalent to a change in range of 2×10^{-6} meters. Clearly, if this is so, the bat has much finer texture discrimination than any organism with vision. It is for exactly this reason that I am somewhat suspicious of these results.

20   The summary below is taken largely from the research of Nobuo Suga and his colleagues; for summaries of this work see Suga (1984, 1988, 1990).

21   Much of the evidence that confirms this hypothesis comes from studies of the Horseshoe bat not the Mustached bat; moreover, neurons in the CF/CF area also show synchronous discharge. I have simplified the evidence for pedagogic purposes.

22   More formally, following Strawson (1959), let us assume that there are two necessary conditions for having a representation of objective particulars or a point of view. First, for an organism to have a conception of *objective* particulars, the organism would need the resources to distinguish between itself and states of itself, on one hand, and that which is not itself or states of itself on the other. In its crudest form, this is the ability of an organism to make a distinction between "me" and "not me." (For example, in the bat's case, the bat ought to be able to distinguish between motion that it makes relative to a stationary target, and motion of a target relative to the bat, i.e. the distinction between

"it's moving" and "I'm moving.") Secondly, a conception of *particulars* – re-identifiable particulars – requires that the organism have the means by which to distinguish reliably, over time, between numerical and qualitative identity, between the same objecte once again and another just like it. (Here, this might be the ability, say, to keep track of and differentiate *this* Lunar moth, now approaching at the right of the sonar field, from *that* Lunar moth, one that just recently made a narrow escape.)

23 One should take this only as a denial of only *large-scale* integration, for integration, on a small scale, must occur given the rapid on-off nature of the sonar "chirps."

24 Given how little we know about bats, however, this conclusion must be taken with a grain of salt. There are many outstanding questions one would like to see answered, about the bat's behavior during the hunt, about its other activities that involve knowledge of permanent objects and structures, and about the integration and overlap of sonar information with other sensory modalities. One might wonder, say, whether, in tracking the moth during the hunt, there is any predictive element involved, a calculation of the moth's trajectory, or whether the bat's behavior is simply guided by an on-line indication of where the moth is at present as the story suggested. Does the bat predict where the moth will go and then base its behavior on its predicted trajectory or are the evasive movements of the moth simply too erratic to make feasible anything but a simple servo-mechanism? Similarly, when a pursued moth actually does manage to evade the bat, there is the problem of the bat's ability to get back on track, to relocate the moth and begin another pursuit. If the bat is distracted during the pursuit phase, does it have the ability to return to the scene, to take up where it left off, or does it simply start the search phase all over again and proceed as it would for a new insect? Then again, bats, we know, live in complex caves, have permanent roosts, hunt in preferred places and can locate and identify their young in a crowded communal roost with thousands of other nearly identical offspring. How, then, do bats find their way around maze-like structures or pick out their own young as their own? What sensory systems are involved in these kinds of tasks and what representational structures underlie this behavior? Finally, we would want to know how the information gleaned by the sonar system linked with visual information and other sensory modalities. What kind of information does the visual system provide and how is it integrated (or is it?) with sonar encodings. All of these questions are pertinent to understanding the bat's conceptual ontology. For a variety of relevant articles, see, for example, on the topic of image formation, Simmons (1989); on the topic of inter-model interaction, Pettigrew (1988) and Surlykke (1988); on tracking strategies, see Masters (1988) and Campbell and Suthers (1988); and on sonar navigation strategies in artificial intelligence, see Mataric and Brooks (1990).

25 This is where my view most clearly conflicts with Denett's understanding of "the intentional stance", for my claim is that the neural system of any organism must have certain representational capacities if it is to be legitimately ascribed intentional states.

26 The notion of a "subjective world" used here is significantly different from what Dennett had in mind when he posited "notional worlds." (For a good explanation of Dennett's concept see "About Aboutness" in Dennett, 1987.) Dennett posited notional worlds as a way of expressing the propositional content of mental events without using "belief that p" statements and their attendant commitments to propositional content. By imagining what world(s) a creature would be *best suited* to survive in, we are supposed to determine between which properties of the world the organism genuinely discriminates. In this way, we can determine what Dennett termed the "organismic contribution" to the semantic content of its belief state. Above, the notion of a "subjective world" is not designed to play any role in a semantic theory of mental states. Rather, it is a notion that is used to show how an organism *without* intentional mental events makes sensory contact with the world: the kind of information available inside the bat under conditions of normal behavior and environment.

REFERENCES

Akins, K. (1993) A bat without qualities? In M. Davies and G. Humphries (eds.), *Consciousness*, Oxford: Blackwell.

Bushnel, R.-G. (ed.) (1967) *Animal Sonar Systems: Biology and Bionics*. France: Laboratoire de physiologie acoustique.

Busnel, R.-G. and Fish, J. F. (eds) (1980) *Animal Sonar Systems*. New York: Plenum Press.

Camhi, J. (1984) *Neuroethology: Nerve Cells and the Natural Behavior of Animals*. Sunderland, Mass.: Sinauer Assoc. Inc.

Campbell, K. A. and Suthers, R. A. (1988) Predictive tracking of horizontally moving targets by the fishing bat. In P. E. Nachtigall and P. W. B. Moore (eds), *Animal Sonar: Processes and Peformance*, New York: Plenum Press.

Churchland, P. M. (1989). *A Neurocomputational Perspective*. Cambridge, Mass.: MIT Press.

Dawkins, R. (1986). *The Blind Watchmaker*. New York: Norton.

Dennett, D. C. (1987) *The Intentional Stance*. Cambridge, Mass.: MIT Press/Bradford Books.

Dennett, D. C. (1991) *Consciousness Explained*. Boston: Little, Brown.

Griffin, D. R., Webster, F. A. and Micheal, C. R. (1960) The echolocation of flying insects by bats. *Animal Behavior*, 8, 141–54.

Grinnell, A. D. and Schnitzler, H.-U. (1977) Directional sensitivity of echolocation in the Horseshoe bat *Rhinolophus Ferrumequinum:* II. Behavioral directionality of hearing. *Journal of Comparative Physiology*, 116, 63–76.

Henson, O. W. (1967) The perception and analysis of biosonar signals by bats. In R.-G. Bushnel (ed.), *Animal Sonar Systems: Biology and Bionics*. France: Laboratoire de physiologie acoustique.

Henson, O. W. (1970) The ear and audition. In W. A. Wimsatt (ed.), *Biology of Bats*, vol. 2, 181–263. New York: Academic Press.

Henze, D. and O'Neill, A. W. (1991) The emission pattern in vocalization and directionality of the sonar system of the echolocating bat, *Pteronotus parnelli*. *The Journal of the Acoustical Society of America*, 89 (5), 2430–4.

Jackson, F. (1982) Epiphenomenal qualia. *Philosophical Quarterly*, 42, 127–36.

Marr, D. (1982) *Vision*. San Francisco: Freeman.

Masters, W. M. (1988) Prey interception: predictive and nonpredictive strategies. In Nachtigall, P. E. and Moore, P. W. B. (eds.), *Animal Sonar: Processes and Performances*, New York: Plenum Press.

Mataric, M. and Brooks, R. (1990) Learning a distributed map representation based on navigation behaviors. *Proceedings of the USA–Japan Symposium on Flexible Automation*, Kyoto, Japan, July 1990.

McGinn, C. (1990) *The Problem of Consciousness*. Oxford: Blackwell.

Nachtigall, P. E. and Moore, P. W. B. (eds) (1988) *Animal Sonar: Processes and Performance*. New York: Plenum Press.

Nagel, T. (1979a) What is it like to be a bat? In *Mortal Questions*. Cambridge: Cambridge University Press.

Nagel, T. (1979b) Objective and subjective. In *Mortal Questions*. Cambridge: Cambridge University Press.

Nagel, T. (1986) *The View from Nowhere*. Oxford: Oxford University Press.

Norris, K. and Evans, E. (1988) On the evolution of acoustic communications systems in vertebrates. In P. E. Nachtigall and P. W. B. Moore (eds), *Animal Sonar: Processes and Performances*, New York: Plenum Press.

Pettigrew, J. (1988) Microbat vision and echolocation in an evolutionary context. In P. E. Nachtigall and P. W. B. Moore, (eds), *Animal Sonar: Processes and Performances*, New York: Plenum Press.

Schnitzler, H.-U. and Grinnell, A. D. (1977) Directional sensitivity of echolocation in the Horseshoe bat *Rhinolophus ferrumequinum:* I. Directionality of sound emission. *Journal of Comparative Physiology*, 116, 51–61.

Schnitzler, H.-U. and Henson, O. W. (1980) Peformance of airborne animal sonar systems. In R.-G. Busnel and J. F. Fish (eds), *Animal Sonar Systems*, New York: Plenum Press.

Schnitzler, H.-U., Menne, D., Kober, R. and Heblich, K. (1983) The acoustical image of fluttering insects in echolocating bats. In F. Hubert and H. Markl, (eds), *Neuroethology and Behavioral Physiology*, Berlin: Springer-Verlag.

Simmons, J. A. (1989) A view of the world through the bat's ear: the formation of acoustic images in echolocation. *Cognition*, 33, 155–99.

Simmons, J. A. and Kick, S. A. (1984) Physiological mechanisms for spatial filtering and image enchancement in the sonar of bats. *Annual Review of Physiology*, 46, 599–614.

Simmons, J. A. et al. (1975) Information content of bat sonar echoes. Am. Sci. 63, 204–15.

Stevenson, S. B. and Altes, R. A. (1990) Discrimination of jittered sonar echoes by the echolocating bat, *Eptesicus fuscus:* the shape of target images in echolocation. *Journal of Comparative Physiology A*, 167, 589–616.

Strawson, P. F. (1959) *Individuals*. New York: Doubleday and Co.

Suga, N. (1984) The extent to which biosonar information is represented in bat auditory cortex. In G. M. Edelman, W. E. Gall and W. M. Cowan (eds), *Dynamics of Neocortical Function*, New York: John Wiley and Sons.

Suga, N. (1988) Auditory neuroethology and speech processing: complex-sound processing by combination-sensitive neurons. In G. M. Edelman, W. E. Gall and W. M. Cowan (eds), *Auditory Function: Neurobiological Bases of Hearing*, New York: John Wiley and Sons.

Suga, N. (1990) Biosonar and neural computation in bats. *Scientific American*, June, 60–8.

Suga, N. and Jen, P. H.-S. (1975) Peripheral control of acoustic signals in the auditory system of echolocating bats. *Journal of Experimental Biology*, 62, 277–311.

Suga, N., Niwa H., Taniguchi, I. and Margoliash, D. (1987) The personalized auditory cortex of the Mustached bat: adaptation for echo location. *Journal of Neurophysiology*, 58, 643–54.

Surlykke, A. (1988) Interaction between echolocating bats and their prey. In P. E. Nachtigall and P. W. B. Moore, (eds), *Animal Sonar: Processes and Performances*, New York: Plenum Press.

Suthers, R. A. (1965) Acoustic orientation by fish-catching bats. *Journal of Experimental Zoology*, 158, 319–48.

Webster, F. A. and Brazier, O. G. (1968) Experimental studies on echolocation mechanisms in bats. Aerospace Medical Res. Lab., Wright-Patterson Air Force Base, Ohio, AD 673373.

Webster, F. A. and Durlach, N. I. (1963) Echolocation systems of the bat. MIT Lincoln Lab Report No. 41-G-3, Lexington, Mass.

Webster, F. A. and Griffin, D. R. (1962) The role of the flight membranes in insect capture in bats. *Animal Behavior*, 10, 332–40.

8
Mind is Artificial

BO DAHLBOM

We come to the full possession of our power of drawing inferences the last of all our faculties, for it is not so much a natural gift as a long and difficult art.

C. S. Pierce, "The Fixation of Belief"

When Daniel Dennett's *Content and Consciousness* was published in 1969, two other books of great importance appeared. Herbert Simon's *The Sciences of the Artificial* was a forceful plea for a radical reorientation of the sciences towards "a science of design" based on an appreciation of the fact that "the world we live in today is much more a man-made, or artificial, world than it is a natural world" and the fact that man himself, or the human mind, is the "most interesting of all artificial systems." W. V. Quine's *Ontological Relativity and Other Essays* expressed a more conservative appreciation of the natural sciences, wanting to "naturalize epistemology," defining it "as a chapter of psychology and hence of natural science" studying "a natural phenomenon, viz., a physical human subject."[1]

Quine's ideas about a naturalized philosophy were perceived as radical by the philosophical community and created quite a commotion. Simon's ideas about cognitive science, as a science of the artificial with a sociological aspect, were much too radical to be perceived at all. The cognitive science coming out of the creative atmosphere of the 1960s was and still remains a natural science. As one of the more forceful proponents of naturalism, Daniel Dennett is original in that he has, over the years, shown a growing appreciation of the artificial.[2] Indeed, the way I like to think of his philosophy, is as being situated in between Quine and Simon, rather closer to Quine but very much aware of the attraction of Simon. In this essay I shall try various strategies to push him further in that direction, and then return at the very end to a discussion of some of Simon's ideas for an artificial science. What I will do, in effect, is outline an artificial, or social, alternative to naturalism, and what would be more natural than to call it "socialism?" That word seems to have no better use at the moment.

1 From Naturalism to Socialism

Dennett is doing "naturalized philosophy" and naturalism is in many ways typically American. Europeans tend to be uneasy with it, with "tough-minded philosophy" as James once put it. When in the late nineteenth century, philosophers were breaking away from transcendental idealism, Americans turned to naturalism, while Europeans returned to the safety of a Lockean "under-labourer" position, trying out different varieties of conceptual analysis. Dennett has rather little patience with this type of meticulous, pedestrian philosophy, with what he now calls "slogan-honing" (Dennett, 1991a, p. 460).

Naturalism in philosophy may mean many things, depending on what other kind of ism – idealism, supernaturalism, platonism, phenomenalism, dualism – one is attacking. When Quine was naturalizing philosophy in the early 1960s, he was arguing explicitly against the idea of a "first philosophy." But very few readers of Quine at that time had much faith in phenomenalism or metaphysics. More important was the fact that Quine's definition of epistemology as "a chapter of psychology" provided an alternative both to epistemology as philosphy of science (Vienna) *and* as linguistic analysis (Oxford), the ruling styles at the time. Thus Quine changed the subject matter of epistemology from scientific products and ordinary language to stimuli, nervous systems, and behavior.[3] But he also changed the very idea of epistemology from being a normative to becoming a descriptive project. The norms of a scientific methodology or the norms of ordinary language no longer had any direct bearing on epistemology. Without much ado, Quine did away with an element generally held to be essential to epistemology – even by fellow Americans such as Wilfrid Sellars, who were otherwise almost as tough as Quine.

When you stress the normative element of epistemology, as Sellars did, the idea of a naturalized epistemology will seem less attractive. Norms are social and consequently demand an epistemology "socialized" rather than naturalized. Quine (1960) stressed that language is a "social art" but only used this fact to defend his behaviorism. His naturalism left epistemology wide open for a more sociological approach. And we have seen a post-Kuhnian philosophy of science develop in direct opposition to the idea of a naturalized epistemology, stressing instead sophistic themes such as: reality is socially constructed; truth is not correspondence; science is continuous with poetry and politics, and like them a search without progress for the best-selling metaphor.

Most American philosophers went with Quine rather than with Sellars, and reading "chapter of psychology" to mean "promise of progress," they did not worry about knowledge as a social phenomenon. Turning to Darwin to define knowledge as an organ, wielded in the struggle for survival,[4] they cut themselves off from the "epistemological" discussion going on in post-Kuhnian philosophy of science.

Now, Dennett has a remedy for this neglect that unfortunately he has not been particularly interested in using. Distinguishing, in "How to Change Your Mind" (1978) between "opinions" and "beliefs," between, roughly, "sentences held true" and "dispositions to behave," he has the distinction he needs to engage in a discussion of knowledge as a social phenomenon. But a naturalized philosophy does not have much to say about opinions. They seem to be peculiarly human, less functional, less biological, than beliefs. And beliefs are certainly important. With wrong ones we die. But then, on the other hand, for most of us, thanks to evolution, the right ones come rather naturally. Most of our dispositions to behave are generally shared, tacit natural habits, not much to fuss about. Opinions, in contrast, are the medium of disagreement, argument, and explicit conflict. Opinions make a difference. Sentences held true are what human beings live and die for. They are what religion, politics, and science are made of, so how can you do epistemology without them?

Dennett can, of course, be excused for not seriously including opinions as objects of study in his philosophy of mind, by the fact that doing so would force him out of his natural habitat, the human organism. The human organism was not designed for language, he will say.[5] The underlying motive, here, seems to be rooted in an unfortunate divide between contemporary psychology and sociology. In psychology, people are organisms with beliefs, while in contemporary sociology they are persons with opinions. It is not easy to cross that divide.

The crucial difference between these two camps seems to be the question of scientific progress. Dennett sees cognitive science as bringing progress to our understanding of the mind, progress as the accumulation of knowledge, while sociology sees all attempts at understanding the mind as part of our attempts at self-understanding and edification, relative to and part of our culture, and changing with the *Zeitgeist*.

I would like to see bridges being built between these two camps. I would like to see a socialized philosophy of mind being developed as a complement to the naturalized philosophy that philosophers like Dennett have turned into the most exciting field within contemporary philosophy. A socialized philosophy of mind studies a social human subject in an artificial environment. In such a philosophy, mind, consciousness, and the mental processes are first and foremost social phenomena and to be studied as such.

I will try to make this view seem plausible by arguing, in section 2, that the theories of mind and consciousness typically put forth in psychology and philosophy are much more revealing about the society of their protagonists than about the human organism, and that this should make one question demarcations between mind and society and think of the mind as part of society. After thus having made a more general case for the social nature of mind, I will go on to show what a socialized theory of mind might look like. I will do this by testing, in section 3, the specific idea that thinking can be viewed as a craft, as a kind of tool use relying on culturally supplied, cognitive, or intellectual artifacts, and by discussing, in section 4, how, like manual crafts, thinking can be automated, resulting in automatic intelligence (AI). In section 5, I will present Simon's conception of cognitive science as artificial and use that presentation to discuss the difference between organisms and artifacts, between a natural and an artificial approach, between a functional stance and a design stance. In section 6, finally, I will try to show how an artificial approach has the implication of adding an "artificial stance" to Dennett's three stances.

2 Society in Mind or Mind in Society?

Dennett is doing naturalized philosophy, but he is not immune to the changes of fashion. And *Consciousness Explained* ends with the declaration that our attempts to understand consciousness is a search for illuminating metaphors:

I haven't replaced a metaphorical theory, the Cartesian Theater, with a *non*metaphorical ("literal, scientific") theory. All I have done, really, is to replace one family of metaphors and images with another, trading in the Theater, the Witness, the Central Meaner, the Figment, for Software, Virtual Machines, Multiple Drafts, a Pandemonium of Homunculi. It's just a war of metaphors, you say – but metaphors are not "just" metaphors; metaphors are the tools of thought. No one can think about consciousness without them, so it is important to equip yourself with the best set of tools available. Look what we have built with our tools. Could you have imagined it without them? (Dennett, 1991a, p. 455)

Quine would *never* have said that. A naturalized philosophy seeks illumination in the experimental results and theorizing of a biologically oriented psychology, that is, in science. Such a philosophy can appreciate the role of metaphors in science, and Quine's certainly does, but the substitution of one set for another is made on the basis of empirical evidence. What empirical evidence motivates the substitution of Multiple Drafts for the Cartesian Theater? Is the substitution Dennett is advocating in *Consciousness Explained* simply a change in fashion?

"Multiple Drafts" – what a wonderful way to summarize the idea of anarchistic liberalism, of a free market! And who would not prefer such a model, in society and in mind, to the "Final Solution" – with all its chilling connotations of a planned, bureaucratic economy? Luring us away from the metaphors of the Cartesian Theater to the metaphors of the Multiple Drafts model, Dennett is obviously in step with a more general ideological shift taking place in the 1980s, in management thinking as well as, to some extent, in management practice. Dennett is inviting us to apply "postfordism" to consciousness, to give up thinking of mind as a centralized, bureaucratic organization of Ford production lines, and begin thinking of it, rather, as a decentralized, flexible, organic organization.

This change of metaphors is radical, but it is by no means the only change since Descartes first drew the outlines of his model of the mind. A comparable change of mental metaphors took place in psychology in the early 1960s. This change was a battle in an ongoing tug-of-war between empiricism and rationalism, between Hume and Descartes. For several decades, behavioristic psychology had managed to stick to its very inductive view of the mind – learning by conditioning – in spite of the success of the so-called hypothetico-deductive method of learning in the empirical sciences.[6] But in the 1960s, people like Noam Chomsky and Ulric Neisser were to annul this discrepancy, bringing psychology back in step with the Cartesian *Zeitgeist*.

The change in metaphors for the mind taking place in the 1960s was motivated, we must say with hindsight, by rather flimsy empirical evidence. Neisser (1967) built his synoptic view of cognition on little more than Sperling's beautiful but rather contrived tachistoscope experiments. And Chomsky had no empirical evidence to motivate his new paradigm for psycholinguistics. Cognition as the reasoned testing of hypotheses, as analysis-by-synthesis, really needed no empirical evidence. People were ready for it, and just waiting for geniuses like Chomsky or Neisser to develop a comprehensive version of the "new" model of the mind.

Analytic philosophers like Quine, Putnam, and Goodman, who had been brought up on Hume and inductivism, were not so easily seduced by the new set of deductive metaphors, and Dennett tended to side with them from the beginning. Now, when the times are changing again, and empiricism is back in favor, Dennett is ready with his, fundamentally inductive, Multiple Drafts model. But is this just another change in fashion? As Dennett admits, his alternative is "initially deeply counterintuitive, but it grows on you." Does it grow on us because his Multiple Drafts model fits better the current ideology of decentralization, flexibility, and postfordism, than the Cartesian theory does? Or is there empirical evidence, less marginal than the Sperling experiments, to motivate a change of metaphors?

Consciousness Explained has rather little to offer in the line of evidence.[7] And the recent developments of computer technology from mainframes to networks, from von Neumann machines to parallel architectures, from classical AI to new connectionism, a vogue for society theories of mind, a general trend from new deal thinking to *laissez faire*, from functionalism to postmodernism, and the collapse of the "planned" economies in East Europe, seem to provide a much more convincing basis for explanation of why a "new" model of the mind "will grow on us."

Dennett is in the best of company, of course, in proposing a theory of the mind matching current ideas about social organization. Plato's theory of mind is a mirror of the social classes of Athens and Freud gives us a striking picture of his society: an enlightened, realistic bourgeoisie trying to negotiate between an aggressive, craving proletariat and a stubborn, conservative feudal class. The current fashion in mind metaphors is heavily influenced by the twentieth century interest in industrial production. A business company is divided into management, production, storage, purchase, and delivery. This is the architecture of the von Neumann machine, but it is also the mind of much contemporary cognitive science. Recently, both computer technology and cognitive science has come under the influence (or is it the other way around?) of the very fashionable philosophy of production called "just-in-time." Adequate communication with suppliers makes expensive long-term storage unnecessary: "It is all in the connections!"

These metaphors for the mind are tools for thought. We cannot think about the mind without them. But are they also right or wrong, that is, do they belong in a naturalized philosophy? Is Dennett's Multiple Drafts model a myth making us all feel more at ease with the "mystery of consciousness," or is it really a theory, generating hypotheses and explaining facts in the sciences of the mind? When we notice the close parallels between, on the one hand, our attempts to understand and organize our societies and, on the other, the theories of mind, we may well begin to wonder if through these changes of fashion we have really learned anything about the mind.

Anthropologists have made much of parallels like these between social phenomena and theories of nature. Maybe we're only trying to understand our own society when we think we are uncovering deep truths about the nature of nature? Maybe Dennett's Multiple Drafts model belongs in sociology rather than in the natural sciences? Well, why not both at the same time? When the metaphors prove valuable they gain strength back home, as when liberal ideas about society after a tour in biology return as Social Darwinism. But when mind is our object of inquiry, it is not clear that we ever leave the social realm. We have learned to distinguish between nature and society, between laws of nature and social customs. That our brains are natural objects we don't doubt, but how about our minds? Dennett has been eagerly contributing to the solution of the mind–body problem, but there is very little in his writings about the mind–society problem.

We begin by thinking of a theory like the Multiple Drafts model as a natural science theory of mental processes, describing brain mechanisms in the language of psychology. We then notice that this theory, like other such theories, is very much the expression of currently fashionable ways of thinking about society. Society is used as a metaphor to describe the mind. We begin to despair: is this kind of theorizing only a fashionable play with metaphors without empirical substance? We then see that if such theories do not teach us anything much about our minds, they at least teach us things about our society. Suddenly we remember that we, and our minds, are very much part of that society, and we begin to view these theories as culturally relative expressions of our attempts at self-understanding rather than as natural science theories. If mind is a social phenomenon rather than a brain process, then the use of social concepts in a theory of mind may not be metaphorical after all.

Psychoanalysis is both a theory of people in *fin de siècle* Europe and a theory of that Europe. It was interesting because of what it said about that society and its minds, about repression, censorship, and class struggle, that people preferred not to see. Theories like Minksy's (1985) society of mind or Dennett's Multiple Drafts model are more obvious expressions of contemporary American self-understanding: free competition in a free market. To the extent that they are true of that society, it is likely that they are true of the minds in that society. To the extent that they teach us things about our times, they tell us things about our minds. If mind is in society, there is no difference here.

If our minds are social rather than natural, then mental life is ruled by social customs rather than by natural laws, and it won't do to identify psychology with brain science. We can still try to distinguish our minds from society by carving out a niche within society for our minds, arguing that our mental life is internal and private, while our social life is external and public. But if, like Dennett, we doubt that there is any deep distinction to be made between the subjective and the objective dimensions of life, we should perhaps take more seriously the relations between mind and society. Rather than developing theories with an isolated subject in focus, we should develop theories which embed the subject in her (social) environment, stressing the way in which mental processes depend on and take place in that environment.

To say that mind is in society, that thinking is a social phenomenon, is to express a view very different from the view of thinking which dominates contemporary naturalistic cognitive science. It is to claim that thinking is regulated by social norms, that much thinking is better understood as a socially organized process involving several individuals (and, of course, their brains) with an organization as "the thinking thing." It is to claim that the process of thinking relies on tools and materials supplied by culture, some of which are internalized but a great deal of which are external, provided by the actual environment. It is to claim that mind is a social artifact, a collection of tools, rather than an organ in a body. It is to claim that the symbols, rules, categories, and objects which human beings use in their thinking belong to their social, artifactual environment, and that therefore questions such as whether human beings think in words or in images are ill formed: human thinking itself is an artifact, done in whatever medium is found suitable.[8]

3   Thinking with Tools

Thinking is a process. A theory of the mind must say something about that process. In *Consciousness Explained*, Dennett concentrates on the structure of mind, and has very little to say about the nature of mental processes. I have tried to indicate how the architecture of mind outlined in the Multiple Drafts model corresponds to the current fashion in organization theory. When you reorganize a business company you rely on the employees to go on producing within the new structure. The vital elements in the process are not supplied by the structure. Similarly, Dennett's new architecture of the mind tells us very little about the processes of mind. And in this case we have no employees to rely on. The Central Meaner in the Cartesian Theater has been fired and even if the Actors are still around somewhere, it is no longer clear what they are doing. Producing drafts, presumably, but what does that amount to?

What little Dennett has to say about the processes of mind is couched in the metaphorical language of speaking, writing, and communicating – perhaps the most popular among the many metaphors applied to thinking. In current cognitive psychology these "office" metaphors are only equalled in popularity by the industrial metaphor "processing." In modern psychology, the latter metaphor has replaced the craftsman as craftsmanship in society has given way to industrial production. Mind is transforming information like an industry processes its material. The metaphor of information processing brings Henry Ford and his production line to mind and invites the use of flow charts to map the mental processes.

A craftsman uses tools. Industrialization replaced both the craftsman and his tools with a machine. As we move into an information society, losing interest in industrialization, the tool metaphor has been revived. It has been used with great commercial success as a metaphor for computer software. This talk has stressed the fact that what you can do depends on the tools you have. I think that the craftsman metaphor, especially if you stress this aspect, can increase our understanding of the mind. Thinking of thinking as the use of tools will give us a richer view of mental processes the more mental tools we come up with.

Dennett wants, of course, a depersonalized architecture, but the craftsman metaphor is only used here to direct our attention to the variety of tools used in thinking. Once we have a rich enough view of that process, we can automate the tools and get rid of the craftsman. So let us consider the following thesis: mind is a social object rather than a natural, it is not a compound of organs but a collection of tools.

When I want to use the craftsman with his tools as a metaphor for the mind – and with tools I mean logic, language, books, logarithm tables, slide-rules, Italian book-keeping, statistical methods, maps, pencils, blackboards, databases – then I don't worry about distinguishing internal tools from external ones. Both mind and society need matter to run on. Society is implemented on buildings, highways, air force bases, law schools . . . and brains. Mind needs a brain to run on, but not just a brain. Some of the matter in which it is realized is inside the skull, some is outside.

Inventors of tools have sometimes been imitating the organs of other species. And mastering the use of a tool means incorporating it as an organ, as an extension of your body, as well noted by Michael Polanyi (1958). But the tool remains an artifact. Cognitive artifacts are no different from other tools in this respect. To learn to master such a tool will, of course, involve an organic change. If that change goes deeply enough it may make sense to view thinking as a brain process, but if not it will be more fruitful to distinguish the artifact in that process, viewing thinking as a craft.

Artifacts are built upon artifacts; we use our intellectual tools to construct more advanced such tools, as Spinoza put it,[9] and, as with most manual tools, very little can be learned about the artifact by studying the organism and vice versa. Even when it comes to such a fundamental cognitive artifact as language it is difficult to tell how much of this artifact is organically incorporated, that is, automated with the brain as mechanism, and how much is accessed only from the outside, as it were, being used as a tool.[10] Dennett expresses this well when he comments on the "virtual architecture" of language:

> So there is nothing *ad hoc* or unmotivated about the acknowledgment that some areas of human cognition require a higher-level "symbolic" virtual architecture; after all, language, arithmetic, logic, writing, map-making – these are all brilliant inventions that dramatically multiply our capacities for cognition, and it should come as no surprise if they invoke design principles unanticipated in the cognitive systems of other animals. They are, in the laudatory sense, *cognitive wheels*. (Dennett, 1991b, p. 27)

Thus when Millikan (chapter 6) argues that the language of thought, for reasons of organic realization, cannot be very language-like, she is not really saying anything about the medium in which we think. We think in all kinds of artificial media, of course. We should not take her advice (at the end of section 7) and "abandon the traditional image of the computing of mental sentences as like a formal system unfolding on paper," since it is on paper that much of our mental inferences are unfolding. I am not denying that our brains play a vital role in thinking. If thinking is tool use, then the role of the brain can best be studied by concentrating on the very complex interface between brain and cognitive artifacts.[11] To Millikan, the question whether our brains can use language is not about this interface, but about the brain itself, as if she were asking if our hands could be screwdrivers.

Millikan is interested in the biology of thinking, and she has (Millikan, 1984) expounded a powerful conception of cognitive science as biology. Normally, Dennett is much closer to Millikan than the positive characterization of cognitive wheels above might indicate. He is wont to stress not only the secondary, dependent nature of opinions, but their secondary importance to cognitive science as well:

> Opinions play a large, perhaps even decisive, role in our concept of a person, but . . . If one starts, as one should, with the cognitive states and events occurring in non-human animals, and uses these as the foundation on which to build theories of human cognition, the language-infected states are more readily seen to be derived, less directly implicated in the explanation of behavior . . . (Dennett, "Self-Portrait," forthcoming)

But certainly our "language-infected states" are seriously implicated in the explanation of verbal behavior and verbal behavior is at center stage in human cognitive affairs, in science, politics, and art. Like Quine, Dennett is caught halfway between language and biology. Wanting to use biology as his foundation, he cannot give to language its proper place as a cognitive artifact, but yet he cannot abandon language completely in view of its obvious importance in human cognitive affairs. He remains uncomfortable with much of the work in the philosophy of language, because he has no real place for language in his theory of the mind. Sometimes, however, as in "Two Contrasts: Folk Craft versus Folk Science, and Belief versus Opinion" (1991), he comes close to seeing the possibility of working out a compromise with a believer in the language of thought such as Jerry Fodor, according to which he and Fodor could both be right, one about natural beliefs, the other about artificial opinions.

When we begin to examine the analogy that thinking is a craft involving the use of intellectual tools, questions jump at us from all quarters. Is it possible to think without tools, with your bare brain so to speak? If you need the tools, the techniques to use them, and judgment to use them well, then how is intelligence distributed between tools, techniques, and judgment? Are there any natural intellectual tools or are all such tools, as I have presupposed above, artifacts? But if so, is not what we generally call "natural intelligence" really "artificial?" Or are the techniques we bring to such tools somehow natural? In order to answer these questions we need a much more careful and concrete examination of the relations between the tools, techniques and judgment of thinking, than I have been able to give. Here I want to consider briefly another aspect of tool use: the division of labor.

A craft is often practiced by a team, and no one expects the lowly apprentice to really understand what she is doing. She is one of those "dumb homunculi," Dennett speaks of, that we know how to replace with a mechanism, like the human computers who were replaced by computing machines. As we move up the hierarchy of a medieval craft system, the members' understanding of what the craft is all about will increase. The person at the top of the hierarchy has a deeper understanding of what goes on and why, but is probably less efficient at the practical task. She may very well use clumsy techniques and tools with the deepest understanding. It is the same with thinking, if it is a craft: it isn't an all or nothing affair.

When we think of thinking as craft, we will stress its productive character. And we will observe that in our modern society most crafts have undergone a process of industrialization. In that process, the idea is to divide and "dequalify" labor by automating techniques and letting management take care of judgment and understanding. Thinking is certainly no exception. What used to be an individual craft using fairly simple tools has become a complex production process performed by organizations relying on advanced rule systems, planning, division of labor and high technology. The more bureaucratic the organization, the more divided the labor, and the more fragmented the understanding will be. Even such anarchistic, conservative craftsmen as philosophers are becoming organized. Their thinking is like traffic: individuals drive the cars, but together they make up a complex system, an organization with many more elements than just people and automobiles (philosophers and their thoughts).

If we think of thinking as a craft, it is a complex process that does not take place in the person or her brain, but in the system which includes the cognitive artifacts used, wherever they may be. So, even if the brain is a machine it is not a thinking machine, except metonymically, as when we say after a long day of sewing: "I am really a sewing machine!" Our tendency to think of thinking as a process in the brain tends to hide from our view its dependence on artifacts. As a brain process, thinking is a *natural* process, and this makes it difficult for us to see that thinking today is about as artificial as anything else – communication, production, consumption – in our modern artificial world. Just as our society will grind to a halt when our artifacts break down, so thinking would be reduced to next to nothing were we to suffer a breakdown of our *intellectual* artifacts. What could we think, how could we reason, if we did not have words, books, diagrams, figures, concrete examples, algebra, logic, lisp, or legal systems?[12]

Thinking of thinking as a brain process makes us think of human intelligence as natural (in spite of the fact that most so-called intelligence tests measure artificial capacities like vocabulary and numerical ability). This has made the discussion of research on artificial intelligence more confusing than it need be. Once it is seen how artificial human thinking is, to what extent it relies on cultural artifacts, the artificial intelligence project to build thinking machines is seen as a rather mundane attempt to automate artifacts, in this case intellectual tools rather than manual ones, but so what? Let us examine the tool metaphor a little more by taking a closer look at that project understood in this way.

4 Automatic Intelligence

The use of tools can be improved by better tools or by better techniques. Thus our history is one of developing tools, of making them more specialized and easier to handle, and of developing educational systems ensuring effective technical training, as well as modern attempts like that of F. W. Taylor (1911) to increase the efficiency of workers by making their behavior stereotypical, more machine-like.

The use of tools can also be improved by better understanding of both tools and their operation: conditions of usage, context, motivations, implications, and so on. This third aspect, often called "judgment," is by many people considered to be particularly human. It is a rag-bag category, and let us leave it like that. If Taylor took a few steps towards the replacement of human workers with industrial robots, it was because he considered the role of judgment to be marginal in manual labor. Taylor concentrated on the techniques at the interface between user and tool.

Tools and techniques develop together by co-adaptation. We can think of automation as the incorporation in the tool of some of the techniques previously demanded of the user. The typical tool is inert. The user puts it in motion. With an automatic sander you don't have to move the sander back and forth. You just hold the machine and the sander moves by itself. With automation, part of the co-adaptation between tool and technique moves into the tool. The tool becomes a machine.

Not all automation transfers techniques from users to tools. Instead of developing the tools into machines, we can leave the tools unchanged and build the techniques of the user into a separate machine, creating a robot. An automobile is a horseless carriage: the techniques of the horse have been incorporated into the tool.[13] But a tractor is more like an imitation horse than a horseless carriage. The tractor replaces the user, while the tools, the carriages, plows, tillers, remain virtually the same, except for slight adjustments of the user interface. Thus, the automation of a work process can either mean the incorporation in the tool of some of the techniques of the user or the replacement of the user with a substitute machine.

This distinction is by no means even as clear as the one between tool and technique. It is a distinction between specialized and more general purpose automation. A Tayloristic approach is an attempt to dequalify work by dividing labor into simple techniques. Each individual worker will perform a single, simple routine with one and the same tool. There is no difference between replacing such a user and automating the tool she is using. But when the worker uses several different tools, relying on several different techniques, having to rely on judgment in selecting tools and techniques, the difference between automating a tool and imitating the user should be clear. Automation has in most cases meant the automation of tools, but there are exceptions. In the future we may see more clear-cut examples of automation by imitation of the user.

Intellectual tools can, of course, be improved by automation. Intellectual operations that can be identified with techniques, algorithms if you like, can be automated and incorporated into the tool. In this regard, there is no difference between intellectual and manual work. The story of the development of the abacus, the desk calculator, the invention of computing machines, and the resulting programmable electronic calculators of today is a good example of how techniques are incorporated, one after the other, in a tool that consequently grows in complexity. This is an example of the automation of a tool rather than the replacement of a user, but of course the first electronic computing machines were built, none the less, with the express purpose of replacing the "computers," a substantial, and growing, profession in the early 1940s.[14]

Electronic calculators are examples of what might be called "automatic intelligence." This is not an expression in wide use. Instead we speak of "artificial intelligence," and we rarely think of common electronic calculators in those terms. We prefer to think of intelligence as a general capacity, and describe the ambition of artificial intelligence research as the imitation of a distinguished user rather than as the automation of some simple tools.

With tool use as a metaphor for thinking, we can define intelligence as the proficiency at using one's tools, whatever they are. The typical way to express your frustration with not being as intelligent as you'd like to be is then: "I *knew* it, why didn't I *think* of it." Intelligence is a matter of having certain techniques.[15] But as those techniques are automated, or more generally, when thinking tools are improved and become more "user-friendly," techniques that used to distinguish the intelligent person will suffer the fate of manual techniques subjected to automation: they no longer confer prestige. And when techniques have lost their prestige, they are no longer signs of intelligence.

Intelligence can, of course, be defined as the general capacity to develop intellectual techniques, rather than as the possession of intellectual techniques and tools. We may still want to describe, as intelligent, the skillful use of intellectual tools. And then, perhaps, calculators deserve to be called intelligent machines in spite of the fact that they rigidly repeat simple combinations of elementary operations. The issue is not what to call these machines, of course, but how we should think of artificial intelligence: as the imitation of a general intelligence or as the piecemeal automation of intellectual tools.

Suppose that we manage to program a computer to solve problems in a certain domain, preferably as general as possible. What have we learned about how human beings solve problems in this domain? We will probably be aided by our computer program in our efforts to determine how human beings solve problems, and we may find that, in our culture at least, people use the very artifact we have been automating. (We may well wonder how our ability to develop the program hinged on the fact that we were already, unwittingly, using this artifect.) But, if that is not the case, our computer program itself has nothing to tell us about human beings. We can learn from it about problem solving, as an artificial discipline, but there is nothing particularly human about that discipline (cf. Simon, 1969, pp. 30f, for this point).

In "classical" or "good old-fashioned" artificial intelligence research, as defined by Allen Newell and Herbert Simon, people study and develop cognitive artifacts and in doing so they study intelligence. Not human intelligence, but just intelligence, as a craft, varying culturally, with certain natural constraints, like other crafts (cf. Simon, 1980, pp. 42f). This is why those in AI never really worry about testing their ideas, principles, systems on human beings. They are developing intelligence techniques, not a psychological theory. It has created unnecessary confusion when people in classical AI have failed to see this.[16]

Even Newell and Simon misdescribed their work on problem solving, viewing the heuristic rules they tested in the Logic Theorist and the General Problem Solver as some sort of psychological laws, while it should be clear that these are better viewed as principles of problem solving and nothing else. Like primitive mathematical theories and legal rule systems, these principles are artifacts, tools, developed for a certain use. Mathematics, generally, is a collection of artifacts, some of which are implemented on some brains, and some even on machines, but this certainly does not make them psychological laws in any interesting sense.[17]

Recently, research in artificial intelligence has begun to shift from automating a variety of different cognitive tools to imitating more general intelligence techniques, or even the brain. This change is radical. To classical AI, thinking is the rule-governed manipulation of symbols, and the implementation is in principle irrelevant. The automation of cognitive tools will naturally take one tool at a time, fulfilling its tasks by "modularization." You learn about the modules by studying the tools. When the project is to imitate the brain, the modules will be different systems in the brain. And the task is typically conceived as an all or nothing affair: "Can artificial intelligence be achieved?" (Waltz, 1988, p. 191).

When artificial intelligence research changes its orientation from automation to imitation, this move can be justified by an interest in the human brain rather than in intelligence, just as when someone initially interested in wood carving turns his attention away from knife and wood to study the human hand. This change seems to me ill advised. Computer technology can no doubt be fruitfully used to study the human brain, but little of relevance to intelligence will result from that research. To reconstruct our cognitive tools from neural net theory is as difficult as reconstructing complex applications from operating systems.

The new technology of parallel architectures, so useful when making large technical calculations, has played an important role in supporting the renaissance of an interest in the brain, in driving artificial intelligence research back to nature. But rather than using this technology to imitate the human brain, we can use it to automate the kind of complex cognitive artifacts exemplified by work organizations such as offices. Artificial intelligence research will then make a substantial contribution to the computerization of society, instead of getting deeply involved in the dream of creating an artificial brain, a dream that may be exciting to neurophysiology, but is otherwise comparatively uninteresting.

Part of the blame for misunderstanding classical AI and for an interest in imitating the human brain must fall on Turing himself. His imitation test makes us think of artificial intelligence as the imitation of human beings rather than as the automation of their cognitive tools. This test, in effect, defines intelligence as the capacity to carry on a conversation, and the aim and nature of artificial intelligence research accordingly. The imitation game is a parlour game of interest to philosophers, but it has very little to do with AI research. Our interest in machine translation or parsing, the ambition to design "automatic English," is not motivated by a desire to have machines as partners in *conversation*.[18]

There is such a lot we still don't know about the cognitive tools we use, looked upon as tools, and the techniques we need to use them. Computers are wonderful devices for automating such tools. And the important task of artificial intelligence research lies not in an attempt to make copies of us, but in an effort to increase our intelligence by improving and automating our cognitive tools, as well as designing new ones.

5 An Artificial Science

I have argued above against the dualism between mind and society, by arguing against naturalism in psychology, trying to show how culture-relative our theorizing in psychology normally is, and by questioning the dominating conceptions of the mind in favor of a view of thinking as a social practice with tools. When mind is seen to be a part of society, then psychology will be a part of (a new kind of) sociology as well. I now want to place this argument within the context of Herbert Simon's ideas about a general, design-oriented science of the artificial.

I began by lining up Simon and Quine as extremes, one introducing artificial science, artifacts, and design, the other advocating natural science, physicalism, and empiricism. I then placed Daniel Dennett in between the two, wanting to push him away from Quine closer to Simon, away from naturalism and biology in the general direction of sociology and technology, away from natural science and a naturalized philosophy towards artificial science and a socialized philosophy.

It is time that we look a little closer at what Simon is actually saying in *The Sciences of the Artificial* about what artificial science is supposed to be. The first thing we then notice is that the contrast I have made between organisms and artifacts is not stressed by Simon. Artifacts or artificial systems are functional, adaptive systems, on Simon's view, systems that "can be characterized in terms of functions, goals, adaptation" (Simon, 1969, p. 6). It is true that he defines artifacts as man-made, but he also claims that, in all other respects, organisms are good examples of artificial systems, being adaptive systems that have "evolved through the forces of organic evolution" (1969, p. 7). Business organizations, machines, and organisms are all exemplary adaptive systems.

An artifact can be thought of as the interface, Simon says, between the substance and organization of the artifact and its environment. The two sides of the interface, its structure and its environment, fall under the province of the natural sciences. But the interface itself belongs to artificial science. While the natural sciences are interested in how things are, the sciences of the artificial are concerned with how things might be – with design. Indeed, artificial science is a science of design.

Simon formulates his task as that of showing how science can encompass both "human purpose" and "natural law," finding "means for relating these two disparate components" (p. 4). In accordance with this project, psychology is first defined as an artificial science studying the internal limits of behavioral adaptation. Then, since these limits are seen to be rather marginal, and the complexity of human thinking to be artificial, "subject to improvement through the invention of improved designs" (p. 26), cognitive science is included in the science of design as a study of (the design of) the cognitive artifacts designed by man attempting to adapt to his environment.

A psychology that studies the internal limits of adaptation is, of course, very different from a psychology that studies (the design of) cognitive artifacts, even if both can be said to study "how things might be." The subject matter of one is "man's relation to his biological inner environment," the subject matter of the other is "man's relation to the complex outer environment in which he seeks to survive and achieve" (p. 81). Thus Simon stresses the role of the environment, internal v. external, in both varieties of psychology. His ideas of how to study the artificial seem to divide into an empirical science about the limits of rationality (or adaptation) on the one hand, and an empirical science of adaptation on the other. The artificial itself, the interface between the internal and the external environment, tends to disappear into the background. And modern evolutionary biology seems like a good model for artificial science, with organisms as exemplary artificial systems. Simon's radical program for a new science of design seems to reduce to a rather well-known theme in contemporary American thinking: functionalism.

Functionalism, the idea that phenomena can be identified and explained in terms of their function, has two rather different roots: biology and engineering. These two forms of functionalism were famously joined by Norbert Wiener in his program for a general science of cybernetics. Dennett is a strong proponent of this marriage, defining biology, and cognitive science, as "a species of engineering: the analysis, by 'reverse engineering,' of the found artifacts of nature" ("Self-Portrait," forthcoming). To Dennett, evolution is a process of engineering, organisms the artifacts designed in that process. Like Simon, Dennett wants to think of both evolution and engineering as processes of adaptation and he ought to feel very comfortable with Simon's ideas for a design-oriented artificial science as I have here described them.

But something is terribly wrong in this description. One of Simon's motives for his campaign for an artificial science is the obvious shortcomings of the natural sciences as a foundation for (education in) engineering:

> In view of the key role of design in professional activity, it is ironic that in this century the natural sciences have almost driven the sciences of the artificial from professional school curricula. Engineering schools have become schools of physics and mathematics; medical schools have become schools of biological science; business schools have become schools of finite mathematics. (Simon, 1969, p. 56)

In the same context he goes on to warn that: "a science of artificial phenomena is always in imminent danger of dissolving and vanishing. The peculiar properties of the artifact lie on the thin interface between the natural laws within it and the natural laws without" (p. 57). Only by holding fast to the "process of design itself" will it be possible to develop an artificial science that is radically different from the natural sciences.

When we look closer at how Simon describes the general science of design, it is substantially different from the two varieties of pscyhology described above. Rather than studying the relations between artifacts and environments, such a science will concentrate on the artifacts themselves and their design. Such an artificial science will stress the important differences between biology and engineering rather than delve into the obvious similarities between them. If one wants to argue, as Simon clearly does, that the idea and methods of an artificial science are importantly different from those of the natural sciences, even if we are only beginning to appreciate how, then one should be careful not to describe evolution by natural selection as a process of design. If we turn to biology to learn about design, then artificial science will collapse into the natural sciences, after all.[19]

But what then are the important differences between natural science and a science of design, between evolution and engineering? The fundamental difference is one of "knowledge interest." In the natural sciences we want to find out what the world is like, while in the artificial we are interested in what could possibly be and how to make it so. In engineering we want to make the impossible, to push further the limits of human imagination. Engineering is radical, utopian, constructive. Evolution is fundamentally conservative. Goldschmidt's hopeful monsters not-withstanding, the design going on in nature is closely tracking the internal and external environment, advancing by "imperceptibly small steps." When we study evolution, we study the environment. In engineering we admire most the radical departures from environmental limitations. And the limitations that count the most are set by the "practical inertia" of previous design decisions.

Organisms are not artifacts for the obvious reason that they are not man-made. All other similarities aside, this difference is important enough to warrant attention. It shows up in fundamentally different attitudes to organisms and artifacts. We look with wonder on complex, beautifully adaptive organs and organisms, wondering how they are at all possible, how they could have evolved. The aim of a biology inspired by evolutionary thinking is to make the wonderful comprehensible. But when we look with wonder at similarly complex artifacts, our wonder has a different, more creative, design-oriented flavor. "If they could make that," we say, "then I should be able to make this!" Artifacts inspire us to improvements. Our interest in how they are made is guided by our interest in making them ourselves, and making them better. In biology it is natural to view organisms from a functional stance, but in engineering the typical stance is a design stance – and these two are funda-mentally different.[20]

The distinction I want to make between biology and engineering is not made in terms of design methods. There are such different methods, to be sure, and some have tried to use them to distinguish between evolution and engineering. But modern engineers are very good at tinkering, so Lévi-Strauss' (1966) distinction between engineering and tinkering does not really draw the line where it should. Similarly misplaced is the rather interesting difference between cultivating a process of growth and imposing a form on an object once and for all. No, the distinction I want to make is blushingly simple, but this does not make it less important.

Of course, I am not saying that this difference between organisms and artifacts, between biology and technology, makes it impossible for us to view organisms as artifacts (or vice versa), to bring to biology an engineering perspective, to organisms a design stance. All I am saying is that when we do this, we should be careful not to reduce the differences between the two, losing what is essential to technology, its creative ambition to explore the space of possibilities, or losing what is essential to biology, its responsibility to keep track of the actual. The risk that biologists begin to think only like engineers does not seem imminent, but the engineers we educate today are certainly lacking in design attitude.

Breeders of animals or plants often become inspired by each others' results: "If she could make that, then I should be able to . . . ." That is, they look upon their organisms as artifacts, with a genuine design orientation. In the course of time we may actually so change our attitude to the organic world as to make it a province of artificial science.[21] This all depends, of course, on the thickness of the interface, on the proportion between the overall complexity of the organism and the internal and external limits to (artificial) adaptation.

The theory of evolution is a theory of how biological organisms develop and change by adaptation to a natural environment. But our environment is artificial rather than natural, our world is an artificial world, and we are to a large extent artificial ourselves. Quine's image of "a biological organism in a physical environment" is complicated by the abundance of artifacts with which we have populated our world. Simon wants us to think of these artifacts as the adaptive interface between their inner and outer environments. The human mind, as well as a person, is an artifact, an interface between a physiological machinery and the natural world. We can think of other artifacts, such as cities, airplanes, colleges, the tools we use and the organizations we belong to, as part of the environment we have to adapt to, but at the same time they are part of ourselves as adaptive systems, part of the artificial interface that we are. So, ironically, we come out defending a sort of dualism between mind and body. But it is a dualism with a twist: mind is material, of course, but it is not natural. Mind is artificial.

6 An Artificial Stance

The modern world is an artificial world, but modern science is a science of nature. Explaining and predicting events in nature, including the behavior of organisms, is very different from explaining and predicting human action in a modern society. The natural sciences, including biology, are of little help in making sense of our artificial world. They tempt us to take society for granted and prevent us from appreciating the role of technology in shaping society, its members, and their actions.

The natural sciences played an important role in revolutionizing thinking in the seventeenth century, but today they act as a conservative brake on our attempts to come to grips with our world. Physicalism, a naturalized philosophy, a biological approach to the study of human cognition, are all expressions of a conservative interest in nature at a time when what we need is a theory of technology, a theory of design, a science of the artificial. Dennett's rightly celebrated intentional systems theory is an excellent example of such a conservative, naturalized attempt to lay the foundation for a study of mind and action. By trying to make clear exactly how this theory falls short, I hope to promote an interest in the artificial.

Dennett is remarkably creative in coming up with examples to illustrate (or generate) his ideas and distinctions, but examples can be seductive. Take the famous chess-playing computer in "Intentional Systems" (1971), for example, used by Dennett to introduce his three stances: the physical stance, the design stance, and the intentional stance. How much hinges on the fact that the machine is playing a familiar parlour game? That it is a computer acting and not a person? Would we come up with different stances were we to use a different type of example?

Before we look at such an example, let us think more generally about human action. In order for an action to appear it must be possible and it must be wanted. An action is possible only if the agent has the competence to perform it and the environment supplies the means needed. The agent must want to perform the action and the social norm system must encourage or at least not prohibit it. In explaining or predicting human action we need consider conditions like these, and the way actions are differentially weighted by them, but sometimes one or more of these conditions will be obviously satisfied, and not in question.

In a game like chess, the overall motivation of the players is to win the game. We know what they want; what is permitted and what is not is rarely in doubt. The norm system is simple and familiar, if we want to explain an action only in its role as a chess move. Likewise there is seldom any problem with the physical environment. Asking for an explanation of a chess move, we do not ask how it was physically possible to move the piece. Only one condition really needs to be considered: the relative competence of the chess players, including what relevant information they may have, or be able to glean, about the opponent.

When we leave the world of games, actions will become more difficult to predict. Motivation and norm system will often be unclear and the environment will be more complex and problematic. When predicting such actions, we have to consider all the four conditions distinguished above, including the three that we can take for granted in predicting chess moves. Norm systems vary and interact with one another and with the desires of the agent in complex ways. People will act under the influence of norm systems that are alien to us, performing surprising and incomprehensible actions. Even in a game of chess we may sometimes need the norm system to explain an action. When someone is cheating, the game can be very puzzling, unless one is daring enough to suggest that there has been a breach of the rules. Similarly, the technical environment becomes important when the action itself was not observed and it was not clear that the environment permitted that kind of action.

The roles of these four conditions are well exemplified in the work of an anthropologist studying a foreign culture, but let us choose a less exotic cliché. When the fictional detective goes about identifying the murderer, he will typically ask about competence, means and opportunity, motive, and moral character. When the detective is reconstructing the crime, possible suspects will be excluded one after the other on the basis of falling short in one or more of these dimensions. At the ensuing trial there will be a replay of sorts of this procedure. The prosecutor will try to convince the jury that the defendant had the competence, means, motive, and character needed to commit the murder. If there is no doubt about the actual sequence of events, then the attorney for the defense still has the possibility of getting the defendant off the hook by claiming temporary insanity, or other mitigating circumstances.

In all these discussions during the criminal investigation and at the trial, there will be a rich variety of explanations and predictions of behavior. The three stances discussed by Dennett will all be used, but in addition, the environment, both physical and social, will figure prominently in these explanations. The design of the culprit, his size, strength, intelligence, special competencies will be referred to, but so will the availability of certain tools and substances. Murder is an immoral act and the likelihood that the suspect would be capable of breaking the norms of his society will also be discussed. Actions are possible only if you are at the right place at the right time, so a lot of time will be spent on the temporal geography of the suspects, the checking of alibis, and so on.

Chess is a parlour game and as such it relies on a simple and standardized physical and social environment. Environmental conditions, external to the agent, tend to drop out when we consider such actions as chess moves. To make things even worse, the pedagogical advantage of having a computer as agent, when explaining the use of the stances, is matched by the disadvantage of having an agent which, at the current state of technology, really has no environment, physical or social. But, when we are not dealing with computers, nor with games, how could we predict behavior unless we had environmental variables in our functions?[22]

The physical and social conditions bring out the role of artifacts in human action. We could take artifacts seriously by adding a fourth, artificial stance, to complement Dennett's three well-entrenched ones. But Dennett would see such a stance as simply an application of the intentional stance suitably provisioned with historical and social contextual details. After all, when you ask, of an intentional system, what it *ought* to believe, given its context, etc., the context includes its personal history, obviously, but also the context (social, environmental, cultural) in which it acts. The principles of interpretation are the same – there is no *special* way in which history or convention enter into it.[23]

But the very same argument can be directed against distinguishing a special design stance. After all, when you ask, of an intentional system, what it *ought* to believe, it seems very natural to consider not only the external context, but the internal as well, what it ought to believe given that it is designed thus and thus. The principles of interpretation will be the same. So, the only motive for distinguishing a design stance but not an artificial stance seems to be a bias in favor of an intentional system as a natural organism rather than a social being. Of course, the point here is not how many stances you want to operate with, but the way you argue for the stances you want to distinguish.

Both the design stance and the artificial stance add information to the intentional stance. The artificial stance looks closer at the various rule systems, instruments, and other environmental features that are involved in the competence of an intentional system, while the design stance goes into the details of the internal implementation of its competence. If you want to predict the behavior of a mouse confronted with combinations of cats and cheese (another of Dennett's early examples), the intentional stance is perfect: the competence involved is simple and we can assume a good design.

In general, if you are trying to keep track of an intentional system, then the more rational or optimal it is, the less interesting will be the properties both of the design and of the physical and social environment.[24] But you must be able to match its competence, of course, in order to use the intentional stance to your advantage. Confronted with an optimally designed chess player, you will lose the game exactly because you will be unable to predict its moves using the intentional stance. The more complex the competence, the more important its role will be in the prediction, and the less relevant will be the beliefs and the desires of the agent, acting as she is as an instrument of her competence.

Explanations and predictions from the artificial stance typically rely on the idioms of the artifacts being referred to. When the artificial stance is couched in an intentional idiom, as it can be, it may seem as if one were ascribing beliefs and desires to the agent. But the particular agent is really not being referred to, except as a vehicle for the relevant artifacts. The intentional stance attributes beliefs and desires to the individual agent, there is never any doubt about that, and it is made quite clear in "True Believers" (in Dennett, 1987), the current "flagship expression" of Dennett's view. But sometimes, as in "Intentional Systems" (1978, p. 13), when Dennett distinguishes between "*human* psychology" and the "'psychology' of intentional systems generally" or, in "Three Kinds of Intentional Psychology" (Dennett, 1987, pp. 58ff), when he describes intentional systems theory as "competence theory," the intentional stance seems much more like, what I here call, an artificial stance. This vacillation, if I may so call it, explains part, but not all, of Dennett's vacillation between realism and instrumentalism in connection with the intentional stance.

To the extent that human beings subject themselves to the rules of their institutions, or to "opportunity," their behavior is predictable from those rules. And to the extent that human beings rely on technology in their actions, their behavior is predictable from the normal functioning of that technology. "Watch her now as the game begins, and you will see her move the pawn in front of her king two steps forward." "Watch how all these cars will begin to move when the lights turn yellow and green." The bureaucrat's stamping of your passport is artificial in the same sense in which the computer's chess move is: the stamping is determined by an institution, the move by a program. Explaining and predicting their behavior, we don't have to assume rationality or posit beliefs and desires. When everything goes well, all we have to rely on is our knowledge of the relevant artifacts and the assumption that people will implement those artifacts. "How do you dare drive here on the highway with all the other cars?" The intentional stance: "I assume that the other drivers are rational and therefore have desires and beliefs that make them drive pretty much the way I do." The artificial stance: "This is traffic, isn't it? The rules of traffic guarantee a reasonable safety."[25]

With most of this Dennett will agree, I think. Indeed, most of the points are from his own writings. Still, he seems unwilling to fully accept the consequences of his position and add a fourth stance to his trio. I interpret this as an indication that, in spite of everything, he is still underestimating the role of artifacts in human life, preferring to think of us as mainly biological organisms. When you introduce a fourth stance, you will have to look closer at artifacts, opinions among them, and you will begin moving towards an attitude very different from the naturalized functionalism dominating contemporary philosophy of mind.

Just seeing how something works will seldom be enough for one to be able to construct it oneself, or even to consider constructing it: there is a long way to go from a functional stance to a design stance. With such a stance you will become more interested in the design of artifacts, than in how they determine human action. Such a design stance is an essential element in Herbert Simon's conception of an artificial science. Artificial science is a science of design. Foreign to the natural sciences as this design attitude is, it is still definitive of human existence. Our ability to negate the actual and think the possible, is what makes us human. Ending this long journey on a high note, we could summarize its message by paraphrasing Heidegger: The essence of *Dasein* is *Design*.

ACKNOWLEDGMENTS

Lars-Erik Janlert gave invaluable advice on a previous version, Svante Beckman has been an unusually stimulating discussion partner, and Susan Dennett heroically checked my English. Olle Edqvist and the Swedish Council for Planning and Coordination of Research have been generous in their support.

NOTES

1 Quotes from Simon (1969), pp. 3, 22 and from Quine (1969), p. 82.
2 Cf. such papers as "Memes and the Exploitation of Imagination" (1990), "The Interpretation of Texts, People and Other Artifacts" (1990), "The Role of Language in Intelligence" (forthcoming) and chapter 7 of *Consciousness Explained*. Ironically, it is a biologist, Richard Dawkins, who (together with Julian Jaynes) has been the important source of inspiration in this process.
3 Verbal behavior to be sure, but still behavior in the service of biological survival.
4 Evolution then comes to play the role of Descartes' benevolent God, ensuring that our beliefs are true. If they were not true we would not be here. Quine puts it thus "Creatures inveterately wrong in their inductions have a pathetic but praise-worthy tendency to die before reproducing their kind" in "Natural Kinds," an essay containing a clearer formulation of the motivation for an "epistemology naturalized," than the essay so named. Both essays are in Quine (1969).
5 But surely that argument can be carried all the way down? The human organism was not designed for sex, or for eating, or for walking – organic structures designed for other purposes, if you forgive the language, were put to new use. All evolution involves exaptation.
6 Sometimes people seem to be confused by the superficial resemblance between the method of hypothesis and instrumental (or operant) conditioning, trial and error, but it is the deduction taking place in the development of hypotheses that makes the difference. Thorndike's kittens do not reason.
7 In appendix B of *Consciousness Explained*, Dennett gives seven predictions ("half-baked ideas for experiment") for scientists to test his theory by. Not bad, when Einstein only had three, you might say, but then, if you look closer at the seven predictions, do they really tell against a Cartesian Theater Model? (The answer, as you might well guess, is no.) And, what does he mean by saying that "as a philosopher I have tried to keep my model as general and noncommital as possible?"
8 The modern source of this kind of thinking is, of course, Hegel and his theory of consciousness in *The Phenomenology of Spirit*. Via Marx this theory has been particularly strong in the Russian school of psychology, often called "activity theory." Two recent, rather different, examples of this kind of thinking are Jaynes (1976) and Suchman (1987). Gregory (1981) is among the few who discuss, rather than just mention, the importance of technology, and the role of tools, in thinking. The theory of intelligence I hint at here, he there develops in more depth, using a fruitful distinction between what he calls "potential" and "kinetic" intelligence.

9 In *Tractatus de Intellectus Emendatione:* "So, in like manner, the intellect, by its native strength . . . makes for itself intellectual instruments, whereby it acquires strength for performing other intellectual operations, and from these operations gets again fresh instruments or the power of pushing its investigations further, and thus gradually proceeds till it reaches the summit of wisdom."

10 This distinction, or difference in degree, is central to my argument, but I have very little to say about it. For a while we thought we had a good handle on it in terms of the distinction between hardware and software, but that was a little simple-minded we have come to realize. Like Dennett's use of the related notion of a "virtual machine," this distinction can serve an educational purpose, but does not really stand up to closer scrutiny. For another attempt, see Haugeland's (1985, pp. 106ff) distinction between, what he calls, type A and type B automation.

11 Dennett's "The Role of Language in Intelligence" (forthcoming) is a hint in the right direction, raising the issue of "the details of the interactions between . . . pre-existing information structures and the arrival of language."

12 This is not a rhetorical question. The answer can be found in classical behavioristic research, with its explicit condemnation, as "cheating," of the use of cognitive tools. This was pointed out by Miller et al. (1960), commenting specifically on behavioristic research on memory. The heritage still plagues our school systems: "This is mental calculation, boys and girls, so let me see your fingers."

13 Let us think of the horse as the user of the carriage. It simplifies the example without biasing the conclusion.

14 Cf. Ceruzzi's (1991) account of the human computers. The computer profession met Taylor's demand for simplicity. A relatively uneducated typist could, according to Ceruzzi, be transformed into a professional computer in just a couple of weeks.

15 Cf. Newell (1990, p. 90): ". . . intelligence is the ability to bring to bear all the knowledge that one has in the service of one's goals."

16 Sometimes I think people in AI should be more careful in defining what they do. Compare standard definitions of AI, e.g. Charniak and McDermott (1985) and Waltz (1988).

17 Unless psychology is viewed as an artificial science, the science of cognitive artifacts, with nothing particularly human about it. But if this is Simon's later view, this was not the view of the Newell and Simon of the late 1950s. There their ambition was to advance functionalism in psychology against a cybernetic interest in the nervous system. Cf. Newell et al. (1958). Cf. also McGinn (chapter 5) for a view of psychology in which it is neither a natural nor an artificial science.

18 I am simplifying. A lot of classical AI effort, particularly by people like Roger Schank, went into attempts to imitate our everyday knowledge, aiming, in effect, to automate an insuperable mess of tacitly acquired artifacts.

19 In spite of the importance of technology in the life of mankind, it remains very difficult to appreciate its nature. The natural sciences continue to determine our way of thinking, to the extent that we still speak of technology as applied science when it would be more appropriate to speak of science as applied technology. Scientific progress is made possible by technical development, and its direction is determined by the direction of that development.

20 Dennett's notion of a design stance tends to coincide with a more passive, functional stance, attending to the mechanisms implementing the competence of an intentional system. This stance is better called a "functional stance," I think, reserving the term "design stance" for an attitude from which you typically ask about the design, meaning how something is made or, better, how to make it, rather than how it functions.

21 Such a change is already on its way, of course, inspired both by genetic engineering and by computer simulation as a method for studying possible life forms. Cf. Langton (1989) and Dennett's review, "Artificial Life: A Feast for the Imagination" (1990).

22   Even if we may not always be as dependent on our environment as Simon's (1969, p. 23f), famous ant making its very complex path across the uneven cliff, certainly most of what we do depends on it.

23   I am paraphrasing Dennett's own words. Similarly, in "The Interpretation of Texts, People, and Other Artifacts" (1990), Dennett wants only two principles of interpretation – an optimality assumption and an ask the author or designer principle – declaring irrelevant what might be called a conventionality principle. But all three principles are normally used to generate and settle conflicts of interpretation.

24   Cf. Simon (1969, p. 11): "To predict how it will behave, we need only ask 'How would a rationally designed system behave under these circumstances?' The behavior takes on the shape of the task environment."

25   Compare the newspaper delivery example discussed by Fodor and Lepore (chapter 4).

REFERENCES

Ceruzzi, P. E. (1991) When computers were human. *Annals of the History of Computing*, 13, 237–44.

Charniak, E. and McDermott, D. (1985) *Introduction to Artificial Intelligence*. Reading, Mass.: Addison-Wesley.

Dawkins, R. (1976) *The Selfish Gene*. Oxford: Oxford University Press.

Dawkins, R. (1982) *The Extended Phenotype*. Oxford and San Francisco: W. H. Freeman.

Dennett, D. C. (1969) *Content and Consciousness*. London: Routledge & Kegan Paul and New York: Humanities Press.

Dennett, D. C. (1978) *Brainstorms. Philosophical Essays on Mind and Psychology*. Montgomery, VT: Bradford Books and Hassocks, Sussex: Harvester.

Dennett, D. C. (1987) *The Intentional Stance*. Cambridge, Mass.: MIT Press/Bradford Books.

Dennett, D. C. (1991a) *Consciousness Explained*. Boston: Little, Brown.

Dennett, D. C. (1991b) Mother Nature versus the walking encyclopedia: A Western drama. In W. Ramsey, S. Stich and D. E. Rumelhart (eds), *Philosophy and Connectionist Theory*. Hillsdale, NJ: Erlbaum.

Gregory, R. L. (1981) *Mind in Science. A History of Explanations in Psychology and Physics*. Cambridge: Cambridge University Press.

Haugeland, J. (1985) *Artificial Intelligence: The Very Idea*. Cambridge, Mass.: Bradford Books/MIT Press.

Jaynes, J. (1976) *The Origin of Consciousness in the Breakdown of the Bicameral Mind*. Boston: Houghton Mifflin Company.

Langton, C. G. (ed.) (1989) *Artificial Life*. Reading, Mass.: Addison-Wesley.

Lévi-Strauss, C. (1966) *The Savage Mind*. London: Weidenfeld and Nicolson.

Miller, G. A., Galanter, E. and Pribram, K. H. (1960) *Plans and the Structure of Behavior*. New York: Holt, Rhinehart and Winston.

Millikan, R. G. (1984) *Language, Thought and other Biological Categories*. Cambridge, Mass.: Bradford Books/MIT Press.

Minsky, M. (1985) *The Society of Mind*. New York: Simon & Schuster.

Neisser, U. (1967) *Cognitive Psychology*. New York: Appleton-Century-Crofts.

Newell, A. (1990) *Unified Theories of Cognition*. Cambridge, Mass.: Harvard University Press.

Newell, A., Shaw, J. C. and Simon, H. A. (1958) Elements of a theory of human problem solving. *Psychological Review*, 65, 151–66.

Polanyi, M. (1958) *Personal Knowledge*. Chicago: University of Chicago Press.

Quine, W. V. O. (1960) *Word and Object*. Cambridge, Mass.: MIT Press.

Quine, W. V. O. (1969) *Ontological Relativity and Other Essays.* New York: Columbia University Press.

Simon, H. A. (1969) *The Sciences of the Artificial.* Cambridge, Mass.: MIT Press. (A second, much enlarged, edition was published in 1981.)

Simon, H. A. (1980) Cognitive science: the newest science of the artificial. *Cognitive Science,* 4, 33–46.

Suchman, L. (1987) *Plans and Situated Behavior.* Cambridge: Cambridge University Press.

Taylor, F. W. (1911) *Principles of Scientific Management.* New York: Harper & Row.

Waltz, D. L. (1988) The prospects for building truly intelligent machines. In S. R. Graubard (ed.), *The Artificial Intelligence Debate.* Cambridge, Mass.: MIT Press.

9

Holism, Intrinsicality, and the Ambition of Transcendence

RICHARD RORTY

1   The Battle Over Intrinsicality

How do we tell when a complete causal explanation must include statements about X and when it is enough for it simply to explain why X is believed to exist, why "X" is in the language? The Copernicans thought that they did not have to explain the sun's motion, because it was enough to explain why the sun was *believed* to move. Their Aristotelian critics suggested that they were confusing the predictive utility of a heliocentric model with the requirements of a genuine causal account. Dennett thinks it enough to explain why there *seems* to be phenomenology – why it seems as if "there's a difference between thinking ... something seems pink to you and something *really seeming* pink to you."[1] His critics think that this strategy shows that *Consciousness Explained* merely explains consciousness away.

It seems reasonable for Dennett to reply that explaining something away – explaining why we do not have to make a place for *it* in our picture, but only for the belief in it – is often a good thing to do. The road of inquiry would have been disastrously blocked if we had forbidden this move to the Copernicans, or to those other seventeenth-century thinkers who attacked traditional beliefs about witches. On Dennett's account, we believe that there is phenomenology, and in qualia, because we adopted a certain set of metaphors for talking about people, just as the Aristotelians believed in solar motion, and witch-hunters in witches, because a certain picture of the cosmos held them captive. The use of these metaphors produced talk about "phenomenological data": about, for example, what it is like to have something pink on display in the Cartesian Theater. But if we can explain people's linguistic and other behavior with the help of other metaphors – for example, those which make up Dennett's Multiple Drafts model – then we are relieved of the obligation to explain qualia. As with the Copernicans, an historico-philosophical gloss on our theory, one which explains why people once talked about things which our theory need talk about no longer, is all that is required.

To those whom Dennett, following Owen Flanagan, calls "the new mysterians," this strategy seems ludicrous. One cannot save the appearances by tossing out phenomenological data, they argue,, for those data *are* the appearances. Reviewing *Consciousness Explained,* Thomas Nagel says that "A theory of consciousness that doesn't include mental data is like a book about Picasso that doesn't mention his paintings." On Nagel's view, the claim "there are no qualities, only judgements," is a product of Dennett's "Procrustean conception of scientific objectivity." Nagel thinks that a non-Procrustean conception would make room for phenomenological data by allowing for "objective standards that combine the first- and third-person points of view" (Nagel, 1991).

The cash-value of the term "first-person point of view," as it is used by Nagel, Searle and others is: a point of view which produces knowledge of *intrinsic,* non-relational properties of mental events. Nagel and Searle see clearly that if they accept the maxim, "To explain all the relational properties something has –all its causes and all its effects – is to explain the thing itself," then they will lose the argument. So non-relational properties, and the irreducibility of those properties to relational ones, are essential to their case. When Nagel says "Of course we would believe that anything that functioned physically and behaviorally like a grown human being was conscious, but the belief would be a conclusion from the evidence, rather than just a belief in the evidence," he is saying that the intrinsic, non-relational, character of an explanandum cannot be reduced to the relational features which permit us to have evidence of its presence. The gap Nagel sees between the evidence and the conclusion from the evidence is the gap between the totality of the relations of consciousness to the rest of the universe and what consciousness is *intrinsically.*

Searle sees the same gap as does Nagel. He thinks we can refute the question-begging claim that "mental states can be entirely defined in terms of their causal relations" by pointing out that no such claim has ever been reached

> by a close scrutiny of the phenomena in question. No one ever considered his own terrible pain or his deepest worry and concluded that they were just Turing machine states or that they could be entirely defined in terms of their causes and effects or that attributing such states to themselves was just a matter of taking a certain stance toward themselves.[2]

But for holists like Dennett, suggesting that we can "scrutinize the phenomena closely" is itself question-begging. That phrase presupposes just the idea of intrinsic, non-relational, features which Dennett questions: the idea of features that were clearly and distinctly scrutable, right up there on the screen of the Cartesian Theater, before you ever learned to talk. It begs the question of whether the behavior which Searle describes as the result of scrutiny is best explained by saying that such scrutiny in fact occurs, or whether the appearance of scrutiny is as illusory as the appearance of phenomenology.

Dennett accepts, as Nagel and Searle do not, the Wittgensteinian dictum that ostensive definition requires a lot of stage-setting in the language, and that ostention without that stage-setting (as when one says "forget about how it might be described; just concentrate on the *feel* of it – on what it's *like*") does not pick out an entity. Holists like Wittgenstein, Ryle, and Dennett – people who specialize in replacing intrinsic features with relational features – recognize their obligation to explain everything anybody has ever talked about. But they think that, just as it counts as an explanation of solar motion to explain why people used the term "solar motion," so it should count as an explanation of qualia to explain why people talk about intrinsic, non-relational features of conscious experience. If the latter explanation succeeds, then the attribution of consciousness to other people (or non-people) can be viewed not as the result of an inference from behavioral evidence (as Nagel views it) but simply as a reformulation of that evidence.

This contrast between inferences from evidence and reformulations of evidence is, however, not quite the contrast we holists want. For putting it this way suggests an un-Quinean, unholistic, contrast between fact and language, between inferring from one fact to another and changing one's description of the same fact. Holists cannot allow themselves the distinction between description and fact which this suggestion presupposes. They cannot allow questions like "Is the organism's actual and possible behavior one fact and its consciousness another, or are they the same fact?" For such questions try to do what Wittgenstein told us not to attempt: to get between language and its object. Holists can only allow questions like: should our best causal account of how things work include the relations of X to Y, or merely an account of the relations of X to Y-talk? In the case at hand: should our account include the relations between brains, behavior, and events in the Cartesian Theater, or just the relations between brains, behavior, and talk about such events?

Nagel would defend his conviction that what Dennett calls "heterophenomenology" is not enough by appealing to his metaphilosophical view that "the sources of philosophy are preverbal and often precultural, and one of its most difficult tasks is to express unformed but intuitively felt problems in language without losing them" (Nagel, 1986, p. 11). This metaphilosophical thesis epitomizes the non-holist, anti-Wittgensteinian picture of language according to which the limits of language are not the limits of thought. For on this picture, as Nagel (1986, p. 102) says, "the content of some thoughts transcend every form they can take in the human mind." This content–form distinction is essential to attempts to resist the encroachments of holism. For the holist wins if he can get you to drop what Davidson calls "the scheme–content distinction," and in particular to admit that what cannot be said cannot be thought. He wins if he can get you to accept Sellars' claim (in "Empiricism and the Philosophy of Mind) that "the appearances" which scientific explanation must save are themselves language-relative: that what appears to you is a matter of how you have been accustomed to talk. The psychological nominalism common to Sellars and Davidson – the view that, as Sellars said, "all awareness is a linguistic affair" – is just holism applied to the relation between language and thought. One will only be able to defend the claim that there are intrinsic, non-relational features of objects if one can claim that knowledge of those features is *not* the same as knowledge of how to use the words which one employs to describe those features.

Early in *Consciousness Explained*, Dennett quotes Nagel as saying that "the attempt to give a complete account of the world in objective terms . . . inevitably leads to false reductions or to outright denial that certain patently real phenomena exist at all" (CE, p. 71, quoting from Nagel, 1986, p. 7) Dennett then suggests that Nagel might be won over to Dennett's own view after grasping the details of the theory which Dennett will proceed to develop. He further suggests that Nagel ought to accept heterophenomenology as a "neutral way of *describing the data*." Both suggestions are misleading and misguided. This becomes clear a bit later in the book when the heterophenomenologist starts claiming the ability to discover that what Nagel thought ineffable is not really ineffable. Nagel can reasonably regard this claim as begging all the interesting questions. From Nagel's point of view, it is not good enough, because not neutral enough, to say, as Dennett says:

> If you retort "I'm not just saying that *I* can't describe it; I'm saying it's indescribable!" we heterophenomenologists will note that at least you can't describe it *now*, and since you're the only one in a position to describe it, it is at this time indescribable. Later, perhaps, you will come to be able to describe it, but of course at that time *it* will be something different, something describable. (CE, p. 97)

Nagel can reasonably rejoin that he isn't interested in "something different, something describable." Rather, he is interested in preventing people from substituting the effable for the ineffable, for the *intrinsically* ineffable. Telling Nagel that he may become able, thanks to mastering Dennett's theory, to describe what he has previously been unable to describe, is like telling Kant that he may become able, after mastering somebody else's theory (Hegel's perhaps, or Sellars') to describe what he had previously claimed was the indescribable thing-in-itself.

In "What Is It Like to Be a Bat?", Nagel says:

> Certainly it *appears* unlikely that we will get closer to the real nature of human experience by leaving behind the particularity of our human point of view and striving for a description in terms accessible to beings that could not imagine what it was like to be us. (Nagel, 1979, p. 174)

Nagel does not think that "the real nature of human experience" could be grasped in language by telling us that what we were *really* talking about when we used metaphors of a Cartesian Theater was something better described without those metaphors. He would presumably agree that the formula invoked by the Copernicans and by Dennett – "What you were describing as A was really B" – makes sense for things identified by non-intrinsic properties, but not for things identified by intrinsic properties. However, when we holists ask Nagel what "intrinsic" means we are led round in a circle: the intrinsic properties are all and only those which we know that we can never explain away. That is, they are properties which we know things to have independently of our knowledge of how to describe those things in language.

This may seem an odd definition of "intrinsic property," since it is epistemological, as opposed to metaphysical definitions such as "property whose presence is necessary for the object being the object it is." But it is the only definition which we holists can accept. For to avoid making a fatal concession to Nagel's essentialism, we must insist that "identity" is always identity under a description. Holists can countenance the notion of "property whose presence is necessary for the application of a certain description to the object," but not that of "property necessary for the object's self-identity, a self-identity it possesses apart from any particular description of it by us." When the non-holist says that the former notion does not capture the relevant sense of "intrinsic," the holist must reply that the only other sense of "intrinsic" which she can make sense of is the one given above: a definition which is still epistemological, but which presupposes the non-holist idea of non-linguistic awareness.

The question of whether metaphysics and epistemology are distinct areas of inquiry is yet another about which holists must disagree with non-holists. It is as useless for a non-holist to tell a holist that she has confused metaphysics and epistemology as for an Aristotelian to tell a seventeenth-century corpuscularian that she has confused substantial change with local motion. The anti-holist, anti-verificationist notion that things have real essences apart from our knowledge of them, a notion shared by Kripke and Nagel and invoked by both in defense of Cartesianism, is required to keep the epistemology–metaphysics distinction – the distinction between objects and the sentences true of them – sharp. The holism and anti-essentialism common to Wittgenstein, Quine, and Sellars breaks down this distinction by telling us that the only way to pick out an object is as that which most of a certain set of sentences are true of. I explore the implications of this latter claim – which I take to be central to the holist's case – in the following section.

Notice that if we once admit that there are such things as intrinsic properties, in the sense of properties, knowledge of which is independent of the language we use, we can no longer think of heterophenomenology as a neutral method. For the heterophenomenologist's privilege of telling you what you were *really* talking about is not compatible with the claim that our knowledge of some things, e.g. of the existence of qualia, is knowledge which cannot be affected by changing the way we talk, abandoning the pictures we have previously used language to sketch. So Dennett's suggestion that he has found neutral ground on which to argue with Nagel is wrong. By countenancing, or refusing to countenance, such knowledge, Nagel and Dennett beg all the questions against each other.

How could Dennett make his refusal to countenance such knowledge look like more than the blinkered stubbornness which Nagel and he must occasionally be tempted to attribute to one another? I do not think he can. At the depth of disagreement which separates these two philosophers, both their spades are turned. It is pointless for Dennett to say "the more you look at the details of the Multiple Draft theory, the more plausible my metaphilosophical presuppositions will become." That would be like a Galilean telling an Aristotelian that she will gradually become willing to settle for a world without final and formal causes, a world of atoms and the void, a world with only nominal essences, as she learns more about the elegant explanations of eclipses, parallax, etc., which a heliocentric model makes possible. Maybe she will, but it is not clear that she should – that there is any compelling reason for her to do so. This is because it is hardly clear when and whether to change one's mind about what to expect explanatory theories to do – and, in particular, about how paradoxical science has a right to be, how far it can go in substituting explanations of X-talk for explanations of X. There is no *general* way of answering the question with which I began this essay. For there is no overarching ahistorical context-free criterion to which one can appeal when asked to shift from one paradigm of explanation to another.

Things become even less clear, and neutral ground even harder to locate, when we leave the philosophy of science and ascend to more abstract, more explicitly metaphilosophical, levels. We ascend thither when we stop asking about the best explanation of the appearance of phenomenology and start asking whether there are such things as intrinsic, non-relational, properties *at all*, whether *any* ascription of any feature to any object is not an implicit description of its relations to something else. Wittgenstein and Sellars assume that it is, because for them to become aware of qualia is the same thing as learning how to make judgments about qualia, a process which involves relating qualia to non-qualia. But the question of whether Wittgenstein and Sellars are right takes us back to the same old clash between holist and non-holist intuitions. For some of us, it is *obvious* that ostensive definition presupposes a lot of stage-setting. For Nagel, on the other hand, the Wittgenstein-like claim that "it makes sense to say that someone is or is not using a concept correctly only against the background of the possibility of agreement and identifiable disagreement in judgments employing the concept" presages disaster. For accepting that claim would mean that "what there is or what is true" is limited to what we "could discover or conceive of or describe in some extension of human language" (Nagel, 1986, pp. 105–6). To believe that, is to give up what Nagel calls "the ambition of transcendence." Nagel thinks that the willingness of recent philosophers (such as Wittgenstein, Ryle, Sellars, Davidson, and Dennett) to renounce this ambition is a sign of spiritual degeneration.

2 Centers of Descriptive Gravity

Even though metaphilosophy is just one more forum in which intutions clash, I think that it may serve the holist cause to which Dennett and I are both devoted to restate our holism in that forum. The high metaphilosophical ground should not be surrendered by default. So I want to commend some dashing metaphilosophical claims to Dennett, claims he might wish to make in an attempt to capture this ground from Nagel.

My principal suggestion is that Dennett put his claim that the self is a "center of narrative gravity" (CE, ch. 11) in the context of the more general claim that *all* objects resemble selves in being centers of *descriptive* gravity. Narratives are just a particular form of description – the one employed by novelists and autobiographers – but the sort of thing that novelists do is not all that different from the sort of thing logicians, physicists, and moralists do. All these people are weaving or reweaving sets of descriptions of objects. The only general truth we know, and the only one we need to know, about the relation between the objects and the descriptions is that the object X is what most of the beliefs expressed in statements using the term "X" are true of.[3] Like heroines whose stories are being told by novelists, and selves whose self-consciousness about their own past character results in the acquisition of a quite different future, objects change as our descriptions of them change. That is to say: their center of descriptive gravity shifts as inquiry proceeds. Just as, for the usual Sartrean reasons, there is no perduring, intrinsic, character of a human self – no "real me," no me *en soi*, for myself to grasp – so there is, for the usual Wittgensteinian–Sellarsian psychological nominalist reasons, no intrinsic character of *any* object to grasp. So Nagel's ambition of transcendence is not the tough-minded commitment to intellectual honesty he thinks it, but rather a tender-minded yearning for an impossible stability and order – the kind of yearning which William James deplored in the opening chapter of his *Pragmatism*.[4]

The view I am suggesting has obvious resemblances to that of the idealists, the founders of the holist tradition in modern philosophy, the first people to question the distinction between the intrinsic and the relational features of objects. The idealists' thesis of the internality of all relations amounts to the suggestion that we think of all objects as physicists think of centers of gravity. On this view, all objects are what they are in virtue of all their relations to everything else in the universe. That was why the idealists often said that "really" there was only One Big Object – the Absolute, the one that didn't shift, because it was non-spatiotemporal, a *totum simul.*

To retain the idealists' holism while junking their metaphysics, all we need to do is to renounce the ambition of transcendence. We can stop suggesting that the four-dimensional All is more of an object, or is "realer," than a dust mote or a patch of pink or Dennett's lost-sock center (the center of the smallest sphere which encompasses all the socks Dennett has lost in his lifetime). We can do this if we cease to think in terms of Appearance and Reality, as Bradley and Royce did, or in terms of sentences made true by Us and sentences made true by The World, as Dummett and his followers do. If we drop such representationalist notions as "appearance" and "making true," then we can let numbers and tables, quarks and stars, lost socks and moral values, share the same "objective" status. The interesting differences between them will be those made by our (often fluctuating) notions of what is relevant and irrelevant to the truth of beliefs about each different sort of object. These notions will not be responsible to something called "the intrinsic character of the object in question," but only to the ordinary process of reweaving our webs of belief and desire, often in unpredictable ways (as when we begin to think of Riemann's axioms as relevant to interstellar distances, or of the origin of the human species as irrelevant to moral values).[5]

Idealism sunk under the burden of its residual attachment to the idea that philosophical reflection might provide a short cut to transcendence, and for a time it took holism down with it. But holism bobbed up again as we gradually freed ourselves from the analytic-synthetic and language-fact distinctions with which neo-empiricist anti-idealist polemics (such as Russell's and Ayer's) had lumbered us. Quine, White, Putnam, Wittgenstein, Kuhn, and the other liberators suggested that we drop the idea of frozen sets of statements (the "analytic" ones, the ones which picked out the "intrinsic" features of an object).

Quine's notion of "the web of belief," like Putnam's notion of "cluster concepts" and Wittgenstein's image of overlapping strands, helped break the hold of the idea that we have, in the back of our heads, Semantical Rules which should enable us to give nice definite answers to questions like "Is it the same sock after being redarned so much?," "Was Dalton talking about the same atoms Democritus was talking about?" and the like. The idea of an Official List of the Semantic Rules for using the word "sock," or the word "atom," was an attempt to do for the meanings of "sock" and of "atom" what we do for Sherlock Holmes and the number seventeen: keep them stable by not letting new Holmes stories into the canon, and not letting physics touch mathematics. Something called "the language" by Carnap and "the eidetic structures" by Husserl was supposed to play the role of canon-fixer, the sort of role which Conan Doyle had played for Holmes. Once this entity was set aside – and especially once Davidson (1986, pp. 445–6) started showing us how to erase "the boundary between knowing a language and knowing our way around in the world generally" – we are in a fair way to eliminating the last refuge of a distinction which helps make the ambition of transcendence possible, the distinction between Us and What We May Not Be In Touch With.

There may seem to be a residue of the bad, metaphysical, side of idealism in the claim that all objects are centers of descriptive gravity. For this may seem to entail saying that objects do not change by being battered or moved about or discolored by other objects, but only by changes in our descriptions of them. Further, the suggestion that they change in the latter way may seem to go against our intuition that "objects exist independently of thought," the intuition which the idealists tried to put in question. But once we think of our uses of words, and of our beliefs, as just worldy objects in constant causal interaction with other worldy objects, battering and being battered, it is no longer clear what "independence" might mean. Obviously it cannot mean "causally independent." But the only other gloss ever offered on "independent of thought" is "having intrinsic qualities unchangeable by our descriptions."

To foreswear intrinsicality is to renounce the realists' ambition of transcending "the human point of view" and reaching objects whose relation to our descriptions of them is utterly external. But it is not thereby to become either an "idealist" or an "anti-realist." It is merely to say that, just as Quine replaced "analyticity" with "centrality to our belief system," so we should replace "intrinsic feature of X" with "feature unlikely to be woven out of our descriptions of X." To insist on a stronger sense of "intrinsic," one which would allow for the gap which Nagel sees between behavioral evidence and the attribution of consciousness, the sort of gap which inspires us with an ambition of transcendence, would be like insisting that "life" might have an intrinsic character to which all the talk about DNA is quite irrelevant (see CE, p. 25 on *elan vital*). Such insistence can, for us holists, mean no more than "some day we may have ways of talking about life which we cannot now imagine," but this gesture toward the future enlargement of the language is not the sort of thing which could gratify Nagel's or Royce's ambitions of transcendence. For they want to transcend themselves in the direction of something that is already *there*, not merely in the direction of a future contingency.

It may seem as if running together the "soft" and the "hard" ways of changing things confuses real and intentional objects. But if we are holist enough to follow Davidson in giving up the scheme-content distinction (the distinction, for example, between what language contributes to the object and what the world contributes, what the mind does by way of constituting the object and what non-minds do to it once it has been constituted), then we no longer have a use for the intentional–real distinction. Once we agree with Davidson that only beliefs can make belief true, then we can get along quite well with what we used to call intentional objects. But we shall no longer call them so, because we shall have no use for the real–intentional contrast. We shall just call them "objects" *tout court*. Analogously, we shall drop the idealists' claim that all relations are internal, for we shall have no use for the external–internal contrast.

Isn't this to drop some useful, necessary, distinctions? No. It is to drop some useless distinctions, distinctions which have made more trouble than they were worth. The ambition of transcendence, in the form it took in modern philosophy, gave us the distinction between the world and our conception of the world, between the content and the scheme we applied to that content, between the truly objective and the merely intersubjective. These distinctions brought with them such nuisances as epistemological skepticism, transcendental idealism, Absolute Idealism, logical constructionism, and phenomenology. Habitual use of these distinctions made us think that if we once gave up on intrinsicality – on the content as something distinct from the scheme – we should no longer have what Nagel calls "a robust sense of reality."[6] But once we are free of the scheme–content distinction we are free to think of robustness as the willingness to let centers of descriptive gravity keep changing. The issue about who is more spiritually degenerate than whom depends on whether you think it more robust to describe yourself in the Darwinian terms which Dewey, Davidson, and Dennett use to describe themselves, or whether you think it more robust to keep your eyes on something on the other side of a gap, the sort of object which is "more" than just a center of descriptive gravity.

Which seems to you more robust will in part be decided by, and in part decide, your reaction to Dennett's discussion of Searle's Chinese Room, to Frank Jackson's example of Mary the Color Scientist, and to all the other intuition pumps which have been designed to enhance or diminish your sense of the importance of phenomenology, qualia, and intrinsicality. Whether you keep or give up the ambition of transcendence is not determined by finding "confusions" or "mistakes" in the work of Nagel or Searle or Dennett or Davidson.[7] Diagnoses of illusion or confusion are just polemical ways of describing your opponent's distinctions, or their failure to make your distinctions. But distinctions are as much up for grabs as anything else. There are no quick fixes. There is only the continual passage back and forth between small intuition pumps like Jackson's description of Mary or Dennett's redescription of Mary (CE, p. 399) and large intuition pumps, for example, large metaphilosophical generalities like those I have cited from Nagel and those which I have been formulating in opposition to his. All we can do is hope to attain reflective equilibrium by trekking back and forth between the low ground, where we haggle about how to describe the Chinese Room, and the high ground, on which we elaborate competing, self-serving, definitions of such virtues as robustness.

3 The Mind as the Last Refuge of Intrinsicality

Full-strength holism, when applied to issues in the philosophy of mind, produces the radical anti-dualism espoused by Davidson.[8] "The most promising and interesting change that is occurring in philosophy today," Davidson says, "is that these dualisms [of scheme and content, and of the objective and the subjective] are being questioned in new ways." These dualisms, he continues, have their common origin in "a concept of the mind with its private states and objects" (Davidson, 1989, p. 163). Commenting on Fodor, Davidson writes:

> it is instructive to find the effort to make psychology scientific turning into a search for internal propositional states that can be detected and identified apart from relations to the rest of the world, much as earlier philosophers sought for something "given in experience," which contained no necessary clue to what was going on outside. The motive is similar in the two cases: it is thought that a sound footing, whether for knowledge or for psychology, requires something inner in the sense of being non-relational. (Davidson, 1989, p. 170)

Suppose we become convinced (by reading CE, perhaps) that persons have no states, propositional or otherwise, which meet this description; that all the properties truly ascribable to people are relational in the relevant respects, and none of them intrinsic. Davidson points out that, despite this conviction, we should still be able to distinguish states of the organism about which the organism has epistemic access and authority of various special sorts. However, we should not explain this access or authority by reference to the "subjective" or "mental" character of the state, for these terms would themselves be explicated entirely by reference to such authority or access.

I argued in *Philosophy and the Mirror of Nature* (1980) that we might well have become convinced of this point a few hundred years ago, in the course of assimilating the implications of Galilean mechanics for the nature of scientific explanation. Had that happened, we should now neither be captivated by the metaphor of the Cartesian Theater nor have a use for Fodor's notion of "psychologically real states." Indeed, we should never have encouraged attempts to develop a science called "psychology" which took itself to be distinct both from the wisdom of the folk and from neurophysiology. In the days when corpuscularians were busy draining the planets and the rocks and the animals of their intrinsic natures, busy driving out formal and final causes, Cartesian philosophers had to work fairly hard (in the face of incredulous stares from people like Hobbes and Gassendi) to create "consciousness" as a refuge for Aristotelian notions of substance, essence, and intrinsicality. But they succeeded. Thanks to their efforts, even after the colorfully diverse contents of Aristotelian nature were smeared together into one big swirl of corpuscles – one big substance called "matter" – there remained, here below, one other substance: the mind. The mind which these philosophers invented was its own place: in the sense that, as Davidson (1989, p. 162) says, it contained "an ultimate source of evidence the character of which can be wholly specified without reference to what it is evidence for." This mind knew both its own contents and its own intrinsic nature independently of its knowledge of anything else.

The cash value of the claim that the mind is its own place is that the mind is capable of swinging free of its environment, capable of standing in relations of "aboutness" or "evidence for" to all kinds of things which have nothing to do with that environment – such things as unicorns and transfinite cardinals. But this ability to swing free of the environment – an ability which Husserl thought was the Achilles' heel of all forms of naturalism – is, on the view of those who (like Dennett and Davidson) think intentionality extrinsic,[9] just as "naturalistic" as the ability to reflect light or to exert gravitational force. For although unicorns do not exist, sentences using the word "unicorn" do, and tokenings of such sentences are no more mysterious or unnatural than collisions of atoms. To attribute a belief in unicorns to someone is to describe her as standing in a relation to a proposition, just as to attribute a dollar value to her is to describe her as standing in a certain relation to a slave-trader or an organ bank. The former attribution is no more "non-natural" than the latter. It is useful to talk about beliefs in unicorns, and thus about unicorns, in order to account for what we find in medieval books and tapestries, just as it is useful to talk about dollar values in order to account for the behavior of businessmen, to talk about propositions in order to account for the linguistic behavior of foreigners, and to talk about atoms to account for, for example, chemical reactions. We do not talk about the internal structure or the evolutionary niche of unicorns, because we have no need to talk about unicorns when we do biology. We do not ask about the intrinsic nature of dollar values, nor of the dollar itself, nor of propositions, any more than about the intrinsic nature of transfinite cardinals. For values and propositions, like numbers, are *obviously* merely slices out of vast webs of relationships.[10]

To see things from Davidson's naturalistic perspective, it helps to consider the analogy between attributing states to a brain and to a mind. Nobody wants to suggest that a *brain* is its own place, or that it could lose touch with the external world. For whether a brain is hooked up to wires, computers, and photoelectric cells, or instead to the rest of a central nervous system and some protoplasmic sense organs, is irrelevant.[11] It is always hooked up to *some* external world. If it ceased to be so hooked, it would cease to be a functioning brain. It would just be a heap of cells. Similarly, if a central processor made of metal, silicon, and plastic were not hooked up to some input and output devices, it would not be a functioning central processor, but just a heap of chips. So one can imagine Davidson arguing as follows: if the mind is just the brain under another description, then both mind and brain are equally incapable of failure to hook up. The most that redescription in mentalistic rather than neural terms could do would be to describe more and more complicated hook-ups, not eliminate them altogether.[12]

Davidson's explanation of why the mind is not its own place hooks up nicely with Dennett's quasi-neurological account of consciousness in terms of parallel distributed processing. The work of these two holists, taken in tandem, should be thought of as the final stage of the attack on Cartesianism which began with Ryle. If this attack succeeds, our descendants will think it unfortunate that the seventeenth century did not carry through on its project of recontextualizing everything by seeing the mind too as just one more slice of a vast web of relationships. If the seventeenth century had treated Descartes' *Meditations* as just an unfortunate bit of residual Aristotelianism, forgiveable in the author of a great treatise on corpuscularian mechanics, we might never have had the notion of "consciousness," or the science of psychology,[13] to worry about.

4   Dennett on Realism

In order to accept the metaphilosophical position I sketched in section 2, and in order to complete the "sea-change" in philosophical thinking which Davidson (1989, p. 159) foresees, we should have to stop worrying about realism and anti-realism. Dennett, alas, still takes controversy about these topics seriously. So in this final section I turn to Dennett's residual attachment to ontology (forgivable in the author of a great treatise on the brain), and in particular to his distinction between illata and abstracta.

I shall begin by trying to rebut something Dennett says about my own views. Dennett describes me as believing that the difference between folk psychology and astrology is "not a significant difference" (Dennett, 1991b, p. 50). He also says that I would not grant to users of folk psychology that their use of this tool gives them "power to understand and anticipate the animate world." I am puzzled to find these views ascribed to me, and puzzled that Dennett should think either view was entailed by my denial that "any brand of 'realism' could *explain* the (apparent?)

success of the intentional stance." Dennett's argument for ascribing these views to me seems to be this:

1 Rorty must admit that if folk psychology is a tool which gives us the power in question, it does so by virtue of accurate representation of the real, rather than of the merely apparent.
2 Admitting that it does so by virtue of accurate representation would contradict his denial of realism.
3 So he must deny that it gives us that power.

I would not admit what (1) claims I must admit. But Dennett thinks that move is not open to me, since:

> Even someone who has transcended the scheme/content distinction and has seen the futility of correspondence theories of truth [like Rorty] must accept the fact that *within* the natural ontological attitude we sometimes explain success by correspondence: one does better navigating off the coast of Maine when one uses an up-to-date nautical chart than one does when one uses a road map of Kansas. Why? Because the former accurately represents the hazards, markers, depths and coastlines of the Maine coast, and the latter does not. Now why does one do better navigating the shoals of interpersonal relations using folk psychology than using astrology? (Dennett, 1991b, p. 50)

The force of Dennett's analogy depends upon whether "accurately represents" can mean the same thing in the case of charts and in the case of the patterns which we folk psychologists, taking the intentional stance, discern in human behavior. In the former case, accuracy of representation can be determined by matching bits of one thing (the chart) with bits of something else (Maine), and finding a procedure for predicting features of the one on the basis of features of the other. My argument for the inability of "any brand of 'realism'" to explain the success of things like particle physics or folk psychology in empowering us to understand and anticipate the world is just that no analogous matching seems possible.

To rehearse once again the hackneyed argument against such matching common to idealists and pragmatists: we cannot go back and forth between our statements about electrons and electrons, or our ascriptions of belief and beliefs, and pair them off as we pair off bits of the chart and bits of Maine. This would be, as Wittgenstein said, like checking what is said in the newspaper against another copy of the same paper. Whereas we have different tests for the presence of a curve on the chart and a curve on the coast, we do not have different procedures for ascribing beliefs and detecting the presence of the beliefs ascribed. That is why "folk psychology represents accurately" seems to me to add nothing to "folk psychology enables us to anticipate the world."

Dennett does nothing to tighten the analogy between mariners and folk psychologists by showing what the relevant sort of pairing or matching would be. Nor does he do much to explain what it is to "tie reality to the brute existence of pattern," something he says that he and Davidson do but Paul Churchland and I do not. The only sense I can make of "tie reality to the brute existence of pattern" is "apply, *ceteris paribus*, the term 'real' to any pattern which helps us anticipate and understand the world." I am as willing to do this as Dennett or Davidson, but I still need an answer to the question: what does thinking of a pattern as *real* do *except* remind us that that pattern has been found useful in anticipating the world? A genuine explanation ought to appeal to something whose presence or absence we can test independently of our tests for the presence of the explanandum, but the pseudo-explanations offered by philosophical "realism" do not.[14]

I also need to know what Dennett (1991b, p. 30) means by "depends on" when he writes "The success of folk-psychological prediction, like the success of any prediction, depends on there being some order or pattern in the world to exploit." Is this sort of "depends on," as they used to ask in Oxford, the "depends on" in "Whether he will show up depends on the weather?" No, because that sort of dependence is a matter of spotting predictively useful regularities. Nobody has ever spotted predictively useful regularities, established by correlating independently isolatable objects, between a bit of success and a bit of exploitable order in the world, any more than anyone has ever spotted such regularities connecting wealth with the possession of material goods. Good Quineans like Dennett and I cannot, of course, speak of "conceptual as opposed to empirical" connections, but we can speak of unhelpful rather than helpful explanations. "That theory is successful because it gets at something real" seems to me as unhelpful as (to use Dennett's example in CE, p. 32) "we laugh because of the hilarity of the stimulus."

I should have thought that the same verificationist impulses which lead Dennett to say that "if we are not urbane verificationists, we will end up tolerating all sorts of nonsense: epiphenomenalism, zombies, indistinguishable inverted spectra ..." (CE, p. 461) would lead him to dismiss the notion of "real patterns as opposed to very useful, but merely apparent, patterns." But he never quite does. Though he often tells us that the terms "realist" and "instrumentalist" are too unclear to be of much use, he is nevertheless prepared to classify himself as more realistic than I, less realistic than Davidson, and so on. He never decides whether he is delicately balanced on a fence which has "irrealists" like (supposedly) me on one side and "realists" like (supposedly) Davidson on the other, or whether he wants (as I do) to help tear down the fence by refusing to use the "irrealist–realist" distinction at all. He sits, so to speak, on a meta-fence.

Pragmatists like myself think that once we stop thinking of true beliefs as representations of reality and instead, with Bain and Peirce, view them as habits of action, we have no use for "real" except as an uninformative, non-explanatory, honorific – a pat on the back for the patterns that we have come to rely upon. Nor, consequently, do we have a use for "only in the eye of the beholder" (a phrase which Dennett, 1991b, p. 50, alas, puts in my mouth). I should have thought that our shared verificationist fervor would have led Dennett to agree with me on these points. But he never quite does. Instead, when asked "Are pains real?" he tells us that "they are as real as haircuts and dollars and opportunities and persons ... but how real is that?" (CE, p. 460).

Nobody would ask "how real is that?" unless he had some invidious contrast in mind between things that are *really* real and things that are (as Royce put it) "not so damned real." Dennett does have such a contrast in mind – the Reichenbachian contrast between illata and abstracta. Haircuts, pains and persons are, for Dennett, like centers of gravity, presumably alike in that they are all abstracta. They differ in this respect from electrons, which enjoy the status of illata. I have never seen Dennett put this abstract–concrete distinction to any use, except to answer questions about his ontological commitments.[15] But if one adopts Fine's "natural ontological attitude," as both Dennett and I do, then one should not answer such questions. A person with that attitude does not *have* "ontological commitments," and never talks, as Dennett still does, about "the furniture of the physical world." Once she has finished anticipating and understanding the world, she feels no impulse to take up a new topic – ontology – nor to make invidious contrasts between the various tools (between, for example, centers of gravity and electrons) which she has been using.

What does the difference between an illatum and an abstractum come to?[16] In "Real Patterns" Dennett (1991b, p. 28) says that abstracts are "definable in terms of physical forces and other properties." This chimes with a passage from Reichenbach he quotes in *The Intentional Stance* (1987, p. 53n) which says that "the existence of abstracta is reducible to the existence of concreta" because "inferences to abstracta" are "equivalences, not probablility inferences." Elsewhere Reichenbach refers to abstracta as "combinations of contreta," and gives "prosperity" as an example of a term which "refers to a totality of observable phenomena . . . is used as an abbreviation which sums up all these observables in their interrelationship" (Reichenbach, 1951, p. 263). By contrast, Reichenbach continues, unobservable illata like electrons are "not combinations of concreta, but separate enties inferred from concreta, whose existence is merely made probable by the concreta."

Reichenbach puts forward two distinctions as if they were coextensive. First, there is the distinction between the referents of terms which you know how to use after being given a short snappy definition phrased mostly in terms of observables and mathematical relations – terms like "the typewriter's center of gravity" or "Dennett's lost sock center" – and terms like "electron," "belief," "pain," "person," and "gene." You can only learn how to use the latter terms by getting the hang of a whole mini-language-game.[17] Secondly, there is the distinction between terms whose referents are such that "their existence is reducible to the existence of concreta" and those whose referents are not so reducible. The first is a pedagogic distinction, the latter a metaphysical one.

We post-Quinean and post-*Philosophical Investigations* holists are not as much at ease with the second distinction as Reichenbach was. The problem is that "referent of a term whose existence is reducible to the existence of observables" only sounds clear as long as you think you have necessary and sufficient conditions for the applications of terms. You have such conditions, at most, only for terms which have nice snappy little definitions in terms of observables (like "Dennett's lost sock center"), and as long as you don't quibble about what counts as observable.

In Reichenbach's day, it seemed obvious that definability and ontological status had something to do with each other. But now it does not. Dennett is not entitled to help himself to the metaphysical part of the Reichenbachian illatum–abstractum distinction, but only to the pedagogical (what we used to call the "semantic") part. But, by itself, this part is no help to him. For pains and persons and beliefs (I am not sure about haircuts) are not entities you can learn to talk about by being given short snappy definitions. From a pedagogical point of view, beliefs are a lot more like electrons than like lost sock centers.

Dennett wants to say that it is as silly to ask whether beliefs are real as to ask whether his lost sock center is real. I quite agree, but not for Dennett's reasons. My reason is that it is silly to ask whether *anything* is real – as opposed to asking whether it is useful to talk about, spatially locatable, spatially divisible, tangible, visible, easily identified, made out of atoms, good to eat, etc. Reality is a wheel which plays no part in any mechanism, once we have adopted the natural ontological attitude. So is the decision to be, or not be, "a realist about" something. So is the decision about what position to occupy on the spectrum which Dennett describes (with Fodor's industrial strength Realism at one end and what he calls, alas, "Rorty's milder-than-mild irrealism" at the other). Dennett should, on my view, drop his claim to have found "a mild and intermediate sort of realism" – the *juste milieu* along this spectrum. He should instead dismiss this spectrum as one of those things which it is not useful to talk about – one of those metaphors which, like those which make up the image of the Cartesian Theater, looked promising but turned out to be more trouble than it was worth.[18]

Why am I quibbling at such length about how Dennett uses, and should use, words like "real" and "realism?" Why am I not as insouciant about Dennett's meta-ontological fence-sitting as he is? Mainly because I should like to convince him that all the reasons we have for getting rid of a captivating but trouble-making picture of the mind, "the Cartesian Theater," are also reasons for getting rid of a captivating but trouble-making picture of human inquiry: "Penetrating the Veil of Appearances." All the reasons why one would want to write a whole book developing a new set of metaphors for talking about consciousness are also reasons for writing a book which offers a new set of metaphors for talking about the goal of science, one which will replace the metaphors which describe the Cartesian "project of pure inquiry" expounded by Bernard Williams – a book like Dewey's *Reconstruction in Philosophy* (1957), for example. I think, in short, that Dennett's "urbane verificationism" is a bit *too* urbane. It stops short of the goal out of what seems to me misplaced courtesy to a half-defeated enemy.

I enjoy metaphilosophy in a way that Dennett seems not to enjoy it. That is why, in section 2 of this chapter, I tried to cloak Dennett's criticism (see 1987, pp. 5–7) of "the new mysterians" such as Nagel in lofty metaphilosophical rhetoric. The rhetoric of mystery-fans like Nagel, McGinn, and Gabriel Marcel – of anti-verificationists who cherish ineffability – should, I think, be countered by an equal and opposite rhetoric, one which denounces the very idea of ineffability. This rhetoric should do what the positivists did, in their day: it should make verification-ism seem glamorous, exciting, and exactly what the age demands. We should not be so urbane as to leave this sort of rhetoric to our opponents.

The sort of rhetoric I commend is, in fact, shadowed forth in the closing paragraph of *Consciousness Explained*. This is one of my favorite passages, for there Dennett robustly resists the natural temptation to announce that he has finally gotten consciousness right – accurately represented it, gotten its intrinsic features straight. Instead, he says that all he has done in CE "is to replace one family of metaphors and images with another." He goes on to say that "metaphors are not 'just' metaphors; metaphors are the tools of thought" (CE, p. 455).

I wish that he had taken one step further, and had added that such tools are all that inquiry can ever provide, because inquiry is never "pure" in the sense of Williams' "project of pure inquiry." It is always a matter of getting us something we want. What do we want out of a theory of consciousness? Not that the intrinsic nature of consciousness be revealed (as the metaphor of science and philosophy joining forces to pierce the veil of appearances would suggest), but simply a way of talking which will, if widely adopted, change our intuitions. Why should we want to change our intuitions? For the usual Kuhnian reasons: our old intuitions are giving rise to too much sterile controversy, too many fancy theories which tack epicycles (such as "narrow content") onto epicycles, too much speculation (like Roger Penrose's) about the need for an as-yet-unimaginable breakthrough before we can hope to reach the light, too much defeatist guff about "the limits of science." In short, we want some new intuitions because the old ones haven't been getting us anywhere.

Mystery-fans, of course, think that we haven't been getting anywhere because of (in a phrase of Colin McGinn's) "our own incurable cognitive poverty," and that philosophers who are content to change metaphors in order to free themselves of inconvenient intuitions are (as Nagel puts it) "sick of the subject and glad to be rid of its problems" and are "turning philosophy into something less difficult and more shallow than it is." Nagel sees attempts (such as Dennett's) to change the language in order to help us actively forget troublesome old intuitions as symptoms of a childish rebellion "against the philosophical impulse itself" (Nagel, 1986, pp. 11–12).

Nagel is identifying "the philosophical impulse" with what he elsewhere calls "the ambition of transcendence." By speaking in such terms, Nagel gears the debate between himself and Dennett up a further metaphilosophical notch. I think it is very helpful to do so. Within the tradition of analytic philosophy, Nagel's *The View from Nowhere* is one of the very few recent books which articulates its author's moral sensibility, and which recognizes that philosophical argument will sooner or later run up against the limits set by such sensibility. My own sense of what it is worthwhile and important for human beings to do requires abjuration of the ambition of transcendence to which Nagel remains faithful. Since which intuitions you think have, or have not, been getting us somewhere depends in part upon where you want to go, your willingness to retain or give up certain intuitions interacts with your willingness to retain or give up certain ambitions. Neither intuition nor ambition, we holists maintain, can provide an Archimedean point.

NOTES

1 Dennett, *Consciousness Explained* (1991a, p. 364). Later references to this book will be as "CE" and will be inserted in the text.
2 Searle (1983), pp. 262–3. The analogy between the Aristotle–Copernicus switch and the Descartes–Dennett switch which I am pursuing is reinforced by Dennett's allusion to Wittgenstein's famous question "how would it look if the sun stood still and the earth moved?" At CE, p. 410, discussing qualia, he follows U.T. Place and J. J. C. Smart in asking: "Well, what do you think it would seem like if it *were* just a combination of electrochemical happenings in your brain?"
3 I develop some of the implications of this dictum in my *Objectivity, Relativism and Truth* (1991, pp. 96ff).
4 Accusations of tender-mindedness and boasts of tough-mindedness are, of course, cheap. I do not wish to make anything of these epithets, but merely to remind the reader of how easily such accusations and boasts can be made by either side, and of how little is ever settled by making them. It is, however, useful to point out the parallel between Dennett's advocacy of the "sort of anti-essentialism that is comfortable with penumbral cases and the lack of strict dividing lines" (CE, p. 421) – an anti-essentialism

encouraged, as Dennett remarks, by Darwin's reinterpretation of biological specification – and James's joy in the fuzziness of the pragmatist's view of things, its lack of sharp clear outlines. Note also Dewey's remarks (1977, pp. 7, 11) that "The influence of Darwin upon philosophy resides in his having conquered the phenomena of life for the principle of transition," thereby enabling us to renounce the sort of explanation which "only abstracts some aspect of the existing course of events in order to reduplicate it as a petrified eternal principle by which to explain the very changes of which it is the formalization." Dewey would have admired Dennett's denunciation of the idea that "consciousness is a special all-or-nothing property that sunders the universe into two vastly different categories: the things that have it (the things that it is like something to be, as Nagel would put it) and the things that lack it" (CE, p. 447). Both James and Dewey thought of themselves as following out the anti-essentialist consequences of Peirce's "principle of pragmatism" ("To attain perfect clearness in our thoughts of an object, then, we need only consider what conceivable effects of a practical kind the object may involve . . ."), a principle which entails the anti-essentialist insistence on relationality which Peirce called "synechism."

5 Here, for example, is how the "physical object" *v.* "non-physical object" distinction looks once it is separated from the distinction between Us and The World. We group Sherlock Holmes, Middle Earth, the number seventeen, the rules of chess, and the interstate commerce clause of the US Constitution together as "non-physical" not because they are all non-spatiotemporal (what's non-spatiotemporal about Middle Earth?), nor because they are all somehow "subjective" or "conventional" objects but because we do not expect our beliefs about them to be altered by the range of cultural activity known as "physical science." We might be wrong in this expectation, but that is all right. Holism and fallibilism go hand in hand, and the object known as "physical objecthood" (also known as "the meaning of the term 'physical object'") is no less a center of descriptive gravity than is any other object.

6 See Nagel (1986) p. 5, where he says that the "present intellectual climate," created both by people who do not regard objectivity "as a method of understanding the world as it is in itself," and by those who think that objectivity "can provide a complete view of the world on its own," is due to "an insufficiently robust sense of reality and of its independence of any particular form of human understanding."

7 Both Nagel and Dennett occasionally accuse their opponents of "confusions," "mistakes," and "illusions." In his review of CE, Nagel (1991) says that Dennett "confuses consciousness with self-consciousness" and is guilty of "a confusion about objectivity." At p. 455 of CE Dennett says that "the illusion that consciousness is the exception [to the rule that whatever is is explicable by being related to other things] comes about, I suspect, because of a failure to understand this general feature of successful explanation [that explanation is in terms of things other than the explanandum]." Such talk is probably inevitable, but its prevalence encourages the continuation of what Janice Moulton calls "the adversarial culture" of analytic philosophy. This is a culture whose inhabitants are impatient with the inconclusiveness of the search for reflective equilibrium, and dream of finding unanswerable arguments – arguments which cannot be vitiated by a new set of distinctions.

8 Portions of this section are adapted from Rorty (1990). That paper offers an account of the recent disagreements between Fodor and Dennett, and a more extended account of Dennett's position in the development of philosophy of mind since Ryle.

9 See Dennett's classification of contemporary philosophers of mind according to whether or not they take intentionality to be intrinsic, in "Evolution, Error and Intentionality" (Dennett, 1987, pp. 287–321).

10 I owe the analogy between assigning intentional states and assigning dollar values to Dennett (1987, p. 208).

11   The difference between these two alternatives creates the familiar problem of how we know that we are not brains in a vat. Davidson's solution is to say that a brain which has always been in a vat will have mostly beliefs about the vat-cum-computer environment which in fact surrounds it, no matter what input it receives from the computer. For discussion and criticism of this Davidsonian line of argument, see Colin McGinn (1986), pp. 369–86. It is significant that McGinn thinks that, to refute Davidson, we need to resurrect the distinction between "experience" and "belief" which Dennett tries to bury. McGinn thinks it necessary, in order to make "interpretation respect the premises on which scepticism rests," to say that "the (phenomenological) content of experience is fixed by the intrinsic condition of the brain" (p. 362). Davidson, by contrast, takes it as his aim to get rid of the premises on which skepticism rests. So for him, both "the problem of the external world" and "the problem of other minds" are problems which repose on a traditional but wrong-headed distinction between "the phenomenological content of experience" and the intentional states attributed to a person on the basis of his causal interactions with his environment.

12   For a defense of the idea of intrinsic mental states against Davidson, see Mark Johnston (1986), pp. 422ff. Johnston is right to say that Davidson's "anomalous monism" takes "the propositional attitudes as constitutive of the mental" (p. 424). He points out that one could take the absence of lawlike connections between mental and physical events, of which Davidson makes much, as showing "that the vocabulary of propositional attitudes is not made to carve out the natural mental properties which stand in lawlike relations to physical properties" (p. 425). One *could*, indeed, so take it. But then one *could* take the incommensurability of Aristotelian and corpuscularian explanations to show that a corpuscularian vocabulary is not suitable for carving out *verae causae*.

13   I am not suggesting that Wundt and Helmholz and James would not have conducted the experiments they conducted, but merely that they would have described what they were doing (as Freud did in the *Project*) as providing place-holders to be filled in by the neurology of the future.

14   See Williams (1986) and Fine (1986), for further defense of the claim that these are pseudo-explanations.

15   See, for example, Dennett (1987), p. 72, where he invokes the notion of "abstracta" in the course of saying why he does not think that beliefs are "part of the 'furniture of the physical world'" and that attributions of belief are "*true* only if we exempt them from a certain familiar standard of literality." Since I think Dennett would be hard pressed to explain what that standard is, I wish that he would fend off questions about his ontological views by saying, as I would, that he no longer has any such views. Someone who has, as Nietzsche says, "actively forgotten" the outworn creed on which she was suckled no longer has any theological convictions; someone who has actively forgotten Quine's distinction between canonical and merely handy notations no longer has any ontological commitments.

16   I once thought that Dennett distinguished the abstracta from "the furniture of the physical world" by the inability of the former to function as causes. But if he ever made the distinction in that way, he no longer seems inclined to do so. In "Real Patterns" (1991b, p. 43n), he says that "if one finds a predictive pattern of the sort just described [the sort that helps you anticipate the world] one has *ipso facto* discovered a causal power." He now seems inclined to grant causal power to anything that appears in a predictively useful explanation, including a belief or a center of gravity (as in "The airplane crashed because the rush of passengers to the bar altered its center of gravity.")

17   Recall Putnam's distinction between "single-criterion concepts" and "cluster concepts" – a somewhat fuzzy distinction, but good enough for present purposes.

18   See the "Introduction" to Rorty (1991) for an expanded statement of this attempt to follow Fine to a position beyond realism and anti-realism. I urge there that we drop

notions like "fact of the matter," "bivalence," and "determinate reality" for the same sorts of reasons as Quine dropped notions like "analyticity," "synonymy," "semantic rule," etc. The same point can be urged by saying that the kind of "determinate reality" which a center of gravity has is all the determinate reality any object could possibly have. To ask for more determinacy than that is to surrender to the ambition of transcendence.

REFERENCES

Davidson, D. (1986) A nice derangement of epitaphs. In E. Lepore (ed.), *Truth and Interpretation*. Oxford: Blackwell.
Davidson, D. (1989) The myth of the subjective. In M. Krausz (ed.), *Relativism, Interpretation and Confrontation*. Notre Dame, Ind.: Notre Dame University Press.
Dennett, D. C. (1987) *The Intentional Stance*. Cambridge, Mass.: Bradford Books/MIT Press.
Dennett, D. C. (1991a) *Consciousness Explained*. Boston: Little, Brown.
Dennett, D. C. (1991b) Real patterns. *The Journal of Philosophy*, 88, 27–51.
Dewey, J. (1957) *Reconstruction in Philosophy*, 2nd edn. New York: Beacon Press.
Dewey, J. (1977) The influence of Darwin on philosophy. In *The Middle Works*, vol. 4. Carbondale: Southern Illinois University Press.
Fine, A. (1986) Unnatural attitudes: realist and instrumentalist attachments to science. *Mind*, 95, 149–79.
Johnston, M. (1986) Why having a mind matters. In E. Lepore (ed.), *Truth and Interpretation*. Oxford: Blackwell.
McGinn, C. (1986) Radical interpreation and epistemology. In E. Lepore (ed.), *Truth and Interpretation*. Oxford: Blackwell.
Nagel, T. (1979) *Mortal Questions*. Cambridge: Cambridge University Press.
Nagel, T. (1986) *The View from Nowhere*. Oxford: Oxford University Press.
Nagel, T. (1991) What we have in mind when we say we're thinking. *The Wall Street Journal*, November 7.
Reichenbach, H. (1951) *The Rise of Scientific Philosophy*. Berkeley and Los Angeles: University of California Press.
Rorty, R. (1980) *Philosophy and the Mirror of Nature*. Oxford: Blackwell.
Rorty, R. (1990) Consciousness, intentionality and pragmatism. In Jose Quiros (ed.), *Modelos de la Mente*. Madrid.
Rorty, R. (1991) *Objectivity, Relativism and Truth*. Cambridge: Cambridge University Press.
Sellars, W. (1963) Empiricism and the philosophy of mind. In *Science, Perception, and Reality*, London: Routledge and Kegan Paul.
Searle, J. (1983) *Intentionality*. Cambridge: Cambridge University Press.
Williams, M. (1986) Do we (epistemologists) need a theory of truth? *Philosophical Topics*, 14, 223–42.

10
Back from the Drawing Board

DANIEL DENNETT

Reading the essays that make up this volume has shown me a great deal, both about the substantive issues I have dealt with and about how to do philosophy. On the former front, they show that I have missed some points and overstated others, and sometimes just been unable to penetrate the fog. On the latter front, they show how hard it is to write philosophy that *works* – and this is the point that stands out for me as I reflect on these rich and varied essays. Philosophical books and articles routinely fail to achieve their manifest goal of persuading their intended audiences of their main points. Does this make philosophy any worse off than other writing endeavors? Most published novels are failures of one sort or another, and the press has reported a recent study (whose methodology I wonder about) that concludes that the *median* number of readers of any paper published in a psychology journal is zero. But it seems to me that philosophy displays a particularly feckless record, with such a huge gap between authorial pretense and effect achieved that it is perhaps more comic than pathetic. In one weak moment I found myself thinking that perhaps some of our French colleagues have the right idea: deliberate obscurantism and the striking of stylized poses – since the goal of persuading by clear, precise analysis and argument is so manifestly beyond us. But that world-weariness passed, I'm happy to say, and my cock-eyed American optimism returned. My ambition continues to be to change people's minds, and not just to win people over to my way of doing philosophy, as Bo Dahlbom suggests. But I admit that it is harder than I had thought. It's hard enough to get a good idea, but sometimes it's even harder, apparently, to get others to see what the idea is, and why it's good.

I view philosophical writing in an engineering spirit: I design and build devices – arguments, intuition pumps, metaphor machines – that are supposed to achieve certain effects. When they work, I'm exultant and when they don't, I'm surprised and annoyed. These essays uncover a variety of failures – mostly mine – and now that I have worked through my initial annoyance, I am ready, like any good engineer, to face the question: why didn't this thing work? What over-optimistic assumptions led me to underdesign the device? Is it worth repairing, or should I junk it and try another tack?

1 Science as a Virus – and Other Metaphors

Let's begin with one of my most striking failures, the twice-quoted passage on metaphor that closes *Consciousness Explained*. Dick Rorty loves it and Bo Dahlbom is, well, almost shocked by it. ("Quine would *never* have said that.") Neither understands it in the way I intended it. I was actually trying for quite a modest little point in that passage. I was not trying to say It's All Just Metaphor or anything remotely like that. I was just pointing out that however precise, literal, and non-metaphorical science may be in *some* of its accounts, it is never free of metaphors; some are good, some bad, and all are potent. I was proposing to replace some of the bad ones with some better ones.

I was not trying to hit a home run. Philosophers are supposed to try to hit home runs, and I guess sometimes that's why I am misunderstood. I seldom swing for the fences; I try to scratch out my runs by a more modest collection of bunts, grounders, and aggressive base running. I'm not noted for modesty – "hubris" and "arrogance" are words that appear all too often in reviews of my books – but in one regard I am more modest than philosophers generally are. I am shy about drawing ultimate conclusions about Reality, Truth, Meaning, Time, Causation, and the other grand topics of metaphysics and epistemology. Those questions are too hard for me to approach with any confidence. I take myself rather to be just working out some of the more surprising implications of the standard scientific picture, roughly the one I was given in school, and I don't even include all of that standard picture. As Dahlbom notes, physics is "none of my business," because I don't think I understand the niceties of contemporary physics well enough to be comfortable holding forth about its ontological presuppositions, and so forth.

Attitudes towards science are at the heart of several of the disagreements expressed in these essays, and perhaps the place to begin is with the contrast between Rorty and Richard Dawkins. The last section of Dawkins' idea-packed essay asks if science is a virus, and answers:

> No. Not unless all computer programs are viruses. Good, useful progams spread because people evaluate them, recommend them and pass them on. Computer viruses spread solely because they embody the coded instructions: "Spread me." Scientific ideas, like all memes, are subject to a kind of natural selection, and this might look superficially virus-like. But the selective forces that scrutinize scientific ideas are not arbitrary or capricious. They are exacting, well-honed rules, and . . . they favor all the virtues laid out in textbooks of standard methodology: testability, evidential support, precision, . . . and so on (p. 26).

When you examine the reasons for the spread of scientific memes, Dawkins assures us, "you find they are good ones." This, the standard, official position of science, is undeniable in its own terms, but question-begging to the mullah and the nun – and to Rorty, who would quite appropriately ask Dawkins: "Where is your demonstration that these 'virtues' are *good* virtues? You note that people evaluate these memes and pass them on – but if Dennett is right, people (persons with fully fledged selves) are themselves in large measure the creation of memes – something implied by the passage from Dennett you use as your epigraph. How clever of some memes to team together to create meme-evaluators that favor *them*! Where, then, is the Archimedean point from which you can deliver your benediction on science?"[1]

There is none. About this, I agree wholeheartedly with Rorty. But that does not mean (nor should Rorty be held to imply) that we may not judge the virtue of memes. *We* certainly may. And who are we? The people created by the memes of Western rationalism. It does mean, as Dawkins would insist, that certain memes go together well in families. The family of memes that compose Western rationalism (including natural science) is incompatible with the memes of all but the most pastel versions of religious faith. This is commonly denied, but Dawkins has the courage to insist upon it, and I stand beside him. It is seldom pointed out that the homilies of religious tolerance are tacitly but firmly limited: we are under no moral obligation to tolerate faiths that permit slavery or infanticide or that advocate the killing of the unfaithful, for instance. Such faiths are out of bounds. Out of whose bounds? Out of the bounds of Western rationalism that are presupposed, I am sure, by every author in this volume. But Rorty wants to move beyond such parochial platforms of judgment, and urges me to follow. I won't, not because there isn't good work for a philosopher in that rarefied atmosphere, but because there is still so much good philosophical work to be done closer to the ground.

Like most cognitive scientists, I'm prepared to take my chances with conservative, standard scientific ontology and epistemology.[2] My project, then, is to demonstrate how a standard, normal respect for science – *Time Magazine* standard, nothing more doctrinaire – leads inexorably to my views about consciousness, intentionality, free will, and so forth. I view science not as an unquestionable foundation, but simply as a natural ally of my philosophical claims that most philosophers and scientists would be reluctant to oppose. My "scientism" comes in the form of a package deal: you think you can have your everyday science and reject my "behaviorism" as too radical? Think again.

Now although I'm not swinging for the fences, I might happen – almost by accident – to hit a home run once in a while. John Haugeland sees me as contributing to ontology, the most Olympian feat in metaphysics, and Rorty and Dahlbom find similar implications to discuss. Maybe Rorty is right that I *ought* to be more ambitious and radical in my conclusions. More on that later, but in the meantime, there is plenty of good work to be done on the basepaths – and plenty of room for instructive failure.

2 A Case from Cognitive Neuroscience: Churchland and Ramachandran

A clear instance of this is found in Pat Churchland and "Rama" Ramachandran's essay (chapter 2) on the metaphor of "filling in", which is ubiquitous in cognitive science, but which I have attempted to condemn. Their essay shows that I'm certainly wrong about one thing: about the effects my own metaphor-machines would have on them, for I have misled them. They don't understand what I was trying to assert (and deny), and if *they* don't understand, what chance do I have of getting through to the uninitiated?

The issues here are not grand metaphysical issues, but rather nagging confusions about how to think about vision. We (scientists and philosophers) have to use metaphors to think about something as complex and puzzling as vision, but the metaphors can also create difficulties for us. The way to overcome these difficulties is not from on high, with sweeping philosophical theses, but in the trenches, looking at the details of how we describe the phenomena and what assumptions we make about them in the process.

They propose to sweep the decks of "needless metaphysical tut-tutting" by claiming that their talk of filling in is only a convenient shorthand; speaking this way does not commit them to any silly view that holds that when someone sees an apple "there might be a little (literal) apple or a (literal) picture of an apple in someone's head which is the thing that is filled in." Good. Then to what does their convenient shorthand refer? "Merely to some property of the brain's visual representation such that the perceiver sees a non-gappy apple." But what does *that* mean? This is the whole issue.

They begin by confronting a choice, an either/or with two alternatives. What is going on, they ask, when one's blind spot is seen as filled in? "Is it analogous to acquiring the non-visual representation (belief) that Bowser, the family dog, is under the bed . . . Or is it more akin to regular visual perception of the whole Bowser in one's *peripheral but non-blind field?* That is, is the representation itself a visual representation, involving visual experiences?" (p. 30). The contrast is not as clear as they may think; there seem to me to be intermediate alternatives. The difference they are alluding to is exemplified, one gathers, by the difference between coming to believe that there is a dog under the table by *deducing* this from various non-visual clues (including, perhaps, a trusted friend whispering in your ear. "There's a dog under the table!") and coming to believe there is a dog under the table by *seeing* it in one's peripheral vision. The latter case, but not the former, involves "visual experiences." And if you just see the dog's tail out of the corner of your eye and infer the rest, this is presumably a mixed case, partly involving visual experience, partly involving visually unclothed inference. What, then, about watching a dog walk behind a picket fence? There is no deliberate, conscious deduction of the hidden bits, certainly, but in some sense they are inferred – *and* your brain accomplishes this (I reckon) without having to draw in, or paint in, or in any other way fill in the hidden bits. You don't "just think" there's a whole dog; you *see* that it's a whole "non-gappy" dog walking behind the fence; this is certainly a "visual experience" even though its completion (so that you see what's in front of you *as* a whole connected dog) involves jumping to a conclusion about what is missing.

At any rate, this is how I would put it, but this courts misunderstanding. Churchland and Ramachandran take the contrast to be between peripheral visual perception and entirely non-visual perception (or just belief), but I am just as insistent that there is no "filling in" in normal peripheral vision as in the blind spot. For instance, there is nothing "non-visual" about your discovery, on entering a room, that it is covered wall-to-wall with identical photos of Marilyn Monroe, but that discovery *must* be way out ahead of the information your eyes have taken in, since your peripheral visual system is simply unable to distinguish the peripheral Marilyns from Marilyn-shaped blobs. I count "jumping to a conclusion" (e.g., jumping to the conclusion that the room is papered with identical Marilyns) as the brain's "doing something positive" but not as "filling in" because, although the brain does indeed add information as it draws the conclusion, it doesn't then go on to draw the Marilyns – nor is its conclusion based on any extrapolative drawing it has already done. Or so I claim.

This is an empirical issue, and there are ways that I could be shown to be wrong. The cases Churchland and Ramachandran describe illuminate the issues, and in some cases force non-trivial clarifications to my position, but for the most part they are either neutral or support my minimalist view, not their alternative. That this should not yet be obvious to Churchland and Ramachandran shows how far from clarity my framing of the issue has been to date.

Consider the case of the field of bagels (their Figure 2.8), in which one bagel is carefully positioned so that its "hole" falls within the subject's blind spot. If they had asked me in advance of the experiment whether the subject would see "just more bagels" or rather a solid disk, I would not have known what to say; I would have recognized an ambiguity in my claim that the brain assumes "more of the same," for it all depends on whether the brain draws this conclusion locally or globally. They assume that my view would have to predict that the bagel would be seen *as* a bagel (globally more of the same), but this does not follow. One can see the alternative by looking at a succession of different cases. Suppose your visual field consisted of solid red; then drawing the conclusion "more of the same" would lead to the same result whether the reasoning was based on global or local conditions. Suppose next that there is a single big red disk off to the side in your visual field. If the brain simply concludes that the property it finds *in the general vicinity* of the blind spot – red – is to be extrapolated, this is a case of concluding "more of the same," and does not also have to involve filling in. Now shrink the disk to the size of a bagel – and, if you like, punch a hole in it, covered by the blind spot. If the brain bases its conclusions on what is in the *immediate vicinity* of the blind spot, then "more of the same" gives just more red, so the brain will indeed conclude it has a solid red disk, which might then "pop out" just as in Ramachandran's experiment. So what the experiment shows is that at least in this instance, the brain bases its extrapolation on local conditions, not global conditions. This is a valuable result; in retrospect we may say it is not surprising, but retrospect doesn't count. I would have said it could go either way before I learned of the experiment, which does indeed show that the brain's conclusion (in this instance) is both locally based and "early," early enough in visual processing to provide the material for "pop out." (One might have predicted that the bagel would be seen as a disk but would *not* pop out, on the supposition that the conclusion *red disk* would be reached too late to provide an odd-one-out premise for pop-out.)

The experiment in which subjects complete the bar through the blind spot, in spite of the fact that the top half is red and the bottom is green, raises a different issue. "Subjects still see the bar as complete, with extensions of both the red and green bar, but they do not see a border where the red and green meet, and hence they cannot say just where one color begins and the other leaves off." Now this way of putting it blurs the distinction I am trying to make. Is it just that "they cannot say" where one color begins and the other leaves off, or is it that the brain itself never "says" where one color begins and the other leaves off? If there is *any* sort of filling in worthy of the name, then each sub-area of the bar-as-represented must be filled in either red or green (or "reddish green" as in the Crane and Piantanida experiment!). Or I suppose areas could flicker back and forth between red and green, but one way or another, filling in requires explicit representation of the color at each "pixel" within the outline of the bar – that is what I mean by filling in (see *Consciousness Explained*, p. 349). But if there isn't filling in, if the brain just concludes that it is a single solid bar with a red top and a green bottom and *does not go into the matter* of where and how the color changes, then there would be no fact of the matter about where "the boundary" was, just as there is no fact of the matter about whether Falstaff had a sister. The brain might even in some sense "recognize" that there had to be a boundary between the two colors (Rule violation! Two color labels on a single region!), but just neglect to resolve that violation and settle where that boundary might be. It is not clear, from Churchland and Ramachandran's formulation, whether they suppose that there must be a boundary in the brain's representation, a boundary that is simply inaccessible to the subjects. I am claiming that while there *might* be – it is an empirical question – there *need not* be. From my reading of other work of Ramachandran's, I expect he agrees, and perhaps Churchland does as well.

The conclusion Churchland and Ramachandran draw from the blind-spot experiments is that "in so far as there is nothing in the visual stimulus correspond-ing to the filled in perception, it is reasonable to infer, in contrast to Dennett, that the brain is 'providing' something, not merely 'ignoring something.'" But their claim does not in fact contrast with mine – or perhaps I should say, it does not contrast with what I intended to convey. The brain certainly provides content regarding the blind-spot region, but it may still be accomplishing this by "ignoring." To ignore an area is to operate without requiring confirmation or disconfirmation from the area – going along as if that bit of space just didn't exist. Jumping to the conclusion that it's more of the same is "adding something" – it is to be distinguished, after all, from not jumping to that conclusion at all – but it is not filling in. The difference I am after is the difference between jumping to a conclusion and stepping to a conclusion by making some bogus steps on which to rest the conclusion (e.g., paint in the region, and then use that painted-in region as one's "evidence" for the conclusion subsequently drawn). The way to test my hypothesis that the brain does not bother filling in the "evidence" for its conclusion is to see if there are effects that depend on the brain's having represented the *step*, rather than just the *conclusion*.

How could this be shown? We might look for inspiration to the famous random-dot stereogram experiments by Bela Julesz. Before Julesz demonstrated that stereo vision could be achieved by simply displacing a region of random dots in the view presented to one eye (creating binocular disparity, interpreted as depth), a minimalist creed prevailed: information about the individual dots on the retinas was not preserved up to the optic chiasm (where the signal streams from both eyes merge for the first time). The brain, it was thought, had already thrown away such pixel-by-pixel information, and replaced it with generalizations, along the lines of "more random dots over here." But since depth perception was demonstrably possible in Julesz's conditions, the pixel-by-pixel information *had* to be preserved this "late" in the visual stream, since if the brain were merely noting that there were "more random dots" there would be no individual dot-representations to match up in order to identify the displaced area. Julesz in effect demonstrated that *each dot* was represented by the information in each stream.

A similarly striking demonstration might prove that the brain actually does fill in pixel-by-pixel values in the region representing the blind spot (or other regions, such as artificial scotomas). The detail would not just *seem* to be there; it would *have* to be there to explain some effect. (Note that Churchland and Ramachandran's essay offers fine examples of the importance of adopting what I call the method of *heterophenomenology* (*Consciousness Explained*, ch. 4). Consider the use they make of subject report; it is not enough to predict phenomenology; you have to show whether the subjects are right about it; you mustn't just assume they are.) I have not yet been able to dream up a plausible experiment that could show this, but Ramachandran will be able to, if anyone can. There are some positive but inconclusive hints in the data he has already presented: the long latency of some filling-in effects, and even more important, the *spatial spread*, such as "the red color bleeding into" the scotoma. This is telling (if not quite conclusive), because you can't assign a label to a region *gradually*, and it is hard to think of a reason why the brain would bind the "gradually" label to a process that wasn't gradual. (It *seems* to be gradual, but maybe it *only* seems to be gradual.)

The Gattass effect and the Gilbert and Wiesel effect, which apparently show that there is much more dynamic migration of receptive fields than heretofore suspected, do indeed add a new set of options to the standard ways of thinking about how the visual system might or must work. As Churchland and Ramachandran say, the options are not exhausted by my "bit map or color-by-numbers" alternatives, but those were not meant to be exhaustive: they were merely meant to be alternative ways of thinking of the *traditional* issue of "filling in." These recent neuroanatomical discoveries are important because they show another possibility: treating input from one area as if it came from another. But Churchland and Ramachandran fail to notice that there are (at least) two very different ways the brain could do this, which we might crudely label "duplication" and "pinching off."

In duplication, the input from one small region is actually *doubled* at a higher level, to represent both its home region and an adopted region. "Pinching off" is a more radical hypothesis: one's visual field can be represented as a space that has no unique mapping onto any portion of the ordinary three-dimensional space in front of your eyes; gaps in one's coverage of that space can be simply "pinched off" in one's visual representation, giving the sense of a seamless, gapless space that simply *leaves out* certain regions of the external world. If I may risk a metaphor: think of printing a map of the USA on a soft rubber sheet, and then, from behind, simply pinching Tennessee out of sight, bringing Kentucky's southern border right down to the northern borders of Mississippi and Alabama, and then smoothing out this infolding, so that a seamless plane resulted. Is that "filling in?" It might be what the brain sometimes does. Ramachandran's most recent researches, conducted after the essay in this volume was completed, show that duplication can occur in other sense modalities, such as phantom limb, so it is possible, but not yet proven, that such duplication occurs in the case of the blind spot.

Each of the other experiments Churchland and Ramachandran describe deserves an equally detailed discussion from me, but since I think I have now expressed all the main themes those detailed discussions would appeal to, instead of "filling in" those details, I will encourage the reader to extrapolate "more of the same" and see if that doesn't provide an adequate response. Churchland and Ramachandran chide me for thinking like a computer engineer and prejudging how the brain might or must deal with its tasks. I plead *nolo contendere*. It's a good way to think – risky, but a fine way of generating hypotheses. I might sometimes forget to admit, in the thrill of the chase, that these hunches need confirmation (and hence court disconfirmation), and, of course, I must take my lumps when I'm proven wrong. But, although the results they describe require me to clarify and disambiguate my hypotheses, they don't *yet* require me to retract them.

The pure philosophers may want to come up for air at this point. Churchland and Ramachandran provide a closing diagnosis of where I went wrong (by their lights) which imputes to me a variety of *behaviorism* which they think has blinded me to the importance of the neuroanatomical details. They contrast my view with "scientific realism," according to which "it is reasonable to consider sensory experiences to be real states of the brain, states whose neurobiological properties will be discovered as cognitive neuroscience proceeds." But I agree wholeheartedly with this, and am, indeed, as scientific a realist as one could find. While I am proud to trace my lineage to Quine and Ryle, I must protest that this identification of my position breeds more misapprehension than enlightenment.

3 Labels: Am I a Behaviorist? An Ontologist?

Am I a behaviorist? Tom Nagel and John Searle have always wanted to insist on it, and now Churchland concurs, and so does Dahlbom, who very accurately describes my position but imposes on it a label I abhor. I agree that there is historical justification for the label, spelled out by Dahlbom, but most people don't appreciate the subtleties of that justification, and hence are drastically misled by the term's connotations.

I once made the mistake of acquiescing, in a cooperative spirit, when Ned Block suggested that I should let myself be called an instrumentalist. Never again. While there are perfectly reasonable doctrines that in fact every right-thinking scientist holds that might reasonably be called instrumentalism (instrumentalism with regard to centers of gravity, instrumentalism with regard to parallelograms of force, etc.), tradition has it that instrumentalism is the all-too-radical dogma that treats electrons (and for that matter, whales and mountains) as in the same ontological boat as the Equator. So when I let myself be counted as an instrumentalist, I then found I had to work very hard to undo the damage. People quite naturally reasoned that if I was a self-professed instrumentalist, and if some dime-store argument refuted instrumentalism, the same argument must refute me. Since people are inclined to reason this way, the tug-of-war about labels (which "ism" do you pledge allegiance to?) is regrettably important.

We all go in for this sort of reasoning. If I learn that somebody is an idealist, or a dualist, my initial working assumption is going to be that this person holds a forlorn view, since the "refutations" of idealism and dualism are well known. So if I held a view that could be seen, in a certain light, to be a *sort* of dualism, I'd be extremely reluctant to "admit it," since the debates that ensued would so boringly gravitate towards defending my view against all the old arguments. The standard arguments against both Skinnerian and Rylean behaviorism do not touch my view; indeed, I am the author of some of those arguments ("Skinner Skinned," "A Cure for the Common Code"). My anti-behaviorist credentials are impeccable.

But people like a memorable label for a view, or at least a slogan, so since I reject the label, I'll provide a slogan: "Once you've explained everything that happens, you've explained everything." Now is that behaviorism? No. If it were, then all physiologists, meteorologists, geologists, chemists, and physicists would be behaviorists, too, for they take it for granted that once they have explained all that happens regarding their phenomena, the job is finished. This view could with more justice be called phenomenology! The original use of the term "phenomenology" was to mark the cataloguing of everything that happened regarding some phenomenon, such as a disease, or a type of weather, or some other salient source of puzzlement in nature, as a useful preamble to attempting to explain the catalogued phenomena. First you accurately describe the phenomena, as they appear under all conditions of observation, and then, phenomenology finished, you – or someone else – can try to explain it all.

So my heterophenomenology is nothing more nor less than old-fashioned phenomenology applied to people (primarily) instead of tuberculosis or hurricanes: it provides a theory-neutral, objective catalogue of what happens – the phenomena to be explained. It does assume that all these phenomena can be observed, directly or indirectly, by anyone who wants to observe them and has the right equipment. It does not restrict itself to casual, external observation; brain scans and more invasive techniques are within its purview, since *everything that happens in the brain* is included in its catalogue of what happens. What alternative view is there? There is only one that I can see: the view that there are subjective phenomena beyond the reach of *any* heterophenomenology. Nagel and Searle embrace this curious doctrine. As Rorty notes: "Nagel and Searle see clearly that if they accept the maxim, 'To explain all the relational properties something has – all its causes and all its effects – is to explain the thing itself;' then they will lose the argument" (p. 185). They will lose and science will win.

Do you know what a zagnet is? It is something that behaves exactly like a magnet, is chemically and physically indistinguishable from a magnet, but is not really a magnet! (Magnets have a hidden essence, I guess, that zagnets lack.) Do you know what a zombie is? A zombie is somebody (or better, something) that behaves exactly like a normal conscious human being, and is neuroscientifically indistinguishable from a human being, but is not consicous. I don't know anyone who thinks zagnets are even "possible in principle," but Nagel and Searle think zombies are. Indeed, you have to hold out for the possibility of zombies if you deny my slogan. So if my position is behaviorism, its only alternative is *zombism.*

"Zagnets make no sense because magnets are just *things* – they have no inner life; consciousness is different!" Well, that's a tradition in need of reconsideration. I disagree strongly with Rorty when he says "Dennett's suggestion that he has found neutral ground on which to argue with Nagel is wrong. By countenancing, or refusing to countenance, such knowledge, Nagel and Dennett beg all the questions against each other" (p. 188). I think this fails to do justice to one feature of my heterophenomenological strategy: I let Nagel have everything he wants about his own intimate relation to his phenomenology *except* that he has some sort of papal infallibility about it; he can have all the ineffability he wants; what he can't have (without an argument) is *in principle* ineffability. It would certainly not be neutral for me to cede him either infallibilty or ineffability *in principle.* In objecting to the very idea of an objective standpoint from which to gather and assess phenomenological evidence, Nagel is objecting to neutrality itself. My method does grant Nagel neutral ground, but he wants more. He won't get it from me.

Are there any good reasons for taking zombies more seriously than zagnets? Until that challenge is met, I submit that my so-called behaviorism is nothing but the standard scientific realism to which Churchland and Ramachandran pledge their own allegiance; neither of them would have any truck with phenomenological differences that were beyond the scrutiny of any possible extension of neuroscience. That makes them the same kind of "behaviorist" that I am – which is to say, not a behaviorist at all!

Labels do seem to have given me a lot of trouble. One of the most frustrating is "realism." Rorty urges me to stop taking the controversy over "realism" seriously. I wish I could, but Haugeland, Fodor and Lepore, and others tug me in the opposite direction. My penchant, so tellingly described by Dahlbom in the introduction, for deflecting objections with storytelling and analogy-drawing instead of responding with clearly marshalled premises and conclusions, sometimes backfires, as I learned in a recent discussion with that metaphysician *par excellence*, Jaegwon Kim. He had complained to me roughly as follows:

> you just give examples and leave it to us to draw the moral; we want you to say what conclusions, what general principles, you think they establish. Instead of answering by stating and defending an ontological position, you just give another example. The examples are very nice, but we want the theory that accounts for them.

My reply: that is not quite the point of my examples. We've been at cross-purposes, for I have not been sufficiently forthright in saying what I take the force of my examples to be. My point is to respond to the challenge from the metaphysicians or ontologists by saying, in effect, Look, when you folks get clear about such non-mysterious cases as smiles, opportunities, centers of gravity and voices, then (and only then) will I feel the obligation to answer your questions. Until that time, the ontological enterprise is nothing I feel obliged to engage in. Are centers of gravity abstract or concrete? Should one be an eliminative materialist about smiles, and then commit oneself to *properties*, the instantiations of which are *events*? Or should one be a realist about them? Are these options ever really serious? I am sure any ontologist worth his salt can provide a rigorous, clear, systematic account of all these cases. (I have tried it out myself, in private, and have some ideas about what might work.) The trouble is that different ontologists come up with different systems, and they are unable to reach consensus. I really am prepared to take instruction on these issues, but not until the instruction is in unison or close to it. I wouldn't want to trot out *my* ontology and then find I had to spend the rest of my life defending or revising *it*, instead of getting on with what are to me the genuinely puzzling issues – like the nature of consciousness, or selves, or free will. The ontological status of fictional characters, haircuts, holes, and the North Pole may be deep and fascinating problems in themselves to some philosophers, but not to me; they are interesting playthings to come back to in one's spare time. *That* is the game I am opting out of, since there seem to me to be better things to do first. When and if professional ontologists agree on the ontological status of all my puzzle examples, my bluff will be well and truly called; I will feel a genuine obligation to make things clear to them in their terms, for they will have figured out something fundamental.

But John Haugeland insists that I am doing ontology whether I like it or not, and I ought to make sure I do it right. One thing is clear; it was at least a tactical mistake for me to describe my alternative to Realism and Eliminativism and Instrumentalism as "mild realism." Both Rorty and Haugeland jump on me for that, and I guess they are right. (Certainly Rorty is right that my description of his view in terms of "irrealism" does it an injustice.) But must I attempt to put my ontological house in order before proceeding further? I don't mean to suggest that this is just a matter of taste; I may be simply wrong about the value of getting ontology straight as a first step. I think, in fact, that ontologists differ in their creeds about this. Some, I gather, really don't care whether ontology is essential to scientific progress; they just find the puzzles intrinsically so interesting that they are prepared to devote their professional lives to trying to sort them out. I see nothing wrong with that attitude. I deplore the narrow pragmatism that demands immediate social utility for any intellectual exercise. Theoretical physicists and cosmologists, for instance, may have more prestige than ontologists, but not because there is any more social utility in the satisfaction of *their* pure curiosity. Anyone who thinks it is ludicrous to pay someone good money to work out the ontology of dances (or numbers or opportunities) probably thinks the same about working out the identity of Homer or what happened in the first millionth of a second after the Big Bang.

Of course, some cosmologists would insist that their researches do – or might well – have social utility in the long run, and in a similar spirit other ontologists seem to think what they are saying is directly relevant to, and important to, the scientists working on empirical theories, for instance, theories of the mind. But I have never seen a persuasive case made for this view, and so far as I can see, ontology has always in fact lagged behind science, whether or not this is a good thing. I have yet to see a case where *first* the metaphysicians got a clear account of the ontology and this *then* enabled the scientists to solve some problem by rendering theory in its terms.

This doesn't mean that I think science is conducted in ontology-neutral terms, or that the ontologies scientists tacitly adopt don't influence (even cripple) their scientific enterprises. Quite the contrary; I think ontological confusions are at the heart of the lack of progress in cognitive science. But I don't think the way to overcome the problem is by stopping the science until the ontology is clear. Here is where we really are in Neurath's boat, and must rebuild it while we keep it sailing.

How, then, do we rebuild it, if not by first developing a "systematic" ontology? By noting pitfalls, looking at analogies, keeping examples close to our attention, etc. This is what I was attempting to do in "Real Patterns," but Haugeland finds my attempt hampered by two sorts of vacillation. In the first instance, I vacillate between talking about the reality of a pattern, and the reality of the elements of the pattern. That's a fair cop. When I asked "When are the elements of a pattern real and not merely apparent?" I meant to be asking about the reality of what we might better call the pattern's *features* (which only exist *as* features-of-a-pattern), since the reality of the ultimate elements of which these features are somehow composed was not at issue. Haugeland thinks this slip of mine interacts in a significant way with the second sort of vacillation he spies, but I am not persuaded. The second vacillation is between two different definitions of pattern: one in which patterns are "recognizabilia" as he puts it, and one that aspires to objectivity (independence from the biases and limitations of any particular recognizer). He is surprised that I don't note the tension between these; in fact, I thought I had resolved the tension and unified them via the mathematical definition of randomness, but I grant that I should have spelled it out. A mathematically random sequence is not a pattern, and any patterns "discerned" in it are strictly illusory, not real; and any sequence that is not mathematically random has a pattern that is recognizable-in-principle by some observer or other, up to and including what we might call the maximal observer: the whole universe considered as a potential observer. Doesn't this keep the tie to recognition while achieving objectivity?

Of course Haugeland wants to treat recognition in its richest garb, as something more than mere discrimination and differential reaction, which is all I wanted to mean by the term. I should perhaps have chosen a more modest or technical term, such as pattern-*transduction*, instead of relying on the standard idiom as it appears in the literature of AI and cognitive science. But then I mightn't have provoked Haugeland's interesting analysis of the foundational role of (rich) recognition in ontology, so it is a fortunate error. One particularly important point he makes is that recognition does not always depend on a process of analysis of elements, but I don't think he draws the right conclusion from it. For this is true even in those cases where the difference between correct and incorrect recognition *can be defined in terms of* such elements. The difference between the written words "boat" and "coat" is nothing other than the occurrence of "b" at the head of one and "c" at the head of the other, but it does not follow that particular acts of visual recognition of either word consist of independent acts of "b"-recognition and "c"-recognition and so forth. Often it is only the wider context that permits a perceiver to recognize a dimly or distantly seen word as "boat" *which then enables* the perception of the leftmost element *as* a "b," something otherwise quite beyond the perceptual capacity of the recognizer. It is even possible for there to be a "boat"-recognizer who hasn't a clue about – and cannot recognize – the individual letters that are the definitive elements of "boat."

Haugeland thinks there is a difficulty for my proposed merger of the two senses of pattern because "if . . . an attempt were made to merge the two notions of pattern, such that recognizable patterns must at the same time *be* arrangements of prior elements, then, arguably, their recognizability would have to be *via* prior recognition of those elements . . ." (p. 59). Arguably, but mistakenly arguably! I think I can accept his observations about the non-algorithmic nature of recognition, while clinging to the conservative default ontology: patterns are patterns of prior elements, even if you don't know what those elements are (yet). The reality of the pattern *features* depends on their being in principle recognizable as features by some pattern recognizer, but this recognizability does not in turn depend on some base recognizability of the atoms, as it were, of which those features are composed.

So I'm not convinced. But if I am wrong and Haugeland is right, then this would be a case in which something of a revolution in ontology came from within, boiling up out of the scientific details, not from on high. And, in the meantime, when people challenge me to announce my allegiance – to eliminative materialism or property dualism or realism or emergentism or even (God forbid) epiphenomenalism, or whatever – I will firmly resist the challenge. Of course, this means that I pass the buck to them; I say, in effect, *you tell me* what category my view falls in. Since I do this, I can't complain *that* they categorize me (I invited them to) but I can complain when they do it wrong. My view is *itself* one of my puzzle examples; I challenge *them* to come up with an ontological interpretation of it that does justice to its subtleties, just as I challenge them to do the same for centers of gravity or voices.

4 Philosophy Drawn and Quartered

That, then, is the strategy I have adopted, but never before been so forthright about. My reticence has cost me some misconstruals, such as those of Jerry Fodor and Ernie Lepore, who work hard to turn me into something I am not. (Fodor believes that doing philosophy is a matter of composing Arguments from Principles, and when he encounters something that purports to be philosophy, he does his best to shoehorn it into that shape.)

Consider the thrashing they give my discussion of adopting the intentional stance towards "Mother Nature" – the process of natural selection. They find it "very puzzling." Why? Because it doesn't fit the mold. They try to turn it into an argument, which they can then rebut by parity of reasoning with their story about Father Erosion and the Tree Fairy. They end with the rhetorical question: "if the story about Father Erosion doesn't legitimize interpretivism about functions in ecology, why, exactly, does the story about Mother Nature legitimize interpretivism about functions in biology?"

This is interesting. Fodor and Lepore think my remarks about Mother Nature's reasons were intended as an *argument* to "legitimize interpretivism" when in fact they were intended to *explain* interpretivism, to make it comprehensible and palatable, not to prove it. How then do I "legitimize interpretivism about functions in biology?" By examining the assumptions and constraints encountered in actual attempts to impute functions in biology. What one discovers is that assertions about function are in the end answers to "why" questions. Such "why" questions can only be satisfied by giving reasons. Whose reasons? Well, nobody's reasons: free-floating rationales, I have called them, but call them what you like, they are ubiquitous and (almost) uncontroversial in biology. My reasons for interpretivism in biology are thus not derived from an argument from general principles. Rather, they are simply to be observed in the details: look and see – the function-ascribers always justify their claims by engaging in interpretation, invoking reasons. Is it acceptable to postulate such reasons that aren't any reasoner's reasons? Well, if it isn't, then we are really in trouble, since then *no* function attributions in biology are acceptable: we can't say the eagle's wings are for flying, or our eyes for seeing. There are indeed biologists who are strongly inclined to this puritanical conclusion, for they see that the only way to open the door to function attributions in biology is to countenance free-floating rationales.[3]

When casting about for materials for an Argument, Fodor begins, naturally enough, with the Principles that are pre-theoretically the most obvious (most obvious to his Granny, as he would say). Not surprisingly, Granny believes that beliefs are real, and really mean what they mean – "period!" as a Granny of my acquaintance would add. Formally rendered and capitalized, that's Intentional Realism.

Fodor and Lepore take themselves, then, to be mounting a Defense of Intentional Realism against its enemy, Interpretivism. Their essay proceeds systematically: first they divide the possible schools of Interpretivism into two camps: Projectivism and Normativism. Then they defeat Projectivism. Then they tackle Normativism, and find two candidate interpretations of my purported defense of it: an evolutionary argument or a transcendental argument. The former they find to yield the wrong conclusion, and the latter, they conclude, "begs the question against intentional laws."

We might call this method *philosophy drawn and quartered*. First you draw a line, dividing the world in half, and make everybody decide which half of the world they want to stand in; then you draw another line, drawing the half they've chosen in half, and demand that they choose one quarter or the other. And so forth. This imposition of either/or is supposed to guarantee that all philosophical positions have good hard edges. You force people off the fences they are sitting on, and make them choose sides for each imposed dichotomy. This does seem to make methodological sense from a certain perspective. The trouble with philosophy is often that it is vague, impressionistic and lacking in rigor, so this seems to be a good way to force precision onto the issues. Fish or cut bait, as the saying goes. Logic teaches us that if you take a well-formed proposition and its negation, exactly one of the pair is true and the other is false, so you'd think that drawing and quartering would be a way of homing in on the truth by a process of elimination.

The trouble is that false dichotomies are hard to spot. When you force people to jump to one side or the other of the fence before they have had a chance to reflect properly on the way the issue has been posed, they may end up not noticing the best alternative – some unimagined third or fourth alternative – because the "only options" are not really exhaustive contradictories, in spite of first appearances.

Fodor and Lepore provide an instructive case of this in their interpretation of the ontology of Interpretivism: "Interpretivism is, *inter alia*, the view that, strictly speaking, we don't really have beliefs and desires" (p. 74). Where do they get this? Well, logic teaches us that exactly one of the following two propositions is true: *beliefs are real* or *it is not the case that beliefs are real*. In other words, they conclude, "strictly speaking" ya gotta be a Realist or an Eliminativist – take your pick. They decide (not surprisingly, given that ultimatum) that Interpretivism falls in the Eliminativist quarter. Then they lower the boom: "Interpretivism is, *inter alia*, the view that, strictly speaking, we don't really have beliefs and desires. But, one supposes, what a creature *deosn't really have* can't help it much in its struggle for survival."

So much, then, for an evolutionary account of belief and desire if one is an Interpretivist. Well, consider an exactly parallel argument regarding centers of gravity. When it comes to centers of gravity, which are you – a Realist or an Eliminativist? Suppose you jump to the right, on the grounds that centers of gravity are "Interpretivist" or "Instrumentalist" posits, not real things like atoms or electrons: "Interpretivism is, *inter alia*, the view that, strictly speaking, nothing really has a center of gravity. But, one supposes, what a sailboat *doesn't really have* (e.g. a low center of gravity) can't help it much in its struggle against capsizing." Persuasive? I trust you feel the urge to back up a step or two and challenge the drawing and quartering that led to this embarrassing conclusion.

After concocting and demolishing a variety of views I don't hold, Fodor and Lepore eventually confront the view I do hold.

Of course, many philosophers who think that charity constrains intentional ascription *a priori* doubt that there *are* intentional laws. We have nothing to say against their doubting this except that they are in need of an argument, and that, whatever this argument is, it mustn't itself depend on assuming that charity is constitutive of intentional ascription . . . In the present context, that assumption would be merely question-begging. (p. 79)

It seems they have cleverly maneuvered me into the deadliest trap in Burden Tennis (burden, burden, who has the burden of proof now?): they have got me where I need an argument (I have the burden), but where only a question-begging argument (in that context) is available. Darn, I lose.

But note that if one is not, at the moment, attempting to refute X but just explain what alternative Y is, it is quite acceptable to beg the question against X. For instance, any compact explanation of the role of DNA in biology would probably beg the question against vitalism. Life, after all, is short. I am accused of begging the question against intentional laws. Again I plead *nolo contendere*. I had thought that the idea of intentional laws was so obviously mistaken that it was not worth arguing against.

5 Intentional Laws and Computational Psychology

Here is the issue that divides us. I have long claimed that the predictive value of belief ascriptions depends on our assuming the underlying (and pervasive) rationality of the believer. Fodor and Lepore do not believe this, and in the course of arguing against it, they say: "We'd get *some* predictive value out of belief ascription even if it only worked, say, 87 percent of the time that a creature that believes ($p \rightarrow q$ and p) believes q" (p. 77). This superficially plausible claim presupposes the independent discoverability of individual beliefs, whereas I hold that it is the assumption of rationality that makes belief-ascription "holistic": you can't attribute a single belief without presupposing the ascription of a host of others, rationally related to it. Let's look more closely at what would be involved in Fodor and Lepore's alternative "atomistic" Intentional Realism. They are supposing in this passage that we might *find* a case of somebody who believes both p and $p \rightarrow q$, and *then* determine independently whether or not he also believes q. Totting up a raft of such individual cases, we might discover that 87 percent of the time, people who believe p and $p \rightarrow q$ also believe q. But this assumes that determining, say, that a particular person didn't believe q wouldn't *ipso facto* undo or at least put into question one's earlier finding that the person believed p and $p \rightarrow q$. Sellars, Quine, Davidson, and I (among others) have always seen – or so we thought! – that individual belief attributions were not anchorable in this imagined way because one always encounters what we might call the Quinian circle: the very best evidence *there could be* that you had made a mistake in attributing to someone the beliefs that p and $p \rightarrow q$ was the evidence that you should also attribute the belief that *not-q*.

Imagine giving a person a huge true–false questionnaire to fill out, the 999-page F-SQUAB (Fodor Self-Questioning Attributor of Belief). Many of the sentences to be checked T or F are logically related to each other, and lo and behold, 13 percent of the time, people who have checked T for pairs of sentences p and $p \rightarrow q$, check F for q. There would be controversy about whether these people *really believed* (or even understood) the sentences in question, given their anomalous performance on them, so we should review those sentences with the subjects, to get clarification. What could be better evidence that they had failed to understand (and hence believe) the sentences in question than their persistence in assigning T and F in the wrong way? Fodor would presumably answer: there *could* be better evidence – we could find those very sentences (or rather, their Mentalese translations) written in the belief boxes inside their heads! (On this score, see the citation of Davidson by

Dennett

Rorty, p. 192.) But identifying something in their heads as the belief box (and not just the memorized sentence box, for instance) is itself a hypothesis that raises the issue of rationality all over again. For one thing, we could never establish rules for translating Mentalese into a natural language without using precisely the assumption about rationality this move to the inside was supposed to avoid. Translating somebody's language of thought into, say, English, would itself be an exercise in Quinian radical translation.

Versions of this claim have been around – and unchallenged – for so long that I have been willing to presuppose it without further ado, but Fodor and Lepore demand an argument. If there were independently discoverable *intentional laws*, they suppose, we could use these as a base from which to get the leverage to break the Quinian circle. There could be logically independent evidence for the attribution of individual beliefs if such attributions were supported by well-confirmed empirical laws. What could an intentional law be? What might some examples be? They give us a template:

being in intentional state A is nomologically sufficient for being in intentional state B.

For such a law to provide leverage against the Quinian circle, we must suppose that it would describe a genuine discoverable regularity in the world, and not just express a disguised constraint on interpretation. For instance,

being in the state of *believing that five is greater than three* is nomologically sufficient for being in the state of *believing that three is less than five*

is unimpressive as a candidate law precisely because, at least in as extreme a case as this, the rival suggestion is compelling that one just *wouldn't count* a person as being in the former state if one was not prepared to count him as being in the latter as well. The evidence for the left half of the "law" would be the same as the evidence for the right half. So let us swing, momentarily, to the other extreme, and imagine the discovery of intentional laws that bore *no* resemblance to such rationality-presupposing norm-approximations. Let us suppose, for instance, that it turns out to be a deep and unfathomable intentional law that

being in the state of *wanting to go to Paris* is nomologically sufficient for being in the state of *deeming candy a better Valentine's Day present than flowers.*

The believer in intentional laws must say "Don't ask *why* people who want to go to Paris think this – as if it were somehow *rational* for this deeming to go with that desire. It just does – it's a law!" I have never seen a plausible example of such a candidate for an intentional law. It provokes suspicion in those of us who are skeptical about intentional laws that all the plausible examples we have encountered look awfully like stand-ins for their nearest normative neighbors. For instance, here is a generalization that is "confirmed by its instances, supports counterfactuals, and so forth":

by and large (*ceteris paribus*) people believe there's a cow standing in front of them whenever they ought to believe there's a cow standing in front of them.

What then of Fodor and Lepore's example of the moon illusion, which they cite as a clear instance of an intentional law? As they say, there is a regular and reliable relationship between the moon's location and its apparent size, but why call it "lawful?" This regular relationship no doubt has some sort of ultimate explanation at the design-stance level. (Fodor and Lepore seem to forget that the intentional stance is one of three stances in my theory, which purports to explain the relations between them.) There is also no doubt a design stance explanation at a somewhat higher level of abstraction of the chess player who is suckered by knight forks – there is a sub-optimal bias in his heuristic search-tree – pruning dispositions, for instance. I never deny that we can take advantage of design stance discoveries; I just insist that they are interpreted *as* design stance implementations of intentional stance competences, and those competences are still describable only in rationality-presupposing language.

The fixation on "laws" by philosophers is a mystery to me. I suspect it is leftover physics envy, but perhaps there is some other explanation. Does anyone suppose that there are laws of nutrition? Laws of locomotion? There are all sorts of highly imperturbable boundary conditions on nutrition and locomotion, owing to funda-mental laws of physics, and there are plenty of regularities, rules of thumb, trade-offs, and the like that are encountered by any nutritional or locomotive mechanisms. But these are not laws. They are like the highly robust regularities of automotive engineering. Consider the regularity that (*ceteris paribus*) ignition is accomplished only by or after the use of a key. There is a reason for this, of course, and it has to do with the perceived value of automobiles, their susceptibility to theft, the cost-effective (but not foolproof) options provided by pre-existing locksmith technology, and so forth. When one understands the myriad cost-benefit trade-offs of the design decisions that go into creating automobiles, one appreciates this regularity. It is not any kind of law; it is a regularity that tends to settle out of a complex set of competing *desiderata* (otherwise known as norms). These highly reliable generalizations are not laws of automotive engineering, nor are their biological counterparts laws of locomotion or nutrition, so it would be surprising if there were laws of cognition – intentional laws. And even if you decide for one reason or another to call such generalizations laws (or "c.p. laws") they won't play the anchoring role needed to break the Quinian circle, for attributions will *still* come down to questions of interpretation (analogous to: is this electronic device that remotely locks the car door and disables the ignition really a *key*?). Such norm-tracking design-stance generalizations abound in biology. The location of the mouth at the bow rather than the stern end of the locomoting organism (*ceteris paribus* – there are exceptions!) gets a similar style of explanation, presumably. And it will turn out that the moon illusion is a tolerable price to pay under normal conditions for other benefits to one's visual system.

This designer's-eye perspective on intentional regularities is familiar to anyone who has confronted the task of creating an information-processing system. One of the primary insights of computer science (or more specifically, Artificial Intelli-gence) is that you have to *arrange for* the mechanisms to generate (approximately) the regularities needed. Sometimes in the quest for such arrangements you may encounter deep, elegant principles or regularities that can be exploited, such as those that ground the enthusiasm for connectionism, but these cannot be Fodor and Lepore's "intentional laws" for they can be observed in entirely non-semantic, non-psychological contexts. Properly exploited, however, such regularities permit one to construct systems that approximate the sought-for intentional regularities in operation. When you succeed – close enough, anyway – you get to *call* the states of the device you have made intentional states. This holism of attribution is obvious in AI, and I have never seen any reason to suppose that cognitive science harbors any other principles of attribution.

Ironically, then, my chief criticism of Intentional Realism is that it is unrealistic; it conjures up an imaginary cognitive science that has never existed, and never will exist – intentional surrealism. This can be discerned from a different perspective in Colin McGinn's essay, which shows, more clearly than ever before, how the truth about the normativity of intentional ascription gets warped by this commitment to Realism into the more luxuriant fantasies of logicism. So close and yet so far! McGinn's comments on the collapse of the problem of mathematical knowledge seem to me to be right on target:

> We can know logical truth only because we embody it, so if we didn't we wouldn't. We know the logical powers of the truth-functions, say, *only* by virtue of the (non-contingent) fact that the corresponding symbols in our heads exhibit causal features that map reliably onto those logical powers. (p. 93)

As McGinn says, "there is a strong sense in which we have to *be* logical if we are to know logic and mathematics," or anything else, I would add. But McGinn conflates the brain's *being logical* (having innately rational mechanisms) with the brain's *using logic*, and this move, which has a distinguished history, of course, creates a major distortion. McGinn notes (in agreement with "Intentional Systems,") that the ultimate explanation of our rationality must be evolutionary: "The reason our minds follow the causal tracks they do is that these tracks are designed to mirror logical relations; would-be minds that followed other tracks failed to pass evolutionary muster." But this is as true of fish minds and bird minds as it is of human minds, and fish and birds do not engage in the practice of abstract logical reasoning, any more than they engage in legal reasoning. The "chains of reasoning" McGinn speaks of are a minor, species-specific manifestation of the rationality evolution designed into us and other fauna. It would be impossible to build the artifacts of logic and language (the meme-structures – see the discussion of Dawkins and Dahlbom below) in a brain devoid of innate rationality, but we mustn't make the mistake of then trying to impose the structural details of those artifacts onto the underlying processes that make them possible. That this can seem to be necessary is itself an artifactual illusion of the meme of Realism: "What makes a belief the particular belief it is is the proposition believed, and propositions are precisely the proper subject-matter of logic." (p. 87).

As we have seen, two ways of reading this have been proposed: as a metaphysical fact about mental states (Realism) or as a constraint on ascription (Interpretivism). Take some particular mental state (the state of Jones when he sees the cow run by the window): one way of going asks: which belief *is* it? the other asks: which belief should we *call* it? The latter says, in effect,

> Don't call it the belief that *p* if you suspect [because of your knowledge of Jones' brain mechanisms, perhaps] that Jones will fail to appreciate some of the important logical consequences of *p*, for this would show that "belief that *p*" would *mismeasure* the actual

state of Jones. Cast about for whatever proposition comes closest to capturing that actual competence of Jones in this regard. Suppose q comes closest; you cannot do better than to call Jones' state the belief that q.

The Realist view, alternatively, supposes that Jones's state *really has* some particular propositional content, so that there is a fact of the matter, independent of all these subsequent psychological states. Although McGinn cites Quine's discussion of radical translation, he apparently doesn't see it as what Fodor and Lepore would call a transcendental argument, for he sees no way of avoiding the Realist view of it:

We must be charitable about other people's reasoning *because* their thoughts are inherently logically defined states. Without mental logicism as an ontological doctrine, logical charity looks like a kind of wishful thinking – or merely [!] a reflection of what the *interpreter* needs to assume about the world. The norms have to be written into the internal structure of the belief system if they are to condition its interpretation. (p. 89)

McGinn's discussion shows clearly that Realism makes sense only in cases in which we have chosen a language *and an interpretation of its terms*, for then we can arrange for particular, pre-identified sentences (whose meanings are already fixed) to be grouped together as axiom sets, etc. Pushed through the template of such a language of thought, *rational norms* get twisted into *logical laws*: "Nakedly stated, logicism says that psychological laws are logical laws" (p. 88).

McGinn imagines a field that postulates an innate logic module, equipped with transducers sensitive to structures isomorphic to the syntactical markers of logical form in formal languages. He calls this field computational psychology, but almost no cognitive or computational psychologist would endorse this vision (for a valuable early discussion, see Johnson-Laird, 1983). What McGinn has actually described is closer to the vision of John McCarthy and his school of logicists in AI. It is curious that for all the varieties of logicism that McGinn considers, he ignores the one that has most explicitly endorsed the identification he proposes between being rational and using logic. The base-level problem facing any intelligent agent is always: now what should I do?, and McCarthy and the AI logicists have supposed that all answers to this question should be generated by theorem-proving machinery operating on an axiom base of the agent's beliefs to date, with the "logical laws" built right in as features of the inference engine that feeds on the axioms and generates new lines of proof. There are many well-known practical or empirical difficulties with this approach (for a discussion of some of them, see my "Cognitive Wheels: an Introduction to the Frame Problem of AI," 1984), and there is also a conceptual difficulty brought to the surface by McGinn's suggestion that such innate logical machinery could account for human prowess in mathematics. If our rationality consisted in our being disposed to entertain sentences in the language of thought that followed logically from the sentences that we had previously entertained – if, in other words, our rationality consisted in our being *hard-wired consistent theorem provers* of one sort or another – we would be bound by the Gödelian limitations that J. R. Lucas, and more recently Roger Penrose,[4] have taken to signal a *reductio ad absurdum* of the hypothesis of mechanism. Our capacity to "produce as true" or "recognize by intuition" the mathematical truths Gödel's Theorem proves to exist could not be explained as the capacity to generate these truths as theorems.

McGinn speculates (in note 7) that perhaps I prefer what he calls an instrumentalist interpretation of mental logicism because I "can't see how a physical system could really, in itself and objectively, be subject to logical norms." On the contrary, I can see all too clearly how logicism runs and what the objections to this move are. And I have seen the alternative, which is really just a nudge of emphasis away from the claim McGinn makes. Why do people who believe *p* and *p* → *q* go on (as it were) to believe *q*? The fact that "such laws actually work" is to be explained, McGinn avers, by the fact that "the causal powers of the two premise beliefs accordingly mirror the logical powers of the premises themselves." The mild and undeniable way of reading this is as the claim that cognitive transition "tracks" sound inference: there will turn out to be an interpretation of the transitions between contentful states in the brain that "mirrors the logical powers" of the propositions used in the interpretation. It is when McGinn insists on a strict Realist interpretation of this explanation that he sets off down the wrong path, as we shall see more clearly when we consider the same issue in Millikan's essay.

6 Millikan on the Bio-mechanics of Representation: Why the Details Matter

The trouble with computational psychology as Fodor and Lepore, and McGinn, imagine it is that they have failed to imagine it in sufficient concrete detail. Principles that seem obvious so long as the investigation is sufficiently general have a way of evaporating when you get down to cases. What might computational psychology really be like? What would a realistic (as opposed to Realistic) theory of mental representation look like?

Ruth Millikan says: "What is needed is not to discover what mental representations *really are* but to lay down some terms that cut between interestingly different possible phenomena so we can discuss their relations." I would say *apparently possible* phenomena, for the deeper we go into the mechanical and ultimately biological details, the more hypotheses we have to discard. Millikan sketches some of the territory, and not surprisingly I approve heartily of most of it, since it elaborates a functionalistic view of content attribution of just the sort I have been recommending as an alternative to Fodor's atomistic Realism. But beyond that, it is full of novel and valuable observations. One of the most seductive metaphors in cognitive science, especially in its most theoretical and philosophical quarters, is the idea of a language of thought. So attractive is it that many have thought it has already begun hardening off into literal science. By taking the hypothesis of the language of thought seriously, as more than just the enabling slogan of various flights of philosophical fantasy, Millikan shows how many pitfalls still beset the notion. She ends up supporting and extending my skepticism about the hypothesis, while also finding and repairing some oversights and misdirection in my account.

> The "content" of an intentional icon is described by telling what sort of structure or feature would have to be in the organism's environment, for the icon to map onto by its mapping rule, in order for its consumer to use it successfully in the normal way . . . . (p. 100)

This supports and illustrates my fundamental point about constraint on interpretation. We are *bound* to ascribe content that makes it come out that there is a free-floating rationale in support of this design. When determining the semantic value of something, "we should refer . . . to the general principles in accordance with which it is *designed* to be guided . . . ." In other words, there simply are no grounds for content ascription beyond those that account for *how well* the devices work at performing their functions when conditions are right.

Content can be defined with "considerable determinacy," she says, according to the following rule: "Consider the content to be that mapped feature to which the icon specifically adapts the *user(s)* of the icon. It is that feature which, if removed from the environment or incorrectly mapped, will guarantee failure for its *users*" (p. 101). She's right, I think. This is a good way of getting at the point. But isn't Millikan's view a species of "atomistic" Intentional Realism? After all, she attributes content to particular, individual "intentional icons" in the brain, one at a time – or so it first appears. But look more closely. Since the content (if any) of an intentional icon (if that is what the item you are looking at really is) depends as much on the "user"-part of the system as on its "producer," no item gets content independently of its role within a larger system. For instance, she notes that "A mental name exists only when its thinker has a competence to reiterate it in a variety of different correct and grounded *whole* representations . . ." (p. 119). Typically, the larger system will only be able to play its "user" role if it includes within itself a variety (yea even a host) of other intentional icons, and then we're right back to "meaning holism." The individual structured items may be picked out "atomistically" but whether they are intentional icons, and if so, what content they carry, is still a holistic matter. In the limiting, simplest case there might be an icon whose "user" could use only one icon; precisely in these simple cases we have what one might call "degenerate" cases of intentionality – like the poor dumb thermostat that we call an intentional system for the same reason we call zero a number: denying it this status makes for worse boundaries than granting it.

Can't we identify an individual spark plug *as* a spark plug without looking at the rest of the engine? Sure. You can't explain the function of a spark plug without at the same time explaining its role within the larger system, but so what? We can detach these items and identify them in their own right. Now why couldn't we do the same thing with beliefs? Or, to use Millikan's term, intentional icons? A comparison with DNA is useful. It is mindboggling to learn that one can splice firefly genes into *plants* that thereupon glow in the dark; here is functional detachment with a vengeance. If there can be a glow-in-the-dark gene that can be moved from insect to weed, why not a belief-that-snow-is-white mechanism that could (in principle) be installed in the head of one who had never even heard of winter?

Suppose, then, you try to install the belief that snow is white in somebody who doesn't already have beliefs about the temperature of snow, its composition as frozen water, etc. If you don't bring all this information along (in some sort of package deal, let's suppose) then whatever else you may have done, the result will *not* be the installation of the belief that snow is white. It will be, perhaps, the disposition to assert "snow is white" (or its canonical translation in whatever language our patient speaks), and also, perhaps, to assent to questions like "Is snow white?" with affirmative answers of one stripe or another. This person still does not believe that snow is white, unless you have a new concept of belief you're selling. After all, *ex hypothesi* this person can't tell snow from bubble gum, hasn't any idea that it is a winter variety of precipitation, etc.

"'You're just changing the concept!' – are you not just making a move in the late and unlamented form of conservatism known as ordinary language philosophy?" Yes I am, and the move was not pointless, but only overused. We *might* want to change the concept of belief in this way, but then let's have the evidence that there really are units, elements, or whatever, that divide nature *this* way. Fodor and Lepore have none to offer, and Millikan's discussion of intentional icons suggests a rather different taxonomy of items.

But still, Millikan seems to suppose that the functional analyses on which she would ground her content-ascriptions bottom out at nice brute facts of the matter – facts of evolutionary history that answer the crucial questions about *the* function of one icon-system or another. Here is the one point of fairly substantial disagreement remaining between us. I have not convinced her that when she looks as closely at the details of her speculative evolutionary histories as she has looked at the details of her representational mechanisms, she will see that functional ascriptions are subject to the same norm-racked questions of indeterminacy of interpretation as intentional ascriptions. I recognize that I have yet to persuade many philosophers that they must take seriously my shocking line on how biology depends, in the end, on adopting the intentional stance towards the evolutionary process itself (that's one reason I am writing my next book on the idea of evolution), so for the time being I will leave matters conditional: if I am right, then Millikan's holism cannot be *quite* as "realistic about content" as it now appears.

Consider her discussion of the perennial question about what the frog's eye tells the frog's brain (p. 107). Is there a *definite content* (i.e. a proposition that is well expressed by a particular English sentence of whatever length) to what the frog's eye tells a frog's brain? Her novel suggestion is that while the particular intentional state – the "telling" – may not even imply (let alone be equivalent to) any definite English sentence or sentences, it might nevertheless be true that "English sentences can be constructed that will imply the truth of what any particular frog's eye is currently telling its brain." This strikes me as an ingenious way of responding to the legitimate demand to say something as definite as possible about the content of this froggy telling without embroiling oneself in the problems of the mismatching "logical spaces" of English and Froggish. I noticed the problem in *Content and Consciousness*, section 10, "Language and Content," and disparaged the quest for *precision* but missed the idea that at least certain one-way implications might be established.

When Millikan attempts to make implications run the other way for people (if not frogs), I have my doubts. "It might still be," she says, "that '*core* information-storage elements in the brain' . . . would strictly entail the belief-ascribing sentences through which we customarily filter their contents" (p. 107). Strictly entail? How would this be understood? The particular information-ladenness of your visuo-motor system at this moment – its content – may in fact contain elements such that, as Millikan puts it, various English sentences entail the truth of those elements, but I don't see how the inverse direction makes sense as a strict entailment. In "Beyond Belief" I imagined someone who had a "thing about redheads," a thought experiment designed to respond to this apparently well-posed question. It was poorly designed, apparently, since Millikan alludes to the example but declines to draw the conclusion I had attempted to enliven: an organism might have a system in its head – we can be deliberately noncommittal about its structure and just call it a "thing" – that quite determinately and systematically contributed in a content-sensitive way to ongoing cognitive processes without that contribution being capturable as the contribution of a particular *proposition*, just because the system in question, and the supersystem of which it is a part, while content-laden, is not a sentential system.

Millikan's main point of disagreement with my view – or with what she takes to be my view – concerns the role I have given rationality. When she asks if, as my early slogan has it, rationality is the mother of intention, she has in mind a reading of rationality as logicality, starting down the same path as McGinn (and a host of others, to be sure). I think this obscures to her the continuum of process types that take us from brute, non-inferential tropism, through various inference-*like* steps, to full-fledged "rational thinking." One can start with the rationality of the design process that produces the mechanisms that do the work. If the thing is wired up rationally, it doesn't need to do any further "thinking;" it will do the rational thing. It doesn't have to (a) identify a state that has meaning; (b) figure out, using "rational thought," what it means; (c) figure out, using more "rational thought," what the implications are on this occasion of a message with that meaning; (d) compose a plan of action rationally justified on the basis of this determination; and finally (e) act on it. If it is rationally wired up, the mechanism will take care of all this. That is the sense in which I view rationality as the mother of intention, but when we look, with Millikan, at more specific ideas about how this wiring-up might be im-plemented, we find distinctions that can be drawn between processes that are in a stronger sense rational, by involving something more like formal inference.

Millikan introduces *mediate inference* as the touchstone of "representations" and gives a fine example; the critter that figures out that the lions are near its water hole by "pivoting" on the icon it has for its den. Her demonstration of the importance of a "middle term" is a good way of getting at what Fodor has long been insisting on: the importance of constituent structure in mental representations. Notice, though, that her way is accomplished without any presupposition of anything like a grammar (unless the mapping rules of map counts as grammar, which I doubt). She does it by semantic-level discussion alone. And the pivoting involved is not *inference* in a narrow, syntactic sense. Or at least I would urge that reading on her discussion:

> Suppose, for example, that, by combining information contained in perception of an object *seen* to be in a certain place, with information about that object as *felt* to be in that same place, one comes to believe, say, that a green apple is hard. Here the premises are percepts and the conclusion is a thought, but the motion turns on a middle term and it is inference. (p. 104)

Would she join me in extending the same account to such phenomena as the "pop out" of the red "disk" in the field of bagels, discussed by Churchland and Ramachandran? One of the "various jobs" of inference, she says, "is to combine with other icons to produce icons carrying new information." In this phenomenon I propose that the process in effect applies the "more of the same" inference rule, and since more of the same in this instance means more red, and since there is a circular outer boundary of red in the immediate vicinity, the system jumps to the conclusion that there is a red disk, and this conclusion then provides an odd-man-out premise for "pop out." Or is it a mistake to call these relatively early visual information-processing steps inferences? This has been a hot debating topic within cognitive science for years – actually ever since Helmholtz.

Certainly "purely perceptual" processes can have the *logical effect* of an inference, including the inferences of identification that Millikan so illuminatingly concentrates on. One of my favorite examples is the experiment by Nielsen (1963), in which, thanks to tricks with mirrors, subjects *misidentify* a hand they see in front of them as their own – and the "conclusions" drawn from this misidentification include "feelings" of "pressure" preventing one's hand from moving where it is supposed to move (*Consciousness Explained*, p. 112n). Were it not for the mistake of identification, the phenomenology of "felt pressure" would not occur. Is this mistake an inference? If so, then inference is ubiquitous in perception; one need have no awareness at all of a passage of rational thought; the effect is experientially transparent or immediate. Presumably this can also be true in the case of the green, hard apple. Although one *might* become aware of – notice – that it was one's own hand (apparently) that picked up the apple, this is surely not required for one "to produce icons carrying new information." Millikan presumably has such cases in mind when she mentions inferencers who "rely heavily" on "tacitly presupposed information." She says that "a correct logical reconstruction of the inference" would require rendering this tacit content explicit. Indeed. This is the rule of rational reconstruction, but it is not a requirement on the mechanism that performs this quasi-inference.[5]

She says that the ability to make inferences is not at all the ability to recognize contradictions or inconsistency, and this can be supported in a way that may not have occurred to her. There are anomalies of perception in which people report, sometimes without wonder, contradictory perceptual states. Or even if they stumble over the contradiction and marvel at it, the effect persists.[6] For example, there are stimuli that generate "paradoxical motion," things that seem very clearly to move without changing their location, or wheel spokes that seem to accelerate their angular velocity of rotation without increasing their RPM. The tolerance of our brains for inconsistent conclusions is often striking.

Millikan's imaginative exercise illustrates a quandary I have faced myself. On the one hand, as she shows again and again, the details count. You are *not* entitled to assume that a "language of thought" system would work just because you think you can dimly see how a little bit of such a system might work. All sorts of dubious assumptions (e.g. about the typing of tokens, about distinctions that make sense for a human language but lapse in the context of brain mechanisms) lie hidden from exposure until you take on the task of describing the machinery of a language of thought with some serious attention to detail. The difficulties that her excursion encounters highlight the shaky position of those who think they can assume some such theory without worrying about details. On the other hand, however, these difficulties also show that the details count even more than she acknowledges! Her pioneering explorations are well stocked with acute observations, and yet in some regards she is going over ground that has been prospected for years by researchers in other disciplines, going back to such classic AI papers as William Woods' "What's in a Link?" (1975). And even these AI investigations, more constrained by mechanical detail than most philosophical explorations of the issues, exhibit the vulnerabilities that Churchland and Ramachandran diagnose in my own top-down ruminations.

The trouble with thought experiments such as Millikan's (and I've been fond of them myself) is that they are unreliable. It is all too easy to imagine them partially, and on the basis of that imagining, conclude either "Oh, then it's possible to do it this way – just in a more complicated version" or "So, you see, it isn't possible to do it this way." But think of how similar this epistemic situation is to one's predicament when having just seen a magic trick. You think about possible mechanisms for awhile, and finally (usually) you give up – and if you didn't know better you'd declare "It just isn't possible. There is *no way* that card could have gotten into that box (or whatever)." And then when the trick is revealed to you, you discover a simple little loophole that you have failed to close, a simple hard-to-think-of alternative. God does not need to be malicious to have exploited lots of these loopholes in nature. So while simple mechanical examples, such as Millikan's sliding board generalizer, may serve a valuable purpose in opening our eyes to (apparent) possibilities, they should be treated with caution.

7 Do Bats Have a *Weltanschauung*, or just a *Lebenswelt?*

Kathleen Akins' essay illustrates how easily I, and others, have had our vision narrowed by ignoring these other perspectives. I have held that adopting the intentional stance towards such creatures as bats is not only harmless but positively useful anthropomorphism. It permits one to "set the specs" – to describe the information-processing tasks – in advance of hypotheses about specific mechanisms. But what if that very setting of the specs already seriously misdescribes the requisite competence, by imputing – along with the bat's beliefs and desires – a human-centered ontology, or other features of our human conceptual scheme that are gratuitous sophistications? This is a more radical version of the hypothesis that the "logical space" of Froggish is too different from our logical space to permit anything like translation. This is the hypothesis that bats (or frogs) might not really have enough of a logical space of concepts to have anything worth calling a "world view" at all.

For instance, Akins asks what evidence would justify the attribution of the concept of an object to the bat. She points (as does Millikan) to the important operations of re-identification and re-location. Do bats *keep track of* individuals? I don't lose track of the individual water molecules I drink; I don't track them at all. I *can* track a particular grain of sand in my shoe, but only under rather special circumstances. The fact that the issue of re-identification for *it* can come up does not mean that I lose track of the other grains on the beach: tracking them is not (except under weird conditions) an option for me at all. "Sand" is a mass noun for me, like "water." If, Akins suggests, bats don't have any use for the concept of an object (a particular object), then they could hardly have beliefs *about* objects. Moreover, without exemplars on both sides, they would have no use for the mass-noun/count-noun distinction. This surprising application of Strawson's metaphysical analysis of the concept of an individual to problems in neuroethology shows that there really is work for "neurophilosophy" to do.

Setting aside discussion of all the discussable details for another occasion, I must comment on two main themes in her essay. First, it demonstrates better than ever how misleading Nagel's wonders are about the *intrinsic* properties of bat experience. At least a great deal of what it is like to be something actually concerns such informational matters as the way opaque objects occlude things, the way distant objects are fuzzy and indistinct, and so forth: "representational problems – *not* problems about inaccessible subjective facts or the intrinsic properties of the experience or the phenomenological 'feel' of a subject's experience." By a careful study of these informational matters, we can close in on the question of what there *could be* in the bat's world. Can we close in all the way? Won't there be an inexplicable residue? Akins' discussion at least suggests a way of shifting the burden of proof: show us, Tom Nagel, *any* interesting subjective fact that will not eventually be pinned down by this process. (I play Burden Tennis when the conditions call for it; I just don't think it's the only game in town.)

That's the positive theme. The negative theme is more striking: there might not be anything at all that it is like to be a bat. "Nagel inadvisedly assumes" that a bat must have a point of view, but, Akins claims, if the bat is well designed in a cost-effective way, this may be gratuitous. Recall the amazing success of the Oak Ridge uranium-enrichment plant during the Manhattan Project. Thousands of workers spent their days controlling the highly complex process, making all manner of timely, appropriate adjustments in the face of a huge repertoire of conditions *and they hadn't a clue what they were doing*! Not only did they not know they were helping to make an atomic bomb; they also didn't know they were enriching uranium, or enriching anything. Never was the motto truer: "Don't ask me, I just work here!" The bat's imagined wingflapper is similarly positioned; it doesn't have to know it is controlling the flight of an insectivorous mammal, or controlling flight at all. "The same kind of story could have been told from the vantage point of some other cortical area . . . [i]n each case, a different story would have unfolded – another 'subjective world' – a story in accordance with the external information available at that particular site" (p. 153). And where in the brain, we feel tempted to ask, does that bat *itself* reside? What makes us think there is any good answer to this question? There are many parallel stories that could be told about what goes on in you and me, and what gives (roughly) one of those stories pride of place at any one time is just that it is the story you or I will tell if asked! If the creature in question isn't a teller – has no language – then the supposition that one of these stories is privileged, in that it would tell what it is actually like to be a bat, dangles with no evident foundation beyond tradition.

It is for just this reason that I insisted, in *Consciousness Explained*, on beginning with human consciousness first, for there we do have a variety of robust and traditional anchor-points for our intuition that a single unified perspective on the world attaches – one-to-a-customer – to each human being. Once we have clarified the sources of *that* intuition, and seen its very real limitations, we can go on to explore the case of consciousness in other animals, less sure of the optimistic assumptions Nagel takes for granted. From the fact that the bat's sonar information is fed directly to the wingflapper without having to pass through some imagined bat-headquarters, one cannot directly infer that it doesn't *also* contribute to a higher level, of course. After all, we human beings can both walk and become conscious of our walking. The new question about bats then becomes: do bats, lacking language and all that comes in the train of language, *have* a higher level, and if so, what is its role in bat life? When we have answered that question – and I see no reason why that question cannot be answered definitively from the third-person point of view – we will know if it is like anything to be a bat, and if so, what it is like.

8   From Biology to Society

The gulf between bats and us is not the gulf Nagel describes, but it is real enough, and Akins expresses from the bats' side much the same criticism that John Haugeland and Bo Dahlbom express from our side: my attempt to span the gap with the intentional stance is at best misleading, at worst a major theoretical error. Resistance to my unification proposal has been around from the beginning, but usually in the unprepossessing form of declared intuitions to the effect that lower animals (and robots) don't *really* have beliefs (not *real* beliefs, not really), a scruple that was easy to shrug off since my position was that whatever we decided to call them, there were informational states the having of which permitted both bats and bartenders to be predicted, manipulated, explained from the intentional stance, and this was what was theoretically important. But the versions of skepticism expressed by Akins, Haugeland, and Dahlbom cut deeper: we are social; bats (and chess-playing computers) are not, or at least not in certain ways that are critical for distinguishing between different *theoretically important* sorts of informational states. While Millikan and Akins concentrate on the confusions that can be engendered when we blithely impose what are essentially social (e.g. linguistic or even metaphysical) categories on biological phenomena, Haugeland and Dahlbom concentrate on the illusions that can arise when we ignore the social dimension and try to biologize all phenomena of human cognition and consciousness.

As Dahlbom notes, it is not that my position has left no room for drawing these important distinctions, but rather that I have failed to exploit the room I had created – in the distinction I had drawn but largely neglected between beliefs and opinions (in my technical sense of the term). My chief regret about the contents of *The Intentional Stance* is that I did not include in it a chapter on opinions, renewing and extending the claims I advanced in "How to Change your Mind" in *Brainstorms*. Now is an opportunity to repair some of that oversight, with the aid of some concepts drawn from Richard Dawkins: the extended phenotype, and the meme.

Both Haugeland and Dahlbom note the necessity of norms, but, unlike McGinn, Millikan and me, they insist that these norms are social at their foundations. But how could this be? How could social norms – and the holding to them that Haugeland describes – become established except on the shoulders of biological norms, of the sort that Millikan has explored? In "Intentional Systems" (1971), I argued that the concept of belief "had a normative cast to it" that was difficult to capture, and went on to propose that far from its being the case that the norms of belief were in any sense *voluntarily followed* (under the sort of mutually acknow-ledged carrot and stick that Haugeland describes), the norms of belief were constitutive at a lower level (the level so well described by Millikan). Only in creatures that *already* were error-shunners or truth-trackers (whether they knew it or not) could the foundations be laid for more self-conscious and sophisticated cognitive transactions.

And "transactions" is, I think, *le mot juste* here. Above the biological level of brute belief and simple intentional icons, human beings have constructed a level that is composed of *objects* that are socially constructed, replicated, distributed, traded, endorsed ("I'll buy that!"), rejected, ignored, obsessed about, refined, revised, attacked, advertised, discarded. Dawkins has given us a generic name for these things – memes – and what I have called opinions are a species of memes: sentences on whose truth a person has, in effect, made a wager. Non-human animals have nothing to do with memes, and hence their minds are vastly simpler than ours, as Akins and Haugeland say, looking across the canyon from opposite sides. One might say that, whereas animals (including human animals) have brains, memes turn brains into minds, arming them with intellectual tools, as Dahlbom says, and *thereby* extending the human phenotype into the larger world of civilization. A human being denied access to memes (by deafness or isolation, say) is like a hermit crab exiled to a world without vacant shells to appropriate, fundamentally incomplete and ill provisioned to face nature in the ways it was designed to do. As Dahlbom says, we are to a large extent artificial ourselves, even if our bodies aren't. We're Catholics, atheists, electrical engineers, licensed drivers, computer-literate, polyglot. Millikan provides a valuable step here: human beings don't just have the benefit of evolution-designed intentional icons; they have the benefit of evolution-designed capacities to *acquire* further intentional icons, and a host of other useful objects, from the social world they grow up in. They can also *abandon* these objects – as Anthony Kenny abandoned his priesthood – in quite sudden revolutionary changes of "psychology" that are unknown in the animal world, where "one-shot learning" of even the simplest "facts" is exceptional.

So I can agree with Dahlbom that it is a mistake to say that thinking occurs (just) in the brain; it is the same mistake as asserting that sexual display occurs in the body (ignoring the bowerbirds' bowers, and the teenagers' hotrods) or that feeding occurs in the mouth (ignoring the spiders' webs and the farmers' plows). But I disagree with his suggestion that explanations of the social world and its objects are discontinuous with or even incompatible with explanations of the biological world. There is indeed a tension between the two perspectives (manifest in Dawkins' question-begging defense of the memes of science), but these two perspectives can be unified. The key to unification lies, I think, in *denying* what seems obvious to Dahlbom:

> If one wants to argue, as Simon clearly does, that the idea and methods of an artificial science are importantly different from those of the natural sciences, even if we are only beginning to appreciate how, then one should be careful not to describe evolution by natural selection as a process of design. (p. 175)

On the contrary, what has to give is the conviction that biology is a "natural science" in the way physics is – with "laws of nature" and "natural kinds." I agree with Dahlbom that there are important differences between the artifacts of engineers and authors on the one hand, and artifacts created by the process of natural selection on the other (see my "Artificial Life: A Feast for the Imagination", (1990), and "Cognitive Science as Reverse Engineering: Several Meanings of 'Top-down' and 'Bottom-up,'" forthcoming), but he has not convinced me that these outweigh the similarities.

A pivotal event in provoking this discussion was my choice of the chess-playing computer as the leading example of an intentional system. Both Dahlbom and Haugeland draw attention to the undeniably important fact that, at least to date, chess-playing computers have existed in a severely truncated version of the real chess-playing environment: they are entirely unequipped to confront such options as cheating, tipping over the table, deliberately losing in order to boost the morale of an old friend, giving up the game in favor of waterskiing, etc. And lacking such complexities, their intentionality is seriously attenuated. But is this really so important? I chose chess-playing computers because they were not science fictional, a qualification always worthy of philosophers' consideration, but not always of overriding significance. What if I had settled instead on firewood-gathering robots? Gone are the subtleties of institution-borne norms (until the robots start venturing onto *your* land for wood for *my* fire), and the concreteness of the objects "considered" and manipulated by the robot would be exemplary. Otherwise, the application of the intentional stance to them would go through in the same fashion, so far as I can see.

But perhaps I cannot see as far as my critics. Both Haugeland and Akins can be read to be claiming something that strikes at the heart of my idea about intentional systems: some intentional systems don't exhibit *intentionality* at all: not all God's critters got ontology, you might say. For Haugeland, the ingredient missing in non-human (and robot) intentional systems is social; in the absence of the memosphere – in the absence of social norms and all that attends them – there is no ontology. This is not the trivially true claim that ontology, as an academic sub-discipline of metaphysics, would not exist unless there were universities, books, etc., but the startling claim that animals (or computers) without social norms "have" no ontology; nothing exists "for" them. The idea that one can speak of, imagine, argue about "the world of the bat" or "the objects that dolphins can conceive of" is a big mistake! I read Akins' essay as consistent with Haugeland's stronger claim, but she may have other complications in mind. If bats don't have an ontology, they lack *something* that is requisite, but she doesn't commit herself to Haugeland's claim that the social realm is the right place to look for it. Now *if* one fails to make the belief–opinion distinction, and hence tends to think of animals' beliefs as sentences-deemed-true by those animals (sentences in their languages of thought), then one will have a vision of what it would mean for a bat or a dolphin to "have an ontology" that does indeed deserve suspicion. (As I once put it, do polar bears *believe that snow is white*? Not the way people do. Polar bears couldn't *think* that snow is white.)[7] As Dahlbom says, *thinking* is an artificial, not a biological, process.

Or, to put the point from Dawkins' perspective, the memes that compose us interact in ways that provide a new layer of complexity on the biological substrate. Here new puzzles confront us. When should we say that a particular "virus of the mind" *exploits* the other memes that it encounters, and when should we say that *we*, masters of our ideas, *evaluate* and *choose* the doctrines we will live by? The idea that there is a *foundational* distinction to be drawn between these two poles is another element of our Cartesian legacy that we must learn to do without. In the context of computer viruses, Dawkins distinguishes the category of Trojan horses, which are not *directly* self-replicating code-strings, but rely on people's choices to get themselves replicated. These viruses are more like pure memes, since the "alternate host" of a human mind is required, but the difference is a matter of degree, in the end, for we choosers have an incomplete knowledge of what lies inside the memes we favor.

Every meme is potentially a Trojan horse. What is "visible" to us, the (willy-nilly) selectors of memes, is one thing; what we thereby actually end up replicating is another – an abstract functional property of our nervous systems that has largely undreamt of powers of combination, subversion, and exploitation. We don't consciously take on all the logical implications of the ideas we adopt, and we can't assay in advance the practical effects of adopting them. Unlike natural selection, we are *somewhat* foresightful choosers of memes, but we should not underestimate the myopia and astigmatism created by the other memes that are our accomplices.

Dawkins overstates the case for the power of scientific rationalism. In his own field of evolutionary biology, not all good scientific ideas spread and not all bad ones are extinguished (Richards, 1987; Cronin, 1991). His own memes have had a rocky career in some niches, and some of those he has combatted have had momentous (if, one hopes, short-lived) population explosions. Fortunately, however, one of the dominant meme-families that compose us – not all people, but those who have been infected by Western rationalism – has the property of being an omni-critical filter of other memes (and even, as Rorty's essay illustrates, of itself).[8] This is the artificial process of deliberately rational thought, a phenomenon idealized by the deductive procedures of academic logic (a family of meta-memes which includes diagrams and methods that *could not* be accomplished without language and even writing systems). It is not directly part of our genetic inheritance, as McGinn imagines, nor do its regularities depend directly on "laws of nature" that mirror the "laws of logic." *That* is the implication of Simon's claim that it belongs to the sciences of the artificial. The potentially unlimited spiral of meta-evaluation that it makes possible (and attractive) is what distinguishes human psychology from that of all other animals.

I am not yet persuaded, however, that attenuated concepts of ontology (and the other sophistications of the human world) don't apply fruitfully to the simpler inhabitants of the planet, but I do grant that the issue has been opened up by Akins, Haugeland and Dahlbom in a way that commands attention, and I have scarcely begun to answer the challenges they raise.

9   Rorty and Metaphilosophy

Dick Rorty is right in his surmise that I like doing metaphilosophy less than he does, perhaps because I'm not nearly as good at it as he is. His historical scenes are delicious: Hobbes and Gassendi staring incredulously at the Cartesians trying to carve out a secure sanctuary for consciousness, Darwin to James to Dewey (the anti-essentialism double-play combination), and the comic suggestion that my modest proposals to Nagel are like Hegel suggesting to Kant that he might, after mastering Hegel's new theory, become able to describe the thing-in-itself. I particularly commend his analysis of the roles that Wittgenstein, Ryle, Sellars, and Davidson play in this drama. If only all the other participants in contemporary debates saw it his way – our way.

He is also a remarkably fairminded and farseeing referee in the sport of Burden Tennis. Rorty's account of the issues that divide Nagel and Searle from me is the best I have encountered. Though these two chief opponents of my views have not contributed directly to this volume, their views get a fine airing by Rorty, I think. The fact that he comes down on my side does not make it less true that he has seen what they have been up to with more sympathy and insight than I have. His strategic comments about which side "wins" under which conditions are always apt (except, as noted above, regarding my claim of neutrality), but slightly in tension with his call for an end to what Janice Moulton calls the "adversarial culture" of philosophy. How can somebody who is so keen on the Sport of Philosophy – who can chide me for "misplaced courtesy to a half-defeated enemy" – issue his call for us to lay down our racquets and have a nice conversation? Robert Nozick once joked about philosophers so combative that their ideal argument would be one so powerful that it set up reverberations in your brain: if you didn't accept its conclusion, you'd die! (1981, p. 4) Rorty suggests that neither Nagel nor I can come up with such a killing argument. "Both their spades are turned," he says, because "it is not clear . . . that there is any compelling reason" to change one's mind about such ultimate matters. I'll settle for that. The reasons I've given are only supposed to be compelling to those who prefer understanding to mystery, and there is actually quite a lot to be said in favor of standing fast for mystery. It doesn't move *me*, but so what? I certainly don't think Nagel is committing some (fatal!) logical gaffe in maintaining his position; there is even something wonderful about it – Horatio at the bridge and all that. If he would rather go on believing in intrinsic and ineffable properties, then he will have to forgo the fun of being in on the kill when we knock off the mind–body problem, but some people are squeamish about myth-murder. (What I can't win by honest argument Rorty encourages me to capture with a rhetoric that makes "verificationism seem glamorous, exciting, and exactly what the age demands." I'm trying, I'm trying.)

Rorty eggs me on in this game, largely approving of the plays I have made to date, but urging me to be more ambitious, more radical, more dashing as a metaphilosopher, than I have been willing to be. Is it ungracious for me to resist such an invitation? The program that would permit me to diagnose Nagel's "ambition for transcendence" as a "tender-minded yearning for an impossible stability" is almost irresistibly attractive, and contains much that I heartily approve of, but I see both general and specific problems with the radical positions Rorty thinks I should hold.

First a specific problem. Once we move beyond the scheme–content distinction, we will have no use, he says, for the intentional–real distinction. "We shall just call them 'objects' *tout court.*" I don't think so, or at least we will still need a more modest distinction between perhaps *mere* intentional objects and other (intentional?) objects. Consider the gold in Fort Knox. One of the interesting facts about it is that its role in the world economy does not depend on its actually being there, but just on people's *believing* that it is there. For instance, much of Belgium's vast gold reserves have been stored at Fort Knox since the beginning of World War II, and it will stay there indefinitely, in all likelihood. If it could somehow be secretly moved to another location, without any leaks to the Belgians or other interested parties, the carefully created intentional object, *the Belgian gold reserves in Fort Knox*, would still be intact to do its stabilizing work, while the real object might be scattered. Yes, of course, there will be circumlocutions that can do justice to such distinctions without reintroducing the old metaphysical divide, but won't they, in the end, let us go right on saying almost everything anybody wanted to say in terms of the intentional–real distinction?

Finally, my general problem. I am not convinced that what is true about consciousness is true about everything. Rorty suggests that my attack on the Cartesian Theater is just one skirmish in the broader attack on the "captivating but trouble-making picture of human inquiry: 'Penetrating the Veil of Appearance'." I do not agree. The well-regarded distinction between Orwellian and Stalinesque tamperings with the evidence lapses, I claim, in the ultra-close quarters of the brain, but in other quarters my allegiance to it is unalloyed. There *is* a fact of the matter about whether Oswald and Ruby were in cahoots, even if it forever eludes investigation. It is not *just* a matter of which story plays well to which audiences, and I would say the same about all the usual quarries of empirical investigation. It is only when we confront the Observer, that, as Kant put it, the distinction between the "for me" and the "in itself" breaks down. As I said at the outset, I'm actually still quite conservative in my adoption of Standard Scientific Epistemology and Metaphysics.

This essay has already overstayed its welcome; doing justice to the many points raised in the essays in this volume would require an essay at least twice as long. It would not be safe to assume that I tacitly agree with all the objections and interpretations I have not discussed. Even more important, no conclusions should be drawn about my sense of the relative importance of these essays or the difficulties they raise for me by counting the pages of discussion I have devoted to them. I discovered problems too minor and too major to deal with in this setting. There will be other occasions, and I hope to be better prepared for them, thanks to the help of these and other constructive critics.

NOTES

1   "Every type of inquiry sets questions which probably only it can solve: how come the sciences can provide solutions, and indeed determine so well what counts as a solution? How do the sciences manage the trick of being, in a way, self-authenticating, internally determining what shall count as true or false?" Ian Hacking, *London Review* May 28, 1992, p. 6 (review of Bryan Appleyard *Understanding the Present: Science and the Soul of Modern Man.* London: Picador, 1992).

2   In my review of Roger Penrose's *The Emperor's New Mind,* in *The Times Literary Supplement,* 1989, I called this orthodoxy to which I subscribe the Cathedral of Science. We are currently experiencing a wave of science-bashing. In England, Bryan Appleyard's recent book (see note 1 above) has the following message on the dust-jacket: "This is an emergency, Appleyard writes, because we must now find our true nature before science crosses the final frontier of the human self." In the light of this contemporary attitude, my relatively uncomplicated "scientism" may appear particularly shallow and unphilosophical. So be it. I have not been able to find a more secure bedrock from which to conduct my investigations.

3   Fodor and LePore say "Well, either ecology does underwrite a notion of function or it doesn't," but elsewhere Fodor has recently opined that the distinction between *selection* and *selection for* cannot be reconstructed (Loewer and Rey, 1991, p. 296). This suggests that he has joined the puritans, and decided that evolutionary biology does not underwrite a notion of function after all.

4   For an analysis of Penrose's error, and suggestions about the nature of the algorithms our brains actually run, see Dennett, "Murmurs in the Cathedral" (1989) and "Betting your

Life on an Algorithm" (1990). In Haugeland's essay, the important discussion of whether recognition could be a matter of rule-following invites the same response (with which I think he would agree): our capacities to recognize things could be based on algorithms without being based on algorithms *for recognizing.*

5 Cf. McGinn, who claims that "since pains and the like are not even links in chains of reasoning" he will set them aside in his discussion. This is a clear case of a philosophical artifact in the making. Step one: by "draw and quarter," force appeals to rationality into appeals to "logical norms" or, better, "logical structures" (and around the bend comes the language of thought). Step two: shelve off pains and the like, since they don't figure in "chains of reasoning" (grounds that would not make sense without the push in step one). Step three: notice that only a "substantial core" of a given subject matter has a logical nature, which then opens the door for postulating "modules" that handle the logical part.

6 There is even a neuropathology of misidentification. In *jamais vu*, one's perceptual experience is pervaded by a sense of unfamiliarity, or lack of affectual tone that can lead to amazing denials of identification. In the Capgras delusion, one becomes convinced that one's spouse or other loved one has been replaced by an identically appearing impostor. (For a sober account and a plausible theory of the mechanism, see Young, 1990.) Shades of Twin-Earth!

7 Cf. Norman Malcolm's (1972) distinction between *thinking that p* and *having the thought that p*, discussed by me in "How to Change your Mind" (in *Brainstorms*).

8 The toxicologist Simon Wolff (1992, p. 44) writes: "Science is no more and no less than one way of systematising knowledge. And modern science is a successful and lasting way of compiling knowledge because it is evolutionary, flexible and internally consistent." But how can it be evolutionary and not be a virus? Whence cometh this internal consistency? It is just that the meme for internal consistency is a part of it.

REFERENCES

Cronin, H. (1991) *The Ant and the Peacock.* Cambridge: Cambridge University Press.
Johnson-Laird, P. (1983) *Mental Models: Towards a Cognitive Science of Language, Inference and Consciousness.* Cambridge: Cambridge University Press.
Loewer, B. and Rey, G. (eds) (1991) *Meaning in Mind: Fodor and his Critics.* Oxford: Blackwell.
Nielsen, T. I. (1963) Volition: a new experimental approach. *Scandinavian Journal of Psychology*, 4, 225–30.
Nozick, R. (1981) *Philosophical Explanations.* Cambridge, Mass.: Harvard University Press.
Richards, R. J. (1987) *Darwin and the Emergence of Evolutionary Theories of Mind and Behavior.* Chicago: University of Chicago Press.
Wolff, Simon (1992) Science as the dustbin of hope. *New Scientist*, May 30, p. 44.
Woods, W. (1975). What's in a link? In D. Bobrow and A. Collins (eds.), *Representation and Understanding*, New York: Academic Press.
Young, A. (1990) Accounting for delusional misidentifications. *British Journal of Psychiatry*, 157, 239–48.

Bibliography of the Publications of Daniel C. Dennett

Books

Content and Consciousness, London: Routledge & Kegan Paul and New York: Humanities Press (International Library of Philosophy and Scientific Method) 1969. Paperback edition with a new preface, Routledge & Kegan Paul, 1986. Translated into Italian (1993).

Brainstorms: Philosophical Essays on Mind and Psychology, Montgomery, VT: Bradford Books and Hassocks, Sussex: Harvester 1978. Translated into Italian (1991) and Swedish (1992).

The Mind's I: Fantasies and Reflections on Self and Soul, with D. R. Hofstadter, New York: Basic Books and Hassocks, Sussex: Harvester 1981. Translated into Japanese (1984), Spanish (1984), Dutch (1985), Italian (1985), German (1986), French (1987), and Chinese (unauthorized, 1989).

Elbow Room: The Varieties of Free Will Worth Wanting, Cambridge, Mass.: Bradford Books/MIT Press and Oxford University Press 1984. Translated into German (1986) and Spanish (1992).

The Intentional Stance, Cambridge, Mass.: Bradford Books/MIT Press 1987. Translated into French (1990), Spanish (1991), Italian (forthcoming), and Japanese (forthcoming).

Consciousness Explained, Boston: Little, Brown 1991 and London: Allen Lane 1992. French, Italian, German and Dutch translations (1993).

Articles and Reviews

1968

"Machine Traces and Protocol Statements," *Behavioral Science*, 13, 155–61, March 1968.

"Geach on Intentional Identity," *Journal of Philosophy*, 65, 335–41, May 31, 1968.

"Features of Intentional Action," *Philosophy and Phenomenological Research*, 29, 232–44, December 1968.

1971

"Intentional Systems," *Journal of Philosophy*, 68, 87–106, February 25, 1971. In *Brainstorms*. German translation, "Intentionale Systeme," in P. Bieri (ed.), *Analytische Philosophie des Geistes*, Heidelberg: Anton Hain 1981. French translation (with a new postscript), "Systemes intentionnels," *Philosophie*, 1, 55–80, Paris: Les Editions de Minuit 1984.

Spanish translation, "Sistemas intencionales," *Cuadernos de Crítica*, 40, Department of Philosophy, University of Mexico, 1985.
"Review of C. O. Evans, The Subject of Consciousness," *Philosophical Quarterly*, 21, 180–1, April 1971.

1972

"Review of J. R. Lucas, The Freedom of the Will," *Journal of Philosophy*, 69, 527–31, September 21, 1972.

1973

"Mechanism and Responsibility," in T. Honderich (ed.), *Essays on Freedom of Action*, London: Routledge & Kegan Paul 1973. In *Brainstorms*. Spanish translation, "Mecanicismo y responsabilidad," *Cuadernos de Crítica*, 42, Department of Philosophy, University of Mexico, 1985.

1974

"Comment on Wilfrid Sellars," *Synthese*, 27, 439–44, July/August 1974.

1975

"Why the Law of Effect Will Not Go Away," *Journal for the Theory of Social Behavior*, 5, 169–87, October 1975. In *Brainstorms*.
"Brain Writing and Mind Reading," in K. Gunderson (ed.), *Language, Mind and Knowledge*, *Minnesota Studies in the Philosophy of Science*, Vol. VII, University of Minnesota Press 1975. In *Brainstorms*.
"Review of G. Warnock and B. F. Skinner, Behavior Control: Freedom and Morality (an Open University film)," *Teaching Philosophy*, 1, 175–7, 1975.

1976

"Are Dreams Experiences?" *Philosophical Review*, 85, 151–71, April 1976. In *Brainstorms*. Spanish translation, "Son experiencias los sueños?" *Cuadernos de Crítica*, 33, Department of Philosophy, University of Mexico, 1984.
"Conditions of Personhood," in A. Rorty (ed.), *The Identities of Persons*, University of California Press 1976. In *Brainstorms*. German translation, "Bedingungen der Personalität," in P. Bieri (ed.), *Analytische Philosophie des Geistes*, Heidelberg: Anton Hain 1981, and in L. Siep (ed.), *Identität der Person*, Basel, Stuttgart: Schwabe 1983.

1977

"Critical Notice of J. Fodor, The Language of Thought," (reprinted in *Brainstorms* as "A Cure for the Common Code"), *Mind*, 86, 265–80, April 1977.
"Review of W. Matson, Sentience," *International Studies in Philosophy*, 9, 182–3, 1977.
"Review of J. Glover, (ed.), The Philosophy of Mind," *Teaching Philosophy*, 2, 196–7, 1977.

1978

"Toward a Cognitive Theory of Consciousness," in C. Wade Savage (ed.), *Perception and Cognition: Issues in the Foundations of Psychology*, *Minnesota Studies in the Philosophy of Science*, Vol. IX, University of Minnesota Press 1978. In *Brainstorms*.
"Why You Can't Make a Computer that Feels Pain," *Synthese*, 38, 415–56, August 1978. In *Brainstorms*.
"Current Issues in the Philosophy of Mind," *American Philosophical Quarterly*, 15, 249–61,

1978. Spanish translation, "Perspectivas Actuales en la Filosofia de la Mente," *Teorema*, 11, 197–230, 1981.

"Requisition for a Pexgo," (commentary on Bindra), *Behavioral and Brain Sciences*, 1, 56–7, 1978.

"Why Not the Whole Iguana?" (commentary on Pylyshyn), *Behavioral and Brain Sciences*, 1, 103–4, 1978.

"Co-opting Holograms," (commentary on Haugeland), *Behavioral and Brain Sciences*, 1, 232–3, 1978.

"What's the Difference: some Riddles," (commentary on Puccetti and Dykes), *Behavioral and Brain Sciences*, 1, 351, 1978.

"Beliefs about Beliefs," (commentary on Premack et al.), *Behavioral and Brain Sciences*, 1, 568–70, 1978.

"Review of M. Boden, Artificial Intelligence and Natural Man," *Philosophy of Science*, 45, 648–9, 1978.

The Philosophical Lexicon, edited with K. Lambert. 7th Edition privately printed and distributed through the *American Philosophical Association* 1978. 8th Edition published by the *American Philosophical Association* 1987. An edited German translation of an early edition, "Das Philosophisches Wörterbuch," *Conceptus*, Graz, Austria, 1974.

1979

"On the Absence of Phenomenology," in D. Gustafson and B. Tapscott, (eds), *Body, Mind and Method: Essays in Honor of Virgil C. Aldrich*, Dordrecht: D. Reidel, 1979.

"The Onus Re Experiences: a Reply to Emmett," *Philosophical Studies*, 35, 315–18, 1979.

"Review of R. Aquila, Intentionality: a Study of Mental Acts, and E. Casey, Imagining: a Phenomenological Analysis," *Southwestern Journal of Philosophy*, 9, 139–43, January 1979.

"Review of Karl Popper and John Eccles, The Self and its Brain," *Journal of Philosophy*, 76, 91–7, 1979.

"Breeding Cognitive Strategies," (commentary on Haber), *Behavioral and Brain Sciences*, 2, 599–600, 1979.

"Artificial Intelligence as Philosophy and as Psychology," in M. Ringle (ed.), *Philosophical Perspectives on Artificial Intelligence*, Atlantic Highlands, NJ: Humanities Press 1979. In *Brainstorms*.

1980

"Passing the Buck to Biology," (commentary on Chomsky), *Behavioral and Brain Sciences*, 3, 19, 1980.

"The Milk of Human Intentionality," (commentary on Searle), *Behavioral and Brain Sciences*, 3, 428–30, 1980.

"Reply to Professor Stich," (reply to S. Stich, Headaches: a Critical Notice of Brainstorms), *Philosophical Books*, 21, 73–6, April 1980.

1981

"True Believers: the Intentional Strategy and Why it Works," in A. F. Heath (ed.), *Scientific Explanation* (the Herbert Spencer Lectures at Oxford), Oxford University Press 1981. In *The Intentional Stance*.

"Wondering Where the Yellow Went," (comment on Wilfrid Sellars's Carus Lectures), *Monist*, 64, 102–8, January 1981.

"Making Sense of Ourselves," (reply to S. Stich, Dennett on Intentional Systems), *Philosophical Topics*, 12, 63–81, 1981. In *The Intentional Stance*.

"Three Kinds of Intentional Psychology," in R. Healey (ed.), *Reduction, Time and Reality*, Cambridge University Press 1981. In *The Intentional Stance*.

1982

"Beyond Belief," in A. Woodfield (ed.), *Thought and Object: Essays on Intentionality*, Oxford University Press 1982. In *The Intentional Stance.*

"Philosophy According to Nozick," *New Boston Review*, 7, 9–11, January/February 1982.

"Grey Matter and Mind," *Radio Times*, 8–14 May, 70–72, 1982.

"Notes on Prosthetic Imagination," *New Boston Review*, 7, 3–7, June 1982.

"The Myth of the Computer: An Exchange," (reply to John Searle's review of The Mind's I), *New York Review of Books*, 29, June 24, 56–7, 1982.

"The Well-Furnished Mind," (review of R. Gregory, Mind in Science), *Contemporary Psychology*, 27, 597–8, 1982.

"Why We Think What We Do about Why We Think What We Do: Discussion on Goodman's 'On Thoughts without Words,'" *Cognition*, 12, 219–27, 1982.

"Correspondent's Report: Recent Work in Philosophy of Interest to AI," *Artificial Intelligence*, 19, 3–5, 1982.

"How to Study Consciousness Empirically: or Nothing Comes to Mind," *Synthese*, 53, 159–80, November 1982.

"Comments on Rorty," *Synthese*, 53, 349–56, November 1982.

"The Imagination Extender," (a revision of "Notes on Prosthetic Imagination"), *Psychology Today*, 16, 32–9, December 1982.

"Review of Gilbert Ryle, On Thinking," *International Studies in Philosophy*, 14, 98–9, 1982.

"Styles of Mental Representation," *Proceedings of the Aristotelian Society, New Series*, 83, 213–26, 1982/83. In *The Intentional Stance.*

1983

"Artificial Intelligence and the Strategies of Psychological Investigation," (an interview by Jonathan Miller), in J. Miller, *States of Mind*, London: BBC and New York: Pantheon Books 1983.

"Intentional Systems in Cognitive Ethology: the 'Panglossian Paradigm' Defended," (with commentaries), *Behavioral and Brain Sciences*, 6, 343–90, 1983. In *The Intentional Stance*. German translation, "Intentionale Systeme in der kognitiven Verhaltensforschung," in D. Münch (ed.), *Kognitionswissenschaft: Grundlagen, Probleme, Perspektiven*, Frankfurt: Suhrkamp 1992.

"When do Representations Explain?" (commentary on Stabler), *Behavioral and Brain Sciences*, 6, 406–7, 1983.

1984

"Formulating Human Purposes: Meta-Engineering Computers for People," in R. E. A. Mason (ed.), *Information Processing 83*, Amsterdam: Elsevier (North-Holland) 1984.

"Cognitive Wheels: The Frame Problem of AI," in C. Hookway (ed.), *Minds, Machines and Evolution*, Cambridge University Press 1984.

"Wishful Thinking," (commentary on Skinner), *Behavioral and Brain Sciences*, 7, 556–7, 1984.

"Foreword," for R. G. Millikan's *Language, Thought and Other Biological Categories*, Cambridge, Mass.: Bradford Books/MIT Press 1984.

"Carving the Mind at its Joints," (review of Fodor, The Modularity of Mind), *Contemporary Psychology*, 29, 285–6, 1984.

"Correspondent's Report: Recent Work in Philosophy II," *Artificial Intelligence*, 22, 231–4, 1984.

"The Role of the Computer Metaphor in Understanding the Mind," in H. Pagels (ed.), *Computer Culture: the Scientific, Intellectual, and Social Impact of the Computer, Annals of the NY Academy of Science*, 426, 266–75, 1984.

"I Could Not Have Done Otherwise – So What?" *Journal of Philosophy*, 81, 553–65, October 1984.

"Computer Models and the Mind – a View from the East Pole," (a condensed version of "The Logical Geography of Computational Approaches: a View from the East Pole"), *The Times Literary Supplement*, December 14, 1453–4, 1984.

"Thinking about Thinking: the Mind as Virtual Machine," in *The Human Mind – the Human Brain and Beyond*, American Broadcasting Companies, Inc., 1984.

1985

"Music of the Hemispheres" (review of M. S. Gazzaniga, The Social Brain), *The New York Times Book Review*, November 17, 53, 1985.

"Can Machines Think?" in M. Shafto (ed.), *How We Know*, San Francisco: Harper and Row, 1985. Dutch translation, "Kunnen machines denken?" *Wijsgerig perspectief op maatschappij en wetenschap*, 24, 98–108, 1983/1984.

"When Does the Intentional Stance Work?" (reply to continuing commentary), *Behavioral and Brain Sciences*, 8, 758–66, 1985.

"Why Believe in Belief?" (review of S. Stich, From Folk Psychology to Cognitive Science: the Case against Belief), *Contemporary Psychology*, 30, 949, 1985.

Commentary in D. G. Bobrow and P. J. Hayes (eds), "Artificial Intelligence – Where Are We?" *Artificial Intelligence*, 25, 375–415 (409–10), 1985. Reprinted in *Abacus* 4, Spring and Summer 1987.

"Where Am I?" *Clinton St Quarterly*, 7, Winter 1985. Reprinted from *Brainstorms*.

1986

"Review of V. Braitenberg, Vehicles: Experiments in Synthetic Psychology," *Philosophical Review*, 95, 137–9, 1986.

"Julian Jaynes's Software Archeology," *Canadian Psychology*, 27, 149–54, 1986.

"The Imagination Extenders," (adapted from "Notes on Prosthetic Imagination"), in D. Flaherty (ed.), *Humanizing the Computer: a Cure for the Deadly Embrace*, Belmont, Calif.: Wadsworth 1986.

"Engineering's Baby," (commentary on Sayre), *Behavioral and Brain Sciences*, 9, 141–2, 1986.

"Who May I say is Calling?" (with K. Akins, commentary on Hoffman), *Behavioral and Brain Sciences*, 9, 517–18, 1986.

"Philosophy as Mathematics or as Anthropology," (forum comment), *Mind and Language*, 1, 18–19, Spring 1986.

"Is there an Autonomous 'Knowledge Level'?" (commentary on Newell), in Z. Pylyshyn and W. Demopoulos (eds), *Meaning and Cognitive Structure: Issues in the Computational Theory of Mind*, Norwood, NJ: Ablex 1986.

"Information, Technology, and the Virtues of Ignorance," *Daedalus, Proceedings of the American Academy of Arts and Sciences*, 115, 135–53, Summer 1986.

1987

"The Logical Geography of Computational Approaches: a View from the East Pole," in M. Harnish and M. Brand (eds), *Problems in the Representation of Knowledge*, University of Arizona Press 1987.

"Skinner Placed," (response to U. T. Place, Skinner Re-Skinned), in S. and C. Modgil (eds), *B. F. Skinner: Consensus and Controversy*, Brighton: Falmer Press 1987.

"Consciousness" (with John Haugeland), in R. L. Gregory (ed.), *The Oxford Companion to the Mind*, Oxford University Press 1987.

"Intentionality" (with John Haugeland), in R. L. Gregory (ed.), *The Oxford Companion to the Mind*, Oxford University Press 1987.

"Comments" (on Pylyshyn, Computers, Knowledge, and the Human Mind) in D. Tuerck (ed.), *Creativity and Liberal Learning*, Norwood, NJ: Ablex 1987.

"Eliminate the Middletoad!" (commentary on Ewert), *Behavioral and Brain Sciences*, 10, 372–4, 1987.
"Commentary on Cam," *Philosophy and Phenomenological Research*, 48, 339–41, December 1987.

1988

"When Philosophers Encounter AI," *Daedalus, Proceedings of the American Academy of Arts and Sciences*, 117, 283–295, Winter 1988.
"The Moral First Aid Manual," in S. McMurrin (ed.), *The Tanner Lectures on Human Values*, vol. 7, University of Utah Press and Cambridge University Press 1988.
"Out of the Armchair and into the Field," *Poetics Today*, 9, 205–21, 1988.
"Quining Qualia," in A. Marcel and E. Bisiach (eds), *Consciousness in Modern Science*, Oxford University Press 1988.
"Précis of The Intentional Stance," (with commentaries), *Behavioral and Brain Sciences*, 11, 495–546, 1988.
"The Intentional Stance in Theory and Practice," in A. Whiten and R. W. Byrne (eds), *Machiavellian Intelligence*, Oxford University Press 1988.
"Why Everyone is a Novelist," *The Times Literary Supplement*, September 16–22, 1988.
"Review of J. Fodor, Psychosemantics," *Journal of Philosophy*, 85, 384–389, July 1988.
"Coming to Terms with the Determined," (review of T. Honderich, A Theory of Determinism: The Mind, Neuroscience, and Life-Hopes), *The Times Literary Supplement*, November 4–10, 1219–20, 1988.
"Why Creative Intelligence is Hard to Find," (commentary on Whiten and Byrne) *Behavioral and Brain Sciences*, 11, 253, 1988.
"Review of W. Lyons, The Disappearance of Introspection," *Philosophy of Science*, 55, 653–4, December 1988.
Dialogue in *The jamais vu papers*, 1, July 1988. Reprinted as "Media-Neutral" in W. Coleman and P. Perrin, *The Jamais Vu Papers*, New York: Harmony Books 1991.
"Intentionality," in *Actes du 3ème Colloque International Cognition et Connaissance: Où va la science cognitive?* Toulouse: CNRS/Université Paul Sabatier 1988.
"Evolution, Error and Intentionality," in Y. Wilks and D. Partridge (eds), *Sourcebook on the Foundations of Artificial Intelligence*, New Mexico University Press 1988. In *The Intentional Stance.*

1989

"Speaking for Our Selves: An Assessment of Multiple Personality Disorder," (with N. Humphrey), *Raritan: A Quarterly Review*, 9, 68–98, Summer 1989. Reprinted (with footnotes), *Occasional Paper 8*, Center on Violence and Human Survival, John Jay College of Criminal Justice, The City University of New York, 1991.
"Murmurs in the Cathedral," (review of R. Penrose, The Emperor's New Mind), *The Times Literary Supplement*, September 29–October 5, 1989.
"Cognitive Ethology: Hunting for Bargains or a Wild Goose Chase?" in A. Montefiore and D. Noble (eds), *Goals, No-Goals and Own Goals: A Debate on Goal-Directed and Intentional Behaviour*, London: Unwin Hyman 1989.
"The Origins of Selves," *Cogito*, 3, 163–73, Autumn 1989.
"Review of R. Richards, Darwin and the Emergence of Evolutionary Theories of Mind and Behavior," *Philosophy of Science*, 56, 540–3, 1989.

1990

"Teaching an Old Dog New Tricks, (commentary on Schull), *Behavioral and Brain Sciences*, 13, 76–7, 1990.

"Thinking with a Computer," in H. Barlow, C. Blakemore and M. Weston-Smith (eds), *Images and Understanding*, Cambridge University Press 1990.

"The Evolution of Consciousness," in J. Brockman (ed.), *Speculations: The Reality Club*, New York: Prentice Hall 1990.

"Ways of Establishing Harmony," in B. McLaughlin (ed.), *Dretske and His Critics*, Oxford: Blackwell 1990. Reprinted (slightly revised), in E. Villaneuva (ed.), *Information, Semantics, and Epistemology*, Oxford: Blackwell 1990.

"The Myth of Original Intentionality," in K. A. Mohyeldin Said, W. H. Newton-Smith, R. Viale and K. V. Wilkes (eds), *Modelling the Mind*, Oxford: Clarendon Press 1990

"The Interpretation of Texts, People, and Other Artifacts," *Philosophy and Phenomenological Research*, 50, Supplement, 177–94, Fall 1990.

"Memes and the Exploitation of Imagination," *Journal of Aesthetics and Art Criticism*, 48, 127–35, Spring 1990.

"Artificial Life: A Feast for the Imagination," (review of G. Langton, (ed.), Artificial Life), *Biology and Philosophy*, 5, 489–92, 1990.

"Dr Pangloss Knows Best," (reply to Amundsen), *Behavioral and Brain Sciences*, 13, 581–2, 1990.

"Abstracting from Mechanism," (reply to de Gelder), *Behavioral and Brain Sciences*, 13, 583–4, 1990.

"Betting your Life on an Algorithm," (commentary on Penrose), *Behavioral and Brain Sciences*, 13, 660–61, 1990.

"Demystifying Consciousness," (interview by John Brockman), *Edge*, 5–8, November 1990.

"Attitudes about ADHD: Some Analogies and Aspects," in K. Conners and M. Kinsbourne (eds), *ADHD: Attention Deficit Hyperactivity Disorders*, Munich: MMV Medizin Verlag 1990.

1991

"Real Patterns," *Journal of Philosophy*, 88, 27–51, January 1991.

"Mother Nature Versus the Walking Encyclopedia: A Western Drama," in W. Ramsey, S. Stich, and D. E. Rumelhart (eds), *Philosophy and Connectionist Theory*, Hillsdale, NJ: Erlbaum 1991.

"A Gadfly's View," in *Teaching and Technology: The Impact of Unlimited Information Access on Classroom Teaching*, Ann Arbor, MI: The Pierian Press 1991.

"Granny's Campaign for Safe Science," in B. Loewer and G. Rey (eds), *Meaning in Mind: Fodor and his Critics*, Oxford: Blackwell 1991.

"Lovely and Suspect Qualities," (commentary on Rosenthal, The Independence of Consciousness and Sensory Quality), in E. Villanueva (ed.), *Consciousness* (SOFIA Conference, Buenos Aires), Atascadero, Calif.: Ridgeview 1991.

"Two Contrasts: Folk Craft Versus Folk Science, and Belief versus Opinion," in J. D. Greenwood (ed.), *The Future of Folk Psychology: Intentionality and Cognitive Science*, Cambridge University Press 1991.

"The Brain and its Boundaries," (review of C. McGinn, The Problem of Consciousness), *The Times Literary Supplement*, May 10, 10, 1991.

"Intencionalidade," (Portuguese translation of "True Believers" from *The Intentional Stance*), in M. M. Carrilho (ed.), *Dicionário do Pensamento Contemporâneo*, Lisbon: Dom Quixote 1991.

"Modelli del Cervello e il Punto di Vista dell'Osservatore," in G. Giorello and P. Strata (eds), *Lautoma Spirituale: Menti, Cervelli e Computer*, Rome: Laterza 1991.

"A Dash to Solve the Puzzle of the Mind," *Boston Globe*, December 8, A21, A24, 1991.

1992

"Moral Thinking under Time Pressure," in *The Kathryn Fraser MacKay Memorial Lecture Series*, St Lawrence University, 1992.

"Hitting the Nail on the Head," (commentary on Thompson, Palacios and Varela), *Behavioral and Brain Sciences*, 15, 35, 1992.

"Temporal Anomalies of Consciousness: Implications of the Uncentered Brain," in Y. Christen and P. S. Churchland (eds), *Neurophilosophy and Alzheimer's Disease*, Berlin: Springer-Verlag 1992.

"Commandos of the Word," (a condensed version of "The Role of Language in Intelligence"), *The Times Higher Education Supplement*, March 27, 15–19, 1992.

"La Compréhension Artisanale," (French translation of "Do-It-Yourself Understanding"), in D. Fisette (ed.), *Daniel C. Dennett et les Stratégies Intentionnelles*, Lekton, 11, Winter, Université de Québec à Montréal, Montréal 1992.

"Time and the Observer: The Where and When of Consciousness in the Brain," (with M. Kinsbourne and with commentaries), *Behavioral and Brain Sciences*, 15, 183–247, 1992.

"Review of F. Varela, E. Thompson and E. Rosch, The Embodied Mind, and G. Edelman, Bright Air, Brilliant Fire," *New Scientist*, 13 June, 48–9, 1992.

"Filling in vs. Finding out: a Ubiquitous Confusion in Cognitive Science," in H. Pick, P. Van den Broek and D. Knill (eds), *Cognition: Conceptual and Methodological Issues*, American Psychological Association, Washington, DC, 1992.

"The Self as the Center of Narrative Gravity," in F. Kessel, P. Cole and D. Johnson (eds), *Self and Consciousness: Multiple Perspectives*, Hillsdale, NJ: Erlbaum, 1992. Danish translation, "Selvet som fortællingens tyngdepunkt," *Philosophia*, 15, 275–88, 1986.

1993

Review of F. Varela, E. Thompson and E. Rosch, The Embodied Mind," *American Journal of Psychology*, 106, 121–6, 1993.

"Living on the Edge" (reply to seven essays on *Consciousness Explained*), *Inquiry*, 36, March, 1993.

FORTHCOMING

"Reply to Ringen and Bennett," (continuing commentary on "Précis of The Intentional Stance"), *Behavioral and Brain Sciences*.

"The Role of Language in Intelligence," (Darwin Lecture, Darwin College, Cambridge) in a volume of Darwin Lectures on Intelligence, Cambridge University Press.

"Self-Portrait," in S. Guttenplan (ed.), *Companion to the Philosophy of Mind*, Oxford: Blackwell.

"Review of A. Newell, Unified Theories of Cognition," *Artificial Intelligence*.

"Producing Future by Telling Stories," in K. Ford and Z. Pylyshyn (eds), *The Robot's Dilemma Revisited: The Frame Problem in Artificial Intelligence*, Norwood, NJ: Ablex.

Definitions of homunculus, intentionality, Mentalese, mentalism, topic-neutral, for R. Audi (ed.), *Cambridge Dictionary of Philosophy*, Cambridge University Press.

"Cognitive Science as Reverse Engineering: Several Meanings of 'Top-Down' and 'Bottom-Up,'" in D. Prawitz, B. Skyrms, and D. Westerståhl (eds), *Proceedings of the 9th International Congress of Logic, Methodology and Philosophy of Science*, Amsterdam: North-Holland.

"Verbal Language as a Communicative System," forthcoming in Italian translation.

"Is Perception the 'Leading Edge' of Memory?" In A. Spadafora (ed.), *Memory and Oblivion*.

"Learning and Labeling" (commentary on A. Clark and A. Karmiloff-Smith, "The Cognizer's Innards"), *Mind and Language*.

"Caveat Emptor" (reply to Mangan, Toribio, Baars and McGovern), *Consciousness and Cognition*.

"Review of J. Searle, The Rediscovery of the Mind," *Journal of Philosophy*.

Index